THE COLLEGE PRESS NIV COMMENTARY

REVELATION

THE COLLEGE PRESS NIV COMMENTARY

REVELATION

CHRISTOPHER A. DAVIS, Ph.D.

New Testament Series Co-Editors:

Jack Cottrell, Ph.D.
Cincinnati Bible Seminary

Tony Ash, Ph.D.
Abilene Christian University

COLLEGE PRESS PUBLISHING COMPANY
Joplin, Missouri

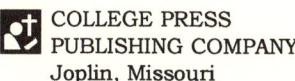

Copyright © 2000 College Press Publishing Co.
All Rights Reserved
Printed and Bound in the United States of America

All Scripture quotations, unless indicated, are taken from
THE HOLY BIBLE: NEW INTERNATIONAL VERSION®.
Copyright © 1973, 1978, 1984 by International Bible Society.
Used by permission of Zondervan Publishing House.
All rights reserved.

The "NIV" and "New International Version" trademarks are
registered in the United States Patent and Trademark Office
by International Bible Society.
Use of either trademark requires the permission of International
Bible Society.

All pseudepigraphal quotes are from THE OLD TESTAMENT
PSEUDEPIGRAPHA by James H. Charlesworth, copyright 1983, 1985
by James H. Charlesworth. Used by permission of Doubleday, a
division of Random House, Inc.

Library of Congress Cataloging-in-Publication Data

Davis, Christopher A., 1958–
    Revelation / Christopher A. Davis
      p.   cm. – (The College Press NIV commentary)
    Includes bibliographic references.
    ISBN 0-89900-641-8
    1. Bible. N.T. Revelation—Commentaries. I. Title. II. Series.
BS2825.3.D37 2000
228'.077—dc21
                                              00-060239

A WORD FROM THE PUBLISHER

Years ago a movement was begun with the dream of uniting all Christians on the basis of a common purpose (world evangelism) under a common authority (the Word of God). The College Press NIV Commentary Series is a serious effort to join the scholarship of two branches of this unity movement so as to speak with one voice concerning the Word of God. Our desire is to provide a resource for your study of the New Testament that will benefit you whether you are preparing a Bible School lesson, a sermon, a college course, or your own personal devotions. Today as we survey the wreckage of a broken world, we must turn again to the Lord and his Word, unite under his banner and communicate the life-giving message to those who are in desperate need. This is our purpose.

To my parents
JERRY AND MARGIE DAVIS
who led me to the King of kings
and called me by his name

PREFACE

This commentary on the Revelation of John has been prepared for general readers of the Bible who desire to deepen their understanding of God's inspired word. It is not a technical commentary, although it draws on the best in current biblical scholarship. It is not a devotional commentary, although the reader will find that Revelation certainly speaks to our day. My primary aim has been to provide a clear, concise explanation of what the biblical text means, showing the evidence on which my conclusions are based.

Extensive cross-referencing makes this volume a convenient reference tool for those seeking insight into a particular passage. However, I strongly recommend that users read through the entire commentary from beginning to end, considering each text in its broader context. It is particularly important to read the Introduction. There I define key terms ("kingdom of God," "labor pains," "apocalypse," etc.) and explain the historical, literary, and theological setting for John's work. Readers who truly desire to understand Revelation will find this approach most productive.

For many years I have taught Revelation at Minnesota Bible College and in other settings. Therefore most of the research for writing this commentary was already done. Nevertheless, completing this project on a tight deadline has been a major undertaking. Many people have provided assistance and support to make this book possible. MBC's President, Mr. Robert Cash, relieved me from certain duties as Vice President of Academics and Professor of New Testament so that I could make a research trip to Virginia. Dr. Mark Mangano, MBC's Professor of Old Testament and Biblical Languages, took over one of my classes to reduce my teaching load. The elders of the Meadow Park Church of Christ in Rochester, Minnesota, granted me a leave of absence from elders' duties so I could devote more time to writing. Dr. Harold Mahan, Director of the G.H. Cachiaras Memorial Library at MBC, provided research assistance. Dr. John Trotti and Mr. Roger Pittard, of Union Theological Seminary in Virginia, also provided library support. My dear wife Cathy read the entire manuscript and provided secretarial assistance. The series editors, Dr. Jack Cottrell and Dr. Tony Ash, also read the manuscript and offered helpful suggestions. Mr. John Hunter of College Press guided me through the publication process. My students and colleagues at MBC, my family members, and so many others offered help and encouragement along the way. The women of the Disciple's Prayer Life Sunday School class have bathed this entire project in prayer. To all these brothers and sisters in Christ, I offer my sincere thanks.

> Christopher A. Davis
> Rochester, Minnesota
> July 2, 2000

INTRODUCTION

I. INTENDED TO REVEAL NOT TO CONCEAL

The Revelation of John is one of the most often read, but least understood books of the Bible. The first three words of the Greek text of Revelation[1] are ἀποκάλυψις Ἰησοῦ Χριστοῦ (*apokalypsis Iēsou Christou*), or "apocalypse from Jesus Christ." *Apokalypsis* is a combination of two Greek terms: The noun καλύπτρα (*kalyptra*) refers to some sort of "covering," particularly a woman's "veil." The preposition ἀπό (*apo*) communicates the idea of "movement away from" or "removing" something from one location to another. The term *apokalypsis* literally means, then, "the removal of that which conceals" or "the removal of the veil" (so that one may see what is under it). In English, the term is usually translated "revelation" — something that does not "conceal" or "cover," but which "unveils" or "reveals." So John's own title for his book is "Apocalypse from Jesus Christ" or "Revelation from Jesus Christ."

Beginning with the very first word of the book, the author claims to be *revealing* something. John expects that his Christian readers will not be puzzled, but able to *comprehend* his meaning. He does not intend the Revelation to be an enigma, but to be *understood*. For centuries, however, the book's mysterious symbolism has served to hide more than it reveals. Anyone who reads interpretations of Revelation — from Irenaeus in the second century, to Joachim of Fiore in the twelfth century, to Hal Lindsey in the twentieth century — finds very little agreement regarding what the book means. The reason is that Revelation is so unusual, so unique in the New

---

[1]Like other New Testament books, Revelation was originally written in *Koiné*, or "common" Greek. *Koiné* served as the trade language for the eastern half of the Roman Empire during the early centuries of the Christian era.

Testament, that many Bible students simply do not know how to approach it. They lack the "key" for unlocking the secrets John intends to share.

II. APPROACH TO REVELATION

A. AN HISTORICAL AND CRITICAL APPROACH

A breakthrough has come in our own time. Before the mid-1800s, the Bible was viewed as little more than a vast collection of proof texts that could be taken apart and used to support the doctrinal systems of the various churches. No serious effort was made to understand each book as a whole or to seek insight into the meaning of the biblical books by examining the historical circumstances in which they were written. Beginning with Ferdinand Christian Baur in the mid-nineteenth century, a new group of scholars has urged a different approach to Scripture — an historical and critical approach. This is the kind of approach to Revelation adopted in this commentary.

By "critical" we do not mean mere "faultfinding." Instead, being "critical" involves asking questions, weighing evidence, and forming judgments. If we ask no questions of Revelation, then we get no answers. Since we wish to understand this word from God, we ask the same kinds of penetrating questions of it that we ask of any other piece of literature, whether it be the orations of Cicero, the plays of Shakespeare, or the novels of Mark Twain. We ask questions such as: Who wrote this book? When? Where? How? For what purpose? To what audience? In what circumstances? Using what sources? Why is the book structured in the way it is? What did the terminology used by the author mean to the readers of his time? What literary techniques does he employ?

We take an "historical" approach to Revelation because we believe that the Bible should not be studied in a vacuum as if it had no relationship to the events surrounding its writing. One of the primary convictions of the Christian faith is that God does not reveal himself in a vacuum, but in history. He is not just "God." He is the God of Abraham, Isaac and Jacob; the God of Moses and the Exodus; the God who made an eternal covenant with King David;

the God who came among us in the person of Jesus Christ in history. For this reason, one of the best ways to gain an understanding of the Bible is to learn something about the historical settings in which it was produced.

In this commentary, we uncover the meaning of Revelation by asking an historical question: What did this book communicate to its *first* readers? What did Revelation *reveal* to the Christians for whom John wrote? How would *they* have understood its message? In order to answer this question, we must learn all we can about who the first readers were. We must acquaint ourselves with their time, their location, their circumstances, their language, their literature, and their culture. Only then will we be able to discern what Revelation meant to the believers for whom it was intended. Only then will we begin to work out an accurate interpretation of Revelation in its historical context. We will find that most of the truths Christ revealed to the first readers are applicable to his modern-day disciples as well.

B. RESOURCES FOR THE STUDY OF REVELATION

What resources from the ancient world assist us in our efforts to correctly understand and interpret Revelation? Primary texts include:

1. The Hebrew Old Testament

The Old Testament contains history and theological reflection regarding God's covenant relationship with the people of Israel.[2] Christians consider the Old Testament and New Testament (see below) to be the inspired, authoritative word of God.

2. The Septuagint

The Septuagint is a Greek version of the Old Testament. This translation was begun in the third century B.C. after Alexander the Great made Greek the common language uniting his empire. According to

---

[2]K. Elliger and W. Rudolph, *Biblia Hebraica Stuttgartensia* (Stuttgart: Deutsche Bibelstiftung, 1977).

legend, seventy Jewish scholars independently produced identical translations of the Hebrew Scriptures, thus attesting to divine inspiration of the Greek text.[3] For this reason, "LXX" (the Roman numeral for "70") serves as the common abbreviation designating the Septuagint translation. The Septuagint was the "Bible" of most of the first Christians, who lived in the Greek-speaking eastern half of the Roman Empire. Nearly every line of Revelation contains allusions to either the Septuagint or the Hebrew Old Testament. The Septuagint also includes the Apocrypha.[4]

3. The Old Testament Apocrypha

The Apocrypha is a collection of Jewish writings, most of which date from the second century B.C. through the first century A.D. Christians from the Roman Catholic and Greek Orthodox traditions consider them part of the authoritative Christian canon. Most Protestants view the Apocrypha as useful, edifying works, but do not give them a status equal to that of the Old and New Testaments.

4. The Old Testament Pseudepigrapha

The Pseudepigrapha is a collection of Jewish and Christian documents, with the majority dating from the third century B.C. through the second century A.D. About one-third are called "apocalypses" because they resemble the Revelation of John in their language, style, use of symbolism, and/or shared concepts. Since they represent the same literary type, or "genre," they prove an invaluable aid to the study of John's vision (as discussed below in Part III).

---

[3]See the Letter of Aristeas, which is part of the *Pseudepigrapha*.

[4]A Greek text of the Septuagint with English translation appears in Launcelot C.L. Brenton, ed., *The Septuagint with Apocrypha: Greek and English* (Grand Rapids: Zondervan, 1851). Our English Bibles (including the NIV) contain translations of the *Hebrew* Old Testament. When New Testament writers quote from the Old Testament, they almost always use the *Greek* Septuagint version. For this reason, there are sometimes differences between the way a biblical text reads in the Old Testament and the way that same passage reads when quoted in the New.

James H. Charlesworth has edited a two-volume collection of these writings in English.[5]

5. Ancient Near Eastern Texts

Texts surviving from the Ancient Near East shed light on the cultural roots of ideas found in Revelation. To illustrate, the Babylonian Creation Myth offers insights into the symbolic meaning of the "sea" and the "sea monster" in John's vision. J.B. Pritchard has edited a useful collection of such texts in English translation.[6]

6. The Dead Sea Scrolls

Called "the greatest manuscript discovery in modern times" by W.F. Albright, the Scrolls were produced by a Jewish community at Qumran on the northwestern shore of the Dead Sea. Some of the texts are biblical manuscripts, while others describe the beliefs and rules of the Qumran sect.[7] Dating from the end of third century B.C. to A.D. 70, the Dead Sea Scrolls shed light on Palestinian Judaism in the years prior to the writing of Revelation.

7. The New Testament

Written in the first century A.D., the New Testament draws together writings of the very first Christian communities.[8] As such, it represents our earliest and most precious witness to Jesus and the church he founded.

---

[5]James H. Charlesworth, ed., *The Old Testament Pseudepigrapha*, 2 vols. (Garden City, NY: Doubleday, 1983).

[6]James B. Pritchard, ed., *Ancient Near Eastern Texts Relating to the Old Testament*, 3d ed. with Supplement (Princeton, NJ: Princeton University Press, 1969).

[7]Geza Vermes provides translations of the community texts in *The Complete Dead Sea Scrolls in English* (New York: Allen Lane/The Penguin Press, 1997).

[8]A particularly useful edition combining the 27th edition of the Nestle-Aland text and the 2nd edition of the English RSV translation is Kurt Aland, et al., eds., *Greek-English New Testament*, (Stuttgart: German Bible Society, 1994).

8. Josephus

A contemporary of John, Flavius Josephus composed valuable histories of the Jewish people.⁹ He provides us, for example, with a vivid, first-hand description of the destruction of Jerusalem in A.D. 70 — an event alluded to in Revelation.

9. The New Testament Apocrypha

The New Testament Apocrypha is a collection of extracanonical Christian writings (some from Gnostic or other heretical groups) from the second century A.D. and beyond.¹⁰ It provides us with additional samples of early Christian apocalypses.

10. Early Christian Fathers

Writings of Christian leaders from the post-New Testament period cast light on the circumstances surrounding Revelation's composition. To illustrate, Eusebius's *History of the Church* (ca. A.D. 325)¹¹ identifies the author and date of Revelation. Eusebius also describes two great persecutions suffered by first-century believers — events that play a role in John's vision.

11. Rabbinical Writings

Although most date to the post-New Testament period, teachings of ancient Jewish rabbis (Mishnah, Talmud, Midrashim, etc.)

---

⁹A popular English version is *Josephus: Complete Works*, trans. William Whiston (Grand Rapids: Kregel Publications, 1978). For a critical edition containing both the Greek texts and English translations by H.St.J. Thackeray and others, consult the Loeb Classical Library of Harvard University Press.

¹⁰Wilhelm Schneemelcher, ed., *New Testament Apocrypha*, Rev. ed., with English translation edited by R.McL. Wilson (Louisville, KY: Westminster/John Knox Press, 1991).

¹¹Eusebius, *The Ecclesiastical History*, trans. Kirsopp Lake, The Loeb Classical Library (Cambridge, MA: Harvard University Press, 1980). Another very readable translation has been produced by G.A. Williamson in Eusebius, *The History of the Church from Christ to Constantine* (Minneapolis: Augsburg, 1975).

sometimes illuminate the biblical text. We turn to them, for example, when interpreting the symbolism of the four living creatures in Revelation 4.

12. Classical Greek and Latin Literature

Ancient Greek and Latin writers open a door to the world of the first readers of Revelation. To illustrate, Suetonius has left us biographies of the first twelve Roman emperors, some of whom play a role in Revelation. The correspondence of Governor Pliny and the Emperor Trajan explains Roman policy toward Christians in the early second century. The nearly five hundred volumes of the Loeb Classical Library (Harvard University Press) make this wealth of knowledge available to English readers.

We will utilize all these resources and more as we interpret the Revelation of John. We study other ancient writings not because we consider them to be inspired or authoritative — not because we place them on an equal level with the Bible. Rather, we study them because they help us to enter the thought world of John's first readers, so that we may understand Revelation as they understood it.

C. STRENGTHS OF THE HISTORICAL AND CRITICAL APPROACH TO REVELATION

The weakness of alternative approaches to Revelation is seen in their failure to create a consensus regarding the meaning of the book. There have been nearly as many interpretations of Revelation as there have been interpreters. The weakness of alternative approaches is further highlighted by the erroneous predictions made on the basis of those approaches. To illustrate, when the former Soviet Union disintegrated, many scholars' interpretations of Revelation perished with it.

The strength of an historical and critical approach to Revelation is demonstrated by several facts: First, there is a great deal of agreement among historical and critical scholars regarding the meaning of John's vision. They have found the key to interpreting Revelation, while others must rely heavily on guesswork. Second, an historical and critical interpretation of Revelation makes sense today, and it would have made sense to the first-century Christians for whom the book was written. Third, an historical and critical interpretation reveals that the message of Revelation is wholly compatible and consistent with the message of the rest of the New Testament. Finally, the accuracy of an historical and critical interpretation of Revelation can be demonstrated with *objective* evidence drawn from other ancient writings. It does not rest on subjective speculation.

III. APOCALYPTIC LITERATURE

Other New Testament writers communicate through narrative or epistle, but in Revelation John employs striking imagery and vivid symbolism. Although Revelation is unique in the New Testament, it was not at all unique in John's time. Revelation belongs to a genre, or type of literature, that was most popular in Palestine from the second century B.C. through the second century A.D. Such writings are called "apocalypses," or "apocalyptic literature," partly because they are revelatory in nature and partly because they resemble the Apocalypse of John (see Part I above).

A. JEWISH AND CHRISTIAN APOCALYPSES

The only apocalyptic writing in the Old Testament is the Book of Daniel. Some believe that Daniel is the oldest apocalypse and that later writers imitate its style. Others argue that the Book of the Watchers (= 1 Enoch 1–36) is older. Whatever the case, Jewish theologians found apocalyptic to be a powerful tool for expressing their convictions concerning God and his dealings with the world. The most important Jewish apocalypses for our purposes are 1 Enoch (a compilation of five originally independent works dating from the second or third century B.C. to the first century A.D.), 2 Enoch (late first century A.D.), 2 Baruch (ca. A.D. 100), 3 Baruch (first to third century A.D.), 4 Ezra (ca. A.D. 100), the Apocalypse of Abraham (ca. A.D. 100), and the Apocalypse of Zephaniah (first century B.C. to first century A.D.). Beyond the apocalypses themselves, other writings from the period contain apocalyptic sections or features. Two examples are the Testaments of the Twelve Patriarchs (second century B.C.) and the Sibylline Oracles (second century B.C. through seventh century A.D.). All of these writings are preserved in the Pseudepigrapha (described above in Part II.B.4).

Early Christian apocalypses include, for example, the Shepherd of Hermas, 5 Ezra, and the Apocalypse of Peter (all dating to the second century A.D.).[12] The Revelation of John appears to be the first Christian apocalypse — the first Christian adaptation of the apocalyptic form. Other New Testament writings certainly contain apocalyptic ideas, but in Revelation alone do we find a fully developed apocalyptic vision. Since John's Christian apocalypse builds on the earlier Jewish apocalyptic tradition, those Jewish documents serve as one of the most valuable resources for understanding the nature and meaning of Revelation.

B. CHARACTERISTICS OF APOCALYPTIC LITERATURE

But what exactly is an "apocalypse"?[13] What sets these books apart and leads us to place them in a special class? First, Jewish apocalyptic literature is characterized by a particular kind of *theology* — a particular understanding of who God is and how he deals with his creation. Apocalyptic theology is rooted in the Jewish Scriptures since apocalyptic was initially a Jewish phenomenon.

---

[12]The Shepherd of Hermas is typically grouped with the writings of the Early Church Fathers. See *The Apostolic Fathers with an English Translation by Kirsopp Lake*, Vol. 2, The Loeb Classical Library (New York: G.P. Putnam's Sons, 1930). The Apocalypse of Peter and 5 Ezra are part of the New Testament Apocrypha. A number of the Jewish apocalyptic writings in the Old Testament Pseudepigrapha also contain Christian revisions (e.g., the Sibylline Oracles).

[13]In 1979 the Apocalypse Group of the Society of Biblical Literature composed the following definition: "'Apocalypse' is a genre of revelatory literature with a narrative framework, in which a revelation is mediated by an otherworldly being to a human recipient, disclosing a transcendent reality which is both temporal, insofar as it envisages eschatological salvation, and spatial insofar as it involves another, supernatural world." See John J. Collins, ed., "Introduction: Towards the Morphology of a Genre," *Semeia* 14 (1979): 9.

Christian apocalyptic writers later modified this theology in significant ways due to their encounter with Jesus Christ (see below).

Second, apocalyptic writers utilize a particular manner of communicating that theology — a *distinctive form or style of writing*. For example, they tend to make heavy use of symbolism.

So apocalyptic theology is a certain network of beliefs about God and the apocalyptic form is a certain means of expressing those beliefs. It is possible to have a message containing apocalyptic theology that is not communicated in the apocalyptic style. (An example would be the gospel preached by the Apostle Paul, which J. Christiaan Beker rightly describes as an "apocalyptic interpretation of the Christ-event.[14]") However, true apocalypses — like the Revelation of John — display both apocalyptic form and apocalyptic theology.

1. Common Characteristics of the Apocalyptic Form

Some of the most common characteristics of the apocalyptic form are described below. Not every apocalypse includes every feature.

a. Visions or Revelations

Apocalypses take the form of visions or revelations from God. Whereas Old Testament prophets experience God directly ("The word of the Lord came to me" or "In the year that king Uzziah died, I saw the Lord"), the apocalyptic seers receive their revelations through an intermediary — often an angel. Their visions usually concern the future, giving apocalyptic a strong "eschatological" element.[15]

---

[14]J. Christiaan Beker, *Paul the Apostle: The Triumph of God in Life and Thought* (Philadelphia: Fortress Press, 1980), p. 135.

[15]The term "eschatological" comes from ἔσχατος (*eschatos*), the Greek word for "last." Apocalyptic visions typically deal with the "last times" or the "eschatological age" (described below under "2. Common Features of Apocalyptic Theology").

b. Symbolism[16]

Apocalyptic visions are filled with vivid symbolism. Over time, as various apocalyptists adopted and adapted the images used by others, a set of common symbols was developed. For example, the sea typically represents the forces of evil and chaos. Stars often represent angels. Beasts symbolize political powers opposed to God and his people. If we read Revelation alone (as so many do), then we may find John's symbolism puzzling and impenetrable. However, if we study other apocalypses as well, then we begin to see the patterns and Revelation becomes less intimidating.

c. Esoteric Elements

Apocalyptic writings are esoteric; they contain an element of mystery or secrecy. They are not meant for the general public, but for "insiders" who are acquainted, for example, with the meaning of the conventional apocalyptic symbols. John apparently considers his readers to be insiders able to grasp his meaning. By acquainting ourselves with their literature and culture, we can become insiders too.

d. Symbolic Numbers

Apocalyptic writers place symbolic meaning in numbers. Here, too, a set of conventional symbols emerge:

> *Two* is the number of valid witness. Its Jewish roots are found in Deuteronomy 19:15 where the Lord requires at least two witnesses for a matter to be established in a court of law.
>
> *Three* often relates to God. This symbol also has Old Testament roots in passages such as Isaiah 6:3 where the Lord receives the threefold worship of the seraphim: "Holy, holy, holy is the LORD Almighty." Christian writers tend to see Trinitarian connotations

---

[16]For a discussion of the evocative, tensive, and polyvalent nature of apocalyptic symbolism, see the comments on "someone 'like a son of man'" in Rev 1:13 and "Summary of Revelation 6 (Seals 1-6) and Comparison with Matthew 24."

in this number since the Lord has revealed himself to us as God the Father, God the Son, and God the Holy Spirit.

Four often symbolizes the world, or God's creation. This goes back to the idea that the "four corners of the earth" (Ezek 7:2; cf. Rev 7:1), the "four quarters of the earth" (Isa 11:12), or the "four winds" (Jer 49:36; Ezek 7:9; Zech 6:5; Dan 7:2; cf. Matt 24:31 // Mark 13:27; Rev 7:1) — i.e., north, south, east, and west — together encompass the whole of creation.

Five, the number of fingers on the human hand, describes a "handful" or a "few."

Ten — two "handfuls" — represents "several." Neither ten nor five should necessarily be interpreted literally in apocalyptic writings.

Seven is the number of "fullness," "completeness," "perfection." In some texts this number carries connotations of goodness or morality, for the author is thinking of persons or things being "complete" in the sense of being everything God intends them to be. However, the dominant meaning for seven is not "perfection" in the sense of being morally faultless, but "perfection" in the sense of being "complete" or "whole." We may trace the origin of this symbol to Old Testament texts such as Genesis 1–2, where seven days form a "complete" week.

Six is one less than seven; it does not "measure up" to seven or attain to the fullness of seven. Six, then, symbolizes "incompleteness," "imperfection," and sometimes evil.

Eight, in Christian apocalypses, symbolizes Jesus Christ. For an explanation, see the comments on Revelation 13:18.

Twelve tends to represent the people of God — those who love him and serve him faithfully (i.e., Law-keeping Jews in Jewish apocalypses and faithful Christians in Christian apocalypses). The idea no doubt comes from the Old Testament, where the twelve tribes of Israel together form the covenant community of God.

Multiples of these numbers typically represent the "fullness" or complete number of the thing symbolized. For example, the 144,000 ($12 \times 12 \times 1000$) in Revelation 7 represent the full number of the people of God. Other symbolic numbers used in Revelation will be explained at appropriate points in the commentary.

e. Pseudonymity

Rather than writing in their own names, apocalyptists typically employ pseudonyms, or false names. They attribute their works to an ancient hero such as Abraham, Jacob, or Ezra. What is the reason for this practice? Various theories have been put forward.

Many apocalypses (including Revelation) were composed in times of persecution. Some suggest that the pseudonyms and mysterious symbols are aimed at hiding the author's identity and message from hostile political authorities. One may question how successful this tactic would have been. Could any of John's neighbors read his description of the Whore of Babylon (Revelation 17) without seeing in it a criticism of Rome?

Apocalyptic literature became popular during the first and second centuries B.C., as Jewish prophecy declined[17] and the Old Testament canon was being finalized. At the same time, Greco-Roman society tended to devalue the present and glorify the past.[18] All of these factors would have made it difficult for newer theologians to gain a hearing. Perhaps they attributed their works to respected ancient luminaries in order to deceive their readers and add authority to their message. They pretended to predict events leading up to their own time, and thereby added credibility to their real predictions concerning the readers' future. The difficulty with this theory is that it assumes a great deal of gullibility on the part of the readers. Would many people really believe that writings of Enoch, the seventh descendant of Adam (Gen 5:18-24), had suddenly appeared in the second century B.C.?

It seems more likely that pseudonymity was openly used as a literary device. In other words, the readers knew very well that the writer was not Jacob or Moses or Ezra. Attributing a book to one of these Jewish heroes was a way of saying: What you are about to read is an apocalypse, so read and understand it as such. The "pen name" was chosen according to the subject matter of the apocalypse. For

---

[17]On the decline of Jewish prophecy, see 1 Macc 4:46; 9:27; 14:41; Josephus, *Against Apion,* I.41.

[18]See John J. Collins, "Jewish Apocalyptic against Its Hellenistic Near Eastern Environment," *Bulletin of the American Schools of Oriental Research* 220 (1975): 27-36.

example, Baruch was the secretary of the prophet Jeremiah, who interprets the destruction of Jerusalem by the Babylonians in the sixth century B.C. (Jer 32:12-16; 36; 43:1-6; 45:1-2). Similarly, the author of the Syriac Apocalypse of Baruch writes of the destruction of Jerusalem by the Romans in A.D. 70. He presents himself as a "second Baruch" helping his readers understand why God again allowed the holy city to fall.

Whereas most apocalypses are pseudonymous, Revelation proves the exception to the rule. As we will see below (Part IV), John writes in his own name.

2. Common Features of Apocalyptic Theology

In addition to sharing a distinctive form of writing, Jewish and Christian apocalyptists tend to hold a number of common convictions concerning God and his ways with the world. This distinctive apocalyptic theology, or worldview, is rooted in the Old Testament. At the risk of oversimplifying a complex matter, we will trace the historical development of the apocalyptic worldview through three primary, overlapping stages: the Old Testament period, the intertestamental period, and the New Testament period.

a. Roots of Apocalyptic Theology in the Old Testament Period

(1) Genesis 1–5. Several key elements of apocalyptic theology appear in the opening chapters of Genesis, the foundational book of the Old Testament. First, God exists and he is the creator of all that is, including human beings. "In the beginning, God created the heavens and the earth" (Gen 1:1). God made humankind, both male and female, in his own image and his own likeness (Gen 1:26-27).

Second, by virtue of the fact that he is creator, God is also the owner, the king, the sovereign Lord over all creation. This truth is implicit in Genesis but is made explicit elsewhere in the Old Testament. For example, the Psalms proclaim that

> The earth is the LORD's, and everything in it, the world, and all who live in it; for he founded it upon the seas and established it upon the waters (Ps 24:1-2).

God is the King of all the earth (Ps 47:7).

As creator and king, God alone has the right to decide what his world should be — what he considers "good" in his creation and what he considers "evil."

Third, as sovereign Lord, God created the world good. "God saw all that he had made, and it was very good" (Gen 1:31) — that is, pleasing to God, perfectly conforming to his will.

Fourth, Genesis does not state that human beings are immortal by nature. Instead, the first humans, Adam and Eve, were created mortal and their lives were sustained only by God's provision. God placed the tree of life in the center of the garden so that, by eating its fruit, the man and the woman could potentially live forever (Gen 2:9; 3:22). Life is the gift of God and is sustained by God alone at his good pleasure.

Fifth, God's creatures have rebelled against his sovereign will, thus introducing "sin" or "evil" into God's "good" creation. According to Genesis 2:16-17, God issued one command to Adam:

> You are free to eat from any tree in the garden; but you must not eat from the tree of the knowledge of good and evil, for when you eat of it you will surely die.

Chapter 3 describes how one of God's creatures, the serpent (discussed below), tempted Eve to sin — that is, to "be like God" by deciding good and evil for herself (Gen 3:5). (Note that the Book of Genesis implies a rebellion against God on the part of the serpent that preceded the rebellion of Adam and Eve.) As a result, she and Adam disobeyed God, ate the forbidden fruit, and thus introduced sin into the human race (Gen 3:6).

Sixth, God has responded to the sin of his creatures by pronouncing several terrible judgments: He cursed the serpent and promised that the woman's "offspring" would crush its head and thereby destroy it (Gen 3:14-15). He condemned the woman to pains in childbearing and domination by her husband (Gen 3:16). He cursed the ground so that it would resist Adam's efforts to cultivate it and would bear fruit only through painful toil (Gen 3:17-19). Finally, God kept the promise made in Genesis 2:17 by condemning Adam and Eve to death. Genesis 3:22-24 reads:

> And the LORD God said, "The man has now become like one of us, knowing good and evil. He must not be allowed to reach out his hand and take also from the tree of life and eat, and live forever." So the LORD God banished him from the Garden of Eden to work the ground from which he had been taken. After he drove the man out, he placed on the east side of the Garden of Eden cherubim and a flaming sword flashing back and forth to guard the way to the tree of life.

Separated from the tree of life, "nature" took its course: Adam and Eve — and their descendants after them — eventually died (see Gen 5:5-31).

Note that, within the framework of Genesis, death is the destruction of God's creation. Furthermore, it is God's penalty for sin, for the idolatrous effort to be one's own "god" by deciding good and evil for oneself. Human beings die as a result of their own sin (e.g., Adam and Eve themselves) *and/or* as a result of their ancestor's sin (Adam and Eve's descendants — including, for example, innocent babies who sometimes die not because they have rebelled against God on their own, but because they have been cut off from the tree of life due to the sin of their ancestors) *and* as a result of the serpent's sin (since the serpent played a role in the fall of Adam and Eve, which led to their death and that of their descendants). As the Apostle Paul would later phrase it, "the wages of sin is death" (Rom 6:23).

(2) Promised Salvation from Sin and Death. However, throughout the Old Testament, God, in his grace and mercy, declares that he will not allow sin and death to have the last word. For example, he vows that Adam and Eve's "offspring" will crush the serpent's head (Gen 3:14-15). He swears to the nomad Abraham that "all people on earth will be blessed through you" (Gen 12:3). He promises King David that, "when your days are over and you rest with your fathers, I will raise up your offspring to succeed you, who will come from your own body, and I will establish his kingdom . . . forever" (2 Sam 7:12-13).[19] To the prophet Isaiah God reveals his future plans: "Behold, I will create new heavens and a new earth. The former things will not be remembered, nor will they come to mind" (Isa 65:17).

---

[19]For the scriptural basis of these promises, see the comments on the title "Christ" in Rev 1:5.

b. Development of Jewish Apocalyptic Theology in the Intertestamental Period

(1) Rebellion in Heaven. In reading the Old Testament and attempting to discern the truths contained in it, Jewish apocalypists draw the logical conclusion that the serpent of Genesis 3 must have been an angel who rebelled against God. After all, the Scripture says that, "in the beginning, God created the heavens and the earth" (Gen 1:1). The "heavens and earth" include *everything* that exists — both the natural, "earthly" realities and the supernatural, "heavenly" realities. Therefore the serpent must have been some sort of creature of God.

This talking "serpent" was certainly unlike other serpents; it apparently did not belong to the natural sphere. Therefore it must have been some sort of supernatural creature — a heavenly or angelic being.

Genesis states that *"all* that [God] had made" was "very *good"* (Gen 1:31), and yet the serpent reveals itself to be very *evil* by tempting humans to sin. Apparently, the "serpent" was an angel who had fallen away from God — a heavenly creature who had surrendered its original goodness and rebelled against the creator. Jewish apocalyptists conclude, then, that the "serpent" must have been a supernatural, angelic being (known to Christians as the "devil" or "Satan"), and that rebellion against God in the heavenly sphere must have preceded Adam and Eve's rebellion against God in the earthly sphere.

This type of interpretation of the Genesis story is found, for example, in 2 Enoch, a Jewish apocalypse dating to the late first century A.D.:

> But [Satanail] from the order of the archangels deviated, together with the division [of angels] that was under his authority. He thought up the impossible idea, that he might place his throne higher than the clouds which are above the earth, and that he might become equal to my [i.e., God's] power.
>
> And I hurled him out from the height, together with his angels [to the earthly sphere] . . . . And he will become a demon, because he fled from heaven; Sotona, because his name was Satanail. In this way he did become different from the angels. His nature did not change, [but] his thought did, since his consciousness of righteous and sinful things changed. And he became aware of his condemna-

tion and of the sin which he sinned previously. And that is why he thought up the scheme against Adam. In such a form he entered paradise, and corrupted Eve (2 Enoch 29:4-5 and 31:4-6 [J]).[20]

This passage from 2 Enoch also illustrates another important aspect of apocalyptic theology: While there was a rebellion against God in the heavenly sphere, this rebellion did not succeed. The rebels were put down and God maintained his sovereignty. Apocalyptic writers often express this conviction by speaking of God binding the devil and his angels in prison (e.g., 1 Enoch 10:4-6; cf. 18:12-19:1; 21:1-6; Test. Levi 18:12; Mark 3:26-27; 2 Pet 2:4; Jude 6) or casting them out of heaven onto the earth (as in the passage quoted above). Defeated on the supernatural plane, they continue their warfare on the natural plane by inciting human beings to join their fight against God.[21]

(2) The Present Evil Age and the Kingdom of Satan. As noted above, Genesis 3 attributes pains in childbearing, painful toil, and human death to God's judgment against the sin of Adam and Eve. Jewish apocalyptists read the Scripture, consider the outcome of the Fall, and draw this conclusion: The sin of Adam and Eve caused the world to be afflicted not only with the judgments mentioned above, but with all manner of evils. To illustrate, 2 Baruch (ca. A.D. 100) maintains that

> When [Adam] transgressed, untimely death came into being, mourning was mentioned, affliction was prepared, illness was created, labor accomplished, pride began to come into existence, the realm of death began to ask to be renewed with blood, the conception of children came about, the passion of the parents was produced, the loftiness of men was humiliated, and goodness vanished (2 Apoc. Bar. 56:6).[22]

---

[20]From THE OLD TESTAMENT PSEUDEPIGRAPHA by James H. Charlesworth, copyright © 1983, 1985 by James H. Charlesworth. Used by permission of Doubleday, a division of Random House, Inc. (hereafter "Charlesworth, *Pseudepigrapha*").

[21]Jesus urges God to complete his victory when he prays: "Your Kingdom come, *your will be done on earth as it is [already done] in heaven*" (Matt 6:10).

[22]Charlesworth, *Pseudipigrapha*. For further discussion of Adam and Eve in the Old Testament and other Jewish literature, see (1) John R. Levison,

Realizing that the entire human race has been adversely affected by Adam's sin, the author of 4 Ezra (ca. A.D. 100) comes close to despair:

> It would have been better if the earth had not produced Adam, or else, when it had produced him, had restrained him from sinning. . . . O Adam, what have you done? For though it was you who sinned, the fall was not yours alone, but ours also who are your descendants (4 Ezra 7:46[116], 48[118]).[23]

Yet Adam does not shoulder the whole blame for warping God's creation. All creatures (both human and angelic) who choose evil over the good, who ally themselves with Satan against God, contribute toward the ruin of God's handiwork. Second Baruch declares:

> . . . although Adam sinned first and has brought death upon all who were not in his own time, yet each of them who has been born from him has prepared for himself the coming torment [i.e., the coming judgment/punishment for sin]. . . . Adam is, therefore, not the cause [of "destruction," or "retribution"], except only for himself, but each of us has become our own Adam (2 Apoc. Bar. 54:15a, 19).[24]

Jewish apocalyptists and other writers of their era refer to this world corrupted with evils, this world marred by death, this world fallen away from its original goodness, using a number of different terms. For example, they call it "the present evil age"[25] — they claim that the "present age" is characterized by "evil." They describe this fallen world as the "kingdom of Satan" — that is, a world where Satan and his allies (both human and angelic) exercise a degree of

---

"Portraits of Adam in Early Judaism: From Sirach to 2 Baruch," *Journal for the Study of the Pseudepigrapha* Supplement Series, 1 (Sheffield: Sheffield Academic Press, 1988); and (2) the author's discussion of "Portraits of Adam Inherited by Paul" in Christopher A. Davis, *The Structure of Paul's Theology: "The Truth Which Is the Gospel"* (Lewiston/Lampeter/Queenston: Mellen Biblical Press, 1995), pp. 73-85.

[23]Charlesworth, *Pseudepigrapha*.
[24]Charlesworth, *Pseudepigrapha*.
[25]This is the phrase employed in Gal 1:4 by the Apostle Paul, whose roots were in apocalyptic Judaism.

"kingdom" or "kingship" or "rule," a degree of power and influence.[26] Human beings have collaborated with Satan to transform God's good creation into the "present evil age," the "kingdom of Satan," a world twisted and ruined by evil and death.

(3) *The Eschatological Age and the Kingdom of God.* The Jewish apocalyptists are hardheaded realists who see more clearly than most the nature and pervasiveness of evil in the created order. Still, they do not despair, for they believe the Old Testament promises of redemption. Though extremely pessimistic about the ability of human beings to purge the world of evil, they are extremely optimistic that God will prove true to his word. They trust that God will someday break into history and radically transform the cosmos, that he will "create new heavens and a new earth" through his promised Redeemer. Then sickness and death will be no more. No more will the untamed forces of nature maim and destroy. God will wipe away all tears and restore broken relationships. He will put an end to sin and evil and demonic activity in the world. Death will give way to eternal life. Now evil is tolerated, but then God will suffer evil no more. Now we are living in the "present evil age," but then God will

---

[26]The idea of the world being the "kingdom of Satan" appears, for example, in Luke 11:18 (cf. 4:5-6). Concerning the meaning of this term, three clarifications are in order:

First, the Greek word translated "kingdom" (βασιλεία, *basileia*) does not refer to the *place* where Satan rules, but to his *exercise of rule* or kingship or sovereignty or influence in the world.

Second, when ancient Jewish and Christian writers speak of the world as being under the "kingdom of Satan," or ruled by Satan, they do not mean that God has lost control over his creation so that he cannot put an end to evil anytime he desires. (Note, for example, the limitations placed on Satan by God in Job 1-2.) Instead, they are simply acknowledging that the world is a place where evil is real. For whatever reason, God has chosen, for the time being, to *tolerate* the presence of evil in the world he created to be good.

Third, when these writers describe the world as the "kingdom of Satan," they are not saying that every single evil thing that happens in the world is *directly* caused by Satan. For example, they are not saying that Satan *forces* human beings to commit sins against one another and against God. Instead, the term "kingdom of Satan" is simply a succinct way of referring to the world in its evil state — whatever the cause of that evil may be. Satan, the primary evildoer, is allowed to stand for all evils, all evildoers.

inaugurate a "new age" or "last age" or "eschatological age" (from the Greek term ἔσχατος [*eschatos*], which means "last"). Now we know only the perversion of creation, but then God will make a "new creation." Now the world is the "kingdom of Satan," but then he will transform it into the "kingdom of God."

(4) The Shift of the Ages. Through what sequence of events will this radical reconfiguration of all things come about? In general, the Jewish apocalyptists anticipate that the world will first undergo a time of terrible "distress" or "tribulation" as Satan and his allies make one last attempt to overcome God and his people. They liken this period of turmoil to the "woes" or "birth pains" that a woman endures in childbirth. In their minds, this time of suffering for God's people will be the "labor pains" preceding the "birth" of the "new creation."[27]

Second, God will send the promised Savior and Redeemer, the Messiah and Christ, the Son of David and Son of Abraham.

Third, they predict that the "labor pains" and the coming of the Messiah will be followed by a great day (sometimes called the "day of the Lord") in which God will suddenly raise the dead (either all the dead or only the servants of God, depending on the writer) to new life.

Fourth, the Messiah will carry out God's final judgment against all his enemies. In other words, God, through his Messiah, will set all wrongs right and put an end to the evil that pollutes his creation. Satan, his angels, and humans allied with them will either be annihilated or forced to suffer an eternal punishment (depending on the writer).

The end result will be a "new age" or "new creation" in which every aspect will conform to God's good and perfect will — the "consummation" of the kingdom of God, or the coming of God's sovereign rule in its fullness.

Who will participate in this new world? Virtually all the Jewish apocalyptists agree that only righteous, covenant-keeping Jews who obey the Law of Moses (not Gentiles) will inherit a place in the consummated kingdom of God (see Fig. 1, overleaf).

---

[27]Some writers refer to this event as the "messianic woes" — namely, the "labor pains" associated with the coming of the Messiah (discussed below).

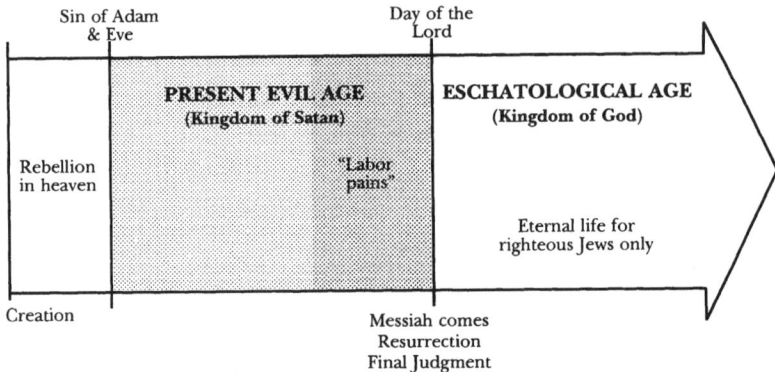

Fig. 1. The Shape of Jewish Apocalyptic Theology

These sorts of expectations are characteristic features of Jewish apocalyptic theology — common elements of the apocalyptists' understanding of God and his dealings with the world. To illustrate, most are found in two passages from the book of Daniel, a Jewish apocalypse included in the Christian canon.

In Daniel 2, King Nebuchadnezzar has a dream in which he sees an enormous statue with a head of gold, chest and arms of silver, belly and thighs of bronze, legs of iron, and feet made partly of iron and partly of baked clay. As the king watches, a rock "cut out, but not by human hands" (i.e., cut out by God) strikes the statue and shatters it to dust. Then the rock becomes a huge mountain that fills the whole earth (see Dan 2:31-35). In verses 36-45 Daniel interprets the vision, telling Nebuchadnezzar:

> . . . You, O king, are the king of kings. . . . You are that head of gold.
>
> After you, another kingdom will rise, inferior to yours. Next, a third kingdom, one of bronze, will rule over the whole earth. Finally, there will be a fourth kingdom, strong as iron — for iron breaks and smashes everything — and as iron breaks things to pieces, so it will crush and break all the others. Just as you saw that the feet and toes were partly of baked clay and partly of iron, so this will be a divided kingdom; yet it will have some of the strength of iron in it, even as you saw iron mixed with clay. . . .
>
> In the time of those kings, the God of heaven will set up a kingdom that will never be destroyed, nor will it be left to another

> people. It will crush all those kingdoms and bring them to an end, but it will itself endure forever.

Daniel predicts that a series of temporal, human kingdoms (represented by the statue) will be replaced (on the "day of the Lord" at the "final judgment") by the eternal kingdom of God (represented by the rock).

Other common elements of Jewish apocalyptic theology appear in Daniel 12:1-3:

> At that time [the archangel] Michael, the great prince who protects your people [= the Jews], will arise. There will be a time of distress such as has not happened from the beginning of nations until then [= the period of "labor pains"]. But at that time your people — everyone whose name is found written in the book — will be delivered. Multitudes who sleep in the dust of the earth will awake [= the resurrection]: some to everlasting life, others to shame and everlasting contempt [= the division made between the righteous and unrighteous at the final judgment]. Those who are wise will shine like the brightness of the heavens, and those who lead many to righteousness [= obedience to the Mosaic Law], like the stars for ever and ever.

(5) Apocalyptic Transcendence, Dualism, and Pessimism. We have seen that the Jewish apocalyptists hold a transcendent worldview. They believe that beyond the visible, material, earthly, physical realities, there lie invisible, immaterial, heavenly, spiritual realities. Spiritual powers influence the material universe in significant ways. The apocalyptic worldview makes room for the supernatural.

Since some angels and some humans oppose God, apocalyptic theology also includes a strong element of dualism. In other words, there are two opposing powers in the world — the evil and the good. What we are witnessing in history is a struggle between the forces of good (God, his angels, his righteous servants) and the forces of evil (Satan, demonic powers, unrighteous persons who do not submit to the Lord). Apocalyptists do not believe in an absolute dualism, for the power of Satan and his allies is not equal to that of the creator and Lord of all. However, evil powers do exercise a degree of influence in the world because the sovereign God — for the time being — permits it. One of the reasons the righteous suffer is that they are being attacked and persecuted by the enemies of God, both human and demonic.

Most apocalypses come out of communities experiencing such persecution firsthand. Their prolonged struggle with evil has led them to a certain kind of pessimism. The Old Testament prophets look for God's good purposes to be worked out within the historical process — in the world as we know it. In contrast, Jewish apocalyptists do not expect the world to improve. They doubt that human beings will *ever* overcome evil to build a good, just, and godly society on their own.

(6) Apocalyptic Optimism, Determinism, and Triumph. Although they are pessimistic about humanity's ability to redeem a fallen world, the apocalyptists are optimistic that God will do just that. From the Old Testament, they know that God is good, just, powerful, and true. If he is good, then he will not allow evil to stand forever. If he is just, then he will punish the wicked and reward the righteous. If he is powerful, then he *can* do it; and if he can do it, then he *will* do it. But if this is so, then why do so many of God's faithful servants suffer hardship, poverty, and even violent death? If this is so, then why do so many of the wicked live prosperous lives and then die peacefully in bed? With remarkable faith, apocalyptic writers conclude that God will be true to himself and true to his promises. He *will* punish evildoers and vindicate his holy people — if not before death then after death, if not in this life then in another, if not in this world then in a new world created just for them. History has a goal predetermined by God:[28] The Sovereign Lord will redeem his fallen creation, purging it from evil and bringing every detail into conformity with his good and perfect will. The Lord will indeed triumph; his kingdom will come.

---

[28]Some apocalyptists have the ancient Jewish hero, in whose name they write (see above under "Pseudonymity"), accurately "predict" the course of history from ancient times to the writer's own time. This is called "*ex eventu* prophecy." Through this literary device, the writers express the twin truths that history has a goal and that God directs history toward that goal.

c. Development of Christian Apocalyptic Theology in the New Testament Period

Against this background, we now turn our attention to the New Testament period. When the German theologian Ernst Käsemann identifies Jewish apocalyptic as "the mother of Christian theology,"[29] he is not far off the mark. When Jesus of Nazareth arrives on the scene, he confirms that much of the apocalyptists' interpretation of the Old Testament is correct. Influenced by Jesus and the first disciples taught by him, New Testament writers introduce many elements of Jewish apocalyptic theology into the Christian Bible. Some elements they adopt wholesale; others they modify or transform as their insight into God's purpose — enacted through Christ — surpasses that of their predecessors. Christian theology, then, is largely *apocalyptic* theology.

(1) Supernatural Forces of Evil. New Testament writers share the apocalyptists' belief in both the earthly and heavenly, the natural and supernatural spheres. Behind the evils plaguing this world — behind the deeply rooted systemic wickedness, behind the sophisticated lies that have for centuries held entire civilizations captive under false worldviews — lies an intelligence, a power beside and beyond that of mere human beings. As Paul says,

> Our struggle is not against flesh and blood [i.e., human beings — creatures of the earthly, natural sphere], but against the rulers, against the authorities, against the powers of this dark world and against the spiritual forces of evil in the heavenly [supernatural] realms (Eph 6:12).

(2) Adam and the Present Evil Age. New Testament writers also hold to the notion of the "kingdom of Satan" or "present evil age" — an era marred by sin and death that begins with the rebellion of Adam and ends with the consummation of God's kingdom. To illustrate, Paul maintains that

> . . . sin entered the world through one man [Adam], and death through sin, . . . many died by the trespass of the one man . . . .

---

[29]Ernst Käsemann, "On the Topic of Primitive Christian Apocalyptic," *Journal for Theology and the Church* 6 (1969): 133. This issue of *JTC* also contains responses to Käsemann by Gerhard Ebeling and Ernst Fuchs.

> The judgment [of God] followed one sin and brought condemnation. . . . by the trespass of the one man, death reigned through that one man . . . (Rom 5:12,15,16,17).

> The creation waits in eager expectation for the sons of God to be revealed [at the resurrection]. For the creation was subjected to frustration, not by its own choice, but by the will of the one who subjected it, in hope that the creation itself will be liberated from its bondage to decay [including death] and brought into the glorious freedom [from decay] of the children of God (Rom 8:19-21).

(3) The Kingdom of God and the Ministry of Jesus. Working from within this kind of apocalyptic worldview, New Testament writers show that Jesus — in his words and even more so in his deeds — claimed to be the promised Messiah, the one sent by God to annihilate the kingdom of Satan and inaugurate the kingdom of God. As 1 John 3:8 words it, "The reason the Son of God appeared was to destroy the devil's work."

That this was Jesus' purpose and mission is seen in every aspect of his ministry. For example, the coming of God's kingdom was the subject of Jesus' preaching, as shown by the summary of his message found in Mark 1:14-15:

> After John [the Baptist] was put in prison, Jesus went into Galilee, proclaiming the good news [or "gospel"] of God. "The time has come," he said. "The kingdom of God is near. Repent and believe the good news!"

Note that the "gospel" message, according to Jesus, is the proclamation of the "good news" — the apocalyptic promise — that God will soon annihilate evil and transform the entire cosmos to conform to his will.

God's coming kingdom was also the focus of Jesus' teaching. For example, in teaching his disciples to pray, Jesus tells them:

> This, then, is how you should pray: "Our Father in heaven, hallowed be your name, your kingdom come, your will be done on earth as it is in heaven" (Matt 6:9-10).[30]

---

[30]This prayer contains one of the best definitions of the "kingdom of God" found in the New Testament: The coming of the "kingdom" means that God's will is done in the natural, "earthly" sphere, as well as in the

When Jesus calls on people to repent and "leave your life of sin" (John 8:11), he is urging them to turn away from evil — to renounce their alliance with Satan (whether conscious or unconscious) and conform their lives to the coming "kingdom" or "rule" or "Lordship" of God. When Jesus forgives sins as only God can (see, e.g., Luke 5:17-26), he shows that God — through his Messiah Jesus — is in the process of doing away with evil, in the process of wiping away the sin that has corrupted his creation for so long. When Jesus gathers disciples to himself and commands them to "love each other as I have loved you" (see, e.g., John 15:12), then he is beginning to form the community of the "eschatological age," when men and women from all nations will live together in peace forever under the beneficent kingship of God.

Jesus' miracles also proclaim the "good news" of God's emerging kingdom. They show that, in the person of Jesus the Christ, God has entered into his sinful, fallen, perverted creation in order to set things right — to reestablish his kingdom rule over it. For example, by healing the sick, Jesus shows that God is going to put an end to the pain and suffering and misery that have warped his good creation. This is why Jesus, in Luke 10:8-9, gives these instructions to his disciples when he sends them out with authority to preach and heal in his name:

> When you enter a town and are welcomed, eat what is set before you. Heal the sick who are there *and* tell them, *"The kingdom of God is near you"* (italics added for emphasis here and throughout the commentary).

He says, when you heal the sick, you must not forget to tell them what it means — what it signifies. The healings are intended to show that the kingdom or lordship of God is near — that it is becoming a reality through the Messiah Jesus (here working through his disciples).

When Jesus exorcises demons, he shows that God is in the process of destroying the kingdom of Satan and establishing the kingdom of God. To illustrate, Luke 11:14-20 recounts how, on one occasion,

---

supernatural, "heavenly" sphere. Rebellion against the creator's lordship ceases throughout creation.

Jesus was driving out a demon that was mute. When the demon left, the man who had been mute spoke, and the crowd was amazed. But some of them said, "By Beelzebub [another name for Satan], the prince of demons, he is driving out demons." Others tested him by asking for a sign from heaven.

Jesus knew their thoughts and said to them: "Any kingdom divided against itself will be ruined, and a house divided against itself will fall. If Satan is divided against himself, how can his kingdom stand? I say this because you claim that I drive out demons by Beelzebub. Now if I drive out demons by Beelzebub, by whom do your followers drive them out? So then, they will be your judges. But if I drive out demons by the finger of God [i.e., by the power of God], then *the kingdom of God has [already] come to you.*"

When Jesus calms the storm and walks on water (see Matt 14:22-33; Mark 6:45-52; John 6:16-21), he shows that even the forces of nature — all God's creation — will be brought under his lordship so that they bend to his will and no longer hurt and destroy. When Jesus resuscitates the dead (e.g., Lazarus in John 11), he points forward to the day when all God's people will be raised up to eternal life in his consummated kingdom.

(4) The Kingdom of God and the Death of Jesus. What is the relationship between Jesus' death on the cross and the kingdom of God? During the Old Testament period, covenants — i.e., formal relationships between two parties — were established or sealed through animal sacrifices. To illustrate, Exodus 24:1-11 describes how God established a covenant with the people of Israel that was mediated by Moses (the so-called "Mosaic Covenant"). The Law of the Lord was read to the people, specifying the behavior that would be required of them in their new relationship with God. Israel then "responded with one voice, 'Everything the Lord has said we will do'" (vv. 3,7). They agreed to enter into the type of covenantal relationship with God described by the Law. Next, animals were sacrificed and Moses sealed the covenant with blood: He "took the blood, sprinkled it on the people and said, 'This is the blood of the covenant that the Lord has made with you'" (v. 8) — i.e., the sacrificial blood that seals or establishes the Mosaic Covenant. Finally, the elders of Israel, on behalf of the entire nation, ascended Mount Sinai, saw God, and ate and drank with him. They shared a

"covenant meal" celebrating the new relationship with God Israel now enjoyed through the blood sacrifices.[31]

During his last meal with his disciples — on the evening before his crucifixion — Jesus took simple bread and a cup of wine, and he used them to offer the most detailed explanation of his death in the Gospels:

> When the hour came, Jesus and his apostles reclined at the table. And he said to them, "I have eagerly desired to eat this Passover with you before I suffer. For I tell you, I will not eat it again until it finds fulfilllment in the kingdom of God."
>
> After taking the cup, he gave thanks and said, "Take this and divide it among you. For I tell you I will not drink again of the fruit of the vine until the kingdom of God comes."
>
> And he took bread, gave thanks and broke it, and gave it to them, saying, "This is my body given for you; do this in remembrance of me."
>
> In the same way, after the supper he took the cup, saying, "This cup is the new covenant in my blood, which is poured out for you" (Luke 22:14-20).

Jesus says, "This is my body given *for you* (ὑπὲρ ὑμῶν, *hyper hymōn*) . . . . my blood, which is poured out *for you (hyper hymōn).*" Although not readily apparent in English translation, this is sacrificial language from the Greek version of the Old Testament. Jesus is saying that his impending death will be a sacrifice. But what kind of sacrifice? The Lord tells them: "This cup is the new covenant in my blood." He uses language nearly identical to that employed in Exodus 24:8 ("This is the blood of the covenant") to identify his death precisely as the kind of sacrifice that establishes a covenant. What covenant? Not the Mosaic Covenant, but a "new covenant."

---

[31]The manner in which the Mosaic Covenant was established may be compared to modern customs for establishing a marriage covenant: The vows — like the Mosaic Law — spell out, in general terms, the nature of the new relationship the bride and groom will share. As Israel responded to the Law by declaring, "We will do everything the Lord has said," the bride and groom respond to the vows with "I do." As the Mosaic Covenant was sealed by blood sacrifices, the marriage covenant is sealed with a kiss. As Israel celebrated their new relationship with God with a covenant meal, a joyful reception or dinner often follows the wedding ceremony.

What, then, is the significance of the ritual meal of bread and wine — the "Eucharist" or "Lord's Supper" Jesus commands his disciples to observe "in remembrance of me"? It is the "covenant meal" celebrating the establishment of the "new covenant" through Jesus' sacrifice. Who participates in this "new covenant"? God, who sent Jesus to establish the covenant, and Jesus' disciples — those from "all nations" (see Matt 28:19), *Jews and Gentiles alike*, who accept God's lordship over their lives as exercised through his Messiah. In other words, those persons to whom the "covenant meal" is offered. Finally, when may Jesus' disciples participate in this "new covenant" relationship with God? The answer is: Both now and, more completely, in the future. The "new covenant" was established in the *past* by Jesus' sacrificial death. It is in place now, in the *present*, so that Jesus' disciples — who were once "God's enemies" — are now at "peace with God" and "reconciled to him through the death of his Son" (Rom 5:1,10). Yet disciples of Christ will experience this new relationship with God on an even deeper, more intimate level, in the *future* — when they are raised from the dead, when they "see him as he is" (1 John 3:2), when the new covenant "finds fulfilllment in the [consummated] kingdom of God."

Who participates in the Kingdom of God — the coming "new creation" in which every detail will *conform to the will of God*? All those who share in the "new covenant." And who participates in the "new covenant"? All those who choose to be disciples of Jesus. All those who *conform to the will of God* as he makes that will known through his Messiah. All those who embrace God's kingdom rule over their lives in Christ. In essence, Jesus offers "all nations" a place in the kingdom of God *now* in the form of the "new covenant" established by his sacrificial death. This truth is extremely important: Jesus' death on the cross forgives sins not merely in the sense that, through it, God pardons wrong deeds. (The sinner receiving such a pardon would still be trapped in a fallen world and doomed to death.) Jesus' death forgives sins in the sense that it provides an escape from the "present evil age" — and entrance into the emerging kingdom of God — in the form of a "new covenant" relationship with God. By his sacrificial death, Jesus shattered the kingdom of Satan, the powers of sin and death, and thus established the kingdom of God. The New Testament writers testify to this wonderful truth:

> . . . the Lord Jesus Christ . . . gave himself for our sins to rescue us from the present evil age, according to the will of our God and Father . . . (Gal 1:3-4).
>
> Since the children have flesh and blood, he too shared in their humanity so that by his death he might destroy him who holds the power of death — that is, the devil — and free those who all their lives were held in slavery by their fear of death (Heb 2:14-15).
>
> [God] has rescued us from the dominion of darkness and brought us into the kingdom of the Son he loves, in whom we have redemption, the forgiveness of sins (Col 1:13-14).
>
> . . . our Savior, Christ Jesus, . . . has destroyed death and has brought life and immortality to light through the gospel (2 Tim 1:10).
>
> Since death came through a man [Adam], the resurrection of the dead comes also through a man [Jesus Christ] (1 Cor 15:21).

Jesus is the full realization of the Old Testament and apocalyptic hopes. He is the "son of Adam" who crushes the serpent's head for his disciples by dying to make a place for them in God's kingdom. He is the "Son of Abraham" who offers this blessing to "all people on earth." He is the "Son of David" who rules over an eternal Kingdom — not through military force, but by dying as a sacrifice for his people. He is the promised one who freely offers "new heavens and a new earth" to all who desire it — to everyone willing to live as his disciple, willing to accept the beneficent rule of God over his or her life.

(5) The Kingdom of God and the Resurrection of Jesus. Jesus died on the cross, and on the third day — much to the surprise of his disciples — God raised him from the dead. What is the meaning and significance of his resurrection? Many answers to that question are found in the New Testament, but we shall mention only four: First, the fact that Jesus was raised from the dead means that he is our contemporary, that he continues to live and work among us. His Spirit is continuously present with us today in accordance with the promise he gave to his first disciples: "Surely I am with you always, to the consummation of the age" (Matt 28:20).

Second, Jesus' return from the grave shows that life after death is possible. Furthermore, such life takes the form of resurrection, by which the biblical writers mean *transformed, bodily existence in the eschatological age*. Resurrection is a *bodily* form of existence in the sense that, like the risen Jesus, raised persons possess bodies (σῶμα, *sōma*). They are not ghosts or disembodied spirits. Like Jesus, they also retain their memories, their personalities, their identities — everything that made them who they were before death, everything that made them some*body*. (The Greek idea of the *sōma* includes both the "body" in the sense of the "physical frame" and the "body" in the sense of the "person.") Resurrection is a *transformed* kind of existence in the sense that, like Jesus, raised persons enjoy a better, higher, more glorious, more exalted, more lasting form of existence than they knew before death.³² Resurrection is existence *in the eschatological age* in the sense described below.

Third, the resurrection of Jesus marks the beginning of the general resurrection of the righteous anticipated by the apocalyptists. Thus Paul calls Christ "the firstfruits of those who have fallen asleep" (1 Cor 15:20) and "the firstborn from among the dead" (Col 1:18) — that is, the first of many to rise from death to eternal life. This is why Christ's resurrection was more than an anomaly, why it gives Christians sure hope for their own resurrection. Jesus' emergence from the tomb shows that the apocalyptists' hopes were not misplaced — that there is indeed such a thing as the resurrection, that it has begun, and that we should expect for many more to be raised in the future. When will this "general resurrection" take place? Jesus indicated that it would occur at his "Second Coming" or "Parousia" (from the Greek term παρουσία for "coming," "arrival" or "appearing"), when he returns to carry out the final judgment and consummate the kingdom of God.³³ Paul describes this event in 1 Thessalonians 4:13-18:

> Brothers, we do not want you to be ignorant about those who fall asleep, or to grieve like the rest of men, who have no hope. We believe that Jesus died and rose again and so we believe that God will bring with Jesus those who have fallen asleep in him. According to the Lord's own word, we tell you that we who are still alive, who are

---

³²See, e.g., the description of the resurrection body/person found in 1 Cor 15:35-56.

³³See, e.g., John 14:2-3; 5:25-29.

left till the coming [*parousia*] of the Lord, will certainly not precede those who have fallen asleep. For the Lord himself will come down from heaven, with a loud command, with the voice of the archangel and with the trumpet call of God, and the dead in Christ will rise first. After that, we who are still alive and are left will be caught up together with them in the clouds to meet the Lord in the air. And so we will be with the Lord forever. Therefore encourage each other with these words (1 Thess 4:13-18).

From that time forward, "there will be no more death or mourning or crying or pain, for the old order of things has passed away" (Rev 21:4).

Fourth, the resurrection of Jesus marks the beginning of the eschatological age and the kingdom of God. The Jewish apocalyptists had predicted that the resurrection of the dead would announce the coming of God's kingdom (see above). The resurrection of Jesus, "the firstborn from among the dead," showed his first disciples that the anticipated event had begun — that God was beginning to fulfilll his eschatological promises, that the kingdom of God had arrived. At the same time, the fact that sin and evil continued to mar the world, the fact that human beings continued to die, demonstrated to first century Christians that the kingdom of Satan had not yet entirely passed away. In light of these two undeniable realities (the continued presence of evil in the world and the eschatological event of Christ's resurrection), they concluded that God's intention must be to establish his kingdom more gradually than the Jewish apocalyptists had anticipated. In other words, the "present evil age" and the "eschatological age" would coexist — or "overlap" — for a time.

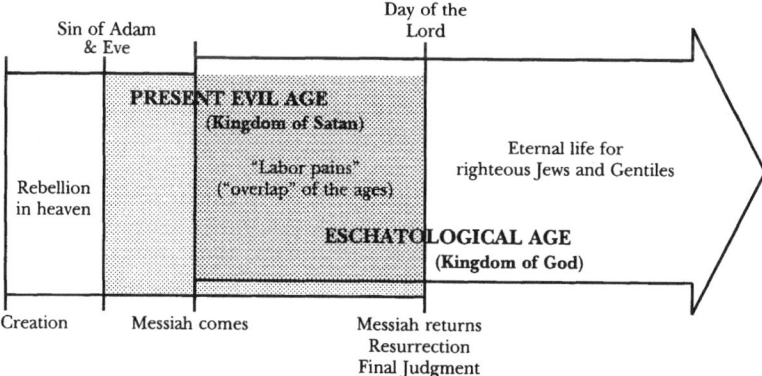

Fig. 2. The Shape of Christian Apocalyptic Theology

In the recent past, the kingdom of God had invaded the kingdom of Satan with the coming, the ministry, the death, and the resurrection of the Messiah.[34] In the present (which becomes the period of "labor pains" in Christian theology — see below), God is allowing the two kingdoms, the two realities, to coexist. The "new covenant" is in place and Christians are embracing the kingdom of God over their lives; but death, the "last enemy," has not yet been completely "destroyed." In the future, however, Christ will return a second time to annihilate the kingdom of Satan and consummate the kingdom of God.[35] In this way, Jesus' resurrection from the dead gave Christian theology its distinctive shape as compared to Jewish apocalyptic theology (compare Fig. 2 with Fig. 1).

Romans 13:11-14 shows that the Apostle Paul arrived at this understanding of God's actions in Christ. In this text, he compares the kingdom of Satan to the darkness or nighttime and the kingdom of God to the light or daytime:

> And do this [i.e., live as kingdom people by obeying Christ's command to "love one another"], understanding the present time [ὁ νῦν καιρός (ho nyn kairos), Paul's technical term for the "overlap" of the ages]. The hour has come for you to wake up from your slumber [i.e., act as if the daytime/kingdom of God has arrived and the nighttime/kingdom of Satan has ended], because our salvation [i.e., our resurrection to eternal life in the consummated kingdom of God] is nearer now than when we first believed. The night is nearly over [i.e., the kingdom of Satan has not entirely ended, but its days are numbered]; the day is almost here [i.e., the kingdom of God has not yet completely arrived, but

---

[34]For this reason, New Testament writers maintain that "this is the last (or 'eschatological') hour" (1 John 2:28, cf. Heb 1:2; 1 Pet 1:20).

[35]If God hates evil, then why does he not transform the cosmos immediately? Why does God delay the consummation of his kingdom? New Testament writers explain that God delays the final judgment in order to give Jews and Gentiles from all nations the opportunity to hear the gospel of Christ, repent of their sins, and embrace the kingdom/new covenant relationship with God made possible by Christ's sacrificial death (see, e.g., 2 Pet 3:9-15). The author further speculates that, by tolerating evil for a season, God ensures the establishment of a redeemed community that — having once experienced the ravages of sin and death — will never turn to evil again.

it has "dawned"]. So let us put aside the deeds of darkness and put on the armor of light. Let us behave decently, as in the daytime [i.e., as if God's kingdom rule had already fully come], not in orgies and drunkenness, not in sexual immorality and debauchery, not in dissension and jealousy. Rather, clothe yourselves with the Lord Jesus Christ, and do not think about how to gratify the desires of the sinful nature.

That the "overlap" of the ages was Jesus' own understanding of God's plan is shown by his masterful Parable of the Weeds:

> Jesus told them another parable: "The kingdom of heaven [= the kingdom of God — the sovereignty God exercises from the heavenly sphere, rather than any human sovereignty exercised from the earthly sphere] is like a man who sowed good seed in his field. But while everyone was sleeping, his enemy came and sowed weeds among the wheat, and went away. When the wheat sprouted and formed heads, then the weeds also appeared.
>
> "The owner's servants came to him and said, 'Sir, didn't you sow good seed in your field? Where then did the weeds come from?'
>
> "'An enemy did this,' he replied.
>
> "The servants asked him, 'Do you want us to go and pull them up?'
>
> "'No,' he answered, 'because while you are pulling the weeds, you may root up the wheat with them. Let both grow together [= the "overlap" of the ages when the kingdom of Satan and kingdom of God coexist — see the interpretation of the parable given below] until the harvest. At that time I will tell the harvesters: First collect the weeds and tie them in bundles to be burned; then gather the wheat and bring it into my barn.'"
>
> Then he left the crowd and went into the house. His disciples came to him and said, "Explain to us the parable of the weeds in the field."
>
> He answered, "The one who sowed the good seed is the Son of Man [i.e., Jesus, the Messiah, who inaugurates the kingdom of God by preaching the gospel and dying as the sacrifice that makes it possible for people to become disciples/participants in the "new covenant"/"sons of the kingdom"]. The field is the world, and the good seed stands for the sons of the kingdom. The weeds are the sons of the evil one, and the enemy who sows them is the devil. The harvest is the end of the age [i.e., the final judgment

when a division is made between the wicked and the righteous, when the "present evil age" is ended and the "eschatological age" comes in its fullness], and the harvesters are angels.

"As the weeds are pulled up and burned in the fire, so it will be at the end of the age. The Son of Man will send out his angels, and they will weed out of his kingdom everything that causes sin and all who do evil. [Note that Jesus considers the field/world to be *his* kingdom. God has never surrendered his good creation to the evil one, but at the final judgment will root out and destroy his evil works.] They will throw them into the fiery furnace, where there will be weeping and gnashing of teeth [i.e., eschatological condemnation for the wicked]. Then the righteous will shine like the sun [i.e., the radiant glory of the resurrection body] in the kingdom of their Father. He who has ears, let him hear" (Matt 13:24-30,36-43).

d. Major Differences between Jewish and Christian Apocalyptic Theology

Jewish apocalyptic is indeed "the mother of Christian theology." The first Christians interpret Jesus in apocalyptic terms, as the Lord himself taught them to do. However, while Jesus does fulfill apocalyptic expectations, he does not do it in the way most Jews expect. Consequently, their first-hand experience with God's Messiah leads the early Christians to recast apocalyptic theology in several significant ways (again, compare Fig. 1 with Fig. 2).

(1) Identity of the Messiah. Christian apocalyptic writers name Jesus of Nazareth as the promised Messiah who destroys the kingdom of Satan and establishes the kingdom of God. Non-Christian Jewish apocalyptists do not, of course, make that identification.

(2) The Coming of God's Kingdom. From the point of view of Jewish apocalyptists, the coming of God's kingdom rule lies in the future, at the long-anticipated "Day of the Lord." In contrast, Jesus' first disciples see the kingdom as both a present and a future reality. They proclaim not that God has made promises that he will *someday* fulfill, but that he has made promises that he has *already begun* to fulfill in their own lifetime. The kingdom of God has begun to appear with the first coming of Jesus. With his Second Coming it will reach its sudden and swift consummation. In other words, for Jewish

apocalyptists the kingdom of God comes suddenly in the future. For Christian apocalyptists it comes more gradually, in two stages.[36]

Scholars sometimes refer to this idea as "the already, but not yet" of Christian theology. The kingdom of God has *already* broken into history with the coming of Jesus, but it has *not yet* come in its fullness. Another way of saying this is that Christian theology contains a strong element of "realized eschatology." This is the belief that many of the eschatological events (e.g., the "labor pains," the coming of the Messiah, the resurrection, the coming of God's kingdom) are already, to some extent, being "realized" or experienced in the present.

(3) The "Labor Pains." Jewish apocalyptists view the period immediately preceding the consummation of God's kingdom as the "labor pains" — a time of intense suffering and persecution for God's people. Christian writers agree that the "labor pains" precede the consummation. However, they differ from their predecessors by identifying the "labor pains" with the period between Christ's first and second comings — the "overlap" of the ages.[37]

(4) Participants in God's Kingdom. Both Jewish and Christian apocalyptists agree that resurrection to eternal life in the consummated kingdom of God is for the "righteous" — that is, for covenant-keepers. They disagree regarding which covenant leads to this salvation. Jewish apocalyptists reserve resurrection to life for persons who participate in the Mosaic covenant and obey the Mosaic Law. In most cases, this limits salvation to Jews, since the Mosaic Law was given to the Jewish people. Christian apocalyptists believe that salvation comes to those who share in the new covenant established by Christ's sacrificial death. This new covenant is based not on Jewish descent, but on "faith" or commitment to God/Christ as Lord. It

---

[36]For the kingdom as a present reality, see, for example, Luke 11:20 and 17:20. For the kingdom as a future reality, see Matt 25:31-33; Luke 19:11-27; and 21:25-31. For the kingdom as both a present and a future reality, see Matt 13:24-30, 36-43; John 5:24-25; and Rom 13:11-14. For the gradual coming of the kingdom, see Matt 13:31-33. For the sudden consummation of the kingdom, see Matt 24:36–25:13.

[37]See the comment on Rev 1:9, as well as Part III.B.3 of the Commentary: "Summary of Revelation 6 and Comparison with Matthew 24."

therefore opens the way for both Jews and Gentiles to enter the rule of God.[38]

(5) Expectation and Fulfillment. The gap between Jewish expectation and the actual fulfilllment of God's promises proved a stumbling block to many Jews of the first century. Luke shows that even John the Baptist was bewildered by the way in which Jesus carried out his messianic mission:

> John's disciples told him about all these things [Jesus was doing]. Calling two of them, he sent them to the Lord to ask, "Are you the one who was to come, or should we expect someone else?"
>
> When the men came to Jesus, they said, "John the Baptist sent us to you to ask, 'Are you the one who was to come, or should we expect someone else?'"
>
> At that very time Jesus cured many who had diseases, sicknesses and evil spirits, and gave sight to many who were blind. So he replied to the messengers, "Go back and report to John what you have seen and heard: The blind receive sight, the lame walk, those who have leprosy are cured, the deaf hear, the dead are raised, and the good news is preached to the poor. [As we have seen, all these activities are manifestations of the end of Satan's rule and the coming of God's rule through Jesus the Messiah.] Blessed is the man who does not fall away on account of me" (Luke 7:18-23 // Matt 11:2-6).

In other words, blessed is the one who does not miss the coming of the Messiah and God's kingdom because Jesus does not fulfill the apocalyptic prophecies in the way that most Jews expect.

The Revelation of John is an expression of Christian apocalyptic theology in the apocalyptic form. For this reason, its message goes

---

[38]Marveling at the faith shown by a Gentile centurion, Jesus articulates this happy reality in Matt 8:10-12: "I tell you the truth, I have not found anyone in Israel [i.e., any Jew] with such great faith. I say to you that many will come from the east and the west [i.e., many Gentiles from outside Israel], and will take their places at the feast with Abraham, Isaac and Jacob in the kingdom of heaven. But the subjects of the kingdom [i.e., Jews who possessed the Scriptures and should have recognized Jesus as Messiah, but who refused to put their faith in him] will be thrown outside, into the darkness, where there will be weeping and gnashing of teeth."

far beyond that of non-Christian apocalypses. Christian theology is rooted in Jewish apocalyptic theology, but Jesus Christ transforms apocalyptic expectation in significant ways.

IV. AUTHOR, DATE, PLACE OF WRITING, OCCASION, AND FIRST READERS

Before examining the message of Revelation, we must first address several important introductory questions concerning this book: Who is the author? When was the book written? Where was the author when he wrote the book? To whom was Revelation written? What occasion or situation does the author address? In seeking answers to these questions, we will examine both internal evidence (i.e., answers found within Revelation itself) and external evidence (i.e., clues to the origin of Revelation from outside the book).

A. INTERNAL EVIDENCE

In the first chapter of Revelation, the author provides us with important information concerning himself and his intended readers:

John,
To the seven churches in the province of Asia: (Rev 1:4)

I, John, your brother and companion in the suffering and kingdom and patient endurance that are ours in Jesus, was on the island of Patmos because of the word of God and the testimony of Jesus. On the Lord's Day I was in the Spirit, and I heard behind me a loud voice like a trumpet, which said: "Write on a scroll what you see and send it to the seven churches: to Ephesus, Smyrna, Pergamum, Thyatira, Sardis, Philadelphia and Laodicea" (Rev 1:9-11).

1. First Readers

The author identifies his audience as "the seven churches in the province of Asia" — specifically the Christian congregations in the cities of "Ephesus, Smyrna, Pergamum, Thyatira, Sardis, Philadelphia and Laodicea." The Roman "province of Asia" made up the western third of Asia Minor (modern Turkey), with Ephesus serving as the provincial capital. The churches here had historical ties to the Apostle Paul, who established several congregations in this region during the late 40s and early 50s. For two or three years, Paul used Ephesus as his base of operations for training leaders and evangelizing the whole province (see Acts 19:8-10).[39] John's "seven churches" may refer to seven literal churches. However, since the number "seven" tends to symbolize "completeness" in apocalyptic literature, these churches probably represent the whole of the Christian community in Asia.[40]

The Asian churches were mixed bodies of Gentile and Jewish believers, reflecting the ethnic diversity of the province. By the late first century, about one million Jews made their homes in Asia Minor where they established more than fifty synagogues.[41] Some had migrated to Asia from Palestine after the Jewish revolt against Rome in A.D. 66-73.[42] Jewish Christians from Palestine would have been familiar with apocalyptic, for many apocalypses were produced in Palestine during this period.

2. Author

The author's name is "John." He calls himself a "brother" — that is, a Christian.[43] He functions as a prophet or spokesman for God.[44]

---

[39] Paul's Letter to the Colossians mentions the church at Laodicea in 4:16.

[40] See the discussion of "Symbolic Numbers" in Part III.B.1 of the Commentary. The number "seven" appears fifty-four times in Revelation. For more information on the seven cities John names, see Part A of the comments on Revelation 2–3.

[41] P.W. van der Horst, "Jews and Christians in Aphrodisias in the Light of Their Relations in Other Cities of Asia Minor," *Nederlands theologisch tijdschrift* 143 (1989): 106-107.

[42] See Josephus, *Jewish Antiquities*, XX.256.

[43] For "brother" and "sister" as designations for believers, see, e.g., Matt 12:50; Rom 14:10; 16:1; 1 Cor 6:6; 1 Tim 5:2; Heb 13:23; 2 Pet 3:15; 1 John 4:20-21 and 5:2.

[44] John "prophesies" in Rev 10:11 and is called a "brother" of the prophets in 22:9. Revelation is called a "prophecy" in 1:3; 22:7,10,18,19.

Revelation contains several indications that the author was a Palestinian Jew: First, the name "John" ('Ιωάννης, *Iōannēs*), a Greek form of the Hebrew "Johanan" (meaning "the LORD is gracious"), was common among first century Jews. Second, the structure and phrasing of Revelation suggest that the author thought in Hebrew (the original language of the Jewish Scriptures) and/or Aramaic (the closely related language spoken by ethnic Jews in Palestine). He spoke Greek only as a second language. Third, through over one hundred allusions to the Scriptures, the author demonstrates extensive knowledge of the Hebrew text of the Old Testament, as well as the Greek. Fourth, John writes in the apocalyptic genre, which was most popular in Jewish circles in Palestine. Finally, symbols such as Armageddon (Rev 16:16), the new Jerusalem (21:2), and the temple (11:1-2) are based on actual places located in Palestine (although such knowledge could have been drawn not from firsthand exposure but from the Old Testament). It may be, then, that the author of Revelation was one of the Jewish Christians who moved to Asia from Palestine due to the war with Rome. Who this "John" was cannot be determined from the book of Revelation in itself.

3. Occasion and Place of Writing

John identifies with his readers by describing himself as their "companion in suffering . . . and patient endurance."[45] John himself has been exiled to the island of Patmos, just off the western coast of Asia, "because of the word of God and the testimony of Jesus." Other portions of Revelation (particularly the letters to the seven churches in chs. 2–3) show that at least some of John's readers are also being persecuted for their faith. To Ephesus and Smyrna the Lord writes:

> You have persevered and have endured hardships for my name, and have not grown weary (Rev 2:3).

> I know your afflictions and your poverty — yet you are rich! I know the slander of those who say they are Jews and are not, but are a synagogue of Satan. Do not be afraid of what you are about to suffer. I

---

[45]For further analysis of this statement, see the comments on Rev 1:9.

tell you, the devil will put some of you in prison to test you, and you will suffer persecution for ten days. Be faithful, even to the point of death, and I will give you the crown of life (Rev 2:9-10).

Christ mentions *past* afflictions, hardships, poverty, and slanders from Jews. When he speaks of "what you are *about* to suffer," he anticipates still more difficulties to come — persecution, imprisonment, and perhaps even death.

The Lord addresses these words to the church in Pergamum:

I know where you live — where Satan has his throne. Yet you remain true to my name. You did not renounce your faith in me, even in the days of Antipas, my faithful witness, who was put to death in your city — where Satan lives (Rev 2:13).

At the time when John writes Revelation, Christians in Asia are under intense pressure to renounce their faith in Christ. At least one martyrdom (Antipas) has already occurred.

Philadelphia and Laodicea receive these assurances:

I know your deeds, your love and faith, your service and perseverance, and that you are now doing more than you did at first (Rev 2:19).

I know your deeds. See, I have placed before you an open door that no one can shut. I know that you have little strength, yet you have kept my word and have not denied my name. I will make those who are of the synagogue of Satan, who claim to be Jews though they are not, but are liars — I will make them come and fall down at your feet and acknowledge that I have loved you. Since you have kept my command to endure patiently, I will also keep you from the hour of trial that is going to come upon the whole world to test those who live on the earth (Rev 3:8-10).

Again we see pressure to deny Christ, troubles with Jews, and an expectation of further hardships to come ("the hour of trial that is *going to come* upon the whole world").

The vision of the fifth seal describes multiple Christian martyrs, whose numbers will continue to grow:

When he opened the fifth seal, I saw under the altar the souls of those who had been slain because of the word of God and the testimony they had maintained. They called out in a loud voice, "How long, Sovereign Lord, holy and true, until you judge the inhabitants of the earth and avenge our blood?" Then each of them was given a white robe, and they were told to wait a little longer, until the number of their fellow servants and brothers who were to be killed as they had been was completed (Rev 6:9-11).

John later sees a woman symbolizing Rome,[46] with a golden cup, "drunk with the blood of the saints, the blood of those who bore testimony to Jesus" (Rev 17:6). She has not merely sipped from her gruesome cup; she has gorged herself with the blood of God's people to the point of intoxication. Numerous Christians are being murdered for their loyalty to Christ.

4. Summary

Internal evidence suggests that Revelation was written by a Jewish Christian from Palestine named "John." John received the Revelation on the island of Patmos, where he had been banished for witnessing to Christ. The book addresses all the churches in the Roman province of Asia. Together with John, these believers are being harassed and persecuted because of their commitment to Christ — some to the point of death. At the time of writing, the author expects the suffering to continue and the number of martyrs to grow.

B. EXTERNAL EVIDENCE

Revelation itself gives us a good start in discovering the origins of this book. Yet important questions remain unanswered: When was Revelation written? Precisely why were the first readers being persecuted and killed? Who is John? For insights into these issues, we turn to "external evidence" from outside the New Testament.

---

[46]See Part III.D.3.f.(1) of the Commentary: "The Great Prostitute (17:1-18)."

1. Author

Regarding the identity of "John," three possibilities seem most likely: First, the author could be John the Apostle, brother of James and son of Zebedee, one of the original Twelve disciples of Jesus (see Matt 10:2). Second, he could be someone writing in the name of John the Apostle, in which case Revelation would be pseudonymous like so many other apocalypses.[47] Third, the writer could be some other person named "John" writing in his own name.

a. "John" a Pseudonym?

Of these three possibilities, we may eliminate the second immediately. Revelation is certainly not pseudonymous — not because such a practice would be unthinkable in a Christian apocalypse, but because the evidence makes this theory untenable. The author of Revelation never gives any indication that he is an Apostle. He simply calls himself a "servant" of God (1:1) and "your brother" (1:9). He recounts no stories or sayings from the ministry of Jesus, nor does he give any other indication that he had known Jesus during his earthly ministry. Many scholars (this writer not included) think that the author actually distinguishes himself from the Apostles in Revelation 21:14: "The wall of the city had twelve foundations, and on them were the names of the twelve apostles of the Lamb" — that is, the *past* founders of the people of God.

If the author of Revelation is someone other than John the Apostle, then this easily explains why he does not identify himself as the Apostle. If the author actually is John the Apostle, then we could attribute his silence to modesty. (The author of the Gospel and letters attributed to John displays similar modesty, being more interested in telling others about Jesus than in telling them about himself.) However, if what we have in Revelation is someone who wants to present himself as John the Apostle, then he fails miserably by never clearly identifying himself as that hero of the faith. The theory of pseudonymity seems quite implausible in the case of Revelation.

---

[47]See the discussion of "Pseudonymity" in Part III.B.1 of the Introduction.

b. Evidence from the Early Christian Fathers

We are left, then, with two possibilities: Is the author of Revelation John the Apostle, or is he some other "John" entirely? Perhaps the Early Christian Fathers can help us with this question. As leaders of the Church in the postapostolic period, they were certainly closer to John in time and space than we are. What do they tell us regarding the origin of Revelation?

(1) Timeline. Before we put the Fathers on the "witness stand," we should acquaint ourselves with the time period in question. Revelation — like all New Testament books — was written during the first century A.D. Thirteen Roman emperors reigned during that century, as outlined below:[48]

Augustus (30 B.C.–A.D 14) was emperor at the time of Jesus' birth (which took place in 4-6 B.C. — see Luke 2:1) and also during his boyhood.

Tiberius (A.D. 14-37) ruled throughout the period of Jesus' adulthood, his public ministry (see Luke 3:1), and his death and resurrection (which occurred in A.D. 33).

Caligula (37-41)
Claudius (41-54)
Nero (54-68)

Caligula, Claudius (mentioned in Acts 11:28 and 18:2), and Nero reigned during the period when the Apostle Paul carried out his mission to the Gentiles and Christianity spread across the Mediterranean world. According to the Church Fathers, both Peter and Paul died under a persecution of Christians sparked by Nero.

Galba, Otho, and Vitellius (68-69) held power only briefly as the Empire suffered through a period of murder, intrigue, and civil war.

Vespasian (69-79) was the Roman general charged with putting down the Jewish revolt that began in A.D. 66. When his forces defeated Vitellius and made him emperor, Vespasian left the siege of Jerusalem to return to Rome.

---

[48]Dates are taken from Bo Reicke, *The New Testament Era: The World of the Bible from 500 B.C. to A.D. 100*, trans. David E. Green (Philadelphia: Fortress Press, 1968).

Titus (79-81), the son of Vespasian, took over his father's command and destroyed Jerusalem in A.D. 70. He later succeeded his father as emperor.

Domitian (81-96)
Nerva (96-98)
Trajan (98-117)

According to the Church Fathers, Domitian (another son of Vespasian), Nerva, and Trajan played a role in the events surrounding the writing of Revelation (see below).

Against this background, what do the Church Fathers tell us about "John" and the writing of Revelation? Justin Martyr, Irenaeus, and Eusebius prove particularly helpful to our inquiry.

(2) The Testimony of Justin Martyr. Our earliest evidence that Revelation was written by John the Apostle comes from Justin Martyr, a teacher of the church at Rome in the mid-second century. In his *Dialogue with Trypho the Jew,* Justin recalls:

> . . . a man among us [Christians] named John, one of Christ's Apostles, received a revelation and foretold that the followers of Christ would dwell in Jerusalem for a thousand years, and that afterwards the universal and, in short, everlasting resurrection and judgment would take place. (Justin refers to John's vision in Rev 20:4-22:5.) [49]

As we will see, some of Justin's fellow believers agree that the Apostle wrote Revelation, while others have their doubts.

(3) The Testimony of Irenaeus. During the late second century, Irenaeus served as bishop of Lyons in what is now France. In *Against Heresies* (ca. 180), a refutation of Gnosticism, he defends the apostolic origin of the Christian gospel. In the process, he provides details concerning the later life of John the Apostle.

> For we learned the plan of our salvation from no others than from those through whom the gospel came to us. They first preached it abroad, and then later by the will of God handed it down to us in

---

[49]The *Dialogue* was composed between A.D. 155 and 161 as the record of a public debate that occurred much earlier in about A.D. 135. For an introduction and English translation, see *Writings of Saint Justin Martyr,* trans. Thomas B. Falls, The Fathers of the Church: A New Translation (New York: Christian Heritage, Inc., 1948), pp. 137-366. The excerpt is taken from *Dialogue,* 81.4 (p. 278).

Writings, to be the foundation and pillar of our faith. For it is not right to say that they preached before they had come to perfect knowledge, as some [Gnostics] dare to say, boasting that they are the correctors of the apostles. For after our Lord had risen from the dead, and they were enclothed with the power from on high when the Holy Spirit came upon them, they were filled with all things and had perfect knowledge. They went out to the ends of the earth, preaching the good things that come to us from God, and proclaiming peace from heaven to men, all and each of them equally being in possession of the gospel of God. So Matthew among the Hebrews issued a Writing of the gospel in their own tongue, while Peter and Paul were preaching the gospel at Rome, and founding the Church. After their decease Mark, the disciple and interpreter of Peter, also handed down to us in writing what Peter had preached. Then Luke, the follower of Paul, recorded in a book the gospel as it was preached by him. Finally John, the disciple of the Lord, who had also lain on his breast, published the Gospel, while he was residing at Ephesus in Asia. All of these handed down to us that there is one God, maker of heaven and earth, proclaimed by the Law and the Prophets, and one Christ the Son of God. If anyone does not agree with them he despises the companions of the Lord, he despises Christ the Lord himself, he even despises the Father, and he is self-condemned, resisting and refusing his own salvation, as all the heretics do.[50]

Note that, according to Irenaeus, the Fourth Gospel was written by the Apostle John (whom he identifies with the "disciple whom Jesus loved," who reclined next to the Lord at the "Last Supper" — see John 13:23). The bishop also identifies John's home at the time of the writing as Ephesus in the Roman province of Asia.

Elsewhere in *Against Heresies*, Irenaeus writes:

> The church in Ephesus also, which was founded by Paul, and where John survived until the time of Trajan, is a true witness of the tradition of the apostles.[51]

---

[50]Cyril C. Richardson, trans. and ed., *Early Christian Fathers*, The Library of Christian Classics, Vol. 1 (New York: Macmillan, 1970). The excerpt is taken from *Against Heresies*, Book III, Part 1, Sections 1-2 (p. 370).

[51]*Against Heresies*, Book III, Part 3, Section 3 (p. 374).

Here the writer again locates John at Ephesus. Furthermore, he dates John's death to the reign of Trajan (A.D. 98-117). If John was as young as fifteen when called to be Jesus' disciple in about A.D. 30, then the Apostle would have been eighty-three years old when Trajan's reign *began* in A.D. 98. The Apostle John could have been in his nineties — or even one hundred years old — when he died (hence the rumors that he would not die mentioned in John 21).

(4) The Testimony of Eusebius, Origen, and Papias. Eusebius was bishop of Caesarea in Palestine and a confidant of Constantine, the first Christian emperor of Rome. After Constantine legalized Christianity, Eusebius wrote a *History of the Church* from its origins with Jesus and the Apostles to his own time in A.D. 325. In constructing this history, he used a number of sources, including the writings of Origen (Christian teacher in Caesarea active during the first half of the third century) and Papias (a bishop from Phyrgia who lived in the early second century). In several passages, Eusebius discusses the authorship of Revelation.

> Meanwhile the holy apostles and disciples of our Saviour were scattered over the whole world. Thomas, tradition tells us, was chosen for Parthia, Andrew for Scythia, John for Asia, where he remained till his death at Ephesus. Peter seems to have preached in Pontus, Galatia and Bithynia, Cappadocia and Asia, to the Jews of the Dispersion. Finally, he came to Rome where he was crucified, head downwards at his own request. What need be said of Paul, who from Jerusalem as far as Illyricum preached in all its fulness the gospel of Christ, and later was martyred in Rome under Nero? This is exactly what Origen tells us in Volume III of his Commentary on Genesis.[52]

Note that Peter and Paul were martyred at Rome during the reign of Nero, who persecuted Christians there. Furthermore, Eusebius — like Irenaeus — places John's death at Ephesus.

Elsewhere Eusebius describes a later persecution carried out against Christians by another emperor after Nero:

---

[52]Reprinted from HISTORY OF THE CHURCH FROM CHRIST TO CONSTANTINE, translated by G.A. Williamson, © 1965 G.A. Williamson (hereafter "Williamson, *History*"). Used by permission of Augsburg Fortress from the 1975 Augsburg Publishing House edition. The excerpt is taken from Book III, Part 1 (p. 107).

> Many were victims of Domitian's appalling cruelty. At Rome great numbers of men distinguished by birth and attainments were executed without a fair trial, and countless other eminent men were for no reason at all banished from the country and their property confiscated. Finally, he showed himself the successor of Nero in enmity and hostility to God. He was, in fact, the second to organize persecution against us, though his father Vespasian had had no mischievous designs against us.
>
> There is ample evidence that at that time the apostle and evangelist John was still alive, and because of his testimony to the word of God was sentenced to confinement on the island of Patmos. Writing about the number of the name given to antichrist in what is called the Revelation of John, Irenaeus has this to say about John in Book V of his *Heresies Answered*:
>
>> Had there been any need for his name to be openly announced at the present time, it would have been stated by the one who saw the actual revelation. For it was seen not a long time back, but almost in my own lifetime, at the end of Domitian's reign. . . .
>
> After fifteen years of Domitian's rule Nerva succeeded to the throne. By vote of the Roman senate Domitian's honours were removed, and those unjustly banished returned to their homes and had their property restored to them. This is noted by the chroniclers of the period. At that time too the apostle John, after his exile on the island, resumed residence at Ephesus, as early Christian tradition records.[53]

According to Eusebius, Domitian carried out an organized persecution against Christians involving confiscation of property, banishment, and executions. He was the second Roman emperor to persecute Christians after Nero. During this time, John the Apostle was exiled to the island of Patmos. There he wrote the Revelation "at the end of Domitian's reign" (i.e., A.D. 95–96). After Domitian's death and during the reign of Nerva (A.D. 96–98), John was released from Patmos and allowed to return to his home at Ephesus.

The author of Revelation identifies himself as "John" (Rev 1:1,4, 9). Eusebius quotes Irenaeus, who suggests that this was probably

---

[53]Williamson, *History*. The excerpt is taken from Book III, Parts 17, 18, 20 (pp. 125, 127).

("ample evidence") the same John who wrote the Fourth Gospel — that is, John the Apostle. Irenaeus also says that the "antichrist" mentioned in Revelation refers to Domitian, and that his identity would have been clear to anyone living at that time.

If Eusebius' information is correct, then we have the author, date, occasion, and an important key to understanding the book of Revelation here in his *History of the Church*. We will see, however, that Eusebius and other Christians of his time were not certain that this tradition was entirely accurate.

The bishop continues:

> Now let me indicate the unquestioned writings of this apostle [John]. Obviously his gospel, recognized as it is by all the churches in the world, must first be acknowledged. . . .
> Of John's writings, besides the gospel, the first of the epistles has been accepted as unquestionably his by scholars both of the present and of a much earlier period: the other two are disputed. As to the Revelation, the views of most people to this day are evenly divided.[54]

Note that, by A.D. 325 (when Eusebius writes his *History*), the fourth Gospel and 1 John are generally considered compositions of John the Apostle. However, the authorship of 2-3 John and Revelation are still disputed. Many Christians doubt the "ample evidence" given by Irenaeus and the other Church Fathers.

Eusebius therefore suggests an alternative theory:

> Papias has left us five volumes entitled *The Sayings of the Lord Explained*. These are mentioned by Irenaeus as the only works from his pen:
>> To these things Papias, who had listened to John and was later a companion of Polycarp, and who lived at a very early date, bears written testimony in the fourth of his books; he composed five.
>
> That is what Irenaeus says; but Papias himself in the preface of his work makes it clear that he was never a hearer or eyewitness of the holy apostles, and tells us that he learnt the essentials of the Faith from their former pupils:

---

[54]Williamson, *History*. The excerpt is taken from Book III, Part 24 (pp. 131, 134).

I shall not hesitate to furnish you, along with the interpretations, with all that in days gone by I carefully learnt from the presbyters and have carefully recalled, for I can guarantee its truth. Unlike most people, I felt at home not with those who had a great deal to say, but with those who taught the truth; not with those who appeal to commandments from other sources but with those who appeal to the commandments given by the Lord to faith and coming to us from truth itself. And whenever anyone came who had been a follower of the presbyters, I inquired into the words of the presbyters, what Andrew or Peter had said, or Philip or Thomas or James or John or Matthew, or any other disciple of the Lord, and what Aristion [the reputed author of the present ending of the Second Gospel — i.e., Mark 16:9-20] and the presbyter John, disciples of the Lord, were still saying. For I did not imagine that things out of books would help me as much as the utterances of a living and abiding voice.

Here it should be observed that he twice includes the name of John. The first John he puts in the same list as Peter, James, Matthew, and the rest of the apostles, obviously with the evangelist in mind; the second, with a changed form of expression, he places in a second group outside the number of the apostles, giving precedence to Aristion and clearly calling John a presbyter. He thus confirms the truth of the story that two men in Asia had the same name, and that there were two tombs in Ephesus, each of which is still called John's. This is highly significant, for it is likely that the second — if we cannot accept the first — saw the Revelation that bears the name of John. Papias, whom we are now discussing, owns that he learnt the words of the apostles from their former followers, but says that he listened to Aristion and the presbyter John with his own ears. Certainly he often mentions them by name, and reproduces their teachings in his writings.[55]

Eusebius raises the possibility that there were two Christian leaders, living in Ephesus, who shared the name "John" — namely, John the Apostle and John the Presbyter.[56] He suggests that perhaps

---

[55]Williamson, *History*. The excerpt is taken from Book III, Part 39 (pp. 149-151).

[56]Note that this is not the only possible interpretation of Papias' words. He calls all the Apostles "presbyters" — including John. Perhaps when he speaks

John the Presbyter is the "John" who was exiled to Patmos and who wrote the Revelation.

c. Conclusions

We possess significant external evidence from the Early Christian Fathers that John the Apostle wrote Revelation. Justin Martyr, Irenaeus, Origen, Papias, and others, together suggest that, later in life, the Apostle moved from Palestine to Ephesus in the Roman province of Asia. There he wrote the fourth Gospel and three New Testament epistles (1–3 John). During the persecution carried out by Domitian, he was exiled to the island of Patmos, where he received the Revelation. After Domitian's death, during the reign of Nerva, John returned to Ephesus. He died during the reign of Trajan after living an unusually long life. The external evidence meshes well with internal evidence suggesting that the author was a Palestinian Jew, exiled to Patmos, writing to Christians in Asia during a time of severe persecution. That John the Apostle wrote Revelation has been the traditional view of the church for centuries.

However, we have seen that — even in ancient times — there were many Christians who doubted this conclusion. As late as A.D. 325, when Eusebius wrote his *History of the Church*, opinions regarding the apostolic origin of Revelation were "evenly divided." As far back as A.D. 250, Dionysius of Alexandria questioned whether the same person who composed the simple yet profound language of the fourth Gospel and Johannine Epistles could have written the complicated prose of Revelation.[57] (Of course, some of the differences must be attributed to the radically different genre of an apocalypse.) The controversy over whether or not Revelation should be included in the Christian canon was not finally settled until the Councils of Hippo (A.D. 393) and Carthage (A.D. 397).

---

of "the presbyter John," he is again referring to John the Apostle. He sets John apart from the other Apostles because, unlike them, John was still living and preaching ("still saying") during his lifetime. However, if this were the case, then would Papias give Aristion precedence over John the Apostle?

[57]Dionysius is quoted in Eusebius, *History of the Church*, Book VII, Part 25 (pp. 309-313).

Did early Church Fathers, such as Justin and Irenaeus, attribute the Revelation to John because they had solid, reliable information that the Apostle did indeed write the book? Or were they making an intelligent (but not necessarily correct) guess based on what evidence they had? For example, did they say that the Apostle John moved to Asia because they *knew* that he did? Or did they *assume* that the "John" who wrote Revelation was the Apostle, take note that this "John" was in Asia, and therefore *assume* that John the Apostle moved to Asia?

The fact that the authorship of Revelation was still heavily debated in Eusebius's time indicates that the early Church lacked solid proof one way or the other. For this reason, we must acknowledge the very real possibility that Revelation was written by someone other than John the Apostle — perhaps by John the Presbyter. We possess very good evidence that Revelation was written by John the Apostle, but not conclusive evidence.

2. Date

According to Irenaeus (see above), John wrote Revelation at the end of Domitian's reign — that is, about A.D. 95 or 96. This date is almost certainly accurate for the reasons given below.

We have already seen that Revelation was written at a time when Christians were beginning to be persecuted and killed by Roman authorities in Asia. The author expected the harassment and killings to escalate. We have also seen that, according to the Church Fathers, second century Christians possessed an historical recollection of two great persecutions during the first century. The earliest occurred during the reign of Nero in A.D. 64 or 65. At that time there was a great fire in Rome. Rumor had it that Nero wanted to build some new buildings, so he had the fire started in order to burn down a lower class part of town to make room for new construction. The fire burned out of control and destroyed a large portion of the city. Nero first tried to use the Jews as scapegoats. When that tactic failed, he blamed the Christians. Large numbers were executed[58] with tor-

---

[58]Including the Apostles Peter and Paul (see above).

tures that sickened even the Romans. Tacitus, a Roman historian writing about fifty years later, describes that terrible time:

> But neither human help, nor imperial munificence, nor all the modes of placating Heaven, could stifle scandal or dispel the belief that the fire had taken place by order [of Nero]. Therefore, to scotch the rumor, Nero substituted as culprits, and punished with the utmost refinements of cruelty, a class of men, loathed for their vices,[59] whom the crowd styled Christians. Christus, the founder of the name, had undergone the death penalty in the reign of Tiberius, by sentence of the procurator Pontius Pilate, and the pernicious superstition was checked for a moment, only to break out once more, not merely in Judaea, the home of the disease, but in the capital itself, where all things horrible or shameful in the world collect and find a vogue. First, then, the confessed members of the sect were arrested; next, on their disclosures, vast numbers were convicted, not so much on the count of arson as for hatred of the human race. And derision accompanied their end: they were covered with wild beasts' skins and torn to death by dogs; or they were fastened on crosses, and, when daylight failed were burned to serve as lamps by night. Nero had offered his Gardens for the spectacle, and gave an exhibition in his Circus, mixing with the crowd in the habit of a charioteer, or mounted on his car[riage]. Hence, in spite of a guilt which had earned the most exemplary punishment, there arose a sentiment of pity, due to the impression that they were being sacrificed not for the welfare of the state but to the ferocity of a single man.[60]

Christians remembered Nero as a bloodthirsty "beast" from this time forward.

The second systematic persecution of Christians occurred late in the reign of Domitian, in A.D. 95-96. Roman historians leave no clear record of Domitian himself ever ordering such a persecution.[61]

---

[59]For a discussion of the early Christians' so-called "vices," see Part 3 below.

[60]Reprinted by permission of the publishers and the Loeb Classical Library from "The Annals," pp. 283-285, in TACITUS: VOLUME IV, Loeb Classical Library Vol. 322, translated by John Jackson, Cambridge, MA: Harvard University Press, 1937 (hereafter "Jackson, *Tacitus*"). The excerpt is taken from Book XIV, Part XLIV.

However, church leaders such as Irenaeus and Eusebius testify to at least a localized persecution, in the province of Asia, carried out in Domitian's name (see above). The question, then, is which persecution prompted the writing of Revelation?

Revelation was probably written during the persecution of Domitian, rather than during the persecution of Nero, for the following reasons: First, John (like the authors of 1 Peter, 4 Ezra, and 2 Baruch) uses "Babylon" as a symbol for Rome.[62] He views Rome as a second "Babylon" because, just as Babylon had destroyed Jerusalem and the temple in 587 B.C., so did Rome destroy Jerusalem and its temple in A.D. 70. At the time of Nero's reign (A.D. 54-68) the temple was still standing, so Rome had not yet become "Babylon." However, by Domitian's rule (A.D. 81-96), this potent symbol had become available to John.

Second, Revelation contains many allusions to Roman emperor worship (discussed below in Part 3). As we shall see, such worship was much more prevalent during the reign of Domitian than it was during the reign of Nero.

Third, Revelation frequently portrays Roman political authorities as *Nero redivivus* ("Nero revivified" or "Nero come back to life") because, like Nero before them, they persecute Christ's church. If he speaks of "Nero come back to life," then John must be writing *after* Nero's death rather than during the persecution he instigated. *Nero redivivus* imagery, then, is a symbolic way of referring to Domitian and his deadly agents. (For a fuller explanation of the *Nero redivivus* idea in Revelation, see the comments on 13:3.)

Finally, the Church Fathers say that John wrote Revelation late in the reign of Domitian (see above), which dates John's Apocalypse to A.D. 95-96.

---

[61]An indirect reference may appear in *Dio [Cassius]'s Roman History,* trans. Earnest Cary, 9 Vols., The Loeb Classical Library (New York: G.P. Putnam's Sons, 1925). Dio mentions that, under Domitian, "atheism" (i.e., refusal to worship the emperor and the other Roman gods) was "a charge on which many . . . who drifted into Jewish ways (Christians?) were condemned . . . to death" or "at least deprived of their property" (LXVII.14.2 [Vol. VIII, p. 349]). For further discussion of this subject, see below.

[62]See Part III.D.3.f.(1) of the Commentary: "The Great Prostitute (17:1-18)."

3. Occasion: Persecution Related to Emperor Worship in Asia Minor

Domitian's persecution of the church was partly due to the Christians' refusal to engage in emperor worship. What were the issues at stake in this practice, and how did believers respond to it?

a. Historical Background

Although worshiping kings as deities had a long history in the east, the practice did not enter the western world until the time of Alexander the Great (late fourth century B.C.). As the young ruler won victory after victory over Babylonia, Persia, and other eastern lands, the conquered peoples began to proclaim him a god. Alexander encouraged such worship because he thought it would help to unify the diverse peoples making up his empire.

Following his assassination on March 15, 44 B.C., Julius Caesar was declared a god by the Roman Senate. Afterwards it became customary to honor dead emperors in this way. On his deathbed Vespasian announced sarcastically, "I am already becoming a god!"[63]

Tiberius and Claudius discouraged worship of living emperors. However, Nero, Vespasian, and Titus tolerated the practice for its political benefits. Caligula, who suffered from mental illness, was the first emperor who actually believed himself divine.

Domitian insisted on being worshiped as a god during his lifetime, which scandalized his biographer Suetonius:

> When [Domitian] became emperor, he did not hesitate to boast in the senate that he had conferred their power on both his father (Vespasian) and his brother (Titus), and that they had but returned him his own; nor on taking back his wife after their divorce, that he had "recalled her to his divine couch." He delighted to hear the people in the amphitheatre shout on his

---

[63]Reprinted by permission of the publishers and the Loeb Classical Library from "Roman History," p. 295, in DIO CASSIUS: VOLUME VIII, Loeb Classical Library Vol. 176, translated by Earnest Cary on the basis of the version of Herbert B. Foster (1905-06), Cambridge, MA: Harvard University Press, 1925 (hereafter "Cary, *Dio Cassius*"). The excerpt is taken from Book LXVIII.17.3.

feast day: "Good Fortune attend our Lord [*Dominus*] and Mistress.". . . With no less arrogance he began as follows in issuing a circular letter in the name of his procurators, "Our Master [*Dominus*] and our God [*Deus*] bids that this be done." And so the custom arose of henceforth addressing him in no other way even in writing or in conversation. He suffered no statues to be set up in his honour in the Capitol, except of gold and silver and of a fixed weight. He erected so many and such huge vaulted passageways and arches in the various regions of the city, adorned with chariots and triumphal emblems, that on one of them someone wrote in Greek: "It is enough."[64]

During Domitian's reign, at least three of the seven cities to which John addressed the Revelation had temples dedicated to the worship of Caesar — namely, Ephesus, Smyrna and Pergamum. Since 29 B.C., Pergamum (called "the place where Satan has his throne" in Rev 2:13) had been the official center of emperor worship in Asia.

b. Emperor Worship in Daily Life

By the late first century, emperor worship touched many aspects of Roman life, embracing the political, the economic, and the social.[65] Civic events and legal transactions included pledges of allegiance to Caesar as "Lord" and "God" (i.e., *dominus* and *deus* in

---

[64]Reprinted by permission of the publishers and the Loeb Classical Library from "The Lives of the Caesars," pp. 367-369, in SUETONIUS: VOLUME II, Loeb Classical Library Vol. 038, translated by J.C. Rolfe, Cambridge, MA: Harvard University Press, 1914 (hereafter "Rolfe, *Suetonius*"). The excerpt is taken from Domitian, XIII.1-2. Compare the parallel account in Dio Cassius' *Roman History*, LXVII.4.7 and 7.8 (Vol. VIII, pp. 329 and 335).

[65]The following texts provide helpful discussions of these matters: R.H. Charles, *A Critical and Exegetical Commentary on the Revelation of St. John*, 2 Vols., The International Critical Commentary (Edinburgh: T. & T. Clark, 1920); J. Massyngberde Ford, *Revelation: Introduction, Translation and Commentary*, The Anchor Bible (Garden City, NY: Doubleday, 1975); Colin J. Hemer, *The Letters to the Seven Churches of Asia in Their Local Setting*, Journal for the Study of the New Testament Supplement Series, 11 (Sheffield: JSOT Press, 1986); and Adela Yarbro Collins, *Crisis and Catharsis: The Power of the Apocalypse* (Philadelphia: The Westminster Press, 1984).

Latin, or κύριος (*kyrios*) and θεός (*theos*) in Greek — the biblical titles Christians used for God the Creator and his Son Jesus Christ). As they entered the theater, sporting competitions, gladiatorial games, or public festivals, citizens tossed a pinch of incense on a small altar as a sacrifice to the "divine Caesar." When animals were slaughtered to provide meat for the marketplace, a small portion was set aside as a sacrifice for the gods. *Collegia* (private men's clubs) and trade guilds (similar clubs made up of people who practiced the same vocation) held banquets honoring the emperor and their patron gods as silent guests.

Such practices were not necessarily taken seriously as major religious events. Rather, they were expressions of patriotism, national unity, and gratitude for the benevolent rule of the Roman emperor. They were the equivalent of saluting the flag or removing one's hat at the playing of the national anthem. However, refusal to participate called into question one's loyalty to the emperor, and this could lead to the most severe of consequences.

c. Exemptions for Jews and Christians

The only groups really troubled by such practices were Jews and Christians, who were monotheists believing in one God alone. To them, honoring Caesar (a mere man) as "Lord and God" was idolatry. To avoid this sin, Jews of the first century B.C. worked out an agreement that convinced the Romans of their loyalty to the empire: They agreed to pray *for* the emperor, but not *to* him. In the temple at Jerusalem they offered sacrifices *for the benefit* of Caesar, but not *to* Caesar. This arrangement satisfied the Romans that the Jews were not dangerous rebels, and it was preferable to fighting a war against irrational religious zealots.[66] So Jews were exempted from worship of the Roman gods — including the emperor — and permitted to practice their own religion. Titus instituted a two-drachma tax on each Jew for continuing this special privilege.[67]

---

[66]See Josephus, *Against Apion*, II.77; cf. *Jewish War*, II.195-198. The cessation of sacrifices for the emperor at the Jerusalem temple signaled the beginning of the Jewish revolt in A.D. 66. See *Jewish War*, II.409.

[67]See Josephus, *War of the Jews*, VII.6.6, and Suetonius, *Lives of the Caesars*, Domitian, XII.2. In the latter document, "those . . . who without publicly

At first, the Romans viewed Christians as simply another variety of Jew — messianic Jews. Christians therefore enjoyed the same exemption from emperor worship given to other Jews. Over time, several events altered their status: First, through the successful missionary activity of Paul and others, Christianity became a predominantly Gentile faith. Second, when Jews rebelled against Rome in A.D. 66-73, Christians began to distinguish themselves from that group in order to keep themselves out of trouble. Finally, after the war, Judaism closed ranks and expelled "heretics" such as Christians from the synagogues. Jews quit saying that the Christians were part of their community, which removed the churches' exemption from emperor worship.

d. Christian Responses to the Emperor Cult

How did Christians respond to this situation? Some favored acknowledging the emperor as "Lord," offering sacrifice to his image, and eating with the *collegia* as harmless expressions of patriotism. After all, they could hail Caesar as "god," giving him that title of honor, without really believing that he was a deity in the literal sense. Did not Jesus himself command us to "Give to Caesar what is Caesar's, and to God what is God's" (Matt 22:21)? Did not our beloved Apostle Paul teach us to "Submit to the governing authorities" (Rom 13:1)? Should we give up our social life, invite financial ruin, and even risk death over a pinch of incense that means nothing?!

Others argued that confessing Caesar as "Lord and god," and offering sacrifice to the "divine Caesar," was rank idolatry. And did not Christ also say, "Worship the Lord your God, and serve him only" (Matt 4:10)? Did not Paul also say that "for us there is but one God (*theos*) . . . and there is but one Lord (*kyrios*)"? John belonged to this latter camp that wanted nothing to do with worshiping the emperor or the other Roman gods. He has harsh words for compromisers in Revelation 2-3.[68]

---

acknowledging [the Jewish] faith yet lived as Jews" may be a reference to Christians, whom the Romans often confused with the Jews.

[68]See the discussion of "Pressures and Opposition from within the Christian Community" found in Part C.1 of the Commentary on Rev 1-2.

To avoid committing idolatry, Christians tended to withdraw from much of the social life of the city. Over time, they gained a reputation for being a rather strange and suspicious group, antisocial and lacking community spirit. Eventually the gossip mill started up, and vicious rumors spread:

> These Christians are so unpatriotic! They refuse to honor the emperor! And what do they do in those secret meetings of theirs? You don't suppose they are plotting some sort of rebellion, do you? Hmmm . . . wasn't their own leader, Christos, crucified for claiming to be a king?

> I heard that those "love feasts" of theirs are incestuous orgies. They say Christos taught them to love their "brothers" and "sisters"!

> It's even worse! I heard them talking about eating the flesh and drinking the blood of the "Son." They are sacrificing babies and practicing cannibalism!

> These "Christ people" are impious atheists! They say idols are not real and refuse to worship any of our gods.

As their neighbors turned against them, Christians became subject to social and economic discrimination, pressures and harassment, unofficial mob violence, and the plundering of their property. Later books of the New Testament mention these kinds of persecution (see, e.g., Heb 10:34; 13:3; 1 Pet 4:14-16; 5:9).

Tensions focused on Christians' refusal to worship the emperor, for this was not simply a religious infraction but apparent political subversion. Domitian, who had once said, "Not good is a number of rulers,"[69] prosecuted this crime without mercy. A possible reference to Christians being punished for such transgressions appears in Dio Cassius' *Roman History*:

> . . . the same year (i.e., A.D. 95) Domitian slew, along with many others, Flavius Clemens the consul, although he was a cousin and had to wife Flavia Domitilla, who was also a relative of the emperor's. The charge brought against them both was that of atheism (i.e., refusal to worship the Roman gods — including the emperor?), a charge on which *many others who drifted into Jewish*

---

[69]Rolfe, *Suetonius*. The excerpt is taken from Domitian, XII.3 (p. 367).

ways (i.e., many Christians?) *were condemned*. Some of these were put to death, and the rest were at least deprived of their property. Domitilla was merely banished to [the island of] Pandateria.[70]

Note that Dio describes events of the year 95, the very time period in which John wrote Revelation. Note also the kinds of penalties Domitian prescribed for "atheism" — namely, confiscation of property, banishment to an island (as John was exiled to Patmos), and death (as Antipas was killed in Pergamum).

There were political, social, and economic benefits to be gained by turning Christians over to the Roman authorities. For example, if there were two silversmiths in a city, and one was a Christian, then the other could eliminate his competitor by accusing the "disloyal" Christian. Jews could purge their synagogues of "heretics" by reporting that Christians were not true Jews and therefore not entitled to exemption from emperor worship. One's social or political rivals could be removed by posting an anonymous notice exposing them as Christians. The emperor cult handed a deadly weapon to anyone with a grudge or petty jealousy against any Christian.[71]

e. The Correspondence of Pliny and Trajan

Unfortunately, we have no historical documents from Domitian's reign detailing governmental policy toward Christians in Asia. However, we do possess a series of official letters exchanged by Pliny Secundus, the Roman governor of Bithynia, and the Emperor Trajan. Bithynia was just north of Asia, and the letters were written only fifteen or sixteen years after Revelation, in A.D. 111-112. So this correspondence may offer a glimpse into the kinds of pressures faced by Christians during John's time.

Pliny to the Emperor Trajan

It is my custom to refer all my difficulties to you, Sir, for no one is better able to resolve my doubts and to inform my ignorance.

I have never been present at an examination of Christians. Consequently, I do not know the nature or the extent of the pun-

---

[70]Cary, *Dio Cassius*. The excerpt is taken from LXVII.14.1-2.
[71]See the discussion of "Pressures and Opposition from outside the Christian Community" in Part C.2 of the Commentary on Rev 2-3.

ishments usually meted out to them, nor the grounds for starting an investigation and how far it should be pressed. Nor am I at all sure whether any distinction should be made between them on the grounds of age, or if young people and adults should be treated alike; whether a pardon ought to be granted to anyone retracting his beliefs,[72] or if he has once professed Christianity, he shall gain nothing by renouncing it; and whether it is the mere name of Christian which is punishable, even if innocent of crime, or rather the crimes associated with the name.

For the moment this is the line I have taken with all persons brought before me on the charge of being Christians. I have asked them in person if they are Christians, and if they admit it, I repeat the question a second and third time, with a warning of the punishment awaiting them. If they persist,[73] I order them to be led away for execution; for, whatever the nature of their admission, I am convinced that their stubbornness and unshakeable obstinacy ought not to go unpunished. There have been others similarly fanatical who are Roman citizens. I have entered them on the list of persons to be sent to Rome for trial.[74]

Now that I have begun to deal with this problem, as so often happens, the charges are becoming more widespread and increasing in variety. An anonymous pamphlet has been circulated which contains the names of a number of accused persons. Among these I considered that I should dismiss any who denied that they were or ever had been Christians when they had repeated after me a formula of invocation to the gods and had made offerings of wine and incense to your statue (which I had ordered to be brought into court for this purpose along with the images of the gods), and furthermore had reviled the name of Christ: none of which things, I understand, any genuine Christian can be induced to do.[75]

---

[72]Or "repenting of his beliefs" (Latin *paenitentiae*, likewise in the last line of the letter). Note that, while Christ commands his followers to "repent" or turn away from sin (e.g., Matt 4:17), the Romans require Christians to "repent" or turn away from Christ.

[73]Latin *perseverantes*, a rough equivalent of the Greek *hypomonē*, which plays an important part in Revelation. See the comments on Rev 1:9.

[74]As the Apostle Paul, a Roman citizen, was sent to Rome in Acts 25:11-12.

[75]Compare 1 Cor 12:3: "No one who is speaking by the Spirit of God says, 'Jesus be cursed,' and no one can say, 'Jesus is Lord,' except by the Holy Spirit."

Others, whose names were given to me by an informer, first admitted the charge and then denied it; they said that they had ceased to be Christians two or more years previously, and some of them even twenty years ago.[76] They all did reverence to your statue and the images of the gods in the same way as the others, and reviled the name of Christ. They also declared that the sum total of their guilt or error amounted to no more than this: they had met regularly before dawn on a fixed day to chant verses alternately among themselves in honour of Christ as if to a god, and also to bind themselves by oath, not for any criminal purpose, but to abstain from theft, robbery and adultery, to commit no breach of trust and not to deny a deposit when called upon to restore it. After this ceremony it had been their custom to disperse and reassemble later to take food of an ordinary, harmless kind;[77] but they had in fact given up this practice since my edict, issued on your instructions, which banned all political societies. This made me decide it was all the more necessary to extract the truth by torture from two slave-women, whom they call deaconesses. I found nothing but a degenerate sort of cult carried to extravagant lengths. I have therefore postponed any further examination and hastened to consult you. The question seems to me to be worthy of your consideration, especially in view of the number of persons endangered; for a great many individuals of every age and class, both men and women, are being brought to trial, and this is likely to continue. It is not only the towns, but villages and rural districts too which are infected through contact with this wretched cult. I think though that it is still possible for it to be checked and directed to better ends, for there is no doubt that people have begun to throng the temples which had been almost entirely deserted for a long time; the sacred rites which had been allowed to lapse are being performed again,[78] and flesh of sacrificial victims is on sale everywhere, though up till recently scarcely anyone could be found to

---

[76]That is, shortly before the writing of Revelation.

[77]Not human blood or the flesh of babies!

[78]Note that, only eighty years after the death and resurrection of Christ, so many people are turning to him that the pagan temples have been largely deserted. Only the severest punishments are turning them back to the Roman gods.

buy it.⁷⁹ It is easy to infer from this that a great many people could be reformed if they were given an opportunity to repent.⁸⁰

Trajan's Reply to Pliny

You have followed the right course of procedure, my dear Pliny, in your examination of the cases of persons charged with being Christians, for it is impossible to lay down a general rule to a fixed formula. These people must not be hunted out; if they are brought before you and the charge against them is proved, they must be punished, but in the case of anyone who denies that he is a Christian, and makes it clear that he is not by offering prayers to our gods, he is to be pardoned as a result of his repentance however suspect his past conduct may be. But pamphlets circulated anonymously must play no part in any accusation. They create the worst sort of precedent and are quite out of keeping with the spirit of our age.⁸¹

The Pliny/Trajan correspondence illustrates that, if Christians were hauled before a Roman magistrate, they were required to prove their patriotism in three basic ways: They must sacrifice wine and incense to images of Caesar and the other Roman gods. They must declare *Kyrios Kaisaros* ("Caesar is Lord," an exact counterpart to the basic Christian confession "Jesus is Lord").⁸² They must "repent" of their faith and curse Christ. If they refused, they would be executed.

f. The Christians' Choice

In such a terrible circumstance, what choices did Christians have? Dr. Boring summarizes them nicely:⁸³ They could surrender

---

⁷⁹Pliny refers to the practice of eating meat offered to idols, so controversial among early Christians (see, e.g., 1 Cor 8:1-13; 10:14–11:1).

⁸⁰Reprinted by permission of the publishers and the Loeb Classical Library from "Letters and Panegyricus," pp. 284-293, in PLINY: VOLUME II, Loeb Classical Library, Vol. 059, translated by Betty Radice, Cambridge, MA: Harvard University Press, 1969 (hereafter, "Radice, 'Letters'"). The excerpt is taken from Book X, Letter XCVI (pp. 284-291).

⁸¹Radice, "Letters," pp. 284-293. The excerpt is taken from Book X, Letter XCVII (pp. 290-293).

⁸²Compare Rom 10:9; 1 Cor 12:3.

⁸³M. Eugene Boring, *Revelation*, Interpretation: A Bible Commentary for Preaching and Teaching (Louisville, KY: John Knox Press, 1989), pp. 21-23.

their faith in Christ, but for John this would be to surrender "the crown of life" (see Rev 2:10). They could lie about their loyalty to Christ, but John reserves a place in the "fiery lake of burning sulfur" for liars (see Rev 21:8). They could try to change the laws, but this was not possible since Rome was not a democracy and Domitian would never accept a rival "Lord." They could fight the Roman government, but this was not practical. They could "adjust" by confessing Caesar as "god" without meaning it, but John rejects even feigned idolatry as unworthy of Christ. Finally, they could die, as Jesus himself had died. John affirms death for Christ's sake as the only truly "Christian" response. There is no other way.

> He who has an ear, let him hear: If anyone is to go into captivity, into captivity he will go. If anyone is to be killed with the sword, with the sword he will be killed. ***Here** is the patient endurance and the faithfulness of the saints.* (Rev 13:10)[84]

This is the challenge faced by the churches of Asia when John writes Revelation. It is a terribly hard book for terribly hard times.

V. THE STRUCTURE OF REVELATION

In Part III of the Introduction we identify Revelation as a Christian apocalypse — probably the first Christian apocalypse. Such writings often incorporate elements of other genres. For example, Daniel 1–6 consists largely of a narrative prologue to the apocalypse proper found in chapters 7–12. In the case of Revelation, John's apocalyptic vision is presented within the framework of a first-century letter.

A. THE FIRST CENTURY HELLENISTIC LETTER FORM IN REVELATION

Letters written today generally bear certain standard features that conform to cultural norms (e.g., the name and address of the sender and receiver, a greeting formula such as "Dear Sir," and a

---

[84]For translation notes, see the Commentary.

closing formula such as "Sincerely yours"). New Testament epistles likewise conform to the standard Hellenistic letter form[85] used in the Roman world of the first century A.D. The elements of this common letter form are listed below, along with examples of each element from Paul's First Letter to the Corinthians and his Letter to Philemon:

The name of the sender(s) (see 1 Cor 1:1; Phlm 1a)

The name of the recipient(s) (see 1 Cor 1:2; Phlm 1b-2)

The prescript, which is a greeting formula (see 1 Cor 1:3; Phlm 3)

The proem, which is a word of thanks, praise, or petition to a god (see 1 Cor 1:4-9; Phlm 4-7).

The introductory formula, which serves as the transition into the primary subject matter of the letter (see 1 Cor 1:10; Phlm 8-9).

The main body of the letter (see 1 Cor 1:11–16:18; Phlm 10-22)

Greetings (see 1 Cor 16:19-20; Phlm 23-24)

Benedictory wishes in the sender's own hand (rather than that of a secretary, if used), which serve to personalize the letter (see 1 Cor 16:21-24; Phlm 25)

Revelation bears most of the features of a first century Hellenistic letter, as shown below. This observation is important because it explains why certain elements appear in Revelation and why they are arranged as they are. John is simply following the conventions of his culture.[86]

---

[85]*Hellēn* (Ἕλλην) is the Greek word for "Greek." *Hellenistic* refers to the Greek language and culture that Alexander the Great spread from Greece and Macedonia in the west, to the borders of India in the east, and to Egypt in the south during the fourth century B.C. The Hellenistic letter form represents one example of this Greek cultural influence on what later became the Roman Empire. For further discussion, see Stanley K. Stowers, *Letter Writing in Greco-Roman Antiquity*, Library of Early Christianity (Philadelphia: The Westminster Press, 1986); and William G. Doty, *Letters in Primitive Christianity*, Guides to Biblical Scholarship (Philadelphia: Fortress Press, 1973).

[86]Why did John write an apocalypse in the form of a letter? Perhaps he was imitating the Apostle Paul, whose influence was so strong in Asia.

Name of Sender (Rev 1:4a):
   John

Name of Recipient(s) (Rev 1:4b):
   To the seven churches in the province of Asia:

Prescript (Rev 1:4c-5a):
   Grace and peace to you from him who is, and who was, and who is to come, and from the seven spirits before his throne, and from Jesus Christ, who is the faithful witness, the firstborn from the dead, and the ruler of the kings of the earth.

Proem (Rev1:5b-6): In this part of the letter, a pagan would often call upon the gods to grant good health and prosperity to the addressee(s). John Christianizes this portion of the standard letter form and transforms it into a doxology of praise to God:

   To him who loves us and has freed us from our sins by his blood, and has made us to be a kingdom and priests to serve his God and Father — to him be glory and power for ever and ever! Amen.

Introductory Formula (Rev 1:9):
   I, John, your brother and companion in the suffering and kingdom and patient endurance that are ours in Jesus, was on the island of Patmos because of the word of God and the testimony of Jesus.

Main Body of the Letter (Rev 1:10–22:20)

Greetings are not found in Revelation.

Benedictory Wishes in the Sender's Own Hand (Rev 22:21):
   The grace of the Lord Jesus be with God's people. Amen.

B. THE STRUCTURE OF JOHN'S VISION

Within the Hellenistic letter form, John structures Revelation in four main parts, as a careful examination clearly shows. The book begins with a Prologue (1:1-20) in which the author describes how Christ commissioned him to deliver a revelation to the seven churches of Asia. Near the end of this Prologue, in 1:19, the Lord summarizes the contents of the revelation itself:

Write, therefore, what you have seen, what is now and what will take place later.

Notice that the vision contains two main elements: First, there is a revelation of the present — a revelation of "what is now." The "present," of course, refers to "what is now" from John's perspective. Christ offers John a vision of the late first century A.D. in Asia. Second, the Lord promises a revelation of the future — a vision of "what will take place later." Again, this is the "future" from John's point of view — the period from A.D. 95-96 through Christ's return and the consummation of the kingdom of God.

Which part of the book reveals John's "present" and which part reveals the "future"? John treats these two subjects in the order in which they are mentioned. His discussion of the "present" appears in 2:1–3:22 and takes the form of seven letters to the churches of Asia. This part of the vision describes the "present" circumstances of the Asian churches from Christ's point of view.

The Lord's revelation of the "future" appears in 4:1–22:6, as the structure of the passage makes clear. The first verse of this section (4:1) reads:

> After this I looked, and there before me was a door standing open in heaven. And the voice I had first heard speaking to me like a trumpet said, "Come up here, and I will show you what must take place after this."

The initial phrase "After this," in and of itself, marks a transition — the end of one discussion and the beginning of another. Christ then introduces the next major portion of the book when he says, "I will show you what must take place *after this*" — that is, "after" the "present" described in chapters 2 and 3. Revelation 4:1 marks the beginning of the promised vision of "what will take place later."

Where does the vision of the future end? After a long series of images we come to Revelation 22:6:

> The angel said to me, "These words are trustworthy and true. The Lord, the God of the spirits of the prophets, sent his angel to show his servants *the things that must soon take place*."

This verse marks the end of John's discussion of the future. The remainder of the book (22:7-21) consists of a short Epilogue.

By far the largest portion of Revelation describes John's vision of the future (4:1–22:6). How has the author structured this important part of the book? The revelation of "what will take place later" begins with an introduction (4:1-5:14) in which John describes his new vantage point in heaven ("Come *up here*, and I will show you"). The prophet will see the future from God's point of view.

The rest of the section (6:1-22:6) contains the revelation of the future itself. However, a careful reading shows that John does not receive one long, sequential vision of the future. Instead, he receives *three separate revelations of the complete future from John's time through the consummation of the kingdom of God.* John describes how the future unfolds in 6:1-8:1. Then he starts over and describes the same period again in 8:2-11:19. Then he reviews the same period a third time in 12:1-22:6. The approach is cyclical, with each vision examining the future from a slightly different angle, and the third vision offering the most detail.

In view of these considerations, we outline Revelation as follows. The Commentary is structured accordingly.

I. Prologue (1:1-20)
II. The Revelation of "What Is Now" (2:1-3:22)
III. The Revelation of "What Will Take Place Later" (4:1-22:6)
   A. Introduction: John's Heavenly Vantage Point (4:1-5:14)
   B. The First Vision of the Future (6:1-8:1)
   C. The Second Vision of the Future (8:2-11:19)
   D. The Third Vision of the Future (12:1-22:6)
IV. Epilogue (22:7-21)

OUTLINE

I. **PROLOGUE** — 1:1-20
  A. **Introduction to the Prophecy** — 1:1-3
  B. **Sender** — 1:4a
  C. **Recipients** — 1:4b
  D. **Prescript** — 1:4c-5a
  E. **Proem** — 1:5b-6
  F. **Prophetic Pronouncement** — 1:7
  G. **The Lord's Self-Introduction** — 1:8
  H. **John's Vision of the Lord** — 1:9-20
    1. John's Circumstances — 1:9-11
    2. John's Vision — 1:12-20
      a. Christ's Voice and His Appearance — 1:12-16
      b. Christ's Words — 1:17-20
      c. Summary: John's Portrait of Christ in Revelation — 1:9-20

II. **THE REVELATION OF "WHAT IS NOW"** — 2:1-3:22
  A. **The Seven Churches**
  B. **The Structure of the Letters to the Seven Churches**
    1. Addressed to the Angels of the Seven Churches
    2. A Renewal of the New Covenant
      a. Typical Elements of Covenants
      b. Covenantal Elements in the Letters to the Seven Churches
      c. The Letter to Ephesus — 2:1-7
      d. The Letter to Smyrna — 2:8-11
      e. The Letter to Pergamum — 2:12-17
      f. The Letter to Thyatira — 2:18-29
      g. The Letter to Sardis — 3:1-6
      h. The Letter to Philadelphia — 3:7-13
      i. The Letter to Laodicea — 3:14-22

C. Pressures and Opposition in Asia
1. Pressures and Opposition from Within the Christian Community
   a. False Apostles and the Nicolaitans – 2:2,6
   b. The Teaching of Balaam – 2:14
   c. The Sins of Jezebel – 2:20-25
   d. Assessment
2. Pressures and Opposition from Outside the Christian Community

D. "Overcomers" in Revelation
1. Satan as "Overcomer"
2. Christ as "Overcomer"
   a. Whom Jesus "Overcomes"
   b. How Jesus "Overcomes"
   c. The Results of Jesus' "Overcoming"
3. Christians as "Overcomers"
   a. Whom Christians "Overcome"
   b. How Christians "Overcome"
   c. The Result of Christians' "Overcoming"

E. Christ's Promises to "Him Who Overcomes"
1. The Tree of Life – 2:7
2. Escape from the Second Death – 2:11
3. The Hidden Manna, White Stone, and Secret Name – 2:17
   a. The Hidden Manna, the Messianic Banquet, Behemoth and Leviathan
   b. The White Stone
   c. The Secret Name
4. Authority over the Nations and the Morning Star – 2:26-28
5. White Garments and the Book of Life – 3:4-5
6. A Pillar in God's Temple – 3:12
7. A Place on Christ's Throne – 3:21

III. THE REVELATION OF "WHAT WILL TAKE PLACE LATER" – 4:1–22:6

A. Introduction: John's Heavenly Vantage Point – 4:1–5:14
1. Transition to the Threefold Vision of the Future – 4:1
2. The Throne of God and the Twenty-Four Elders – 4:2-6a
3. The Four Living Creatures – 4:6b-8

4. The Heavenly Worship — 4:9-11
5. The Scroll with Seven Seals — 5:1
6. The Lion of Judah and the Root of David — 5:2-5
7. The Lamb Who Was Slain — 5:6-14
B. **The First Vision of the Future** — 6:1-8:1
   1. The "Labor Pains:" Seals One through Five — 6:1-11
      a. The Four Horsemen of the Apocalypse — 6:1-8
      b. The Souls of the Martyrs — 6:9-11
   2. The Final Judgment: Seal Six — 6:12-17
   3. Summary of Revelation 6 (Seals 1-6) and Comparison with Matthew 24
   4. Interlude: The 144,000 Sealed for Salvation — 7:1-17
      a. The Sealing of the 144,000 — 7:1-8
      b. A Song of Salvation — 7:9-17
   5. The Consummation of God's Kingdom: Seal Seven — 8:1
   6. Summary: John's First Vision of the Future — 6:1-8:1
C. **The Second Vision of the Future** — 8:2-11:19
   1. The Structure of the Second Vision
      a. Seven Trumpets versus Seven Seals
      b. Major Elements of the Vision
      c. The Dominant Image: God's Coming Kingdom as a "Second Exodus" for His People
      d. Subordinate Imagery in Revelation 8:2-9:21
   2. The "Present Evil Age/Labor Pains": Trumpets One through Six — 8:2-9:21
      a. Hail, Blood, Bitter Waters, Darkness, Locusts, and Death: The "Present Evil Age" and "Labor Pains" as Eschatological "Plagues"
         1) Present Evils as "Plagues"
         2) The First Trumpet — 8:6-7
         3) The Second Trumpet — 8:8-9
         4) The Third Trumpet — 8:10-11
         5) The Fourth Trumpet — 8:12
         6) The Fifth Trumpet — 8:13-9:12
         7) The Sixth Trumpet — 9:13-21
         8) Heightened Imagery Portraying Eschatological Events

9) Partial Destruction versus Total Destruction
   b. Earth, Trees, Grass, Springs, Rivers, Sea, and Sea Creatures: The Effect of the "Present Evil Age" and "Labor Pains" on the Natural World
   c. The "Present Evil Age" and "Labor Pains" as God's Judgment on Sin and Call to Repentance
   d. The "Present Evil Age" and "Labor Pains" as a Source of Hope and a Call to Perseverance
   e. The Blazing Mountain, Falling Stars, Wormwood, Demon Locusts from the Abyss, Abaddon, Apollyon, and a Demon Army: The "Present Evil Age" and "Labor Pains" as God's Unleashing Demonic Forces on the Earth
   f. Fire from the Altar: The "Present Evil Age" and "Labor Pains" as an Answer to Prayer
   g. The Sounding of Seven Trumpets: The "Present Evil Age" and "Labor Pains" as the Announcement of the Day of the Lord
   h. The Eagle and the Three "Woes"
   3. Interlude: The Mighty Angel and the Two Witnesses — 10:1–11:14
      a. The Mighty Angel with the Little Scroll — 10:1-11
         1) The Angel's Appearance
         2) The Angel's Voice
         3) The Little Scroll
         4) Comparison with Daniel 12
      b. The Measuring of the Temple and the Two Witnesses — 11:1-14
         1) A Note on the "Rapture"
         2) A Note on the "Protection" of the "New Israel" from the "Plagues"
   4. The Final Judgment and Consummation of God's Kingdom: Trumpet Seven — 11:15-19
   5. Summary: John's Second Vision of the Future — 8:2–11:19
D. The Third Vision of the Future — 12:1–22:6
   1. The Structure of the Third Vision
   2. The "Labor Pains": The Dragon's War against the Saints — 12:1–13:18

a. The Dragon, the Woman, and the Male Child — 12:1-17
   1) The Identity of the Male Child
   2) The Identity of the Red Dragon
   3) Five Theories Regarding the Identity of the Woman
   4) A Sixth Theory: John's Adaptation of the Apollo Myth
   5) Interpretation of Revelation 12
b. The Beast from the Sea — 13:1-10
c. The Beast from the Land — 13:11-18
d. Satan's Parody of Christ
e. Summary of Revelation 12–13: The "Labor Pains"
3. The Final Judgment and Consummation of God's Kingdom — 14:1-22:6
   a. The Relationship between Salvation and Condemnation, Final Judgment and Consummation
   b. The Structure of Revelation 14:1-22:6
   c. Announcement of the Final Judgment — 14:1-13
      1) The 144,000 — 14:1-5
      2) Threefold Announcement of the Judgment — 14:6-13
   d. The Harvest of the Earth — 14:14-20
   e. The Seven Last Plagues or Seven Bowls of God's Wrath — 15:1-16:21
      1) The Structure of Revelation 15–16
      2) The Sea of Glass and Fire — 15:1-4
      3) The Heavenly Tabernacle — 15:5-8
      4) The Meaning of the Seven Bowls of God's Wrath — 16:1
      5) The First Bowl of Wrath — 16:2
      6) The Second Bowl of Wrath — 16:3
      7) The Third Bowl of Wrath — 16:4-7
      8) The Fourth Bowl of Wrath — 16:8-9
      9) The Fifth Bowl of Wrath — 16:10-11
      10) The Sixth Bowl of Wrath — 16:12-14,16
      11) Interlude — 16:15
      12) The Seventh Bowl of Wrath — 16:17-21
   f. God's Final Judgment against Babylon — 17:1-19:4
      1) The Great Prostitute — 17:1-18

        2) The Scarlet Beast — 17:1-18
        3) The Fall of Babylon — 18:1–19:4
    g. Announcement of the Wedding Supper of the Lamb — 19:5-10
        1) The Wedding of the Lamb — 19:5-9
        2) The Testimony of Jesus — 19:10
    h. The Victorious Christ — 19:11-21
        1) The King of Kings — 19:11-16
        2) The Great Supper of God — 19:17-21
    i. Deliverance from Babylonian Captivity — 20:1–22:6
        1) Element One: The Binding of Satan — 20:1-3
        2) Element Two: The Resurrection of Christian Martyrs — 20:4a
        3) Element Three: The Millennial Reign of Christ — 20:4b-6
        4) Element Four: God's Judgment of Gog and Magog — 20:7-15
        5) Element Five: The New Jerusalem — 21:1–22:5
        6) Comparison of Revelation 20:1–22:5 with Ezekiel 37–48
        7) Conclusions Regarding the Meaning of Revelation 20:1–22:5
        8) Climax: The Consummated Kingdom of God — 21:1–22:5
        9) Conclusion of the Third Vision of the Future — 22:6

IV. EPILOGUE — 22:7-21

BIBLIOGRAPHY

APOCALYPTIC LITERATURE

Barr, J. "Jewish Apocalyptic in Recent Scholarly Study." *Bulletin of the John Rylands University Library of Manchester* 58 (1975): 9-35.

Charlesworth, James H., ed. *The Old Testament Pseudepigrapha: Volume 1 – Apocalyptic Literature and Testaments*. Garden City, NY: Doubleday, 1983.

Collins, John J., ed. "Apocalypse: The Morphology of a Genre." *Semeia* 14. Missoula, MT: Scholars Press, 1979.

――――――. *The Apocalyptic Imagination: An Introduction to the Jewish Matrix of Christianity*. 2nd ed. The Biblical Resource Series. Grand Rapids: Eerdmans, 1998.

――――――. "Apocalyptic Literature." In *Early Judaism and Its Modern Interpreters*. Eds. Robert A. Kraft and George W.E. Nickelsburg, 345-370. Atlanta: Scholars Press, 1986.

Collins, John J., and James H. Charlesworth, eds. *Mysteries and Revelations: Apocalyptic Studies Since the Uppsala Colloquium*. Journal for the Study of the Pseudepigrapha Supplement Series, 9. Sheffield: JSOT Press, 1991.

Funk, Robert W., ed. *Journal for Theology and the Church* 6 (1969) [issue on "Apocalypticism"].

Hanson, Paul D. *The Dawn of Apocalyptic*. Philadelphia: Fortress Press, 1975.

――――――. *Old Testament Apocalyptic*. Interpreting Biblical Texts. Nashville: Abingdon Press, 1987.

Hellholm, David, ed. *Apocalypticism in the Mediterranean World and the Near East: Proceedings of the International Colloquium on*

Apocalypticism, Uppsala, August 12-17, 1979. Tübingen: J.C.B. Mohr (Paul Siebeck), 1983.

Koch, Klaus. *The Rediscovery of Apocalyptic: A Polemical Work on a Neglected Area of Biblical Studies and Its Damaging Effects on Theology and Philosophy*. Studies in Biblical Theology, Second Series, 22. London: SCM Press Ltd, 1972.

Marcus, Joel, and Marion L. Soards, eds. *Apocalyptic and the New Testament: Essays in Honor of J. Louis Martyn*. Journal for the Study of the New Testament Supplement Series, 24. Sheffield: JSOT Press, 1989.

Minear, Paul S. *New Testament Apocalyptic*. Interpreting Biblical Texts. Nashville: Abingdon, 1981.

Morris, Leon. *Apocalyptic*. Grand Rapids: Eerdmans, 1972.

Murphy, Frederick J. "Apocalypses and Apocalypticism: The State of the Question." *Currents in Research: Biblical Studies* 2 (1994): 147-179.

Rowley, H.H. *The Relevance of Apocalyptic: A Study of Jewish and Christian Apocalypses from Daniel to the Revelation*. New York: Association Press, 1964.

Russell, D.S. *Divine Disclosure: An Introduction to Jewish Apocalyptic*. Minneapolis: Fortress Press, 1992.

_____. *The Method and Message of Jewish Apocalyptic: 200 B.C.–A.D. 100*. The Old Testament Library. Philadelphia: The Westminster Press, 1964.

Yarbro-Collins, Adela, ed. *Early Christian Apocalypticism: Genre and Social Setting. Semeia* 36. Atlanta: Scholars Press, 1986.

THE APOCALYPSE OF JOHN

Aune, David. *Revelation*. 3 Vols. Word Biblical Commentary. Dallas: Word, 1997-98.

Barclay, William. *Letters to the Seven Churches*. New York: Abingdon Press, 1957.

_____. *The Revelation of John.* 2 Vols. The Daily Bible Study Series. Rev. ed. Philadelphia: The Westminster Press, 1976.

Bauckham, Richard. *The Theology of the Book of Revelation.* New Testament Theology. Cambridge: University Press, 1993.

Boring, M. Eugene. *Revelation.* Interpretation: A Bible Commentary for Teaching and Preaching. Louisville, KY: John Knox Press, 1989.

Caird, G.B. *The Revelation of St. John the Divine.* Harper's New Testament Commentaries. New York and Evanston: Harper & Row, 1966.

Hemer, Colin J. *The Letters to the Seven Churches of Asia in Their Local Setting.* Journal for the Study of the New Testament Supplement Series, 11. Sheffield: JSOT Press, 1986.

Murphy, Frederick J. "The Book of Revelation." *Currents in Research: Biblical Studies* 2 (1994): 181-225.

Pilch, John J. *What Are They Saying about the Book of Revelation?* New York: Paulist Press, 1978.

Ramsay, W.M. *The Letters to the Seven Churches.* Updated ed. Edited by Mark W. Wilson. Peabody, MA: Hendrickson, 1994.

REVELATION 1

I. PROLOGUE (1:1-20)

Revelation begins with a Prologue (1:1-20) in which John relates how the risen Christ appeared to him on the island of Patmos, bringing an apocalyptic vision of the present and future. In describing this vision, John organizes the book according to the standard first century Hellenistic letter form. For further discussion of the Structure of Revelation, see Part V of the Introduction.

A. INTRODUCTION TO THE PROPHECY (1:1-3)

¹The revelation of Jesus Christ, which God gave him to show his servants what must soon take place. He made it known by sending his angel to his servant John, ²who testifies to everything he saw—that is, the word of God and the testimony of Jesus Christ. ³Blessed is the one who reads the words of this prophecy, and blessed are those who hear it and take to heart what is written in it, because the time is near.

1:1 The revelation of Jesus Christ

The author's title for his book is "The Revelation of Jesus Christ." Old Testament prophets place similar titles at the beginning of their writings.[1] By imitating such men, John places himself in their company as an authoritative spokesman for God. He describes Revelation as "words of prophecy" in 1:3 and himself as a "brother of the prophets" in 22:9.

In the first words of the book, John tells us the nature of his prophecy. It is a "revelation" (ἀποκάλυψις, *apokalypsis*), which was a

---

[1] See, for example, Isaiah 1:1 and Jeremiah 1:1.

recognized type of literature most popular from the second century B.C. through the second century A.D. Apocalyptic writings reflect a certain type of theology, or understanding of God and his dealings with the world. They communicate that theology in a distinctive manner by, for example, making heavy use of symbolism. They also focus on the future — on "what must soon take place" as God moves human history toward the goal of his kingdom rule. The Revelation of John probably represents the first Christian adaptation of the apocalyptic form. For a detailed discussion of these matters, see Parts I and III of the Introduction.

In Greek, the initial phrase (ἀποκάλυψις Ἰησοῦ Χριστοῦ, *apokalypsis Iēsou Christou*) may mean either "the revelation *about* Jesus Christ" (genitive of description) or "the revelation *from* Jesus Christ" (ablative of source). John probably means it in the second sense because the rest of verse 1 focuses on the *source* of John's apocalyptic prophecy.

which God gave him [i.e., Jesus] to show his servants what must soon take place. He made it known by sending his angel to his servant John,

Ultimately the message comes from God, but notice the chain of revelation involved: God gives the revelation to Jesus, who passes it on to an angel, who delivers it to John, who communicates it to the churches ("his servants"). John plays the role of a "servant" prophet, who brings a revelation from God to others. An angel is involved, but John does not seem to place as much importance on the mediating role of angels as do other apocalyptists.[2] In this book, Jesus often bypasses the angel and speaks to John directly.

In the chain of revelation, Jesus stands between God and his creation. John's Apocalypse is theocentric, or "God-centered." The book reveals what God says and what God does, but Jesus is the one through whom God speaks and through whom God carries out his will. John emphasizes this mediating role of Jesus throughout the book.

He made it known

The Greek term translated "made known" is σημαίνω (*sēmainō*),

---

[2]See Part III.B.1.a of the Introduction: "Visions or Revelations."

which is the verb form of the noun σημεῖον (*sēmeion*). A *sēmeion* is a "sign" that points beyond itself to some deeper reality, some deeper truth. For example, a traffic sign picturing a truck on a steep grade points beyond itself to a real hill. In the same way, the Gospel of John describes a number of miraculous "signs" (*sēmeion*) performed by Jesus. The healing of the man born blind (John 9) points beyond the miracle itself to the truth that Jesus is "the light of the world." The resuscitation of Lazarus (John 11) points to Jesus as "the resurrection and the life."

John says that the Revelation was "signed" to him. If we view John's kaleidoscope of symbols only on the surface, then we miss a major portion of what the Lord intends to "reveal" to us. Revelation was never meant to be read literally — it is an *apocalypse*. The symbols point beyond themselves to deeper realities. We will try to uncover those truths as we work our way through the book.

1:2 who testifies to everything he saw—

In contrast to many Old Testament prophets who *heard* the word of the Lord, the revelation to John was largely an optical experience — an apocalyptic *vision*. As G.B. Caird writes, "Much of the New Testament is written for those who have ears to hear, but this book is written for those who have eyes to see."[3]

that is, the word of God and the testimony of Jesus Christ.

Since the Revelation comes ultimately from God through his mediator Christ (see above), John calls it "the word of God and the testimony of Jesus Christ." The fact that John shares "the word of God," rather than the word of a mere human being, is extremely significant. We humans may say, "Let this pig sprout wings and fly," but our speaking the words will not make it happen. However, when the sovereign God speaks a word, then whatever he says is done. This is called "performance language" — language that accomplishes what it says. We see it, for example, in Genesis 1:3, where "God said, 'Let there be light,' and there was light." The same idea appears in Isaiah 55:10-11:

---

[3]G.B. Caird, *The Revelation of St. John the Divine*, Harper's New Testament Commentaries (New York and Evanston: Harper & Row, 1966), p. 13.

> As the rain and the snow
>   come down from heaven,
> and do not return to it
>   without watering the earth
> and making it bud and flourish,
>   so that it yields seed for the sower and bread for the eater,
> so is my word that goes out from my mouth:
>   It will not return to me empty,
> but will accomplish what I desire
>   and achieve the purpose for which I sent it.

Jesus is called "the Word of God" (e.g., in John 1) because he "performs" or accomplishes God's will. In like manner, John calls Revelation "the word of God," which means that what God says in this book concerning the present and the future is reality. It *will* be accomplished.

1:3 Blessed is the one who reads the words of this prophecy, and blessed are those who hear it and take to heart what is written in it, because the time is near.

John expects the Revelation to be read aloud in the churches' assemblies (compare 1 Tim 4:13), just as the Jewish Scriptures were read aloud in the synagogues (see Acts 13:15). So he prays a blessing — a good gift from God — on "the one who reads," the one who shares God's word with others. The prophet also pronounces a blessing not on those who merely "hear" the word, but on those who "hear it *and take [it] to heart.*" Those who allow the Revelation to penetrate their minds and hearts so that it reshapes their lives — *they* are the ones who will be blessed.

Reader, this blessing is available for you as the time of Christ's return grows "near." However, the verse also contains an implicit warning — a warning that the person who refuses to hear, who refuses to act on God's word, will not be blessed.

B. SENDER (1:4a)

1:4 John,

The author identifies himself simply as "John." The Early Church Fathers provide significant evidence — but not conclusive evidence

— that the author is John the son of Zebedee, one of the original Twelve Apostles of Jesus. For a more detailed discussion of authorship, see Parts IV.A.1 and IV.B.1 of the Introduction.

C. RECIPIENTS (1:4b)

To the seven churches in the province of Asia:

In verse 4 John addresses the Apocalypse "to the seven churches in the province of Asia." The Roman province of Asia made up the western third of Asia Minor (modern Turkey). In verse 11, John locates the seven churches in the cities of "Ephesus [the provincial capital], Smyrna, Pergamum, Thyatira, Sardis, Philadelphia and Laodicea." The Revelation may be intended for these seven congregations alone. However, since "seven" often symbolizes "completeness" in apocalyptic literature,[4] the seven churches of Asia probably represent the entire body of Christian believers in that part of the Roman world. For further discussion of the recipients and their circumstances, see Part IV of the Introduction, along with the Commentary on Revelation 2–3.

D. PRESCRIPT (1:4c-5a)

Grace and peace to you from him who is, and who was, and who is to come, and from the seven spirits before his throne,[a] ⁵and from Jesus Christ, who is the faithful witness, the firstborn from the dead, and the ruler of the kings of the earth.

[a]4 Or *the sevenfold Spirit*

1:4c Grace and peace to you

"Grace" (χάρις, *charis*) was the common greeting used by Greeks or Gentiles (non-Jews) in the first-century Roman world. The term meant "goodwill," so the greeting was simply a way of expressing positive feelings toward another person. In Christian circles, however, "grace" took on added meaning as the "goodwill" God has shown toward sinners, particularly by sending Christ to die as the

---

[4]See Introduction, Part III.B.1.d: "Symbolic Numbers."

sacrifice for sins (see, e.g., Rom 5:1-2; Eph 2:8). In a culture where the deities were often seen as wrathful gods, who must be constantly appeased through sacrifice, the message that God actually had "goodwill" toward his creatures was "good news" or "gospel" (εὐαγγέλιον, *euangelion*).

"Peace" (Greek, εἰρήνη [*eirēnē*], Hebrew, *shalom*) was the common greeting used by Jews. In Christian circles, the word became a technical term for the peaceful reconciliation to God and to one another that believers enjoy through the cross of Christ (see, e.g., Rom 5:1; Eph 4:3).

Combining "grace" and "peace" creates a universal greeting that takes in both Jews and Gentiles. In this greeting, the threefold God (see below) offers "grace and peace" to the entire world — to "every nation, tribe, people and language" (see Rev 7:9).

from him who is, and who was, and who is to come,

John describes God, both here and in verse 8, as "him who is, and who was, and who is to come." On one level, the author is simply saying that God is eternal — that he *has* always existed and *will* always exist, that he has no beginning and no end. Greeks would affirm the same about their gods. For example, Pausanias writes, "Zeus was, Zeus is, Zeus shall be; O mighty (μεγάλη, *megalē*) Zeus."[5] In this way, he expresses the god's eternity and immutability.[6]

Yet John has more in mind than God's eternal *existence*. John's God is a God who also *acts* — he will "come." The prophet is thinking within his apocalyptic framework:[7] God "was" — that is, he existed prior to "the beginning," when he acted to "create the heavens and the earth" (see Gen 1:1). God "is"[8] — that is, he has continued to be

---

[5]Reprinted by permission of the publishers and the Loeb Classical Library from the "Description of Greece," pp. 436-437, in PAUSANIUS: VOLUME IV, Loeb Classical Library, Vol. 297, translated by W.H.S. Jones (Cambridge, MA: Harvard University Press, 1969) (hereafter, "Jones, 'Description'"). The excerpt is taken from Phocis, Ozolian Locri, Book XII.10.

[6]This statement resembles the Hebrews writer's declaration that "Jesus Christ is the same yesterday and today and forever" in Heb 13:8.

[7]See the Introduction, Part III.B.2.

[8]When Moses asks God's name in Exod 3:13-14, the LORD calls himself "I AM WHO I AM." It is interesting to note that the translators of the Septuagint interpreted this name to mean "He who is."

alive and present during world history, when Adam's sin launched the "present evil age," but God acted through Christ to redeem his fallen creation. God will one day "come," in the person of Christ, to consummate his eternal kingdom. God's being and his actions embrace all of time and eternity. He shapes all and he directs all.

John communicates similar truths about God in verse 8, where the Lord calls himself "the Alpha and the Omega" and "the Almighty." Alpha and Omega are the first and last letters of the Greek alphabet. (The English equivalent would be for the Lord to say, "I am the A and the Z.") The fuller formula appears in Revelation 22:13 (cf. 21:6):

> I am the Alpha and the Omega,
> the First and the Last,
> the Beginning and the End.

God is our "Alpha and Omega," our "First and Last," our "Beginning and End," in the sense that he gives his creation both its origin (creation) and its goal (God's kingdom).

The Greek term translated "the Almighty" is παντοκράτωρ (*pantokrator*), a combination of πᾶς (*pas*, "all") and κρατέω (*krateō*, "power"). God is "all powerful" or "almighty" in the sense that he holds ultimate power over all of creation for all of time and eternity. You exist right now, at this moment, reading this commentary, only because God – right now – actively wills it and sustains his creation! And what is the attitude of this God toward us – this God "who is, and who was, and who is to come," the "Alpha and the Omega," the "Almighty"? In verse 4 he wishes all nations "grace and peace."

and from the seven spirits before his throne,

The same greeting comes "from the seven spirits before his throne." Here in Revelation 1:4 (and again in 3:1) John speaks of "seven spirits" – that is, the Spirit of God in his fullness and completeness.[9]

In 4:5 he writes: "Before the throne, seven lamps were blazing. These are the seven spirits of God." John uses seven lamps as a

---

[9] For a discussion of "seven" as the symbolic number for "completeness," see Part III.B.1.d of the Introduction.

symbol for the sevenfold Spirit of God — that is, the Spirit of God in his fullness as one who "enlightens" like a lamp.

In 5:6 John speaks of Jesus' having "seven horns and seven eyes, which are the seven spirits of God sent out into all the earth." The "horn" is an ancient symbol for power.[10] Picturing God's Spirit as "seven horns" speaks of his omnipotence, or his having all power. Portraying God's Spirit as "seven eyes . . . sent out into all the earth" speaks of his omniscience, his being all seeing and all knowing.

Much of this symbolism echoes Zechariah 4, where the prophet speaks of the Holy Spirit (v. 6) in the context of a lampstand with seven lights (v. 2) that represent the seven "eyes of the Lord which range throughout the earth" (v. 10). When we view John's Spirit imagery as a whole, it becomes clear that the "seven spirits" in Revelation 1:4 symbolize God the Holy Spirit, in the fullness of his omniscience and omnipotence, present and active throughout all the earth.

1:5 and from Jesus Christ,

Finally, the greeting of "grace and peace" comes to the readers "from Jesus," whom John identifies as the "Christ." This title has its roots in a long series of Old Testament promises regarding the Messiah as a descendant of David the king. John refers to these promises again and again in his Apocalypse. In order to gain the necessary scriptural background for understanding Revelation, we will examine several key texts.

The foundational passage appears in 2 Samuel, chapter 7. At this point in his life, David has conquered his enemies and his kingdom is secure. So David decides that he wants to build a great house, a great temple for the Lord. However, God has other plans. He speaks to David through the prophet Nathan and says, "No, you will not build me a house. Instead, I will build *you* a house." Yet God is not thinking of a house of wood or stone. He intends to build for David a royal "house," a kingly dynasty:

---

[10]See, for example, 1 Sam 2:10 ("[The Lord] will give strength to his king and exalt the horn of his anointed") and Lam 2:3 ("In fierce anger [God] has cut off every horn of Israel. He has withdrawn his right hand at the approach of the enemy.").

The LORD declares to you that the LORD himself will establish a house for you: When your days are over and you rest with your fathers, I will raise up your offspring to succeed you, who will come from your body, *and* I will establish his kingdom. He is the one who will build a house for my Name, *and* I will establish the throne of his kingdom forever (2 Sam 7:11b-13).

Solomon was the particular "offspring" of David who built a temple at Jerusalem, but the Lord's words do not concern Solomon alone. God *also* promises to establish a royal "house," or dynasty of kings descended from David through Solomon. Since they are blood descendants of David, we refer to these rulers as "Davidic kings." The Lord describes how he will treat Solomon and the other Davidic kings in verses 14-16:

I will be his father, and he will be my son. When he does wrong, I will punish him with the rod of men, with floggings inflicted by men.[11] But my love will never be taken away from him, as I took it away from Saul, whom I removed from before you. Your house and your kingdom will endure forever before me; your throne will be established forever.

This prophecy contains several specific promises of great importance: First, in verse 12 God says he will "raise up" David's "offspring" — blood descendants who will come from David's "own body." Each Davidic king will be, then, a "son of David." Second, in verse 14 God promises: "I will be his father, and he will be my son." Each king descended from David will be a "son of God," receiving his heavenly "Father's" love and (if necessary) his discipline. In contrast to other ancient Near Eastern peoples who considered their kings to be literal blood descendants of gods, we will see that the Jewish people considered kings from David's line to be *adopted* "sons of God." Third, verses 12, 13, and 18 say that these "sons of God," these descendants of David, will rule as kings and their kingdom will never end.

These divine promises shaped the way that the Jewish people viewed David and his heirs for centuries. One place we see that influence is in the Book of Psalms. The Psalter served as the "hymnbook"

---

[11]Such as the Babylonian Exile inflicted by Nebuchadnezzar.

for the Jewish people. The songs it contains were used in their worship services at the temple and elsewhere. Some of these songs are called "Royal Psalms" because they were sung at the coronation ceremonies when David's descendants were placed on the Jewish throne at Jerusalem. They include Psalms 2, 18, 20, 21, 45, 72, 101, 110, and perhaps others.[12] We will briefly examine three such Psalms, beginning with Psalm 2.

King David and some of his heirs conquered their Gentile neighbors (e.g., the Moabites and Ammonites) and compelled them to pay tribute or provide forced labor for the Jewish kingdom. When a Davidic king died and his son took the throne, these surrounding nations hoped for a weak ruler so that they could break free from his influence. Psalm 2 warns subject peoples against such rebellion. The first part of the Psalm was sung by the people or the worship leaders:

> Why do the nations conspire / and the peoples plot in vain? / The kings of the earth take their stand / and the rulers gather together / against the LORD [i.e., God] / and against his Anointed One [i.e., the Davidic king]. / "Let us break their chains," they say, / "and throw off their fetters."
>
> The One enthroned in heaven laughs; / the Lord scoffs at them. / Then he rebukes them in his anger / and terrifies them in his wrath, saying, / "I have installed my king / on Zion, my holy hill [a reference to the Jews's capital city, Jerusalem, which King David established on a hill called 'Zion']."

At this point in the coronation service, the newly-crowned Davidic king stepped forward and sang:

> I will proclaim the decree of the LORD: / He said to me, "You are my Son; / today I have become your Father. / Ask of me, / and I will make the nations your inheritance, / the ends of the earth your possession. / You will rule them with an iron scepter; / you will dash them to pieces like pottery."

And then the people joined in again:

> Therefore, you kings, be wise; / be warned, you rulers of the earth. / Serve the LORD with fear / and rejoice with trembling. / Kiss the Son,

---

[12]See Bernhard W. Anderson, *Out of the Depths: The Psalms Speak for Us Today*, Rev. ed. (Philadelphia: The Westminster Press, 1983), pp. 186-192, 237.

lest he be angry / and you be destroyed in your way, / for his wrath can flare up in a moment. / Blessed are all who take refuge in him.

This "Royal Psalm" offers several important insights concerning the Jews' understanding of David's dynasty: First, in verse 2, the Davidic king is called the Lord's "Anointed One." At his coronation, the Jewish king was anointed with oil as a symbol of God's setting him apart for a special work. The oil represented the Holy Spirit, whom God would send upon the king in order to empower him to carry out his duties as ruler and shepherd of God's people.[13] The Hebrew word here translated "anointed one" is "messiah." The Greek equivalent is "christ." All the Davidic kings were called "the Lord's anointed one" or "messiah" or "christ" for this reason.

Second, the Psalm refers to the Davidic king as God's "son." In verse 7 the king says: "I will proclaim the decree of the LORD: He said to me, 'You are my Son.'" This proclamation of divine sonship simply repeats the promise of 2 Samuel 7:14, where God says to David: "I will be his father, and he will be my son."[14] Notice that the Davidic king was not considered to be the "son of God" from birth. The Lord says, "Today" — that is, on this coronation day — "I have become your Father." The Jews viewed the Davidic king as the *adopted* "son of God" — adopted on the day he took the throne.

Third, God gives his "son," the Davidic king, authority to rule over the "nations." The Greek word rendered "nations" is ἔθνη (*ethnē*), from which we get the English term "ethnic groups." In the Bible, the word is often translated "Gentiles." Jews tended to think of themselves as God's covenant people and all other ethnic groups as outsiders —

---

[13]See, for example, 1 Samuel 10:1-11, which describes how, after Saul was anointed king, the Holy Spirit came upon him in power.

[14]Older translations, such as the King James Version, render verse 7b as "Thou art my son; this day have I *begotten* thee." The term "begotten" (γεννάω, *gennaō*) refers to the father's role in procreation. It could be translated into English as "this day I have *sired* you," but the term "sired" is usually used of animals rather than human beings. The NIV's "today I have become your Father" captures the idea well.

All of the Davidic kings were considered "begotten" sons of God. However, the writer of the fourth Gospel uses a slightly different term to set Jesus apart from his royal ancestors. The author refers to him as the "only begotten" or "uniquely begotten (μονογενής, *monogenēs*) Son of God" (see John 1:14,18; 3:16,18; cf. 1 John 4:9).

as the *other* "nations." Therefore the term "nations" or "Gentiles" refers to non-Jews. Psalm 2 shows that God had made the king descended from David ruler — at least in theory — over not only Israel, but over all other nations as well. "Ask of me, and I will make the nations your inheritance, the ends of the earth your possession."

Psalm 110, another "Royal Psalm," also sheds light on the Jewish understanding of the Davidic kings. For our purposes, we will examine only verse 1:

> The LORD [i.e., God (*Yahweh* in Hebrew or *kyrios* in the Greek Septuagint)] says to my Lord [i.e., the Davidic King (*adonai* in Hebrew or *kyrios* in Greek)]: "Sit at my right hand until I make your enemies a footstool for your feet."

Note, first of all, that God seats the Davidic king at his right hand, the place of the second in command under the king. God allows David's heir to rule over all nations as God's "vicar," God's representative, God's "right hand man." Note also that, in the Greek version used by most early Christians, both God and the Davidic King are called "Lord" (*kyrios*). Using the same title for the earthly ruler that is used for the heavenly ruler shows that the Davidic king bears the authority of God himself. How long will the Davidic king reign? Until God makes his enemies "a footstool for his feet" — until God subdues them all, bringing them under his "son's" kingly authority.

Psalm 72 — another "Royal Psalm" — contains many of the same ideas described above. For example, the author calls the Davidic king "the royal son" (v. 1) and declares that "all nations will serve him" (v. 11). However, verse 17 introduces a new concept: "All nations will be blessed through him, and they will call him blessed." The Psalmist here identifies the Davidic king as the one through whom God's promise to Abraham would be fulfilled: ". . . all peoples on earth will be blessed through you" (Gen 12:3).

We have seen that God's promises to David in 2 Samuel 7, together with the "Royal Psalms" that interpret those promises, describe the Davidic kings as persons "raised up" by God; offspring or descendants of David; and kings who sit at the right hand of God, ruling over all nations in a kingdom that lasts forever. They are "lords" who exercise the authority of God himself. They are "anointed ones" — "messiahs" or "christs" — on whom God's Spirit rests. Finally, they are adopted "sons of God," whom the Deity treats as his own and disciplines as needed. These promises form the beginnings and foundation of the Jewish expectation of *"the* Messiah" — the hope that one of David's descendants would not require God's discipline, but would fully realize his promise of a universal kingdom under a godly ruler.

There were many descendants of David, and many of them ruled over Israel, and many of them fulfilled the biblical promises — or fit the description of the "messiah" — to one extent or another. However, the first Christians saw for themselves that there is only one descendant of David who fulfills these promises completely — namely, Jesus of Nazareth. Jesus "full-fills" the Scriptures both in the sense of accomplishing what the biblical writers predict and also in the sense of "filling" the words of Scripture "full" of new meaning not grasped before his coming. In light of what Jesus said and did, the early Christians gained a new understanding of the Old Testament prophecies.[15]

For example, they knew that Jesus was born to Mary, a descendant of David, and belonged to the family of Joseph, also a descendant of David. On both counts, Jesus was a "son of David" and a possible heir to David's throne (see the genealogies in Matt 1:1-17 and Luke 3:23-37).

Jesus was conceived by the Holy Spirit of God and born to the virgin Mary, so that he lacked a human father (see Matt 1:18-25; Luke 1:26-35). This made him Deity, the "Son of God" in a fuller sense than any other Davidic king. Indwelt by the Spirit of God from his conception, Jesus was also the "Anointed One," the "Messiah," and the "Christ" in the deepest sense. His public anointing at his baptism simply confirmed this fact (see Matt 3:16-17; Luke 3:21-22).

The first disciples were present at the "Last Supper" when Jesus explained that his death on the cross would establish a "new covenant" offering eternal life to both Jews and Gentiles.[16] This new covenant, based on faith in Christ as Lord, is the "blessing" for all nations promised to Abraham (see Gal 3:6-9).

---

[15]For additional samples of early Christian interpretations of Jesus based on the Davidic promises, see Matt 16:13-20; Luke 1:26-35; John 18:33-37; Acts 2:22-36; Rom 1:1-4; 1 Cor 15:24-28; Heb 1:1-5,13-14.

[16]See Part III.B.2.c.(4) of the Introduction: "The Kingdom of God and the Death of Jesus."

The first Christians were witnesses to Jesus' death and then to his victorious emergence from the tomb. Not only was this descendant of David "raised up" by God in history (2 Sam 7:12); he was "raised up" from the dead to eternal life.

The first disciples also saw Jesus ascend into heaven, where he sat down at the right hand of God and began ruling over all nations as God's representative (see, e.g., Acts 7:56 where Stephen saw Jesus at God's right hand as he was being stoned). In other words, Jesus inaugurated the kingdom of God — not a temporary, earthly, Jewish kingdom, but a kingdom that includes people from all nations and that lasts forever and ever.

In view of these experiences, it is no wonder that the first disciples called Jesus "Lord," which refers both to his deity and his kingly authority. It is no wonder that they called Jesus "the Anointed One," "the Messiah," "the Christ." It is no wonder that they called him the "Son of David" and the "Son of God." These titles are abbreviated ways of referring to the entire complex of ideas surrounding God's promises to David. They have a very specific meaning and content grounded in the Old Testament promises. When John calls Jesus the "Christ" in Revelation 1:5, he is identifying Jesus as the ultimate Davidic King.

Christ, who is the faithful witness, the firstborn from the dead, and the ruler of the kings of the earth.

In these titles, John reflects language and imagery from Psalm 89 in order to communicate certain truths about Jesus. Concerning the Davidic king the Psalmist writes:

> I will sing of the LORD's great love forever; / with my mouth I will make your faithfulness known through all generations. / I will declare that your love stands firm forever, / that you established your faithfulness in heaven itself. / You said, "I have made a covenant with my chosen one, / I have sworn to David my servant, / 'I will establish your line forever / and make your throne firm through all generations'" [a reference to the promises God gives to David in 2 Samuel 7]. . . .
>
> Once you spoke in a vision, / to your faithful people you said: / "I have bestowed strength on a warrior; / I have exalted a young man from among the people. / I have found David my servant; / with my sacred oil I have anointed him. / My hand will sustain

him; / surely my arm will strengthen him. / No enemy will subject him to tribute; / no wicked man will oppress him. / I will crush his foes before him / and strike down his adversaries. / My faithful love will be with him, / and through my name his horn will be exalted. / I will set his hand over the sea, / his right hand over the rivers. / He will call out to me, 'You are my Father, / my God, the Rock my Savior.' / I will also appoint him my firstborn, / the most exalted of the kings of the earth. / I will maintain my love to him forever, / and my covenant with him will never fail. / I will establish his line forever, his throne as long as the heavens endure.

"If his sons forsake my law / and do not follow my statutes, / if they violate my decrees / and fail to keep my commands, / I will punish their sin with the rod, / their iniquity with flogging; / but I will not take my love from him, / nor will I ever betray my faithfulness. / I will not violate my covenant / or alter what my lips have uttered. / Once for all, I have sworn by my holiness— / and I will not lie to David— / that his line will continue forever / and his throne endure before me like the sun; / it will be established forever like the moon, / the faithful witness in the sky" (vv. 1-4, 19-37).

In Revelation 1:5 John first calls Jesus the "Christ" (Greek) — that is, the "Messiah" (Hebrew) or "Anointed One" (English). The title "Christ" identifies Jesus as the one who fulfills God's promises to David regarding the king who rules over an eternal kingdom (see above). The idea of the "Christ" appears in Psalm 89:20, where the writer describes David himself as "anointed" with "sacred oil."

Second, Psalm 89:27 says that God will appoint David and his descendants "the most exalted of the kings of the earth." In very similar fashion, John calls Jesus "the ruler of the kings of the earth." In doing so, he again ties Jesus to the Davidic prophecies. He also exalts Christ over Caesar as the true Lord of all.

Third, Psalm 89:27 says that God will appoint the Davidic king his "firstborn" son, exalting him over the other "kings of the earth." John likewise calls Jesus "firstborn," but he alters the title slightly by referring to him as "the firstborn from the dead".[17] He is the one

---

[17]Compare Col 1:18, where Paul calls Christ "the firstborn from among the dead," and 1 Cor 15:20, where the Apostle describes him as "the firstfruits of those who have fallen asleep."

whom God has "raised up" (2 Samuel 7:12) to eternal life as the first participant in the eschatological age, the inaugurator of the kingdom of God.[18]

Finally, John introduces Jesus as "the faithful witness." The language comes from Psalm 89:37 (cf. Isa 55:3-4), where the moon is called "the faithful witness in the sky." John borrows this phrase from Scripture, but fills it with new content.

The Greek word here translated "witness" is μάρτυς (*martys*), the noun form of the verb μαρτυρέω (*martyreō*). It means "one who gives testimony" as in a court of law. Jesus was a "witness" in the sense that he testified concerning who God is (Creator and Lord) and what he is doing in the world (establishing his eternal kingdom or rule). That witness resulted in his death (see, e.g., John 18:37; 1 Tim 6:13). Jesus was "faithful" in his "witness" even to the point of death. He is "the faithful witness."

The first readers of John's Apocalypse face similar circumstances. They are called to be "witnesses," to testify to the world that Jesus Christ — not the Roman Caesar — is the true King of kings and Lord of lords. The only way that John's readers are able to faithfully carry out that witness in the face of Roman emperor worship is by dying like Jesus did.[19] *Martys* (from which we get the word "martyr") is on its way to becoming a technical term for Christians who die in the process of carrying out their witness to the Lord. John's readers, in many cases, are being called upon to follow in the footsteps of Jesus by dying because of their testimony to him. By calling Jesus "the faithful witness," John reminds his readers that Jesus is not asking them to do anything that he himself has not already done.

E. PROEM (1:5b-6)

To him who loves us and has freed us from our sins by his blood, ⁶and has made us to be a kingdom and priests to serve his God and Father—to him be glory and power for ever and ever! Amen.

---

[18]See Part III.B.2.c.(5) of the Introduction: "The Kingdom of God and the Resurrection of Jesus."

[19]See Part IV.B.3.f of the Introduction: "The Christians' Choice."

1:5b-6 In his proem, or word of praise to God, John describes what Christ has done for his people. First, he "loves us." The term translated "love" is ἀγάπη (*agapē*), which is the selfless, giving kind of love Christ commands his disciples to show to one another (see John 13:34-35), to their neighbors (see Matt 19:19), and even to their enemies (see Matt 5:44-48). How has Christ demonstrated his own *agapē* love for us? The Lord "has freed us from our sins by his blood" and given us a place in God's eternal "kingdom" (compare Rev 1:9). For further discussion of Christ's sacrificial death and its relationship to the coming kingdom of God, see Part III.B.2.c.(4) of the Introduction, as well as the discussion of "Christ as 'Overcomer'" in the Commentary on Revelation 2-3.

John also says that Christ has made us "priests to serve his God and Father."[20] He does not elaborate on just how Christians function as "priests" beyond saying that we "serve" God. However, there are many ways in which believers resemble priests. For example, we enter into God's presence through the death of Christ. We represent God to the world, testifying to who he is and his eternal purpose. Furthermore, we offer to the creator the worship from his creation that is rightfully his. It is with this kind of worship that John ends his proem in verse 6: "To him be glory and power for ever and ever! Amen."

F. PROPHETIC PRONOUNCEMENT (1:7)

> [7]Look, he is coming with the clouds,
>   and every eye will see him,
> even those who pierced him;
>   and all the peoples of the earth will mourn because of him.
>   So shall it be! Amen.

1:7 Here we have a sort of prophetic pronouncement in which the prophet John introduces the Lord who speaks through him. He borrows language from two Old Testament passages — namely, Daniel 7:13 and Zechariah 12:10. Jesus himself combines these two texts in Matthew 24:30.

---

[20]John makes similar statements in Rev 5:10 and 20:6. Compare also 1 Pet 2:9, where the writer describes the church as "a royal priesthood."

John proclaims that Jesus is "coming with the clouds," which is a reference to his imminent Second Coming. When the Lord returns, "*every eye* will see him," for there will be a universal revelation of Christ. That will be a day of victory and vindication for Christ's faithful servants. However, in this verse, John focuses on the defeat of Christ's enemies. "Those who pierced him" and "all the peoples of the earth will mourn because of him."

G. THE LORD'S SELF-INTRODUCTION (1:8)

⁸"I am the Alpha and the Omega," says the Lord God, "who is, and who was, and who is to come, the Almighty."

1:8 John introduces Christ to the readers in verse 7. Here in verse 8 the Lord, who speaks through the prophet, identifies himself. For analysis of "the Alpha and the Omega" and the other divine titles, see the comments on Revelation 1:4.

H. JOHN'S VISION OF THE LORD (1:9-20)

Revelation 1:9-20 describes the circumstances in which John receives his revelation from the Lord. In verses 9-11 John describes his own situation, and then in verses 12-20 he focuses on the words and appearance of the risen Christ.

1. John's Circumstances (1:9-11)

⁹I, John, your brother and companion in the suffering and kingdom and patient endurance that are ours in Jesus, was on the island of Patmos because of the word of God and the testimony of Jesus. ¹⁰On the Lord's Day I was in the Spirit, and I heard behind me a loud voice like a trumpet, ¹¹which said: "Write on a scroll what you see and send it to the seven churches: to Ephesus, Smyrna, Pergamum, Thyatira, Sardis, Philadelphia and Laodicea."

1:9 I, John, your brother[21] and companion in the suffering and kingdom and patient endurance that are ours in Jesus

---

[21]For the identity of "John" and the meaning of the term "brother," see the Introduction, Parts IV.A.1 ("First Readers") and IV.B.1 ("Author").

In describing the circumstances of himself and his fellow Christians in Asia, John says that they are "in Jesus" (ἐν Ἰησοῦ, *en Iēsou*). The only real parallel to this expression is found in Revelation 14:12-13, where John speaks of persons who are "in the Lord" (ἐν κυρίῳ, *en kyriō*):

> This calls for patient endurance on the part of the saints who obey God's commandments and remain faithful to Jesus.
> Then I heard a voice from heaven say, "Write: Blessed are the dead who die in the Lord from now on."

The context shows that, for John, to be "in the Lord" or "in Jesus" means to "obey God's commandments," to "remain faithful to Jesus," and to be a "saint" — that is, a person devoted to the Lord even to the point of "death." In other words, when John talks about people who are "in Jesus," he is simply talking about committed Christians.

John indicates that, "in Jesus," he and his fellow Christians are "companions" (literally "sharers," συγκοινωνός, *synkoinōnos*) in three kinds of experiences — namely, "suffering and kingdom and patient endurance." The Greek word translated "suffering" is θλίψις (*thlipsis*) (cf. 2:9,10,22). Elsewhere in the New International Version, this term is translated "tribulation." For example, Revelation 7:13-14 reads:

> Then one of the elders asked me, "These in white robes—who are they, and where did they come from?"
> I answered, "Sir, you know."
> And he said, "These are they who have come out of the great *tribulation* [*thlipsis*]; they have washed their robes and made them white in the blood of the Lamb."

For John and other apocalyptic writers, *thlipsis* ("suffering" or "tribulation") is a technical term for the "labor pains," the time of intense suffering and persecution of God's people that immediately precedes the consummation of God's kingdom. This period of hardship begins with the First Coming of Christ and ends with his Second Coming. In other words, it is the period when the kingdom of God and kingdom of Satan coexist — the "overlap" of the ages.[22]

---

[22] For a full explanation, see Part III.B.2.d.(3) of the Introduction: "The 'Labor Pains.'" See also Figure 2: The Shape of Christian Apocalyptic Theology, p. 41.

Some interpreters of Revelation claim that a great "Tribulation" will come upon the world sometime in the *future*. Some even say that Christians will be "raptured" out of the world so that they will not have to endure the Tribulation. In Revelation 1:9 we find John's view: The "tribulation" is *present*. It is already under way in A.D. 95 or 96. Christians are not immune to it any more than Christ himself was immune to suffering. Christians are right in the middle of the tribulation, "sharing" in suffering together.

Believers are also "companions" or "sharers" in "patient endurance." The Greek term is ὑπομονή (*hypomonē*), a key word in Revelation that is translated either "patient endurance" or "perseverance" (see Rev 2:2,3,19; 3:10; 13:10; 14:12). *Hypomonē* is the attitude that John encourages Christians to adopt in the face of the "tribulation" or "suffering" of the "labor pains." It is more than just stoicism — more than just "gritting your teeth and bearing it." It is persisting in faithfulness to God because we know that he is in control and his kingdom will ultimately prevail.

John and his fellow Christians are also participating in the "kingdom" (βασιλεία, *basileia*) of God as they live their lives "in Jesus," or under the rule of God in Christ. Note that, for John, both the "labor pains" and the "kingdom" occur *simultaneously in the present*. What we have here is John expressing the Christian apocalyptic idea of the "overlap" of the two ages — the "present evil age" and the "eschatological age."[23] As Christ was crucified under a placard proclaiming him king (see John 19:19), so do Christians — for the moment — "reign" from the "cross."

was on the island of Patmos because of the word of God and the testimony of Jesus.

Here John describes his own individual "suffering" during the "labor pains." John is a "martyr," a "witness" to Christ. (See the comment on Jesus as the "faithful witness" in Rev 1:5.) As a result of his "witness," John is being forced to "patiently endure" banishment on Patmos, one of the Southern Sporades islands off the southwest-

---

[23]See the Introduction, Parts III.B.2.c-d: "Development of Christian Apocalyptic Theology in the New Testament Period" and "Major Differences between Jewish and Christian Apocalyptic Theology."

ern coast of Asia Minor.²⁴ He fears that his Christian brothers and sisters in Asia may have to endure worse than that.

1:10a On the Lord's Day

John receives his apocalyptic revelation from Christ "on the Lord's Day." This term most probably refers to Sunday, the first day of the week. Even as early as the 50s, Sunday was the customary day of Christian worship in commemoration of the resurrection of Christ.²⁵ The designation, "the Lord's Day," may have been patterned after the practice in Asia Minor of referring to the first day of the month as "Emperor's Day."²⁶ Revelation 1:10 marks the first occurrence of this term in Christian literature.

I was in the Spirit,

The phrase "in the Spirit" occurs four times in the Revelation (1:10; 4:2; 17:3; 21:10). On each occasion it refers to John's exercising his prophetic gift.²⁷ God always initiates this activity; John does not prophesy at will. God is the primary actor behind John's Revelation.

---

²⁴Roman writers indicate that the Sporades and the nearby Cyclades were regularly used for the exile of political offenders. See, for example, (1) Tacitus, *The Annals*, 5 Vols., trans. John Jackson, The Loeb Classical Library (Cambridge, MA: Harvard University Press, 1979-91), Book III, Part LXVIII (Vol. 3, 630-631); Book IV, Part XXX (Vol. IV, 52-53); Book XV, Part LXXI (Vol. V, 328-329); and (2) Juvenal, *Satires*, trans. G.G. Ramsay, The Loeb Classical Library (Cambridge, MA: Harvard University Press, 1940), I.73-174 (pp. 8-9); VI.560-564 (pp. 128-129); X.168-172 (pp. 206-207).

²⁵See, e.g., Mark 16:2; Acts 20:7; 1 Cor 16:2; and the letter of Pliny quoted in Part IV.B.3.e of the Introduction. For further discussion, see Willy Rordorf, *Sunday: The History of the Day of Rest and Worship in the Earliest Centuries of the Christian Church* (Philadelphia: The Westminster Press, 1968).

²⁶For details see G. Adolf Deissmann, *Bible Studies: Contributions Chiefly from Papyri and Inscriptions to the History of the Language, the Literature, and the Religion of Hellenistic Judaism and Primitive Christianity*, trans. Alexander Grieve, The Alpha Greek Library (Winona Lake, IN: Alpha Publications, 1979), pp. 217-219.

²⁷Compare Rom 12:6; 1 Cor 12:10,28; 13:2; 14:1-39.

1:10b-11 and I heard behind me a loud voice like a trumpet, which said: "Write on a scroll what you see and send it to the seven churches: to Ephesus, Smyrna, Pergamum, Thyatira, Sardis, Philadelphia and Laodicea."

John first hears a voice. (On the sound of the voice, see the comment on 1:12.) He then turns around and, beginning in verse 12, receives a vision of the risen Christ. John describes what he sees in the language of Scripture. He bombards us with Scripture, leading the person who is familiar with God's word to think of passage after passage, promise after promise, prophecy after prophecy.

2. John's Vision (1:12-20)

a. Christ's Voice and His Appearance (1:12-16)

¹²I turned around to see the voice that was speaking to me. And when I turned I saw seven golden lampstands, ¹³and among the lampstands was someone "like a son of man,"ᵃ dressed in a robe reaching down to his feet and with a golden sash around his chest. ¹⁴His head and hair were white like wool, as white as snow, and his eyes were like blazing fire. ¹⁵His feet were like bronze glowing in a furnace, and his voice was like the sound of rushing waters. ¹⁶In his right hand he held seven stars, and out of his mouth came a sharp double-edged sword. His face was like the sun shining in all its brilliance.

ᵃ*13* Daniel 7:13

1:10,12 a loud voice like a trumpet . . . the voice that was speaking to me

John describes the Lord's voice using language from the Septuagint version of Exodus 19:16-19. This passage describes what Israel saw and heard at Mount Sinai when the nation received the Ten Commandments from God:

> And it came to pass on the third day, as the morning drew nigh, there were voices and lightnings and a dark cloud on mount Sina[i]: *the voice of the trumpet sounded loud,* and all the people in the camp trembled. And Moses led the people forth out of the camp to meet God, and they stood by under the camp. The mount of Sina[i] was altogether on a smoke, because God had descended

upon it in fire; and the smoke went up as the smoke of a furnace, and the people were exceedingly amazed. And the [voices (Brenton has "sounds")] of the trumpet were waxing very much louder. Moses spoke, and *God answered him with a voice.*

The meaning of the symbol of the "loud voice like a trumpet" is that, when John turns around and sees Jesus, he is in the presence of God, hearing the voice of God speaking the words of God.

1:13 And among the lampstands was someone "like a son of man"
John describes the Lord as "someone 'like a son of man'" (cf. 14:14). This symbol is capable of carrying several different shades of meaning: First, this language identifies Jesus as a human being. In Jewish idiom, the phrase "son of . . ." can express the idea of *nature*. To illustrate, Jesus calls James and John "sons of thunder" (Mark 3:17). Apparently their loud and boisterous personalities — or perhaps their fiery tempers — remind Jesus of characteristics of thunder. "Son of . . ." can also communicate *function*. For example, Jesus refers to young men in charge of a wedding celebration as "sons of the bride chamber" (Matt 9:15). Such language may also communicate *destiny*. For example, John 17:12 and 2 Thessalonians 2:3 speak of the "son of perdition" — that is, the person whose end is destruction. By calling Jesus a "son of man," John identifies him as a human, as one bearing human nature.[28] Yet he is not quite the same as other humans — he is one *"like* a son of man." Jesus is human, but at the same time he is set apart from all other humans.

Second, the title "son of man" is a common designation in apocalyptic literature for the Messiah (e.g., in 1 Enoch 37:71, part of which is quoted below in the discussion of Jesus' hair and head). John may intend for the phrase "son of man" to carry messianic overtones as well.

Third, the Old Testament passage that the phrase "like a son of man" immediately brings to mind is in Daniel 7. In this passage, Daniel receives a vision of four great beasts, the last of which has a little horn that speaks "boastfully." Verses 9-14 tell what happens to this beast and its horn:

---

[28]In like manner, God addresses the prophet as "son of man" in Ezek 2:1, and throughout the rest of the prophecy. "Son of man" is a way of drawing a sharp contrast between the human creature Ezekiel and the divine Creator God.

As I looked,
> thrones were set in place,
>> and the Ancient of Days took his seat.
> His clothing was as white as snow;
>> the hair of his head was white like wool.
> His throne was flaming with fire,
>> and its wheels were all ablaze.
> A river of fire was flowing,
>> coming out from before him.
> Thousands upon thousands attended him;
>> ten thousand times ten thousand stood before him.
> The court was seated,
>> and the books were opened.

Then I continued to watch because of the boastful words the horn was speaking. I kept looking until the beast was slain and its body destroyed and thrown into the blazing fire. (The other beasts had been stripped of their authority, but were allowed to live for a period of time.)

In my vision at night I looked, and there before me was one like a son of man, coming with the clouds of heaven. He approached the Ancient of Days and was led into his presence. He was given authority, glory and sovereign power; all peoples, nations and men of every language worshiped him. His dominion is an everlasting dominion that will not pass away, and his kingdom is one that will never be destroyed.

In the rest of the chapter, Daniel receives the interpretation of this vision. The four beasts represent a succession of four world empires.[29] The "one like a son of man" represents "the saints of the Most High" (see vv. 18,22,27). The first readers no doubt understood these "saints" to be righteous, Law-keeping Jews, who are faithful to the Mosaic Covenant. According to the vision, these Jewish saints are hated and persecuted by world rulers (one of which is represented by the "little horn"), but they will be vindicated by God, caused to enter his presence, highly exalted, and then given the everlasting kingdom of God. By using the language of Daniel 7 to describe Jesus as one "like a son of man," John may be representing Jesus as the embodiment of righteous Israel, ideal Israel, the one who fulfills everything

---

[29]Much like the statue of gold, silver, bronze, iron and clay represents a series of four empires in Daniel 2 (discussed in Part III.B.2.b.[4] of the Introduction).

that God intended Israel to be. Jesus is the first of many "saints of the Most High" to be raised and exalted to the kingdom.

By describing Jesus as "someone 'like a son of man,'" John invites his readers to think of Jesus' humanity, his messiahship, and his identity as the one who embodies God's hopes for Israel. Which is the correct interpretation of this symbol? In the case of Jesus, all three meanings apply equally well, and so John may intend for the symbol to communicate all three truths simultaneously. If so, this image serves as a very fine illustration of how apocalyptic symbols function. Eugene Boring states it well: "Revelation's symbols are tensive, evocative and polyvalent."[30] They are "evocative" in that they draw forth, or elicit from the reader's mind, a number of different mental images from the Old Testament, apocalyptic literature, and/or Greco-Roman life. They are "tensive" in the sense that they create a tension in the mind, forcing the reader to reflect on the various possible interpretations and the relationship between them. In other words, the symbols force the reader to meditate on the meaning of the apocalyptic vision. The symbols are "polyvalent" in that they are able to communicate multiple meanings at the same time.

dressed in a robe reaching down to his feet

The Greek word translated "a robe reaching down to his feet" is ποδήρης (*podērēs*). In the Greek Old Testament and Apocrypha, this term is used to describe only one kind of garment — namely, the garments worn by the Jewish priests, and notably the High Priest.[31] A person familiar with the Scriptures would read this verse in Revelation and immediately realize that Jesus is being pictured as the High Priest. That is the point of the symbol: Jesus is the Great High Priest, the Mediator through whom we approach God and through whom God deals with us. The Hebrews writer communicates this truth through didactic language (see Heb 2:14-18; 4:14–10:18). John, in Revelation, communicates that same truth through apocalyptic symbolism.

---

[30]Boring, *Revelation*, 54-57.

[31]See Exodus 28:4,27; 29:5; Ezek 9:2-3,11; Zech 3:5; Wisd. Sol. 18:24; Sirach 45:8 (LXX). Sirach 27:8 departs from the norm by using *podērēs* as a symbol for righteousness: "If you pursue righteousness, you will attain it and wear it as a glorious robe (*podērēs*)."

a golden sash around his chest

How would John's first readers have interpreted the Lord's "golden sash"? They may have viewed it as a royal garment. In Joseph and Aseneth 10:10 (a Jewish "romance novel" dating somewhere from the second century B.C. to A.D. 200), the Egyptian princess Aseneth wears such a sash when she weds Joseph.

They may have linked it with John's identification of Jesus as "someone 'like a son of man'" (see above). Daniel 10:5 uses similar (but not identical) language to describe a golden belt worn by "the likeness of a son of man" (v. 16). However, in this text, "the likeness of a son of man" does not represent "the saints of the Most High," as in Daniel 7. Instead, he appears to be some sort of heavenly being — perhaps an archangel — in the company of the archangel Michael.

Christians in Asia may have linked the "golden sash" with John's identification of Jesus as the Great High Priest (see the comment on Christ's robe given above). In Exodus 39:5 the High Priest wears a similar (but not identical) garment around his waist.

The "golden sash" adds to the overall majesty of Jesus' appearance, and the symbol may carry some of these other connotations as well.

1:14 His head and hair were white like wool, as white as snow

This language is like that in Daniel 7:9, which is part of the vision of the four beasts and the "one like a son of man" discussed above. In Daniel, the Person with hair as white as wool is God himself, whom Daniel refers to as the "Ancient of Days." The prophet writes:

> As I looked, thrones were set in place, and the Ancient of Days took his seat. His clothing was as white as snow; the hair of his head was white like wool.

The same sort of language appears in 1 Enoch 46:1-4. This passage resembles Daniel 7 inasmuch as God and the Son of Man are discussed together. It differs in that Daniel 7 uses the title "Son of Man" to refer to righteous Israelites, while 1 Enoch 46 uses the title "Son of Man" to refer to one particular righteous Israelite — the Messiah.

> At that place, I saw the One [God] to whom belongs the time before time [i.e., he is preexistent, existing prior to creation]. And his head was white like wool [the mark of extreme old age, of an

eternity], and there was with him another individual, whose face was like that of a human being. His countenance was full of grace like that of one among the holy angels. And I asked the one — from among the angels — who was going with me, and who had revealed to me all the secrets regarding the One who was born of human beings, "Who is this, and from whence is he who is going as the prototype of the Before-Time?" [The Messiah is a human, "born of human beings," but at the same time he is "like" the angels. Furthermore, he is "the prototype of the Before Time" — the very image of God.] And he answered me and said to me, "This is the Son of Man, to whom belongs righteousness, and with whom righteousness dwells. And he will open all the hidden storerooms; for the Lord of the Spirits [i.e., God] has chosen him, and he is destined to be victorious before the Lord of the Spirits in eternal uprightness. This Son of Man whom you have seen is the One who would remove the kings and the mighty ones from their comfortable seats and the strong ones from their thrones. He shall loosen the reigns of the strong and crush the teeth of the sinners. [In other words, he executes the eschatological judgment of God.] He shall depose the kings from their thrones and kingdoms. For they do not extol and glorify him, and neither do they obey him, the source of their kingship [In the language of Revelation, the Messiah is "King of the kings and Lord of the lords."] (1 Enoch 46:1-4).[32]

By describing Jesus' "head and hair" as "white like wool" and "white as snow," John communicates the fact that Jesus is "Ancient of Days," eternal and preexistent. He is "the Alpha and the Omega, the First and the Last, the Beginning and the End" (see the comment on Rev 1:4). He is God.

1:14b,16 his eyes were like blazing fire. His feet were like bronze glowing in a furnace . . . . His face was like the sun shining in all its brilliance.

These symbols together speak of an intensely bright light radiating from the Lord. The Greek term for such light is δόξα (*doxa*), which is usually translated "glory." The term also carries connotations of "honor," for ancient peoples associated radiant light with

---

[32] Charlesworth, *Pseudepigrapha*.

honor. To illustrate, they placed many-pointed gold or silver crowns on the heads of kings. As the sun reflected off these crowns, it would create a "halo" of glory around the rulers' heads, signifying the honor associated with their position.

In the Old Testament and apocalyptic literature, basically three kinds of persons are described as "glorious." First, heavenly beings, such as the "archangel" (see v. 13) in Daniel 10:4-6, display this glorious radiance:

> On the twenty-fourth day of the first month, as I was standing on the bank of the great river, the Tigris, I looked up and there before me was a man dressed in linen, with a belt of the finest gold around his waist. His body was like chrysolite, his face like lightning, his eyes like flaming torches, his arms and legs like the gleam of burnished bronze, and his voice like the sound of a multitude.

The "cherubim" (see 10:20) of Ezekiel 1 also emit this heavenly glory.

Second, Jewish writers often describe God himself as "glorious." Psalm 104:1-2 illustrates this point:

> Praise the LORD, O my soul. / O LORD my God, you are very great; / you are clothed with splendor and majesty. / He wraps himself in light as with a garment . . . .

Exodus 24:15-17 also speaks of God's radiant glory:

> When Moses went up on the mountain, the cloud covered it, and the glory of the LORD settled on Mount Sinai. For six days the cloud covered the mountain, and on the seventh day the LORD called to Moses from within the cloud. To the Israelites the glory of the LORD looked like a consuming fire on top of the mountain.

Another example comes from Ezekiel 1:26-28 (cf. 8:2), which describes "the likeness of the glory of the LORD":

> Above the expanse over their heads [i.e., the heads of the four living creatures] was what looked like a throne of sapphire, and high above on the throne was a figure like that of a man. I saw that from what appeared to be his waist up he looked like glowing metal, as if full of fire, and that from there down he looked like fire; and brilliant light surrounded him. Like the appearance of a rainbow in the

clouds on a rainy day, so was the radiance around him. This was the appearance of the likeness of the glory of the LORD.

Third, Jewish writers — particularly apocalyptic writers — use "glory" language to describe persons who have been raised from the dead to eschatological life in the kingdom of God. These theologians employ many adjectives to characterize the resurrection body, but the three ideas that appear most often are immortality, exaltation, and glory. Whereas our current bodies are subject to sickness, disease, aging, and death, the resurrection body will be immortal. Resurrection life will also be exalted — that is, a better, higher form of existence than what we have experienced thus far. Finally, the resurrection body will be characterized by "glory" (*doxa*), both in the sense of radiance and in the sense of the honor it signifies.[33] The most detailed description of the resurrection body in Jewish apocalyptic appears in 2 Baruch 51. The most detailed description in first-century Christian literature appears in 1 Corinthians 15:39-44a:

> Not all flesh is alike, but there is one kind for men, another for animals, another for birds, and another for fish. There are celestial bodies and there are terrestrial bodies; but the glory of the celestial is one [a bright light], and the glory of the terrestrial is another [a dimmer light]. There is one glory of the sun, and another glory of the moon, and another glory of the stars; for star differs from star in glory.
>
> So is it with the resurrection of the dead. What is sown is perishable, what is raised is imperishable [i.e., immortal]. It is sown in dishonor, it is raised in glory. It is sown in weakness, it is raised in power. It is sown a physical body, it is raised a spiritual body (RSV).

When John, in Revelation 1:14-16, describes Jesus as having a "glorious" body, the symbolism communicates several truths: First, the Lord is a heavenly, supernatural being. Second, he is a divine being, the manifestation of the glory of God on earth. Third, he is a

---

[33]Note that, when the risen Jesus appears to Paul on Damascus Road, the future Apostle sees exactly what a first-century Jew would expect to see when viewing a person raised from the dead — namely, a light so bright that it blinds him for several days (see Acts 9:1-18).

person who has already been raised from the dead to glorious eschatological life[34] in the kingdom of God.

1:15 His voice was like the sound of rushing waters

This beautiful symbol comes from the prophecy of Ezekiel and concerns the temple of the Lord. Patterned after the tabernacle of Exodus, Solomon's temple in Jerusalem was divided into two rooms separated by a curtain. In the inner room, the "Most Holy Place," stood the Ark of the Covenant. The Ark was a wooden box, covered with gold, that held the tablets engraved with the Ten Commandments. Its lid was also made of gold and featured two golden cherubim with their wings overshadowing the Ark.[35] This lid was called the "Atonement Cover." Over the Atonement Cover, the glory of the Lord hovered. This bright light signified the presence of the invisible God with his people Israel. The Psalmist refers to God's radiant glory in Psalm 80:1: "You who sit enthroned between the cherubim, shine forth."

In 587 B.C. the Babylonians destroyed Jerusalem and the temple and took most of the Jews into exile. Among their number was the prophet Ezekiel. In Ezekiel 10 the prophet receives a vision of the "glory of the Lord" departing from over the Ark of the Covenant. This symbolizes God removing his presence from his people because of their sin and idolatry. However, in Ezekiel 43 the prophet sees another vision of the Lord's glory returning to the temple. This latter vision shows that, in spite of their sin, God will not abandon his people forever. Verses 1-5 describe the Lord's return:

> Then the man brought me to the gate facing east, and I saw the glory of the God of Israel coming from the east. *His voice was like the roar of rushing waters* [cf. 1:24], and the land was radiant with his glory. The vision I saw was like the vision I had seen when he came to destroy the city and like the visions I had seen by the Kebar River, and I fell facedown. The glory of the LORD entered the temple through the gate facing east. Then the Spirit lifted me

---

[34]See the discussion of "The Kingdom of God and the Resurrection of Jesus" in Part III.B.2.c.(5) of the Introduction.

[35]For a discussion of the symbolism of the Ark of the Covenant, see footnote 10 under the comment on Rev 4:6b,8.

up and brought me into the inner court, and the glory of the LORD filled the temple.

Echoing Ezekiel, John describes Jesus in Revelation 1:15 as having a voice "like the sound of rushing waters." Through this symbol, he communicates the idea that Jesus is the "glory of God" — the visible manifestation of God's presence on earth.

1:16 Out of his mouth came a sharp double-edged sword

The sword symbolizes the fact that Christ speaks the word of God (the gospel of the kingdom), which is both a word of salvation to those who serve God and — at the same time — a word of judgment to those who oppose him. The primary evidence for this interpretation appears in Revelation 19:11-16:

> I saw heaven standing open and there before me was a white horse, whose rider is called Faithful and True. With justice he judges and makes war. His eyes are like blazing fire, and on his head are many crowns. He has a name written on him that no one knows but he himself. He is dressed in a robe dipped in blood, and his name is the Word of God. The armies of heaven were following him, riding on white horses and dressed in fine linen, white and clean. Out of his mouth comes a sharp sword with which to strike down the nations [i.e., the nations who oppose God and his Messiah — see the context of the following quote from Psalm 2:9, which is discussed above in the comment on the title "Christ" in Rev 1:5]. "He will rule them with an iron scepter." He treads the winepress of the fury of the wrath of God Almighty. On his robe and on his thigh he has this name written: KING OF KINGS AND LORD OF LORDS.

Note that, in verse 13, the Lord is identified as "the Word of God." Out of his mouth — where words are formed — comes a "sword," which apparently represents the words of God. With this "sword," Christ executes God's wrath against his enemies.[36]

1:12-13,16,20 . . . And when I turned I saw seven golden lampstands, and among the lampstands was someone "like a son of man" . . . . In his right hand he held seven stars . . . . "The mystery

---

[36]For similar ideas, see Isa 11:4; 49:2; 4 Ezra 13; Eph 6:17; Heb 4:12-13.

of the seven stars that you saw in my right hand and of the seven golden lampstands is this: The seven stars are the angels of the seven churches, and the seven lampstands are the seven churches."

In many apocalypses, God assigns a different angel responsibility for each nation. Evil angels, who have rebelled against God, direct their corresponding nations in evil paths. Good angels, who remain faithful to God, discharge their duties according to God's will. Each angel is rewarded or punished according to how he carries out his responsibility over his corresponding nation. In this way, apocalyptic writers communicate at least two theological truths: First, God is sovereign over all. He rules over the nations through his servants, the angels. Second, there is a spiritual world beyond the physical world. This spiritual world, which has been partially corrupted by sin, influences the physical world.[37]

We find an example of this kind of thinking in Daniel 10:12-14. Here the archangel, who brings God's revelation to Daniel, explains that he has been delayed in his coming by demonic resistance:

> Then he continued, "Do not be afraid, Daniel. Since the first day that you set your mind to gain understanding and to humble yourself before your God, your words were heard, and I have come in response to them. But the prince of the Persian kingdom [i.e., the fallen angel who has charge over Persia — which explains why Persia persecutes God's people, the Jews] resisted me twenty-one days. Then Michael, one of the chief princes [the archangel who has charge over the nation of Israel], came to help me, because I was detained there with the king of Persia. Now I have come to explain to you what will happen to your people in the future, for the vision concerns a time yet to come."

The Apostle Paul expresses the same sort of an idea in Ephesians 6:10-12, where he reminds Christians that they are dealing with more than just the realities that can be seen:

> Finally, be strong in the Lord and in his mighty power. Put on the full armor of God so that you can take your stand against the

---

[37]For further discussion of these ideas, see the Introduction, Parts III.B.2.b.(1) "Rebellion in Heaven" and III.B.2.c.(1) "Supernatural Forces of Evil."

devil's schemes. For our struggle is not against flesh and blood, but against the rulers, against the authorities, against the powers of this dark world and against the spiritual forces of evil in the heavenly realms.

Against this background, we can now understand the meaning of the symbolism in Revelation 1. The Lord explains that the seven golden lampstands represent the seven churches of Asia. The symbol of the lampstands carries connotations of "witness." Compare Isaiah 42:6, where the Servant of the Lord serves as "a light for the Gentiles," and Matthew 5:16, where Jesus instructs his disciples to "Let your light shine before men." By picturing them as lampstands, John indicates that the churches function as witnesses for Christ.

Note that Christ is "among the lampstands." He is not far away from the churches, but close at hand and present with them. Jesus expresses the same truth in a different manner in his Great Commission: "And surely I will be with you always, to the very end of the age" (Matt 28:20).

The "seven stars" are seven angels who direct the churches of Asia. These angels are in Christ's right hand, which means that Christ is in control of the churches' angels, and thus in control of the churches. We will see him exercise this lordship in chapters 2 and 3 as he addresses words of commendation and rebuke to the seven angels and, through them, to the churches themselves.

The image of the seven stars in Christ's right hand would have also spoken to the people of John's time in other ways. First, this is an antiastrology message. The stars do not control our destiny and are not to be feared. Christ is the Lord who holds the stars in his hand. Second, the symbol of the stars challenges the divine claims of certain Roman Caesars. To illustrate, the young son of the Emperor Domitian died in A.D. 83. Domitian proclaimed the child a god and minted coins picturing his mother, Domitia, as queen of heaven, and the child holding the stars in his hands. In Revelation 1, John removes the stars from human hands and places them where they rightfully belong – in the hand of Christ. He thus declares the Roman Caesars to be false imitations of the true cosmic ruler, who is Christ the Lord.

b. Christ's Words (1:17-20)

¹⁷When I saw him, I fell at his feet as though dead. Then he placed his right hand on me and said: "Do not be afraid. I am the First and the Last. ¹⁸I am the Living One; I was dead, and behold I am alive for ever and ever! And I hold the keys of death and Hades.

¹⁹"Write, therefore, what you have seen, what is now and what will take place later. ²⁰The mystery of the seven stars that you saw in my right hand and of the seven golden lampstands is this: The seven stars are the angels[a] of the seven churches, and the seven lampstands are the seven churches.

[a]20 Or *messengers*

1:17 When I saw him, I fell at his feet as though dead.

This is a typical response of persons who encounter the Deity. (Compare, for example, Daniel 8:17-18 [LXX]; Ezekiel 1:28; Luke 5:8.) As such, the action itself serves to highlight the divine nature of Christ.

Then he placed his right hand on me and said: "Do not be afraid. I am the First and the Last.

See the comment on "him who is, and who was, and who is to come" in Revelation 1:4.

1:18 I am the Living One; I was dead, and behold I am alive for ever and ever! And I hold the keys of death and Hades.

Jesus endured a painful death for his "faithful witness" to God,[38] but then God raised him up to eschatological life. Where Christ once was, John's readers are now. The suffering Christians of Asia may be facing death,[39] but John lays before them the certainty that — like Jesus — they will be raised up to victorious new life.

Why will they escape from death? Because Jesus holds "the keys of death and Hades." In Hellenistic mythology, "Hades" was the

---

[38]See the comment on "the faithful witness" in verse 5.

[39]See Part IV.B.3 of the Introduction: "Persecution Related to Emperor Worship in Asia Minor."

grave, the place of the dead. It is the Greek equivalent of the Hebrew "Sheol." Even if John's readers are dragged before the authorities and put to death for their faith, Jesus has the power to unlock the gates of the grave and set them free — forever.

1:19 "Write, therefore, what you have seen, what is now and what will take place later.

Christ promises to give John a revelation of the present ("what is now") and a revelation of the future ("what will take place later"). The revelation of the present appears in chapters 2–3, while the revelation of the future is found in 3:1–22:6. For further discussion of the Structure of Revelation, see Part V of the Introduction.

1:20 The mystery of the seven stars that you saw in my right hand and of the seven golden lampstands is this: The seven stars are the angels of the seven churches, and the seven lampstands are the seven churches."

See the comments given above on Revelation 1:12-13,16,20.

c. Summary: John's Portrait of Christ in Revelation 1:9-20

In Revelation 1:9-20 John presents a striking portrait of Christ in apocalyptic symbolism. We have searched out the literary and cultural roots of these symbols in an effort to discern the truths they would have communicated to John's first readers in Asia. Who, then, is Jesus? Who is this person who will speak to us through the Revelation?

According to chapter 1, Jesus is *divine*. He is the presence of God himself with his spokesman John. As such, he is eternal ("head and hair white as wool, as white as snow"), preexistent or "ancient of days" ("head and hair white as wool, as white as snow"), and glorious ("eyes like blazing fire," "feet like glowing bronze," "face like the sun shining in its brilliance"). Christ is the visible manifestation of God's presence among his people ("voice like the sound of rushing waters"). He speaks with the voice of God ("a loud voice like a trumpet"), pronouncing the words of God, which are words of salvation for his people and words of judgment for those who oppose him ("out of his mouth came a sharp double-edged sword").

At the same time, Jesus is *human* ("someone 'like a son of man'"). As a human being, Jesus was susceptible to death ("I was dead"). However, he is the first of the "saints of the Most High" to be raised and exalted to glorious eschatological life in the kingdom of God ("someone 'like a son of man,'" "face like the sun shining in its brilliance," "alive for ever and ever"). Christ is the embodiment of righteous Israel — everything God wanted his covenant people to be ("someone 'like a son of man'").

Jesus is also the *Messiah* or "Anointed One" ("someone 'like a son of man'"). As Messiah, he functions as a prophet inasmuch as he speaks the words of God ("a loud voice like a trumpet"). He also serves as High Priest, as the Mediator between God and human beings ("a robe reaching down to his feet"), the person through whom we approach God and through whom God relates to us. He is also the ultimate Davidic King ("a golden sash around his chest"). He is sovereign over heaven and earth. He is sovereign over the churches, holding our lives and our destiny in his hand ("in his right hand he held seven stars"). He is sovereign over life and death ("I hold the keys of death and Hades").

REVELATION 2-3

II. THE REVELATION OF "WHAT IS NOW" (2:1–3:22)

In Revelation 1:19 Christ offers John a vision of both the present ("what is now") and the future ("what will take place later"). The vision of the future appears in 4:1–22:6, where John watches history unfold from God's vantage point in heaven. The vision of the present appears in 2:1–3:22 and takes the form of seven letters to churches in Asia. The phrase "what is now" refers not to what is "present" from our point of view, but to what was "present" for John at the time he received the Revelation. In the letters, the Lord offers his assessment of the situation faced by Christians in the Roman province of Asia during A.D. 95-96.[1] For a more detailed discussion of the Structure of Revelation, see Part V of the Introduction.

Christ's letters to the churches display several recurring themes. For example, the Lord highlights the kinds of pressures and opposition faced by his Asian disciples. He also promises rewards for those who meet and "overcome" those challenges. Studying the letters individually is certainly a worthwhile exercise. However, studying them as a group yields a clearer, more comprehensive understanding of both the situation in Asia and Christ's response to it. For this reason, we have adopted a topical approach — rather than a verse-by-verse approach — to Revelation 2 and 3.

A. THE SEVEN CHURCHES

Christ addresses his letters to the Christian congregations in Ephesus, Smyrna, Pergamum, Thyatira, Sardis, Philadelphia, and

---

[1] On the date of Revelation, see Part IV.B.2 of the Introduction.

Laodicea.² Some believe that the Lord is speaking to these seven churches alone because each letter seems tailor-made for its specific destination. To illustrate, after years of decline, Smyrna had revived to enjoy a "second life." Christ compares himself to the city as one "who died and came to life again" (2:8). Pergamum was the center of the emperor cult in Asia, and so Christ identifies it as the place "where Satan has his throne" (2:13). In contrast with the medicinal hot springs of nearby Hierapolis and the clear, cold streams of nearby Colossae, Laodicea's water supply was tepid, impure, and barely drinkable. Accordingly, the Lord rebukes the Laodicean church for its inadequacies by calling it "lukewarm." Several excellent books are available, which discuss these historical, geographical, and religious details at great length.³

While acknowledging the local connections, others point out that "seven" is the apocalyptic number for "completeness." The seven congregations probably symbolize *all* the churches in the Roman province of Asia. This theory seems to be supported by the substance of the letters, which reflect the kinds of challenges faced by Christians *throughout* Asia late in the first century. If this is the case, then why does Christ choose these particular cities to represent the whole of the Asian Church? First, all were communities of some prominence, located along the main Roman road system. Second, at least three of these cities (Ephesus, Smyrna, and Pergamum) contained temples dedicated to emperor worship. Third, all seven cities held a Roman law court, where believers could be put on trial for the capital crime of being a Christian. Perhaps the Lord singles out these particular churches because they are at the center of the crisis facing Christians late in the reign of Domitian.⁴

---

²Compare Rev 1:4b,11.
³See William Barclay, *Letters to the Seven Churches* (New York: Abingdon Press, 1957); Colin J. Hemer, *The Letters to the Seven Churches of Asia in Their Local Setting*, Journal for the Study of the New Testament Supplement Series, 11 (Sheffield: JSOT Press, 1986); W.M. Ramsay, *The Letters to the Seven Churches*, rev. ed., ed. Mark W. Wilson (Peabody, MA: Hendrickson, 1994); Roland H. Worth, Jr., *The Seven Cities of the Apocalypse and Greco-Roman Culture* (Mahwah, NJ: Paulist Press, 1999) and *The Seven Cities of the Apocalypse and Roman Culture* (Mahwah, NJ: Paulist Press, 1999).
⁴For further discussion of "Persecution Related to Emperor Worship in Asia Minor," see Part IV.B.3 of the Introduction.

B. THE STRUCTURE OF THE LETTERS TO THE SEVEN CHURCHES

1. Addressed to the Angels of the Seven Churches

The Lord addresses each letter to the angel of the corresponding church (see 2:1a,8a,12a,18a; 3:1a,7a,14a). Through the commendations and rebukes of the letters, Christ exercises his sovereignty over the angels. Through the angels, he exercises lordship over the churches. For a further explanation of this apocalyptic idea, see the comment on Revelation 1:12-13,16,20 concerning the "seven stars."

2. A Renewal of the New Covenant

a. Typical Elements of Covenants

A "covenant" is a formal relationship between two persons or groups. The Mosaic Covenant between God and Israel includes five main elements — namely, a preamble, historical prologue, stipulations, witnesses, and blessings and/or curses. As such, it closely resembles Hittite suzerainty treaties — that is, treaties between a superior and inferior, between a king and his subjects.[5] The renewal of the Mosaic Covenant in Joshua 24:1-27 serves to illustrate:

First, there is a preamble in which the king is identified. In verse 2a Joshua declares: "This is what the LORD, the God of Israel, says."

The second element is an historical prologue, which reviews the past relationship between God the king and his people Israel (vv. 2b-13). Joshua describes what the Lord has done for Israel, beginning with his promises to Abraham and ending with the Exodus and conquest of Canaan in fulfillment of those promises.

Third, Joshua names the terms or stipulations for a continued relationship with God (v. 14). The Israelites must rid themselves of idols and serve the LORD alone.

Fourth, Joshua warns the people of the curse that will fall on them if they break the covenant. He declares, "If you forsake the

---

[5]See, for example, the treaty between the Hittite lord Mursilis and his vassal Duppi-Tessub of Amurru that appears in Pritchard, *Ancient Near Eastern Texts*, pp. 203-205.

LORD and serve foreign gods, he will turn and bring disaster on you and make an end of you, after he has been good to you" (v. 20). This particular passage names no blessings that will come from upholding the covenant. However, the blessings and curses of Deuteronomy 27–28 are fine examples of these typical elements of ancient covenant agreements.

Fifth, Joshua names the people themselves as witnesses of the covenant, and he also sets up a large stone to serve as a witness (vv. 22-27).

b. Covenantal Elements in the Letters to the Seven Churches

William H. Shea shows that the letters to the churches in Revelation 2 and 3 include all five elements of ancient covenants. This suggests that, in the letters, the risen Christ is offering to renew his new covenant relationship with the suffering Christians of Asia.[6]

First, each letter begins with a preamble in which Christ appears in the role of king. Many of the titles used to identify the Lord repeat symbols that appear in Revelation 1. So the apocalyptic description of Christ in that chapter sets the tone for the seven letters that follow.

Second, the letters feature historical prologues beginning with "I know your deeds" (or "I know your afflictions" in the case of Smyrna, or "I know where you live" in the case of Pergamum). After describing the kinds of pressures and opposition faced by Christians in Asia (discussed below), the king reviews the churches' performance.

Third, Christ issues a series of commands ("Remember! Repent! Be faithful! Wake up! Hold on!"), which should be understood as stipulations for remaining in a right covenant relationship with the Lord.

Fourth, most of the letters include a warning — a curse for those who refuse to meet the stipulations. However, all of the letters place much more emphasis on the blessings that come through covenantal faithfulness. In each letter, the Lord offers a promise "to him who overcomes" (discussed below).

---

[6]See William H. Shea, "The Covenantal Form in Revelation 2–3," *Andrews University Seminary Studies* 21 (1983): 71-84.

Fifth, each letter includes a type of appeal that Jesus was fond of using during his earthly ministry: "He who has an ear, let him hear what the Spirit says to the churches."[7] In a covenantal context, it should be understood as a call for everyone to act as witnesses to the renewal of the covenant between Christ and the churches of Asia.

The NIV translations of the seven letters are printed below, along with a few comments. The contents of the letters are arranged in a way that highlights their covenantal elements.

c. The Letter to Ephesus (2:1-7)

"To the angel[a] of the church in Ephesus write:

Preamble (2:1b): **These are the words of him who holds the seven stars in his right hand and walks among the seven golden lampstands:**[8]

Historical Prologue (2:2-4,6): **I know your deeds, your hard work and your perseverance. I know that you cannot tolerate wicked men, that you have tested those who claim to be apostles but are not, and have found them false. You have persevered and have endured hardships for my name, and have not grown weary.**

Yet I hold this against you: You have forsaken your first love. . . . But you have this in your favor: You hate the practices of the Nicolaitans, which I also hate.

Stipulations (2:5a): **Remember the height from which you have fallen! Repent and do the things you did at first.**

Curse (2:5b): **If you do not repent, I will come to you and remove your lampstand from its place.**

Witnesses (2:7a): **He who has an ear, let him hear what the Spirit says to the churches.**

Blessing (2:7b): **To him who overcomes, I will give the right to eat from the tree of life, which is in the paradise of God.**

[a]*1* Or *messenger*, also in verses 8, 12 and 18

---

[7]Compare, for example, Matt 11:15; 13:9.
[8]See the comment on Rev 1:12-13,16,20 concerning the "seven stars" and "seven golden lampstands."

d. The Letter to Smyrna (2:8-11)

"To the angel of the church in Smyrna write:

Preamble (2:8b): **These are the words of him who is the First and the Last, who died and came to life again.**[9]

Historical Prologue (2:9): **I know your afflictions and your poverty—yet you are rich! I know the slander of those who say they are Jews and are not, but are a synagogue of Satan.**

Stipulations (2:10a): **Do not be afraid of what you are about to suffer. I tell you, the devil will put some of you in prison to test you, and you will suffer persecution for ten days. Be faithful, even to the point of death,**

Witnesses (2:11a): **He who has an ear, let him hear what the Spirit says to the churches.**

Blessing (2:10b, 11b): **and I will give you the crown of life. . . . He who overcomes will not be hurt at all by the second death.**

The "crown" (στέφανος, *stephanos*) is the "wreath" of the victor in athletic games. It here symbolizes eternal life.

e. The Letter to Pergamum (2:12-17)

"To the angel of the church in Pergamum write:

Preamble (2:12b): **These are the words of him who has the sharp, double-edged sword.**[10]

Historical Prologue (2:13-15): **I know where you live—where Satan has his throne. Yet you remain true to my name. You did not renounce your faith in me, even in the days of Antipas, my faithful witness, who was put to death in your city—where Satan lives. Nevertheless, I have a few things against you: You have people there who hold to the teaching of Balaam, who taught Balak to entice the Israelites to sin by eating food sacrificed to idols and by committing sexual immorality. Likewise you also have those who hold to the teaching of the Nicolaitans.**

Stipulation (2:16a): **Repent therefore!**

---

[9]See the comment on "him who is, and who was, and who is to come" in Rev 1:4c. See also the comment on Rev 1:18.

[10]See the comment on the "sharp, double-edged sword" in Rev 1:16.

Curse (2:16b): **Otherwise, I will soon come to you and will fight against them with the sword of my mouth.**

Witnesses (2:17a): **He who has an ear, let him hear what the Spirit says to the churches.**

Blessings (2:17b): **To him who overcomes, I will give some of the hidden manna. I will also give him a white stone with a new name written on it, known only to him who receives it.**

f. The Letter to Thyatira (2:18-29)

"To the angel of the church in Thyatira write:

Preamble (2:18b): **These are the words of the Son of God, whose eyes are like blazing fire and whose feet are like burnished bronze.**[11]

Historical Prologue (2:19-21): **I know your deeds, your love and faith, your service and perseverance, and that you are now doing more than you did at first. Nevertheless, I have this against you: You tolerate that woman Jezebel, who calls herself a prophetess. By her teaching she misleads my servants into sexual immorality and the eating of food sacrificed to idols. I have given her time to repent of her immorality, but she is unwilling.**

Curse (2:22-23): **So I will cast her on a bed of suffering, and I will make those who commit adultery with her suffer intensely, unless they repent of her ways. I will strike her children dead. Then all the churches will know that I am he who searches hearts and minds, and I will repay each of you according to your deeds.**

Stipulation (2:24-25): **Now I say to the rest of you in Thyatira, to you who do not hold to her teaching and have not learned Satan's so-called deep secrets (I will not impose any other burden on you): Only hold on to what you have until I come.**

Blessings (2:26-28): **To him who overcomes and does my will to the end, I will give authority over the nations—**
  'He will rule them with an iron scepter;
     he will dash them to pieces like pottery'[a]**—**
  just as I have received authority from my Father. I will also give him the morning star.

---

[11]See the comment on the similar imagery found in Rev 1:14-16.

Witnesses (2:29): **He who has an ear, let him hear what the Spirit says to the churches.**

ᵃ27 **Psalm 2:9**

g. The Letter to Sardis (3:1-6)

"To the angel of the church in Sardis write:

Preamble (3:1b): **These are the words of him who holds the seven spiritsᵃ of God and the seven stars.**[12]

Historical Prologue (3:1c,2b,4a): **I know your deeds; you have a reputation of being alive, but you are dead. . . . for I have not found your deeds complete in the sight of my God. . . . Yet you have a few people in Sardis who have not soiled their clothes.**

Stipulations (3:2a,3a): **Wake up! Strengthen what remains and is about to die . . . . Remember, therefore, what you have received and heard; obey it, and repent.**

Curse (3:3b): **But if you do not wake up, I will come like a thief, and you will not know at what time I will come to you.**

> Compare Matthew 24:43 // Luke 12:39; 1 Thessalonians 5:2,4; 2 Peter 3:10; and Revelation 16:15, which also liken Christ's Second Coming to the surprise appearance of a thief.

Blessings (3:4b-5): **[Yet you have a few people in Sardis who have not soiled their clothes.] They will walk with me, dressed in white, for they are worthy. He who overcomes will, like them, be dressed in white. I will never blot out his name from the book of life, but will acknowledge his name before my Father and his angels.**

Witnesses (3:6): **He who has an ear, let him hear what the Spirit says to the churches.**

ᵃ1 Or *the sevenfold Spirit*

h. The Letter to Philadelphia (3:7-13)

"To the angel of the church in Philadelphia write:

Preamble (3:7b): **These are the words of him who is holy and true,**

---

[12] See the comment on the "seven spirits" in Rev 1:4c, as well as the comments on Rev 1:12-13,16,20 concerning the "seven stars."

who holds the key of David. What he opens no one can shut, and what he shuts no one can open.

> The "key" is a symbol of authority and power — the ability to "open" and "shut," the ability to do what others cannot do. In Revelation 1:18 (discussed above); Christ "holds the keys of death and Hades" — the ability to "open the door" of the grave and release people from death. John calls this "key" the "key of David" (a phrase borrowed from Isaiah 22:22) because it is held and used by the Messiah, the Son of David. On Jesus as the ultimate Davidic King, see the comments on "Christ," "the faithful witness," and "the ruler of the kings of the earth" in Revelation 1:5.

Historical Prologue (3:8,10a): **I know your deeds. See, I have placed before you an open door that no one can shut. I know that you have little strength, yet you have kept my word and have not denied my name. . . . Since you have kept my command to endure patiently,**

Blessings (3:9,10b): **I will make those who are of the synagogue of Satan, who claim to be Jews though they are not, but are liars—I will make them come and fall down at your feet and acknowledge that I have loved you. . . . I will also keep you from the hour of trial that is going to come upon the whole world to test those who live on the earth.**

Stipulation (3:11a): **I am coming soon. Hold on to what you have,**

Curse (3:11b): **so that no one will take your crown.**

Blessings (3:12): **Him who overcomes I will make a pillar in the temple of my God. Never again will he leave it. I will write on him the name of my God and the name of the city of my God, the new Jerusalem, which is coming down out of heaven from my God; and I will also write on him my new name.**

Witnesses (3:13): **He who has an ear, let him hear what the Spirit says to the churches.**

i. The Letter to Laodicea (3:14-22)

"To the angel of the church in Laodicea write:

Preamble (3:14b): **These are the words of the Amen, the faithful and true witness,**[13] **the ruler of God's creation.**

---

[13] See the comment on Jesus as "the faithful witness" in Rev 1:5.

The word "Amen" means "truly" or "so be it." Compare 2 Corinthians 1:20, where Paul says that Jesus adds the "Yes" or the "Amen" to the promises of God — that is, he makes those promises come true.

The Greek term translated "ruler" is ἀρχή (*archē*), which means "first" or "primary." If the writer is speaking of someone who is "primary" in authority, then the term may be translated "ruler" (as in the NIV). If the writer is speaking of someone or something that is "first" in time, then the term may be translated "beginning." In Revelation 21:6 and 22:13, this title is applied to Christ as "the Beginning and the End." (For an explanation, see the comment on "him who is, and who was, and who is to come" in Rev 1:4.) Here in 3:14, the basic truth contained in the title "ruler of God's creation" is that Christ holds preeminence over all.

Historical Prologue (3:15,17): **I know your deeds, that you are neither cold nor hot. I wish you were either one or the other! .... You say, 'I am rich; I have acquired wealth and do not need a thing.' But you do not realize that you are wretched, pitiful, poor, blind and naked.**

Curse (3:16): **So, because you are lukewarm—neither hot nor cold—I am about to spit you out of my mouth.**

Stipulations (3:18-20a): **I counsel you to buy from me gold refined in the fire,[14] so you can become rich; and white clothes to wear, so you can cover your shameful nakedness; and salve to put on your eyes, so you can see. Those whom I love I rebuke and discipline. So be earnest, and repent. Here I am! I stand at the door and knock. If anyone hears my voice and opens the door,**

> Laodicea was famous for the black wool garments produced by its clothing industry and for the Phyrgian eye salve distributed by its medical school. Christ reminds the Laodicean church that he is the true giver of sight and the "clothier" who can truly remove their shame.[15]

---

[14] Note that the treasure or reward that Christians receive comes from having passed through the "fire." Compare Rev 15:2.

[15] For studies of the many local references in the seven letters, see the third footnote in this chapter.

Blessings (3:20b-21): **I will come in and eat with him, and he with me. To him who overcomes, I will give the right to sit with me on my throne, just as I overcame and sat down with my Father on his throne.**

> To eat with someone expresses a willingness and desire to enter into a close relationship with that person. (This is why Jewish leaders were scandalized when Jesus ate with prostitutes, tax collectors, and other sinners — see, e.g., Matthew 9:11 and 11:19.) Here Christ offers a covenant relationship to anyone who will "open the door." Compare Luke 22:14-30, where Jesus explains that he is about to establish the new covenant, and then says to his disciples: "I confer on you a kingdom, just as my Father conferred one on me, so that you may eat and drink at my table in my kingdom . . . ."

Witnesses (3:22): **He who has an ear, let him hear what the Spirit says to the churches."**

C. PRESSURES AND OPPOSITION IN ASIA

Throughout the letters to the seven churches, John mentions certain persons whom he considers to be enemies of Christ and enemies of the churches. The author does not provide a detailed description of the situation because the readers know full well what they are facing. Nevertheless, we will survey the contents of the letters and try to reconstruct the circumstances in which Asian Christians found themselves in A.D. 95-96. It appears that they were enduring pressures and opposition both from within the Christian community and from outside the community of faith.

1. Pressures and Opposition from Within the Christian Community

a. False Apostles and the Nicolaitans (2:2,6)

In his letter to the Christians in Ephesus, the Lord says:

> I know your deeds, your hard work and your perseverance. I know that you cannot tolerate wicked men, that you have tested those who claim to be apostles but are not, and have found them

false. . . . But you have this in your favor: You hate the practices
of the Nicolaitans, which I also hate (Rev 2:2,6).

Note that Christ commends the church for testing and detecting false apostles. The Greek term ἀπόστολος (*apostolos*, "apostle") literally means "sent one." It refers to a person sent out with a commission as the authoritative representative of the sender. The term could be translated into English as "ambassador" or "missionary." In the New Testament we read of two types of "apostles": First, "Apostles of Christ" are chosen and commissioned by Jesus himself to be authoritative eyewitnesses of his resurrection, to preach the gospel, and to establish churches in his name. Peter, John, the rest of the Twelve, and later Paul are examples of this kind of "Apostle" (see, e.g., Mark 3:14-19; Acts 1:21-26; 1 Cor 9:1; Gal 2:8). Second, "apostles of the churches" are chosen and commissioned by churches to serve as authorized missionaries, evangelists, and teachers. Barnabas (Acts 14:14), Andronicus and Junias (Rom 16:7), and Epaphroditus (Phil 2:25) belong to this group of "apostles."

The "false apostles" John mentions in Revelation 2 are probably not claiming to be "Apostles of Christ." They are most likely roving "missionaries" who enjoy the backing of one or more Christian congregations. We know nothing about these apostles other than the fact that John calls them "false" (i.e., untruthful) and "wicked men." The teaching of these apostles apparently conflicts with John's, and he commends the Ephesian church for rejecting them. They are people whom John considers enemies, and they are operating from *within* the Christian community.

Through John, Christ also commends the Ephesians for hating "the practices of the Nicolaitans." This group is mentioned here in Revelation 2:6 and again in 2:15. John says nothing about them except that they were spreading some sort of false teaching. We will return to the question of their identity below.

b. The Teaching of Balaam (2:14)

In the letter to Pergamum, Christ says:

Nevertheless, I have a few things against you: You have people there who hold to the teaching of Balaam, who taught Balak to entice the Israelites to sin by eating food sacrificed to idols and by committing sexual immorality (Rev 2:14).

John mentions people "who hold to the teaching of Balaam." Balaam was the prophet from the region of the Euphrates River described in Numbers 22–25. When Israel was preparing to come out of the wilderness and invade the land of Canaan, Balak, king of Moab, grew afraid. So he summoned Balaam to come and call down a curse on Israel. Balaam came, but instead of cursing Israel the Lord caused him to bless Israel. His plans thwarted, Balaam later tried to defeat God's people through a different tactic: He encouraged the Moabite women to seduce the men of Israel, to get them involved in sexual immorality and the worship of Moabite idols (see Num 25:1-3; 31:16).

John indicates that there are Christians in the church at Pergamum repeating the sins of Balaam: First, they are participating in the worship of false gods "by eating food sacrificed to idols." Second, they are practicing "sexual immorality." The latter sin may refer to literal fornication or adultery in the believers' personal lives. It may refer to literal sexual sins with temple prostitutes, who played a role in many pagan religions. However, "sexual immorality" was also a common Old Testament figure of speech for unfaithfulness to God. As husbands or wives break the marriage covenant with their spouses by having "affairs" with other lovers, so do the people of God break their covenant relationship with the Lord by having "adulterous affairs" with other gods. In other words, the biblical writers often use "sexual immorality" or "adultery" or "fornication" or "prostitution" as synonyms for idolatry. An example may be found in Hosea 4:12, where the Lord complains: "[My people] consult a wooden idol and are answered by a stick of wood. A spirit of prostitution leads them astray; they are unfaithful to their God." John seems to use sexual sins as symbols for idolatry quite often in the Book of Revelation.[16]

c. *The Sins of Jezebel (2:20-25)*

In Revelation 2:20-25 the Lord rebukes the church at Thyatira:

---

[16]See Rev 2:20-22; 9:20-21; 14:8; 17:1-5,15-16; 18:3,9; 19:2; 21:8; 22:15.

> Nevertheless, I have this against you: You tolerate that woman Jezebel, who calls herself a prophetess. By her teaching she misleads my servants into sexual immorality and the eating of food sacrificed to idols. I have given her time to repent of her immorality, but she is unwilling. So I will cast her on a bed of suffering, and I will make those who commit adultery with her suffer intensely, unless they repent of her ways. I will strike her children dead. Then all the churches will know that I am he who searches hearts and minds, and I will repay each of you according to your deeds. Now I say to the rest of you in Thyatira, to you who do not hold to her teaching and have not learned Satan's so-called deep secrets (I will not impose any other burden on you): Only hold on to what you have until I come.

Jezebel was the wife of King Ahab and queen over Israel in the time of Elijah the prophet. 1 Kings 16:29-33 records that

> In the thirty-eighth year of Asa king of Judah, Ahab son of Omri became king of Israel, and he reigned in Samaria over Israel twenty-two years. Ahab son of Omri did more evil in the eyes of the Lord than any of those before him. He not only considered it trivial to commit the sins of Jeroboam son of Nebat [who set up golden calf idols in Bethel and Dan – see 1 Kings 12:26-33], but he also married Jezebel daughter of Ethbaal king of the Sidonians, and began to serve Baal and worship him. He set up an altar for Baal in the temple of Baal that he built in Samaria. Ahab also made an Asherah pole and did more to provoke the Lord, the God of Israel, to anger than did all the kings of Israel before him.

As the text suggests, the Phoenician princess Jezebel became a great promoter of idol worship in Israel. Later, after Elijah defeated the prophets of Baal on Mount Carmel, Jezebel tried to have Elijah killed (see 1 Kings 18-19). She was a corrupter and persecutor of the people of God.

According to Revelation 2, there is a prophetess in the church at Thyatira whom John considers to be promoting idolatry. As in the case of "Balaam" (see above), he picks the name of a villain from the Jewish past, who committed similar sins, and calls the prophetess by that name – "Jezebel." (John employs a similar literary device later in Revelation when he speaks of "Babylon" and alludes to Pharaoh.) Specifically, this "Jezebel" woman is encouraging Christians to eat food sacrificed to idols and participate in "adultery" or sexual "immorality" — which, again, probably refers to a lack of covenant faithfulness to God (see above). This prophetess is also teaching what John calls "Satan's deep secrets." Of course, Jezebel herself was probably claiming to be revealing the mysteries of God, but John identifies her teaching as the work of Satan.

d. Assessment

Based on the preceding evidence, what conclusions should we draw concerning the situation in Asia at the time Revelation was written? All the opponents John has mentioned so far seem to be people within the churches, people who call themselves "Christians," people who think they are serving God. These believers are probably encouraging other Christians to go ahead and eat meat offered to idols, or say "Caesar is Lord," or offer incense to Caesar at the public festivals and trade guild banquets and other social events. In support of this position, they could appeal to Jesus himself, who commands his followers to "Give to Caesar what is Caesar's" (Matt 22:21). They could also appeal to the Apostle Paul's admonition to "submit to the governing authorities" as ministers of God (Rom 13:1). (For further discussion of Emperor Worship in Daily Life, Christian Responses to the Emperor Cult, and the Christian's Choice, see Part IV.B.3 of the Introduction.)

In the letters to the seven churches, John attacks this point of view. He offers the churches a revelation of the present in which he helps believers to see their behavior as Christ sees it. What his readers may be brushing off as harmless accommodation to Greco-Roman culture, Christ identifies as the work of Satan, the idolatry of Balaam and Jezebel, adultery committed against God.

We know nothing about the "Nicolaitans," but they were probably promoting a similar accommodation. The Greek term "Nicolaitans" literally means "conquerors of the people" or "ones who overcome the people." ("Overcoming" is a major theme in Revelation, as discussed below.) It is roughly equivalent to the Hebrew name "Balaam" (*Baal-am*), which means "lord over the people." Like "Balaam" and "Jezebel," the "Nicolaitans" may be John's symbolic name for his opponents.

2. Pressures and Opposition from Outside the Christian Community

The letters to Ephesus, Pergamum, and Thyatira describe opposition to Christ from *within* the churches. The letters to Smyrna and Philadelphia describe opposition from *outside* the Christian community. In Revelation 3:9 the Lord solemnly declares:

> I will make those who are of the synagogue of Satan, who claim to be Jews though they are not, but are liars—I will make them come and fall down at your feet and acknowledge that I have loved you.

The Lord refers to opposition from Jews, who claim to belong to God and to be the people of God, but who are actually serving Satan by opposing Christ's church. We discussed the reasons for Jewish opposition to the church in the Introduction.[17] As the pressure on believers increases, Jews in Asia are probably beginning to deny that Christians are part of the Jewish community. This strips the churches of special protections under Roman law, making them vulnerable to persecution for refusing to worship Caesar.

Christ has more to say about Jewish opposition to the church in the letter to Smyrna:

> These are the words of him who is the First and the Last, who died and came to life again. I know your afflictions and your poverty—yet you are rich! I know the slander of those who say they are Jews and are not, but are a synagogue of Satan. Do not be afraid of what you are about to suffer. I tell you, the devil will put some of you in prison to test you, and you will suffer persecution for ten days [a round number in apocalyptic literature that is not to be taken literally[18]]. Be faithful, even to the point of death, and I will give you the crown of life (Rev 2:8-10).

The Lord expects the opposition in Smyrna to grow worse. Christians there will face persecution, imprisonment, and even death — as did Christ before them. Jews will be involved. It is their slander that will

---

[17]See Part IV.B.3.c of the Introduction: "Exemptions for Jews and Christians."

[18]See the discussion of Symbolic Numbers in the Introduction, Part III.B.1.d.

cause many Christians to be dragged before the Roman authorities on charges of subversion.

Everything that Christ foresaw did actually occur within the next few years. In his *History of the Church*, Eusebius describes the murder of many Christians in Smyrna — the very city addressed here — in about A.D. 156. He focuses especially on the martyrdom of Polycarp, who at that time was bishop over the church at Smyrna. Quoting from a letter prepared by Christians from that city, he writes:

> After this, before giving an account of Polycarp's death, they relate what happened to the other martyrs, vividly describing the heroism with which they faced their torments, to the amazement of the spectators on every side. Sometimes they were torn with scourges to the innermost veins and arteries, so that even the secret hidden parts of the body, the entrails and internal organs, were laid bare; sometimes they were forced to lie on pointed seashells and sharp spikes. After going through every kind of punishment and torture, they were finally flung to the beasts as food.
>
> Special mention is made of the noble Germanicus, who by divine grace overcame his natural physical fear of death. The proconsul tried to dissuade him, stressing his youth and begging him as one still in the very prime of life to spare himself; but without a moment's hesitation he drew the savage beast towards him, well nigh forcing and goading it on, the more quickly to escape from their wicked, lawless life. After this glorious death the whole crowd were so astounded by the heroism of God's beloved martyr, and the courage of Christian people everywhere, that a shout went up from all sides: "Away with the godless! [Note that Christians were considered to be 'godless' or 'atheists' because they refused to worship the Roman gods.] Fetch Polycarp!". . .

From that point the letter tells us the rest of the story as follows:

> [Polycarp] was met by Herod the chief of police and his father Nicetes, who after transferring him to their carriage sat beside him and tried persuasion. "What harm is there in saying 'Lord Caesar' and sacrificing? You will be safe then." At first he made no answer, but when they persisted he replied: "I have no intention of taking your advice." Persuasion having failed they turned to threats, and put him down so hurriedly that in leaving the carriage he scraped his shin. But without even looking

round, as if nothing had happened, he set off happily and at a swinging pace for the stadium. There the noise was so deafening that many could not hear at all, but as Polycarp came into the arena a voice from heaven came to him: "Be strong, Polycarp, and play the man." No one saw the speaker, but many of our people heard the voice.

His introduction was followed by a tremendous roar as the news went round: "Polycarp has been arrested!" At length, when he stepped forward, he was asked by the proconsul if he really was Polycarp. When he said yes, the proconsul urged him to deny the charge [of being a Christian]. "Respect your years!" he exclaimed, adding similar appeals regularly made on such occasions: "Swear by Caesar's fortune; change your attitude; say: 'Away with the godless!'" But Polycarp, with his face set, *looked at the crowd* in the stadium and waved his hand *towards them*, sighed, looked up to heaven, and cried: "Away with the godless!" The governor pressed him further: "Swear, and I will set you free: execrate Christ." "For eighty-six years," replied Polycarp, "I have been His servant, and He has never done me wrong: how can I blaspheme my King who saved me?". . .

As he said this and much besides, he was filled with courage and joy, and his features were full of grace, so that not only did he not wilt in alarm at the things said to him, but on the contrary the proconsul was amazed, and sent the crier to stand in the middle of the arena and announce three times: "Polycarp has confessed that he is a Christian." At this announcement the whole mass of Smyrnaeans, Gentiles *and Jews* alike, boiled with anger and shouted at the tops of their voices: "This fellow is the teacher of Asia, the father of the Christians, the destroyer of our gods, who teaches numbers of people not to sacrifice or even worship". . . . Then a shout went up from every throat that Polycarp must be burnt alive. . . .

The rest followed in less time than it takes to describe: the crowds rushed to collect logs and faggots from workshop and public baths, *the Jews as usual joining in with more enthusiasm than anyone.* . . .

When [Polycarp] had offered up the Amen and completed his prayer the men in charge lit the fire and a great flame shot up . . . .[19]

---

[19]Williamson, *History*. The excerpt is taken from Book 14, Part 8, through Book 15, Part 40 (pp. 168-173).

D. "OVERCOMERS" IN REVELATION

Throughout Revelation, John speaks of those who "triumph" or "conquer" or "overcome." The Greek verb translated "overcome" is νικάω (*nikaō*). Three persons or groups of persons are identified as "overcomers" — namely, Satan and the forces of evil, Jesus Christ, and Christians. In tracing the contours of this important theme, we will focus on three questions: First, who or what do they "overcome"? Second, how do they "overcome"? Third, what is the result of their "overcoming"? For further discussion of the texts involved, see the appropriate portions of the Commentary.

1. Satan as "Overcomer"

Two sections of Revelation describe Satan as an "overcomer."[20] First, Revelation 13:1-10 describes "a beast coming out of the sea," which symbolizes one of the agents of the "red dragon" Satan. According to verse 7, "He was given power to make war against the saints and to conquer (*nikaō*) them."

This theme appears again in chapter 11, which describes "two witnesses" who represent the church and who testify concerning Christ. Verses 7 and 11 read:

> Now when they have finished their testimony, the beast that comes up from the Abyss will attack them, and overpower [*nikaō*] and kill them. . . . But after three and a half days a breath of life from God entered them, and they stood on their feet, and terror struck those who saw them.

In light of these two texts, we may draw some conclusions about Satan as an "overcomer." Whom does he "overcome"? The answer is Christians, the saints of God. How does Satan "overcome" the saints? He does so by killing them. What is the result of his "overcoming" Christians? Ultimately, Satan accomplishes nothing because God raises his servants from the dead.

Below, we will see that Christ and Christians "overcome" in quite different ways with quite different results.

---

[20]Compare also Rev 6:2, where the rider on the white horse represents a particular type of evil — namely, political struggle and "conquest" (*nikaō*).

2. Christ as "Overcomer"

a. Whom Jesus "Overcomes"

According to the Book of Revelation, whom does Jesus "overcome"? First, he "overcomes" Satan and his angels, the spiritual forces of darkness that pervert and destroy God's good creation.[21] John communicates this truth in the vision of the woman and the dragon found in Revelation 12:

> The great dragon was hurled down—that ancient serpent called the devil, or Satan, who leads the whole world astray. He was hurled to the earth, and his angels with him.
> Then I heard a loud voice in heaven say:
>
> "Now have come the salvation and the power and the
>   kingdom of our God,
> and the authority of his Christ.
> For the accuser of our brothers,
>   who accuses them before our God day and night,
>   has been hurled down.
> They overcame [*nikaō*] him
>   *by the blood of the Lamb*
>   and by the word of their testimony;
> they did not love their lives so much
>   as to shrink from death.
> Therefore rejoice, you heavens
>   and you who dwell in them!
> But woe to the earth and the sea,
>   because the devil has gone down to you!
> He is filled with fury,
>   because he knows that his time is short"
>   (Rev 12:9-12).

We will discuss this vision in much more detail later in the commentary. For now, let the reader note that Satan and his angels are the ones who are "overcome" (v. 9). Furthermore, Christ is the one who ultimately "overcomes" them — an act he accomplishes by his bloody sacrificial death (v. 11).

---

[21]On this subject, see the Introduction, Parts III.B.2.b.(1) "Rebellion in Heaven" and III.B.2.c.(1) "Supernatural Forces of Evil".

In addition to "overcoming" Satan himself, Jesus also "overcomes" human beings who ally themselves with Satan against God. This is seen in the vision of the woman on the beast with seven heads and ten horns found in Revelation 17. Verses 12-14 read as follows:

> The ten horns you saw are ten kings[22] who have not yet received a kingdom, but who for one hour will receive authority as kings along with the beast. They have one purpose and will give their power and authority to the beast. They will make war against the Lamb, but the Lamb will overcome them because he is Lord of lords and King of kings—and with him will be his called, chosen and faithful followers.

Note that the ten horns represent ten humans — ten kings who ally themselves with the "beastly" forces of evil and "make war against the Lamb." However, Christ the Lamb "overcomes" them.

To summarize, then, Christ, in the Book of Revelation, "overcomes" Satan and all who join him in his rebellion against God, the true Creator and Lord of all. In other words, he "overcomes" all those powers that stand behind the "present evil age," seeking to prevent the coming of God's universal kingdom rule.

b. How Jesus "Overcomes"

How does Jesus "overcome" Satan and his allies? He does so by shedding his blood in his sacrificial death on the cross. We see this idea in Revelation 12:11 (quoted above), where Satan is beaten "by the blood of the Lamb." This truth also appears in Revelation 5:5-6:

> Then one of the elders said to me, "Do not weep! See, the Lion of the tribe of Judah, the Root of David, has triumphed [or "overcome," *nikaō*]. He is able to open the scroll and its seven seals."
>
> Then I saw a Lamb, *looking as if it had been slain*, standing in the center of the throne, encircled by the four living creatures and the elders.

---

[22]That is *several* kings. The number ten symbolizes "two handfuls," so it should not necessarily be taken literally. See Part III.B.1.d of the Introduction: "Symbolic Numbers."

It is the Christ *who has been slain* who is able to "overcome." Once again, John links Christ's victory to his death.

c. The Results of Jesus' "Overcoming"

What is the outcome or result of Christ's "overcoming" Satan and the forces of evil on the cross? First, God has responded to Christ's sacrificial death by raising him up to eschatological life and exalting him to the position of King of kings and Lord of lords. We see this, for example, in Revelation 3:21:

> To him who overcomes, I will give the right to sit with me on my throne, *just as I overcame and* [after being raised from the dead] *sat down with my Father on his throne.*[23]

A second result of Christ's death is that he is able to open the scroll with seven seals, which symbolizes God's redemptive plan for creation (see the Commentary on Revelation 5). In other words, he is able to destroy the kingdom of Satan and establish the kingdom of God. This seems to be the force of Revelation 5:9-10:

> "You are worthy to take the scroll
>   and to open its seals,
> because *you were slain,*
>   *and with your blood you purchased men for God*
>   from every tribe and language and people and
>   nation.
> *You have made them to be a kingdom* and priests to serve
>   our God,
>   and *they will reign* on the earth."

How exactly does Christ's death on the cross "overcome" Satan and his allies, bring the "present evil age" to an end, inaugurate the kingdom of God, and give believers a place in that kingdom? John, in Revelation, never gives a clear answer to that question. He does not offer a detailed explanation of precisely how the Cross "works." Drawing on other parts of the New Testament, we have explained the relationship between the kingdom of God and the death of Jesus in Part III.B.2.c.(4) of the Introduction. Our explanation goes

---

[23]Compare Phil 2:5-11.

beyond what John says in Revelation, but it does not contradict the message of Revelation.

3. Christians as "Overcomers"

a. Whom Christians "Overcome"

Like Christ himself, Christians "overcome" Satan and his angels. As John says in Revelation 12:10-11 (quoted above),

> . . . the accuser of our brothers [i.e., Satan], who accuses them before our God day and night, has been hurled down. They [i.e., Christians] overcame him by the blood of the Lamb.

Moreover, Christians "overcome" human beings who ally themselves with Satan against God and his people. Revelation 17:14 (also quoted above) highlights this truth:

> [The ten human kings who serve the beast] will make war against the Lamb, but the Lamb will overcome them because he is Lord of lords and King of kings—*and with him will be his called, chosen and faithful followers.*

With Christ, believers will "overcome," will conquer, will gain the victory over all the powers responsible for the "present evil age."

b. How Christians "Overcome"

How do Christians gain the victory over their enemies, both natural and supernatural? Revelation 12:11 answers this question very nicely:

> They overcame him by the blood of the Lamb and by the word of their testimony; they did not love their lives so much as to shrink from death.

First, Christians "overcome" Satan and his allies "by the blood of the Lamb." We do not — and, in fact, cannot — end the kingdom of Satan and establish the kingdom of God by our own power. Christ conquers Satan by his blood. Christians, by his grace, simply share in the Lord's victory.

Second, Christians "overcome" Satan and his allies "by the word of their testimony" — that is, by their μαρτυρία (*martyria*), their "witness" to Christ. By proclaiming the "good news" of what God has accomplished in Christ, we enable others to embrace God's emerging rule, and thus share in Christ's victory and kingdom with us. We participate in Christ's work of "overcoming" Satan by helping to free people from the devil's power.

Third, Christians "overcome" Satan and his allies by remaining faithful to Christ until death, and by remaining faithful to Christ even if it brings death. In other words, we "overcome" by not allowing Satan to reestablish his hold on us even through threats of persecution and martyrdom. As verse 11 states it, the "overcomers" "did not love their lives so much as to shrink from death." Revelation 2:26 expresses the same idea when it speaks of "him who overcomes and does my will *to the end*."

c. The Result of Christians' "Overcoming"

What is the outcome when Christians embrace Christ's sacrifice and thereby "overcome" the forces of evil? The Lord gives his people the right to sit down with him on his throne, to share in his beneficent rule over the universe, to experience the fullness of the kingdom of God:

> To him who overcomes, I will give the right to sit with me on my throne, just as I overcame and sat down with my Father on his throne (Rev 3:21).

> He who overcomes will inherit all this [i.e., the "new heaven and new earth"], and I will be his God and he will be my son (Rev 21:7).

These are amazing promises! Our God is a God who does not keep the blessings and joys of lordship to himself, but who freely shares them with us, his creatures! Jesus lets us reign as kings with him, giving us dominion over all creation. The whole universe — with all its joys and limitless possibilities — will be ours to relish! (For further discussion of Christ's promises to "him who overcomes," see Part E.)

E. CHRIST'S PROMISES TO "HIM WHO OVERCOMES"

We have seen that, in the Book of Revelation, Christians "overcome" the forces of evil through the death of Christ and through remaining faithful to him. Each of the letters to the seven churches contains a promise to "him who overcomes" in this way. We will examine each promise below.

1. The Tree of Life (2:7)

2:7 To him who overcomes, I will give the right to eat from the tree of life, which is in the paradise of God.

"Paradise" is the Greek word for "garden." (The term literally means "a walled enclosure.") The "Paradise" or "Garden of God" Christ refers to in Revelation 2:7 is the Garden of Eden. Genesis 2:8-9 explains that the "tree of life" was one of the trees found in this Garden:

> Now the LORD God had planted a garden in the east, in Eden; and there he put the man he had formed. And the LORD God made all kinds of trees grow out of the ground—trees that were pleasing to the eye and good for food. In the middle of the garden were the tree of life and the tree of the knowledge of good and evil.

As we saw in the Introduction,[24] the first humans were not created immortal. Instead, they were created mortal, or subject to death. God sustained Adam and Eve through his gift of the "tree of life," and he presumably would have sustained them forever.

However, after Adam and Eve sinned, God decided that he would not continue their lives indefinitely while they were in that evil state.

> The LORD God said, "The man has now become like one of us, knowing good and evil. He must not be allowed to reach out his hand and take also from the tree of life and eat, and live forever." So the LORD God banished him from the Garden of Eden to work the ground from which he had been taken. After he drove the man out, he placed on the east side of the Garden of Eden cherubim

---

[24]See Part III.B.2.a.(1) of the Introduction: "Genesis 1–5."

and a flaming sword flashing back and forth to guard the way to the tree of life (Gen 3:22-24).

One of the characteristics of the "present evil age" is that human beings have been cut off from the "tree of life" because of their own sin and the sin of Adam and Eve.[25]

Jewish apocalyptic writers predict that one of the blessings of the kingdom of God will be that the righteous are given access to the tree of life, so that they may live forever. This idea appears, for example, in 1 Enoch 25:4-7. Here the prophet is shown a vision of seven mountains made of precious stones and surrounded by fragrant trees. Among them is the tree of life. The angel Michael tells Enoch:

> "And as for this fragrant tree, not a single human being has the authority to touch it until the great judgment, when [God] shall take vengeance on all and conclude [everything] forever. This is for the righteous and the pious. And the elect will be presented with its fruit for life. He will plant it in the direction of the northeast, upon the holy place — in the direction of the house of the Lord, the Eternal King.
>
>> Then they shall be glad and rejoice in gladness, and they shall enter into the holy [place]; its fragrance shall [penetrate] their bones, long life will they live on earth, such as your fathers lived in their days."
>
> At that moment, I [Enoch] blessed the God of Glory, the Eternal King, for he has prepared such things for the righteous people, as he had created [them] and given it to them.[26]

We find a similar prediction in the Testament of Levi, a Jewish apocalyptic work dating to the second century B.C. The author of this book believes that God will send two Messiahs to Israel — namely, a kingly Messiah from the tribe of Judah (David's tribe) and a priestly Messiah from the tribe of Levi. In Testament of Levi 18:10-11, the writer anticipates that the priestly Messiah "shall open the gates of paradise; he shall remove the sword that has threatened since Adam, and he will grant to the saints to eat of the tree of life."

---

[25] For further discussion of this point, see the Introduction, Part III.B.2.b.(2): "The Present Evil Age and the Kingdom of Satan."

[26] Charlesworth, *Pseudepigrapha*.

Christ makes a similar prediction in Revelation 2:7: "To him who overcomes, I will give the right to eat from the tree of life, which is in the paradise of God."

2. Escape from the Second Death (2:11)

He who overcomes will not be hurt at all by the second death.
John tells what "the second death" is in Revelation 20:11-15:

> Then I saw a great white throne and him who was seated on it. Earth and sky fled from his presence, and there was no place for them. And I saw the dead, great and small, standing before the throne, and books were opened. Another book was opened, which is the book of life. The dead were judged according to what they had done as recorded in the books. The sea gave up the dead that were in it, and death and Hades gave up the dead that were in them, and each person was judged according to what he had done. Then death and Hades were thrown into the lake of fire. *The lake of fire is the second death.* If anyone's name was not found written in the book of life, he was thrown into the lake of fire.

The "second death" refers to "the lake of fire" — to *not* having one's name written in the "book of life." The "fire" is a symbol for eschatological condemnation at the final judgment — the punishment God will carry out against those who oppose his kingdom when Christ returns. In his letter to the church at Smyrna, the Lord makes a promise to Christians who "overcome," who forsake the kingdom of Satan and embrace the emerging rule of God. These persons "will not be hurt at all by the second death."

3. The Hidden Manna, White Stone, and Secret Name (2:17)

To him who overcomes, I will give some of the hidden manna. I will also give him a white stone with a new name written on it, known only to him who receives it.

a. *The Hidden Manna, the Messianic Banquet, Behemoth and Leviathan*

The symbol of the "hidden manna" has deep roots in Jewish history and legend. Manna first appears in the Bible in Exodus 16, where the Israelites cry out for food during their wilderness wanderings. The Lord responds by sending them "bread from heaven" that falls like dew, looks like frost, and tastes like wafers made with honey. When the people find it on the ground, they ask, "*Manna?*" (Hebrew for "What is it?") and so the miraculous food takes on that name. In Exodus 16:32-35, the Israelites store some of the manna in a jar as a reminder of God's provision:

> Moses said, "This is what the LORD has commanded: 'Take an omer of manna and keep it for the generations to come, so they can see the bread I gave you to eat in the desert when I brought you out of Egypt.'"
>
> So Moses said to Aaron, "Take a jar, and put an omer of manna in it. Then place it before the LORD to be kept for the generations to come."
>
> As the LORD commanded Moses, Aaron put the manna in front of the Testimony [that is, within the Ark of the Covenant, which also contained the stone tablets bearing the Ten Commandments – the so-called "tablets of the Testimony"; cf. Heb 9:3-5], that it might be kept. The Israelites ate manna forty years, until they came to a land that was settled; they ate manna until they reached the border of Canaan.

What happened to the Ark and its jar of manna? According to Jewish legend, the prophet Jeremiah later took them to Mount Nebo and hid them in a cave to prevent them from falling into the hands of the invading Babylonians. The story appears in 2 Maccabees 2:4-8:

> It was also in the writing that the prophet [Jeremiah], having received an oracle, ordered that the tent [i.e., the Tabernacle] and the ark should follow with him, and that he went out to the mountain where Moses had gone up and had seen the inheritance of God. And Jeremiah came and found a cave, and he brought there the tent and the ark and the altar of incense, and he sealed up the entrance.
>
> Some of those who followed him came up to mark the way, but could not find it. When Jeremiah learned of it, he rebuked them and declared: "The place shall be unknown until God gathers His people together again and shows His mercy. And then the Lord will disclose these things, and the glory of the Lord and the cloud will appear, as

they were shown in the case of Moses, and as Solomon asked that the place should be specially consecrated" (RSV).[27]

This is how the jar of manna became the "hidden manna." Note that, in this text, the prophet predicts that the manna will be found again "when God gathers His people together" at some future time.

The manna likewise appears in texts that describe the Messianic Banquet. In Jewish apocalyptic literature, the Messianic Banquet is a symbol for the consummated kingdom of God.[28] The symbol communicates the joy and fellowship and abundance of the kingdom by picturing it as a great feast presided over by the Messiah. The basic Old Testament text that inspires the apocalyptic writers' descriptions of the Messianic Banquet is Isaiah 25:6-8:

> On this mountain the LORD Almighty will prepare
>   a feast of rich food for all peoples,
> a banquet of aged wine—
>   the best of meats and the finest of wines.
> On this mountain he will destroy
>   the [burial] shroud that enfolds all peoples,
> the sheet that covers all nations;
>   he will swallow up death forever.
> The Sovereign LORD will wipe away the tears
>   from all faces;
> he will remove the disgrace of his people
>   from all the earth.
>   The LORD has spoken.

Notice that, when this "Banquet" is served — when the kingdom of God comes in its fullness — it will mark the end of death and sadness and disgrace.

---

[27]We call this story a "legend" because it appears to contradict 1 Kings 8:9, which suggests that the jar of manna had already disappeared by the time of Solomon.

[28]Examples of New Testament texts that use the Messianic Banquet as a symbol for the kingdom include Matt 22:1-14; 25:1-13; and Rev 19:6-9. In addition to being a "covenant meal" (see Part III.B.2.c.[4] of the Introduction), the Lord's Supper is also a foretaste of the Messianic Banquet. In Luke 22:16 the Messiah Jesus promises his disciples: "I will not eat it again until it finds fulfillment in the kingdom of God."

Building on Isaiah's vision, the author of 2 Baruch (a Jewish apocalypse dating to about A.D. 100, which is very close to the writing of Revelation] offers his vision of the great Feast:

> And it will happen that when all that which should come to pass in these parts has been accomplished, the Anointed One [i.e., the Messiah] will begin to be revealed. And Behemoth will reveal itself from its place, and Leviathan will come from the sea, the two great monsters which I created on the fifth day of creation and which I shall have kept until that time.[29] And they will be nourishment for all who are left. The earth will also yield fruits ten thousandfold. And on one vine will be a thousand branches, and one branch will produce a thousand clusters, and one cluster will produce a thousand grapes, and one grape will produce a cor [i.e., about 6 bushels] of wine. And those who are hungry will enjoy themselves and they will, moreover, see marvels every day. For winds will go out in front of me every morning to bring the fragrance of aromatic fruits and clouds at the end of the day to distill the dew of health. And it will happen at that time that the treasury of manna will come down again from on high, and they will eat of it in those years because these are they who will have arrived at the consummation of time (2 Bar 29:3-8).[30]

According to this vision, the menu at the Messianic Banquet will include some unusual items: First, there will be wine in extraordinary abundance. Second, the meat dishes served will be the sea serpent Leviathan and the land monster Behemoth.[31] Apocalyptic writers (including John) often use these mythical beasts to represent the forces of evil and chaos — the enemies of God. The meaning of the symbolism here in 2 Baruch is that, when the kingdom comes in its fullness, God and his people are going to "have their enemies for lunch." Finally, the Messianic Banquet will feature manna, which the Messiah provides for those who "have arrived at the consummation of time."

Against this background, we may now interpret the promise of Revelation 2:17. Christ says, "To him who overcomes, I will give

---

[29]Compare 4 Ezra 6:49-52.
[30]Charlesworth, *Pseudepigrapha*.
[31]The names appear also in Job 40:15–41:34 as the greatest of God's creatures.

some of the hidden manna." In literature of the time, the persons who receive the "hidden manna" are servants of the Lord who inherit the kingdom of God. Christ is promising "overcomers" a seat at the Messianic Banquet, new life in the eschatological age.

b. The White Stone

What would the symbol of the "white stone" have communicated to the first readers of Revelation? Some suggest that a "white stone" with a "name written on it" refers to a magical amulet. Greeks engraved the names of deities on such amulets and wore them as sources of divine power and protection.[32] However, if John is thinking of the name of the Deity, then would he describe it as a name "known only to him who receives it"? Perhaps so, if his idea is that only Christians truly "know" God and truly have a relationship with him.

To this author, a different meaning seems more likely: In the Greco-Roman world, white and black stones were used in courtrooms for rendering verdicts. To acquit the defendant, jurors tossed a white stone into a basket. To condemn the accused, they used a black stone. Luke mentions this practice in Acts 26:9-10, where the Apostle Paul describes his earlier life as a persecutor of the church:

> I too was convinced that I ought to do all that was possible to oppose the name of Jesus of Nazareth. And that is just what I did in Jerusalem. On the authority of the chief priests I put many of the saints in prison, and when they were put to death, I cast my vote against them [lit., "I cast the stone against them"].[33]

In his *Sayings of Kings and Commanders*, Plutarch refers to the same practice in an amusing quote from Alcibiades:

---

[32] See, for example, K. Preisendanz, ed., *Papyri graecae magicae*, 2 Vols., 2d ed. (Stuttgart: Teubner, 1973-74), I.146; XII.6-20.

[33] Josephus uses similar language in *Jewish Antiquities*, II.163 (Vol. IV, 234-235); X.60 (Vol. VI, 190-191). See also Philo, *[The Works of] Philo*, trans. F.H. Colson and G.H. Whitaker, The Loeb Classical Library, 12 Vols. (Cambridge, MA: Harvard University Press, 1960), *The Unchangeableness of God*, 75 (Vol. III, 46-47).

Summoned from Sicily by the Athenians to be tried for his life, [Alcibiades] went into hiding, saying that it is silly for a man under indictment to seek a way to get off when he can get away.

When somebody said, "Don't you trust your fatherland to decide about you?" he replied, "Not I; nor would I trust even my mother, lest in a moment of thoughtlessness she unwittingly cast a black ballot [lit., 'black stone'] instead of a white one [lit., 'white stone']."[34]

John and his fellow Christians in Asia are being hauled into the Roman courts and having the black stone cast against them. Jesus promises that, if they "overcome" by remaining faithful even to death, then he will cast the white stone in their favor. Having once received imprisonment, death, and condemnation from the Roman king, they will one day receive acquittal, release, and vindication from the King of kings.[35]

c. The Secret Name

The "white stone" has "a new name written on it." The Greek term translated "new" is καινός (*kainos*), which John uses throughout Revelation to describe realities of the eschatological age.[36] He speaks of a "new song" (5:9; 14:3), "new names" (2:17; 3:12), the "new Jerusalem" (3:12; 21:2), "a new heaven and a new earth" (21:1), and the consummation of the kingdom of God in which the Lord makes "everything new" (21:5). When Christ promises "overcomers" a "new name," he is offering them a share in the coming redemption and transformation of all creation.

---

[34]Reprinted by permission of the publishers and the Loeb Classical Library from "Sayings of Kings and Commanders," pp. 100-101, in PLUTARCH, MORALIA: VOLUME III, Loeb Classical Library Vol. 245, translated by Frank C. Babbitt, Cambridge, MA: Harvard University Press, 1931 (hereafter, "Babbitt, 'Sayings'"). The excerpt is taken from Alcibiades 5-6.

[35]Note: It is possible that, by placing the "new name" on the verdict stone, John intends to combine the idea of acquittal with the protective power of the magical amulet.

[36]On the "eschatological age," see Parts III.B.2.b.(3) "The Eschatological Age and the Kingdom of God," and III.B.2.d.(2) "The Coming of God's Kingdom" of the Introduction.

And yet there is more, for the "new name" is "known only to him who receives it." In the ancient world, the ability to name some person or some thing was associated with power. To illustrate, the Greek magical papyri include lists of the names of various deities so that the sorcerer may invoke their names in casting spells. They also contain the secret "true names" of various creatures, which were thought to give the magician power over those creatures.

We find hints of this idea in the Bible. For example, in Genesis 2:19-20 God grants Adam the right to name the animals, which is a sign of his "dominion" over them (see Gen 1:26). In Luke 8:26-39 a man possessed by a "Legion" of demons cries out to Jesus, "What do you want with me, Jesus, Son of the Most High God?" Since the demons know Jesus' true name ("Son of God"), the ancient reader would expect them to have power over Jesus — and yet they do not! Instead, Christ asks, "What is *your* name?" When they give it, the Lord expels them from the region.

In A.D. 95-96, the Christians in Asia are suffering under the power of their enemies, but Jesus promises to give them a new name "known only to him who receives it." In other words, the Lord promises them freedom, self-determination, deliverance from those who would oppress them.

4. Authority over the Nations and the Morning Star (2:26-28)

2:26-28 To him who overcomes and does my will to the end, I will give authority over the nations—"He will rule them with an iron scepter; he will dash them to pieces like pottery"—just as I have received authority from my Father. I will also give him the morning star.

In verse 27 Christ quotes from Psalm 2:9, a "Royal Psalm" describing the God-given authority of the Davidic King or Messiah.[37] Here the Lord promises to share that authority with his people — to give them dominance over their enemies and a share in his kingdom rule. Compare the similar promise found in Revelation 3:21 (discussed below).

---

[37]For a detailed discussion of this Psalm, see the comment on the title "Christ" in Revelation 1:5.

"The morning star" refers to the planet Venus, a symbol of victory and domination in the ancient world. So in verse 28 the Lord promises his people that they will triumph over their enemies, the human and angelic forces of darkness. In Revelation 22:16 Christ himself is called the Victor, "the bright, morning star."

5. White Garments and the Book of Life (3:4-5)

3:4-5 Yet you have a few people in Sardis who have not soiled their clothes. They will walk with me, dressed in white, for they are worthy. He who overcomes will, like them, be dressed in white. I will never blot out his name from the book of life, but will acknowledge his name before my Father and his angels.

In Revelation 19:8, "bright and clean," unsoiled garments symbolize "the righteous acts of the saints" — that is, a way of life consistent with covenant faithfulness. White garments also appear in Revelation 3:18; 4:4; 6:11; 7:9,13; and 19:14. The "book of life" is the "list" of people to whom Christ will give eschatological life (see Rev 13:8; 20:12,15). "Overcomers" receive, then, a covenant relationship with God in the present, followed by eternal salvation in the future.

6. A Pillar in God's Temple (3:12)

3:12 Him who overcomes I will make a pillar in the temple of my God. Never again will he leave it. I will write on him the name of my God and the name of the city of my God, the new Jerusalem, which is coming down out of heaven from my God; and I will also write on him my new name.

The "temple" is the place where God is *present* with his people (see, e.g., Exod 29:44-46; 1 Kings 9:3). A "pillar" is a fixture in the temple, something that "never leaves" God's presence. Christ promises "overcomers" the eternal presence and fellowship of God.

The "new Jerusalem" is a symbol for the consummated kingdom of God, which John describes more fully in Revelation 21:1-22:5. This heavenly, supernatural city is a "temple" (see particularly the comment on the symbolic dimensions of the city in Rev 21:16) because the Lord God Almighty and the Lamb are always there.

Writing one's name on something is a mark of ownership and belonging. The Lord's promise to those who "overcome" is that they will belong to God, and belong to Christ, and belong in the "new Jerusalem." They will have a place in the kingdom, the community of God's people.

7. A Place on Christ's Throne (3:21)

3:21 To him who overcomes, I will give the right to sit with me on my throne, just as I overcame and sat down with my Father on his throne.

For a discussion of this promise, see Section D.3.c above, which describes "The Result of Christians' 'Overcoming.'"

REVELATION 4

III. THE REVELATION OF "WHAT WILL TAKE PLACE LATER" (4:1–22:6)

A. INTRODUCTION: JOHN'S HEAVENLY VANTAGE POINT (4:1–5:14)

1. Transition to the Threefold Vision of the Future (4:1)

¹After this I looked, and there before me was a door standing open in heaven. And the voice I had first heard speaking to me like a trumpet said, "Come up here, and I will show you what must take place after this."

4:1 In Revelation 1:19 Christ says that he will give John a revelation of both the present and the future: "Write, therefore, what you have seen, what is now [i.e., the Lord's view of circumstances in the Roman province of Asia in A.D. 95-96] and what will take place later [i.e., a vision of the future from A.D. 95-96 to the consummation of God's kingdom]." The vision of the present appears in chapters 2–3 and takes the form of letters to the seven churches. The vision of the future begins here in 4:1 and continues through 22:6.

The vision of the future has two main parts: First, 4:1–5:14 forms an introduction in which John describes his new vantage point in heaven. Second, 6:1–22:6 describes the future itself. This description of the future has three main parts – namely, Revelation 6:1–8:1, Revelation 8:2–11:19, and Revelation 12:1–22:6. Here the Lord gives three revelations of the complete future – from John's time to the final consumation – seen from three slightly different angles. (For a more detailed discussion of the Structure of Revelation, see Part V of the Introduction.)

I looked, and there before me was a door standing open in heaven. And the voice I had first heard speaking to me like a trumpet said, "Come up here,

The Lord, with a voice "like a trumpet,"[1] calls John up into heaven, to the throne room of God. Everything John sees from this point onward (namely, the vision of the future) is seen from the vantage point of heaven — from a "God's eye view." John's description of the future will not be his own, but a product of the foreknowledge of God.

2. The Throne of God and the Twenty-Four Elders (4:2-6a)

²At once I was in the Spirit, and there before me was a throne in heaven with someone sitting on it. ³And the one who sat there had the appearance of jasper and carnelian. A rainbow, resembling an emerald, encircled the throne. ⁴Surrounding the throne were twenty-four other thrones, and seated on them were twenty-four elders. They were dressed in white and had crowns of gold on their heads. ⁵From the throne came flashes of lightning, rumblings and peals of thunder. Before the throne, seven lamps were blazing. These are the seven spirits^a of God. ⁶Also before the throne there was what looked like a sea of glass, clear as crystal.

ᵃ5 Or *the sevenfold Spirit*

4:2 At once I was in the Spirit

God's Spirit again enables John to exercise his prophetic gift (see under 1:10).

and there before me was a throne in heaven with someone sitting on it.

"The One seated on the throne" is John's favorite description of God. He uses it throughout the book, emphasizing the Lord's divine sovereignty. The fact that John will see the future from the vantage point of God's heavenly throne room is extremely significant, for it means that we cannot possibly understand the goal of history unless

---

[1] See the comment on Rev 1:10.

we realize that God is in control of history. God rules; God is king; God's sovereign will shall be done.[2]

In describing his heavenly surroundings, the imagery John uses to describe God's throne is much the same as that of Ezekiel's vision in Ezekiel 1. Compare 1 Enoch 14 (which also similarly echoes Ezekiel) and Daniel 7:9-10.

4:3 And the one who sat there had the appearance of jasper and carnelian. A rainbow, resembling an emerald, encircled the throne.

We cannot know with certainty the precise color and significance of the gems mentioned in Revelation because we do not necessarily know to what precious stones the Greek names refer. The "jasper" (ἴασπις, *iaspis*) may actually be diamond because this stone is described as "clear as crystal" in Revelation 21:11. The "carnelian" (σάρδιον, *sardion*) was probably red.

The glittering light that would be given off by all these stones together — the "jasper," the "carnelian," and the "rainbow resembling an emerald" — may together be intended to describe the radiance of God's glory.[3] This seems to be the significance of the rainbow in Ezekiel 1:28:

> Like the appearance of a rainbow in the clouds on a rainy day, so was the radiance around him. This was the appearance of the likeness of the glory of the LORD.

It is very likely that the "rainbow" is also intended to remind us of the covenant God made with Noah and all creation in Genesis 9:8-17:

> Then God said to Noah and to his sons with him: "I now establish my covenant with you and with your descendants after you and with every living creature that was with you—the birds, the livestock and all the wild animals, all those that came out of the ark with you—every living creature on earth. I establish my covenant with you:

---

[2]This is an example of the apocalyptic determinism discussed in Part III.B.2.b.(6) of the Introduction: "Apocalyptic Optimism, Determinism, and Triumph."

[3]On "glory," see the comments on Christ's radiant eyes, feet, and face in Rev 1:14-16.

Never again will all life be cut off by the waters of a flood; never again will there be a flood to destroy the earth."

And God said, "This is the sign of the covenant I am making between me and you and every living creature with you, a covenant for all generations to come: I have set my rainbow in the clouds, and it will be the sign of the covenant between me and the earth. Whenever I bring clouds over the earth and the rainbow appears in the clouds, I will remember my covenant between me and you and all living creatures of every kind. Never again will the waters become a flood to destroy all life. Whenever the rainbow appears in the clouds, I will see it and remember the everlasting covenant between God and all living creatures of every kind on the earth."

After destroying nearly all of creation through the Flood, God "hangs up" his war-bow, signifying that he will not use this watery weapon again. Very shortly in Revelation we are going to see terrifying visions of judgment; but the "rainbow" over God's throne reminds us from the start that the ultimate goal of God, the King, is not to destroy his creation, but to save it.

4:4 Surrounding the throne were twenty-four other thrones, and seated on them were twenty-four elders. They were dressed in white and had crowns of gold on their heads.

A number of theories have been put forward as to the meaning and significance of the "twenty-four elders." The theories range from angels, to Old Testament heroes, to God the King's heavenly court. The following evidence makes clear that the elders actually represent the church:

First, there are twenty-four elders. The number twenty-four is a multiple of twelve, and throughout Revelation multiples of twelve are used to designate the People of God.[4] (See below for the significance of this particular multiple of twelve.)

Second, the twenty-four elders are "dressed in white." This is the garment of redeemed saints in Revelation 3:4-5,18; 6:11; 7:9,13-14.

Third, the twenty-four elders wear "crowns of gold on their heads." They are kings who sit on "thrones" in the presence of God's

---

[4]See, for example, the twelve tribes of Israel (12×1) and the 144,000 ($12 \times 12 \times 1000$) in Rev 7. For a discussion of the symbolic significance of numbers in apocalyptic literature, see the Introduction, Part III.B.1.d.

throne, sharing in God's kingdom rule. We saw in chapters 2 and 3 that Christians will be given this privilege. For example, in Revelation 3:21 Christ says: "To him who overcomes, I will give the right to sit with me on my throne, just as I overcame and sat down with my Father on his throne" (cf. 2:26-27).

Fourth, in Revelation 5:8, John says that each of the elders holds a "harp." This is the instrument played by the redeemed saints in Revelation 14:2 and 15:2.

Fifth, in Revelation 5:8 the elders also hold "golden bowls full of incense, which are the prayers of the saints." Here the twenty-four elders are acting as priests, offering incense to God. 1 Chronicles 24 names twenty-four divisions of priests, so the particular multiple of twelve given here (12×2) also serves to identify the priestly function of the elders. Throughout the Apocalypse, John says that God has made Christians "priests" (e.g., 5:10). The "incense" these priestly figures offer up to God are "the prayers of the saints." These twenty-four elders symbolize the praying children of God.

Sixth, throughout Revelation, these twenty-four elders offer the same kind of praise to the Lord that the church offers to him (e.g., praises to God as creator in 4:11 and to Jesus as redeemer in 5:9-10).

The above evidence suggests that the twenty-four elders together represent the church. What, then, is the significance of this symbol? Seen from God's point of view, Christians are already in heaven with him, participating in his eschatological rule. The kingdom of God has not yet been consummated, but it has begun. Christians have a share in it.

4:5 From the throne came flashes of lightning, rumblings and peals of thunder. Before the throne, seven lamps were blazing. These are the seven spirits of God.

Regarding the theophany of thunder and lightning, see the explanation of the "loud voice like a trumpet" in Revelation 1:10,12. For the "seven lamps," see the comment on Revelation 1:12-13,16,20.

4:6a Also before the throne there was what looked like a sea of glass, clear as crystal.

The "sea" is an ancient Near Eastern symbol for the forces of evil and chaos. The origin of this symbol goes back at least as far as the

Babylonian creation myth.[5] According to that myth, the heavens and the earth came into existence when Marduk, the god of light and order, defeated Tiamat, the great sea monster and goddess of darkness and chaos. When Marduk killed Tiamat, he sliced her body into two halves and made heaven out of one and earth out of the other. From the Ras Shamra tablets[6] we learn that this myth was also told in Canaan, where the part of Tiamat was played by Lotan, a seven-headed sea monster otherwise known as "Leviathan."[7]

A number of biblical passages use language and imagery from this myth in order to describe the greatness and power of God. To illustrate, Psalm 74:12-15 describes Israel's successful crossing of the Red Sea and the destruction of the pursuing Egyptian army as a victory of God over "Leviathan," the forces of evil:

> But you, O God, are my king from of old;
>   you bring salvation upon the earth.
> It was you who split open the sea by your power [a
>   reference to God's miraculous parting of the
>   Red Sea in Exodus 14];
>   you broke the heads of the monster in the waters.
> It was you who crushed the heads of Leviathan [i.e.,
>   destroyed the Egyptian army]
>   and gave him as food to the creatures of the desert.
> It was you who opened up springs and streams;
>   you dried up the ever flowing rivers.

Psalm 104:5-9 uses the same sort of imagery to describe God's creation of the earth and separation of the sea from the dry land as his victory over the sea. Similar ideas appear in Genesis 1:1-10 (where God brings order and goodness to a world that was "formless and empty" and chaotic); Job 9:13; 38:8-11; Psalms 89:10; 104:5-9; Proverbs 8:27-29; Isaiah 27:1; 51:9-10; Ecclesiasticus 39:17. As Caird explains,

---

[5] An English translation appears in Pritchard, *Ancient Near Eastern Texts*, 60-72.

[6] Cuneiform texts dating to 1500-1200 B.C., which were found in the ruins of Ugarit on the Mediterranean coast of Syria.

[7] On Leviathan, see the comment on Rev 2:11 (i.e., Section E.2 of the Commentary on Revelation 2-3).

Israel believed that her national history was the scene where God was continuing to wage war on the powers of evil until the day of final victory. "On that day the Lord with his great, strong, relentless sword will punish Leviathan the fleeing serpent, Leviathan the twisting serpent, and will kill the dragon in the sea" (Isa 27:1).[8]

The sea — and the sea monster — are very ancient symbols for the forces of evil and chaos that threaten to engulf God's good creation. In Revelation, the sea stands for everything that opposes the kingdom of God: It is the reservoir of evil out of which the seven-headed beast arises in 13:1. It is the fiery trial through which the saints must pass in 15:2. And yet notice the way John describes the "sea" here in Revelation 4:6: It is "before God's throne" — subject to his will, under his control and his sovereignty. Furthermore, it looks like "a sea of glass, clear as crystal." It is perfectly calm, perfectly still, thoroughly tamed. Why? Because Jesus Christ has died on the cross as the sacrifice that cancels sin in the sense that it destroys the kingdom of Satan and the present evil age.[9] The decisive battle against evil has already been won on the cross. In Revelation 21:1, when John describes the final consummation of God's kingdom, he says that there will "no longer" be "any sea." Evil will vanish from God's creation altogether.

3. The Four Living Creatures (4:6b-8)

[6]In the center, around the throne, were four living creatures, and they were covered with eyes, in front and in back. [7]The first living creature was like a lion, the second was like an ox, the third had a face like a man, the fourth was like a flying eagle. [8]Each of the four living creatures had six wings and was covered with eyes all around, even under his wings. Day and night they never stop saying:

> **"Holy, holy, holy**
> **is the Lord God Almighty,**
> **who was, and is, and is to come."**

---

[8]Caird, *Revelation*, 67.
[9]See the discussion of the "Kingdom of God and the Death of Jesus" in Part III.B.2.c(4) of the Introduction.

4:6b,8 In the center, around the throne, were four living creatures . . . Each of the four living creatures had six wings

In describing the "four living creatures," John combines imagery also used in two parts of the Old Testament: Isaiah's vision of God's throne room in Isaiah 6 includes six-winged seraphim who call out: "Holy, holy, holy is the Lord Almighty; the whole earth is full of his glory" (v. 3). Ezekiel's vision of God in Ezekiel 1 includes "four living creatures" (called "cherubim" in chapter 10), each of which has four faces — the faces of a man, lion, ox and eagle.[10]

and they were covered with eyes, in front and in back, . . . and was covered with eyes all around, even under his wings. Day and night they never stop saying: "Holy, holy, holy is the Lord God Almighty, who was, and is, and is to come."

The many eyes signify that the four living creatures never sleep, but praise God continually forever and ever. The basis for this interpretation appears in verse 8: *"Day and night they never stop* saying: 'Holy, holy, holy is the Lord God Almighty'" (see also Ezek 10:12; 1 Enoch 39:12; 2 Enoch 21:1). On the threefold description of God, see the comment on Revelation 1:4c.

4:7 The first living creature was like a lion, the second was like an ox, the third had a face like a man, the fourth was like a flying eagle.

---

[10]Ezekiel pictures God's throne as a great, wheeled chariot, being supported in heaven by these four cherubim. In this vision, the cherubim arrive in a great "windstorm" (Ezek 1:4), so part of the symbolism may be that the cherubim represent the four winds and therefore the four corners of the earth. Together, they hold up the heavens, which are God's "throne." The Lord's throne may then move on the winds like a heavenly chariot. (One may easily picture ancient Israelites looking into the sky, watching the winds blowing the clouds about, and imagining God mounted on the clouds/heavens and being carried where he wills by the winds/cherubim.) David expresses this idea in 2 Samuel 22:10-11 // Psalm 18:9-10: "He parted the heavens and came down; dark clouds were under his feet. He mounted the cherubim and flew; he soared on the wings of the wind."

The Ark of the Covenant, with its golden cherubim, serves as a visual representation of this idea: The cherubim symbolize the winds holding aloft God's heavenly throne. The glory of God — the bright light that is a visible manifestation of the invisible God's presence — hovers over the cherubim. God is therefore enthroned above the cherubim (see 1 Sam 4:4; Ps 80:1; 99:1).

To John's original readers, the lion, ox, man, and eagle each represent the pinnacle or apex of a different facet of God's creation. The Jewish rabbinical document *Midrash Shemoth* illustrates this point:

> Four kinds of exalted beings have been created in the world. The most exalted of all living creatures is man; of birds, the eagle; of cattle [i.e., of domestic animals], the ox; and of wild beasts, the lion. All of these received royalty and had greatness bestowed upon them, and they are set under the chariot [i.e., the throne] of God. . . .[11]

All participate in God's sovereignty over creation, and yet are themselves creatures under God's rule. The four living creatures with their four faces together represent all God's creation offering praise to him. For further discussion of the number four symbolizing creation, see Part III.B.1.d of the Introduction.

4. The Heavenly Worship (4:9-11)

⁹Whenever the living creatures give glory, honor and thanks to him who sits on the throne and who lives for ever and ever, ¹⁰the twenty-four elders fall down before him who sits on the throne, and worship him who lives for ever and ever. They lay their crowns before the throne and say:
¹¹"You are worthy, our Lord and God,
    to receive glory and honor and power,
for you created all things,
    and by your will they were created
    and have their being."

4:9-11 Throughout Revelation, the songs sung in heaven serve to interpret the visions that precede them by highlighting the main point that the visions are intended to communicate. In this case, what are we to make of the vision of God's throne room in Revelation 4? Verse 11 tells us: "You are worthy, our Lord and God,

---

[11]H. Freedman and Maurice Simon, eds., *Midrash Rabbah: Exodus*, 3d ed., trans. S.M. Lehrman (New York: The Soncino Press, 1983), *Beshallach* XXIII.13 (p. 291).

to receive glory and honor and power, for you created all things, and by your will they were created and have their being."

From a heavenly point of view God is, both now and forevermore, Lord over all creation. It is quite appropriate for all creation (here symbolized by the four living creatures) — and especially the church (symbolized by the twenty-four elders) — to ascribe glory, honor, power, and thanks to him. The essence of sinfulness is not to recognize God as creator and Lord.[12] Those who oppose him are not being realistic.

In verse 10, the twenty-four elders lay their crowns before God's throne. What is the meaning and significance of this gesture? At the beginning of the Bible, in Genesis 1:26-27, we find an account of how God created human beings:

> Then God said, "Let us make man in our image, in our likeness, and let them rule over the fish of the sea and the birds of the air, over the livestock, over all the earth, and over all the creatures that move along the ground."
> So God created man in his own image, in the image of God he created him; male and female he created them.

What does the text mean when it says, "God created man in his own image," in his own "likeness"? In what way are human beings "like" God? We are like our creator in many ways, but the Lord tells us what *he* had in mind in this text, in verse 26:

> Then God said, "Let us make man in our image, in our likeness, *and let them rule* over the fish of the sea and the birds of the air, over the livestock, over all the earth, and over all the creatures that move along the ground."

Human beings are created in the "image" of God in the sense that he has given us the ability to "rule" as he rules — the ability to think, and reason, and manipulate creation, and exercise dominion over creation, and shape the world according to our will. Human beings are created in the "image" of God in the sense that he has made us *lords* as he himself is a *Lord*.

---

[12]For a classic expression of this truth, see Rom 1:18-32.

We can cut wood, and quarry stone, and dig clay, and mine ore, and fashion these simple materials into houses and tools and machines with amazing abilities — jet airplanes that can carry us thousands of miles in a single day, computers that can perform millions of complex calculations in the blink of an eye. We can harness the energy in sunlight, fossil fuels, running water, the wind, the atom. We can record and transmit events and ideas through written language, radio waves, microwaves, photography, optic fibers, and information storage and retrieval systems.

Our God-given, God-like ability to shape the world according to our will holds incredible potential for good, but also incredible potential for evil. The next few chapters of Genesis tell how human beings chose to use their dominion — their lordly abilities — against God and against other human beings.

At the end of the Bible, in Revelation 4, John pictures twenty-four elders seated on "thrones" and wearing "crowns" on their heads. The elders represent the church. God's people have been given dominion and lordship and rule, as the Scripture says in Genesis.

But what do Christians do with their "crowns," their lordship, their rule? Christians lay their "crowns" before God's throne. They *voluntarily* subordinate their wills to God's will, *voluntarily* place their dominion under his dominion, *voluntarily* allow "the kingdoms of this world" to become "the kingdom of our Lord and of his Christ," who "will reign for ever and ever" (see Rev 11:15).

REVELATION 5

5. The Scroll with Seven Seals (5:1)

¹Then I saw in the right hand of him who sat on the throne a scroll with writing on both sides and sealed with seven seals.

5:1 The "scroll with writing on both sides and sealed with seven seals" evokes a plurality of Old Testament and apocalyptic images, including the following: First, this document reminds us of the scroll God gives to Ezekiel in Ezekiel 2:9-10. That scroll has words written on both sides, but it is not sealed with seven seals like the one in Revelation. In Ezekiel, the scroll written on both sides contains the word of God that Ezekiel the prophet must deliver to the house of Israel — in this case, "words of lament and mourning and woe." By describing the scroll in Revelation 5 using the language of Ezekiel, John leads us to believe that it contains a word from God.

In a similar fashion, Exodus 32:15-16 describes the two stone tablets on which the Ten Commandments were engraved as "inscribed on both sides, front and back." These tablets are "the work of God; the writing was the writing of God, engraved on the tablets." If John intends for us to think of this passage, then he wants us to view the writing on both sides of the scroll as put there by God.

Finally, Roman law required last wills and testaments to be sealed with the seals of seven witnesses. A seal is a dab of wax placed over the edge of the scroll and then stamped with a signet ring or some other mark of the witness. The scroll could not be opened without breaking the seal. If John intends for his readers to think of the scroll with the seven seals as a will, then it is the "last will and testament of God." The scroll will be opened only when God's will is to be put into effect — and that time has come, as John is about to show us.

If the "scroll with writing on both sides and sealed with seven seals" is a word from God — the will of God written with God's own hand — then what is the content of that will? What exactly is written on the scroll? That question is relatively easy to answer because Revelation 6:1–8:1 describes exactly what happens when the scroll is opened and God's will is executed. What we have in those chapters is a complete revelation of the future from John's time to the final consummation of the kingdom of God. The scroll, then, contains God's redemptive plan for all of creation, leading to the goal of the kingdom of God. Now all we need is someone to break the seals, open the scroll, and put that plan into effect.

6. The Lion of Judah and the Root of David (5:2-5)

²And I saw a mighty angel proclaiming in a loud voice, "Who is worthy to break the seals and open the scroll?" ³But no one in heaven or on earth or under the earth could open the scroll or even look inside it. ⁴I wept and wept because no one was found who was worthy to open the scroll or look inside. ⁵Then one of the elders said to me, "Do not weep! See, the Lion of the tribe of Judah, the Root of David, has triumphed. He is able to open the scroll and its seven seals."

5:5 the Root of David

"The Root of David" is a messianic title.[1] The Jews expected the Messiah to be a descendant of David, a member of David's kingly line. If we picture David's family as a great tree, with David as the root and his descendants as the branches, then David's "tree" was "cut down" by events like the Babylonian Exile, when many of David's descendants were either killed or scattered throughout the earth. However, the prophets predicted that God would keep his promise to David (found in 2 Samuel 7) of establishing his kingly dynasty forever. They said that a "shoot" would sprout up from the "stump" or the "root" of David. That "shoot," or "root" that bears a "shoot," would be the Messiah, whom God would place on David's throne and cause to reign forever. We see this idea in Isaiah 11:1-14:

---

[1] For a discussion of messianic titles, see the comments on Rev 1:5.

A shoot will come up from the stump of Jesse [i.e., David's father
  — Isaiah is speaking of David's family line];
    from his roots a Branch will bear fruit.[2]
The Spirit of the LORD will rest on him—
    the Spirit of wisdom and of understanding,
    the Spirit of counsel and of power,
    the Spirit of knowledge and of the fear of the LORD—
and he will delight in the fear of the LORD.

. . . .

In that day the Root of Jesse will stand as a banner for the peoples; the nations will rally to him, and his place of rest will be glorious. In that day the Lord will reach out his hand a second time to reclaim the remnant . . . [i.e., he will gather all the scattered Jews together again].

Ephraim's [i.e., the northern kingdom's] jealousy will vanish,
    and Judah's [i.e., the southern kingdom's] enemies will be cut
        off;
Ephraim will not be jealous of Judah,
    nor Judah hostile toward Ephraim. [The Jews will be reunited.
        Now note what they will do to the Gentiles, their enemies:]
They will swoop down on the slopes of Philistia to the west;
    together they will plunder the people to the east.
They will lay hands on Edom and Moab,
    and the Ammonites will be subject to them.

Here the Messiah — the "Shoot," the "Branch," the "Root" — is pictured as a David-like warrior, who will fight and conquer God's/Israel's enemies.

Sirach 47:22 describes the Messiah in similar terms:

But the Lord will never give up his mercy, nor cause any of his works to perish; he will never blot out the descendants of his chosen one, nor destroy the posterity of him who loved him; so he gave a remnant to Jacob, and to David a root of his stock.

Compare also Testament of Judah 24, in which the Messiah is called "the Shoot of God Most High" (v. 4) and "the Shoot" from the "root" of Jesse (v. 6).

---

[2]"The Shoot," "the Root," and "the Branch" are all messianic titles virtually equivalent to one another in meaning.

Against this background, we conclude that, when John calls Jesus "the Root of David" in Revelation 5:5, he is identifying Jesus as the Messiah — and particularly a David-like warrior Messiah.

the Lion of the tribe of Judah

"The Lion of the tribe of Judah" is another messianic title rooted in Genesis 49:8-10. In this passage, Jacob blesses his son Judah with these words:

> "Judah, your brothers will praise you;
> your hand will be on the neck of your enemies;
> your father's sons will bow down to you.
> You are a lion's cub, O Judah;
> you return from the prey, my son.
> Like a lion he crouches and lies down,
> like a lioness—who dares to rouse him?
> The scepter will not depart from Judah,
> nor the ruler's staff from between his feet,
> until he comes to whom it belongs
> and the obedience of the nations is his."

Later Jews understood Jacob's words to be a prophecy concerning the Messiah. First, he would be a descendant of David, who himself was a descendant of Judah. Second, the Messiah would be a king because "the scepter will not depart from Judah." Finally, he would be a "lion," a powerful warrior like his ancestor Judah.

Fourth Ezra 12:31-32 is one example of a later Jewish text that understands the "Lion of Judah" mentioned here in Genesis 49 to be a reference to the Messiah:

> And as for the lion whom you saw rousing up out of the forest and roaring and speaking to the eagle and reproving him for his unrighteousness, and as for all his words that you have heard, this is the Messiah whom the Most High has kept until the end of days, who will arise from the posterity of David, and will come and speak to them; he will denounce them for their ungodliness and for their wickedness, and will cast up before them their contemptuous dealings.[3]

Compare also Testament of Judah 24:5, which identifies the "scepter" as the "Shoot" of Judah — that is, the Messiah.

---

[3]Charlesworth, *Pseudepigrapha*.

In light of these texts, we conclude that, when John calls Jesus "the Lion of the Tribe of Judah," he is again identifying him as the Messiah by using a common Jewish image for the Messiah.

Both titles for Jesus discussed thus far picture the Messiah as a mighty warrior — a soldier like David and a "king of beasts" like the lion. So when one of the twenty-four elders in Revelation 5 introduces Christ as "the Lion of the tribe of Judah" and "the Root of David," the next thing we expect to see is Christ appearing in the form of a conquering king. Instead, John turns and sees a little Lamb.

7. The Lamb Who Was Slain (5:6-14)

⁶Then I saw a Lamb, looking as if it had been slain, standing in the center of the throne, encircled by the four living creatures and the elders. He had seven horns and seven eyes, which are the seven spirits^a of God sent out into all the earth. ⁷He came and took the scroll from the right hand of him who sat on the throne. ⁸And when he had taken it, the four living creatures and the twenty-four elders fell down before the Lamb. Each one had a harp and they were holding golden bowls full of incense, which are the prayers of the saints. ⁹And they sang a new song:
"You are worthy to take the scroll
    and to open its seals,
because you were slain,
    and with your blood you purchased men for God
    from every tribe and language and people and nation.
¹⁰You have made them to be a kingdom and priests to serve our God,
    and they will reign on the earth."
¹¹Then I looked and heard the voice of many angels, numbering thousands upon thousands, and ten thousand times ten thousand. They encircled the throne and the living creatures and the elders. ¹²In a loud voice they sang:
"Worthy is the Lamb, who was slain,
to receive power and wealth and wisdom and strength
and honor and glory and praise!"
¹³Then I heard every creature in heaven and on earth and under the earth and on the sea, and all that is in them, singing:
"To him who sits on the throne and to the Lamb
be praise and honor and glory and power,
    for ever and ever!"

¹⁴**The four living creatures said, "Amen," and the elders fell down and worshiped.**

ᵃ6 Or *the sevenfold Spirit*

5:6 Then I saw a Lamb, looking as if it had been slain, standing in the center of the throne,

The Lamb has died; he has the marks of being slain on him. The Greek word here translated "slain" is σφάζω (*sphazō*), which is a technical term for being "slaughtered as a sacrifice."⁴ John is here describing Christ as a *sacrificial* Lamb.

The word for "lamb" used throughout the rest of the New Testament is ἀμνός (*amnos*), but John here uses the term ἀρνίον (*arnion*), which means "little lamb" — or even "lambykin."⁵ By calling Jesus *arnion* — "little lamb" — John emphasizes Christ's vulnerability, his victimization, his defenselessness as the sacrificial lamb. "The Lamb" is John's definitive title for Christ. He uses it twenty-nine times in Revelation.⁶

The Lamb has died as a sacrifice, but now he is "standing" — he is alive again, raised from the dead. Furthermore, he is "standing in the center of the throne," having been exalted to share in God's heavenly rule.

encircled by the four living creatures and the elders.

The "four living creatures" symbolize all creation gathered around the Lord's throne (see under 4:6b-8).The twenty-four "elders" represent the church, which participates in the worship of the Lamb (see under 4:4).

He had seven horns and seven eyes, which are the seven spirits of God sent out into all the earth.

---

⁴A form of this word appears, for example, in Isaiah 53:7 (LXX): "He was oppressed and afflicted, yet he did not open his mouth; he was led like a lamb to the slaughter [σφαγή, *sphagē*], and as a sheep before her shearers is silent, so he did not open his mouth."

⁵When people were plotting to murder Jeremiah, the prophet used this term to describe himself in Jer 11:19 (LXX): "I had been like a *gentle lamb* led to the slaughter; I did not realize that they had plotted against me, saying, 'Let us destroy the tree and its fruit; let us cut him off from the land of the living, that his name be remembered no more.'"

⁶The term occurs only one other place in the New Testament — namely, in John 21:15.

This image identifies Jesus as the one who bears and gives the complete Spirit of God (i.e., "the seven spirits of God"). He is omnipotent, having complete power ("seven horns"). He is omniscient, having complete insight or knowledge ("seven eyes"). He is omnipresent, with no place in heaven or earth beyond his influence ("sent out into all the earth"). For further discussion of the symbolism in this verse, see the comment on the "seven spirits" in Revelation 1:4.

5:9-10 And they sang a new song: "You are worthy to take the scroll and to open its seals, because you were slain, and with your blood you purchased men for God from every tribe and language and people and nation. You have made them to be a kingdom and priests to serve our God, and they will reign on the earth."

How can Jesus be the warrior Messiah — "the Root of David" and "the Lion of the tribe of Judah" — and be a little sacrificial Lamb at the same time? Once again, the hymn serves to interpret the preceding vision. Jesus is the Messiah who makes war, who conquers, who "overcomes" by dying. The Lamb conquers by dying on the cross as the sacrifice that cancels sin in the sense of annihilating the "present evil age" and inaugurating the kingdom of God.[7] It is Christ, then, who is able to open the scroll with seven seals and put into effect God's plan of redemption for his creation.

5:11-14 Then I looked and heard the voice of many angels . . . . and the living creatures and the elders. In a loud voice they sang: "Worthy is the Lamb . . . !" Then I heard every creature in heaven and on earth and under the earth and on the sea . . . "To him who sits on the throne and to the Lamb be praise and honor and glory and power, for ever and ever!" The four living creatures said, "Amen," and the elders fell down and worshiped.

Note that the angels, the church (i.e., the elders), and the whole of creation (i.e., the living creatures) offer the same worship to the Lamb that they offer to God himself. In doing so, they acknowledge Christ as the divine Messiah who shares God's kingly authority.[8]

---

[7]For a discussion of this point, see Part III.B.2.c.(4) of the Introduction: "The Kingdom of God and the Death of Jesus."

[8]For further discussion of this truth, see the comment on the title "Jesus Christ" in Rev 1:5.

REVELATION 6

B. THE FIRST VISION OF THE FUTURE (6:1–8:1)

In our study of Revelation 4–5, we saw that the "scroll with writing on both sides and sealed with seven seals" symbolizes the redemptive will of God for his creation.[1] Christ, the "Lamb who was slain," is able to open that scroll — or put God's plan into effect — because he died on the cross as the sacrifice for sin. Christ's sacrificial death cancels sin in the sense of ending the old age and inaugurating the new age of God's kingdom.[2] In Revelation 6:1–8:1 we have John's description of the opening of that scroll — the execution of God's redemptive plan. This part of the book contains the first of three revelations of the future from John's time to the consummation. In the opening of the seven seals (seven being the number of completion[3]), John gives us a picture of the complete future in abbreviated form. Later in the book, he will describe two more visions of the same period (8:2–11:19 and 12:1–22:6), each with more detail and each focusing on different aspects of the future.[4]

1. The "Labor Pains": Seals One through Five (6:1-11)

a. The Four Horsemen of the Apocalypse (6:1-8)

[1]I watched as the Lamb opened the first of the seven seals. Then I heard one of the four living creatures say in a voice like

---

[1]See the comment on Rev 5:1.
[2]For an explanation, see the Introduction, Part III.B.2.c.(4): "The Kingdom of God and the Death of Jesus."
[3]See Part III.B.1.d of the Introduction: "Symbolic Numbers."
[4]For a more detailed discussion of the "Structure of Revelation," see Part V of the Introduction.

thunder, "Come!" ²I looked, and there before me was a white horse! Its rider held a bow, and he was given a crown, and he rode out as a conqueror bent on conquest.

³When the Lamb opened the second seal, I heard the second living creature say, "Come!" ⁴Then another horse came out, a fiery red one. Its rider was given power to take peace from the earth and to make men slay each other. To him was given a large sword.

⁵When the Lamb opened the third seal, I heard the third living creature say, "Come!" I looked, and there before me was a black horse! Its rider was holding a pair of scales in his hand. ⁶Then I heard what sounded like a voice among the four living creatures, saying, "A quart[a] of wheat for a day's wages,[b] and three quarts of barley for a day's wages,[b] and do not damage the oil and the wine!"

⁷When the Lamb opened the fourth seal, I heard the voice of the fourth living creature say, "Come!" ⁸I looked, and there before me was a pale horse! Its rider was named Death, and Hades was following close behind him. They were given power over a fourth of the earth to kill by sword, famine and plague, and by the wild beasts of the earth.

[a]6 Greek *a choinix* (probably about a liter)   [b]6 Greek *a denarius*

In this passage, John uses imagery similar to that found in Zechariah 1:7-15 and 6:1-8. He states clearly what he intends the four horsemen to represent:

6:2 I looked, and there before me was a white horse! Its rider held a bow, and he was given a crown, and he rode out as a conqueror bent on conquest.

The first horseman symbolizes political struggle and conquest.

6:4 Then another horse came out, a fiery red one. Its rider was given power to take peace from the earth and to make men slay each other. To him was given a large sword.

The second horseman symbolizes conflict and war.

6:5b-6 I looked, and there before me was a black horse! Its rider was holding a pair of scales in his hand. Then I heard what sounded like a voice among the four living creatures, saying, "A quart of wheat for a day's wages, and three quarts of barley for a day's wages, and do not damage the oil and the wine!"

The third horseman symbolizes limited famine and economic hardship. The rider holds in his hand a pair of scales, a common symbol of famine or food rationing.[5] John hears a voice saying, "A quart of wheat for a day's wages, and three quarts of barley for a day's wages." A quart of grain was considered a day's ration and a denarius a day's wage. Barley was cheaper than wheat and was the food of the poor. Oil and wine were also considered staples. The voice continues "and do not damage the oil and the wine!" presumably because they are scarce and thus precious. John paints a picture of limited famine. Food is selling for eight to sixteen times its normal price, but it is still available.

6:8 I looked, and there before me was a pale horse! Its rider was named Death, and Hades was following close behind him. They were given power over a fourth of the earth to kill by sword, famine and plague, and by the wild beasts of the earth.

The rider on the "pale" horse (literally "green," apparently meaning sickly pale) symbolizes death — and particularly tragic, unnatural death in all its various forms (sword, famine, plague, and wild beasts). "Hades" is the Greek place of the dead, and thus a synonym for "death."[6]

6:2,4,8 he was given a crown . . . . Its rider was given power . . . . To him was given a large sword. . . . They were given power . . . .

In Greek literature of John's time, verbs in the passive voice often indicate that the Deity is performing the action. These so-called "divine passives" appear throughout John's description of the four horsemen. As the seven seals are opened and God's redemptive plan for creation is put into effect, John shows us that God will permit the kind of troubles represented by the four horsemen to continue in the world for a period of time. Political struggle, war, economic hardship and tragic death will continue to be a part of the

---

[5]See, for example, Leviticus 26:26, where God says to Israel: "When I cut off your supply of bread, ten women will be able to bake your bread in one oven, and they will dole out the bread by weight [using a scale]. You will eat, but you will not be satisfied."

[6]Compare Rev 1:18, where Christ holds "the keys of death and Hades."

future John envisions for humankind. In other words, the "labor pains"[7] will continue beyond A.D. 95-96 until the Second Coming of Christ. The prophecy is true, for this is exactly the way the world has been from John's time to the present.

6:1,3,5,7 I watched as the Lamb opened the first of the seven seals. Then I heard one of the four living creatures say in a voice like thunder, "Come!". . . When the Lamb opened the second seal, I heard the second living creature say, "Come!". . . When the Lamb opened the third seal, I heard the third living creature say, "Come!". . . When the Lamb opened the fourth seal, I heard the voice of the fourth living creature say, "Come!"

Before each horseman appears, one of the "four living creatures" cries out in a thunderous voice, "Come (ἔρχου, *erchou*)!" Are the creatures addressing the horsemen, summoning them to come forth? Or are they addressing John, calling him to "come" and see each horseman? This second possibility seems most likely because, in at least three of four cases, the action that immediately follows this command is one taken by John ("I looked" – in response to the command?).

However, a third possibility should also be considered: Perhaps the four living creatures – together representing all God's creation (see under 4:6b-8) – are addressing Jesus, calling for his return. In support of this theory, the creatures do use the exact same language employed by John in Revelation 22:20, where he prays, "Come (*erchou*), Lord Jesus!" If this is John's intended meaning, then how should we interpret the vision of the four horsemen? These verses communicate the fact that, throughout the course of history, not only human beings, but all of creation (symbolized by the four living creatures), will be calling on Jesus to return and put an end to the hardship and suffering of the "labor pains" (symbolized by the four horsemen). In other words, John here communicates in apocalyptic symbolism the same truth the Apostle Paul expresses in Romans 8:22: "We know that the whole creation has been groaning as in the pains of childbirth right up to the present time."

---

[7]For an explanation of the "labor pains," see the Introduction, Parts III.B.2.b.(4) "The Shift of the Ages" and III.B.2.d.(3) "The 'Labor Pains.'" See also the comments on Rev 1:9.

b. The Souls of the Martyrs (6:9-11)

⁹When he opened the fifth seal, I saw under the altar the souls of those who had been slain because of the word of God and the testimony they had maintained. ¹⁰They called out in a loud voice, "How long, Sovereign Lord, holy and true, until you judge the inhabitants of the earth and avenge our blood?" ¹¹Then each of them was given a white robe, and they were told to wait a little longer, until the number of their fellow servants and brothers who were to be killed as they had been was completed.

6:9 When he opened the fifth seal, I saw . . . the souls of those who had been slain because of the word of God and the testimony they had maintained.

The souls under the altar are the souls of Christian martyrs. They have been killed because of their witness to Christ — "slain because of the word of God and the testimony they had maintained." (John says in Revelation 1:9 that he has been banished to Patmos for the same reason.)

under the altar

In the Jewish system, the bodies of sacrificial animals were burned on the altar and their blood was poured out at the base of the altar (see Leviticus 4). The life or "soul" of the animal was considered to be in the blood. As the Lord says in Leviticus 17:11, "The life of a creature is in the blood, and I have given it to you to make atonement for yourselves on the altar; it is the blood that makes atonement for one's life." So Hebrews would think of the "life" or "soul" of the sacrificial animals as being in the pool of blood at the base of the altar.

When John pictures the souls of martyred Christians under an altar, he is portraying their deaths as blood-sacrifices poured out to God. He reinforces this idea in verse 9 when he says that these Christians have been "slain." The Greek verb here translated "slain" is σφάζω (*sphazō*), the same word used earlier to describe the crucified Jesus as "a Lamb, looking as if it had been *slain*" (see above under Rev 5:6). *Sphazō* is a sacrificial term communicating the idea of being "slaughtered as a sacrifice."

In using the same terminology to describe both the murdered Jesus and murdered Christians, John is not saying that the deaths of martyred Christians are "sacrifices" in the same sense that Christ's death was a sacrifice — i.e., deaths that cancel sin in the sense of destroying the "present evil age" and inaugurating the kingdom of God.[8] Revelation makes it very clear that the kingdom comes not through the death of Christians, but through the death of Christ. We see this truth in, for example, Revelation 12:10-11:

> Then I heard a loud voice in heaven say:
>
> "Now have come the salvation and the power and the
>   kingdom of our God,
>   and the authority of his Christ.
> For the accuser of our brothers [i.e., Satan],
>   who accuses them before our God day and night,
>   has been hurled down.
> They overcame him
>   *by the blood of the Lamb*
>   and by the word of their testimony;
> they did not love their lives so much
>   as to shrink from death.

The kingdom of God does not come apart from the death of Christ. The deaths of Christians alone cannot accomplish the universal reign of God.

So when John describes Christians as being "slain" as sacrifices like Christ, he is not putting their deaths on an equal plane with Christ's regarding what their deaths accomplish. He is, however, making a comparison between the death of Christ and the deaths of Christian martyrs: Just as Christ himself was slain for his witness to God, so have these Christians followed in their Lord's footsteps by being slain for their witness to the truth. Christians will be treated like Christ himself was treated.

6:10-11 They called out in a loud voice, "How long, Sovereign Lord, holy and true, until you judge the inhabitants of the earth and avenge our blood?" Then each of them was given a white robe, and they were told to wait a little longer, until the number of their fellow servants and brothers who were to be killed as they had been was completed.

---

[8]See Part III.B.2.c.(4) of the Introduction: "The Kingdom of God and the Death of Jesus."

From under the altar, the souls of the slain martyrs cry out to God for vindication and vengeance — just as the blood of murdered Abel cried out to God from the ground in Genesis 4:10. However, God's vengeance on those who have mistreated his servants will not come yet. Verse 11 says: "They were told to wait a little longer, until the number of their fellow servants and brothers who were to be killed as they had been was completed."

2. The Final Judgment: Seal Six (6:12-17)

¹²I watched as he opened the sixth seal. There was a great earthquake. The sun turned black like sackcloth made of goat hair, the whole moon turned blood red, ¹³and the stars in the sky fell to earth, as late figs drop from a fig tree when shaken by a strong wind. ¹⁴The sky receded like a scroll, rolling up, and every mountain and island was removed from its place.

¹⁵Then the kings of the earth, the princes, the generals, the rich, the mighty, and every slave and every free man hid in caves and among the rocks of the mountains. ¹⁶They called to the mountains and the rocks, "Fall on us and hide us from the face of him who sits on the throne and from the wrath of the Lamb! ¹⁷For the great day of their wrath has come, and who can stand?"

6:12-17 Using the language of cosmic catastrophe, John here describes the final judgment, the day of Christ's "wrath" against the enemies of God (v. 16), or the end of the world as we know it.[9] For Christians who serve God it will be the dawn of salvation, but for those who oppose God — described here — it will be terrifying judgment and condemnation.

3. Summary of Revelation 6 (Seals 1-6) and Comparison with Matthew 24

The contents of the scroll with seven seals — the contours of the future, the shape of God's redemptive plan — are becoming clear as we work our way through John's vision: The kind of suffering and

---

[9]For a more complete discussion of the final judgment, see in the Introduction, Parts III.B.2.b.(4), "The Shift of the Ages," and III.B.2.d.(2), "The Coming of God's Kingdom."

tribulation represented by the four horsemen will continue (seals 1-4). Christians will not be immune from these troubles; they will not be taken out of the world to escape the suffering therein. Instead, believers may suffer even more than others because of their faith. Christians may be required to endure the persecution and death Christ himself endured because of their faithful witness to God and his Messiah (seal 5). However, these hardships of the messianic woes will not continue forever. Christ will one day return to end the suffering of his people and carry out God's final judgment (seal 6).

This is the same basic scenario Christ himself predicts a few days prior to his crucifixion and resurrection. In Matthew 24:3, Jesus' disciples ask him two questions: First, "When will this happen?" — that is, when will the temple be destroyed, as Jesus predicted in verse 2? Second, "What will be the sign of your coming and of the end of the age?"

Jesus answers the second question in verses 4-31, where he indicates that the only sign announcing his Second Coming will be the "labor pains" described in verses 4-29. Immediately after the "distress" of the labor pains, the "sign of the Son of Man" himself will appear as Christ returns to carry out the final judgment and consummate God's kingdom (see vv. 29-31).

The Lord answers the first question in verses 15-22, where he anticipates the destruction of the temple by the Romans in A.D. 70. This event is preceded by "the abomination that causes desolation" — i.e., the detestable thing that causes God's presence to leave the temple. This phrase (borrowed from Daniel 9:27; 11:31; and 12:11) refers to the bringing of Gentile idols into Jerusalem by the Roman armies, just as Antiochus Epiphanes had brought them into Jerusalem in about 167 B.C. The destruction of the temple is itself a part of the "labor pains," which enables Jesus to answer his disciples' first question in the course of answering the second.

Against this background, note the similarities between John's first vision of the future and Jesus' prediction in Matthew 24:

> You will hear of wars and rumors of wars [compare the first seal and horseman in Rev 6:1-2], but see to it that you are not alarmed. Such things must happen, but the end is still to come. Nation will rise against nation, and kingdom against kingdom [compare the second seal and horseman in Rev 6:3-4]. There will be famines

[compare the third seal and horseman in Rev 6:5-6] and earthquakes in various places. [Compare the deadly realities of verses 6-7 with the fourth seal and horseman in Rev 6:7-8.] All these are the beginning of birth pains [i.e., the beginning of the "labor pains" — Jesus calls on his disciples to understand the period between his first and second comings in apocalyptic terms].

Then you [disciples] will be handed over to be persecuted and put to death, and you will be hated by all nations because of me [compare seal 5 in Rev 6:9-11]. At that time many will turn away from the faith and will betray and hate each other, and many false prophets will appear and deceive many people. Because of the increase of wickedness, the love of most will grow cold, but he who stands firm to the end will be saved. And this gospel of the kingdom will be preached in the whole world as a testimony to all nations, and then the end will come.

Immediately after the distress of those days
"the sun will be darkened,
and the moon will not give its light;
the stars will fall from the sky,
and the heavenly bodies will be shaken [compare the
cosmic catastrophe that accompanies the
opening of the sixth seal in Rev 6:12-17]."

At that time the sign of the Son of Man will appear in the sky, and all the nations of the earth will mourn. They will see the Son of Man coming on the clouds of the sky, with power and great glory. And he will send his angels with a loud trumpet call, and they will gather his elect from the four winds, from one end of the heavens to the other (Matt 24:6-14,29-31).

Jesus reveals the same vision of the future to his disciples that he later reveals to John — namely, the unfolding "labor pains" immediately followed by the final judgment and consummation. Regarding the exact time of the latter, we would be wise to keep in mind the Lord's words in verse 36: "No one knows about that day or hour, not even the angels in heaven, nor the Son, but only the Father."

REVELATION 7

4. Interlude: The 144,000 Sealed for Salvation (7:1-17)

The Book of Revelation contains three visions of the complete future from John's time in A.D. 95-96 to the consummation of the kingdom of God.[1] At one point or another within each vision, John includes a series of seven elements. There are seven seals in 6:1-8:1, seven trumpets in 8:2-11:19, and seven bowls of wrath in 15:1-16:21. Between the sixth and seventh elements in each series, John places an "interlude" that interrupts the flow of events. The first interlude appears in 7:1-17, the second in 10:1-11:14, and the third in 16:15.[2] These interludes perform several functions: First, they create suspense leading up to the climactic seventh element in each series. Second, they draw a sharp distinction between Christians and non-Christians. Third, they encourage the readers to view their present circumstances in light of what God will do in the future. The interludes thus enable the readers to place their suffering in proper perspective, which encourages faithful endurance and hope for the future.

The first interlude (Rev 7:1-17) answers the question concerning the final judgment posed in 6:17: "The great day of their wrath has come, and *who can stand?*"

---

[1] For further discussion of the "Structure of Revelation," see Part V of the Introduction.

[2] On the interludes in Revelation, see Kevin J. O'Brien, "An Examination of the Meaning, the Purpose, and the Function of the Interlude within the Sevenfold Series of the Book of Revelation," Ph.D. diss., Union Theological Seminary in Virginia, 1996.

a. The Sealing of the 144,000 (7:1-8)

¹After this I saw four angels standing at the four corners of the earth, holding back the four winds of the earth to prevent any wind from blowing on the land or on the sea or on any tree. ²Then I saw another angel coming up from the east, having the seal of the living God. He called out in a loud voice to the four angels who had been given power to harm the land and the sea: ³"Do not harm the land or the sea or the trees until we put a seal on the foreheads of the servants of our God." ⁴Then I heard the number of those who were sealed: 144,000 from all the tribes of Israel.
⁵From the tribe of Judah 12,000 were sealed,
from the tribe of Reuben 12,000,
from the tribe of Gad 12,000,
⁶from the tribe of Asher 12,000,
from the tribe of Naphtali 12,000,
from the tribe of Manasseh 12,000,
⁷from the tribe of Simeon 12,000,
from the tribe of Levi 12,000,
from the tribe of Issachar 12,000,
⁸from the tribe of Zebulun 12,000,
from the tribe of Joseph 12,000,
from the tribe of Benjamin 12,000.

7:1-8 The opening of the sixth seal marks the end of the universe and everything in it (see Rev 6:12-14, discussed above), but here in chapter 7 the land and sea and trees are again in their normal places. In this "interlude," John looks back to something that happened *before* the final judgment — namely, the sealing of the 144,000. Angels are set to unleash destructive forces against the earth, but they are restrained until this "sealing" is complete.[3]

The 144,000 represent the totality of Christ's church. John makes his meaning clear in a number of different ways: First, in verse 4, he identifies the 144,000 as "Israel." The nation of Israel entered into the Mosaic Covenant with God at Mount Sinai. In like

---

[3]Compare 2 Baruch 6:4–7:1, where four angels with torches are kept from burning the temple until the sacred furnishings have been removed. See also 1 Enoch 66:1-2, where angels are commanded to hold back the waters of the Flood until Noah's ark is complete.

manner, the church has entered into the new covenant with God through the sacrificial death of Christ.[4] Because of the similarity between these two groups, New Testament writers sometimes speak of Christians — both Jews and Gentiles — as the new "Israel"[5] or true "Israel."[6] In Old Testament times, most of the twelve tribes of Israel were either dispersed or destroyed because of their sin.[7] However, prophets predicted that, with the coming of the eschatological age, God would gather his people from all parts of the earth and again make them one.[8] New Testament writers see in the church the fulfillment of this hope. Why should we interpret "Israel" in verse 4 as a symbol for the church, rather than as the literal Jewish nation? Because John describes the 144,000 in verse 9 as a multitude "from *every* nation, tribe, people and language."

Second, John, in verse 3, identifies the 144,000 as "the servants of our God." The Lord's "servants" consist of a larger group than his Jewish servants alone.

Third, we have seen that twelve is the apocalyptic number symbolizing the people of God. It has its roots in the Old Testament, where the twelve tribes of Israel make up the totality of God's covenant people. The number 144,000, being a multiple of twelve ($12 \times 12 \times 1000$), signifies the full number of God's people — that is, *all* Christians.[9] John further emphasizes the idea of completeness by saying that the 144,000 are from "*all* the tribes of Israel" (v. 4). No part of "Israel" — no part of the church — is excluded. Why should we interpret "144,000" as a symbolic number, rather than as the

---

[4] See the Introduction, Part III.B.2.c.(4): "The Kingdom of God and the Death of Jesus."

[5] See, e.g., John 11:51-52; Rom 11:25-26; Gal 3:29; 6:15-16; Eph 2:11-22; James 1:1; 1 Pet 2:9-10.

[6] In Rev 2:9 and 3:9 the Lord speaks of "those who say they are Jews and are not, but are a synagogue of Satan." He indicates that true "Jewishness," in his eyes, is not simply a matter of ethnic identity. The Lord also implies that faithful Christians — both Jews and Gentiles — make up the true "Israel," the true covenant people of God.

[7] See, e.g., 2 Kgs 17,25; 2 Bar 67; Test. Mos. 2:3–3:1.

[8] See, e.g., Jer 16:10-15; Bar 4-5; 4 Ezra 13:39-47; 2 Bar 78; cf. Matt 19:28; Luke 22:30; John 11:49-52.

[9] On the symbolic significance of numbers in apocalyptic literature, see Part III.B.1.d of the Introduction.

literal number of true Christians? Because John makes clear in verse 9 that the number is not to be taken literally. There he describes the 144,000 as "a great multitude *that no one could count.*"

In the vision, the angels put "the seal of the living God" on the foreheads of his servants. The seal is a mark of ownership, showing that all Christians — the entirety of "Israel" — belong to the Lord. The point of the vision is that, before the cosmic catastrophe that will mark the end of the present evil age, God will place his seal of ownership on his people. Before the Lord intervenes in history to carry out his final judgment, God will take note of who belongs to him.[10] John is reminding the persecuted Christians of Asia that, in the midst of their suffering, God has not forgotten them. The Lord knows his own.[11]

Why are Christians being "sealed"? Why do they receive the sign of God's ownership? Verses 9-17 show that they are being marked for salvation.

b. A Song of Salvation (7:9-17)

⁹**After this I looked and there before me was a great multitude that no one could count, from every nation, tribe, people and language, standing before the throne and in front of the Lamb. They were wearing white robes and were holding palm branches in their hands.** ¹⁰**And they cried out in a loud voice:**

"**Salvation belongs to our God,**
who sits on the throne,
and to the Lamb."

¹¹**All the angels were standing around the throne and around the elders and the four living creatures. They fell down on their faces before the throne and worshiped God,** ¹²**saying:**

"**Amen!**
Praise and glory
and wisdom and thanks and honor
and power and strength

---

[10]Compare the vision in Ezekiel 9. God commands that a mark be placed on the foreheads of those who grieve over Jerusalem's sin before he sends executioners through the city to kill the wrongdoers.

[11]Compare John 10:14, where Jesus says, "I am the good shepherd; I know my sheep and my sheep know me."

be to our God for ever and ever.
Amen!"
¹³Then one of the elders asked me, "These in white robes—who are they, and where did they come from?"
¹⁴I answered, "Sir, you know."
And he said, "These are they who have come out of the great tribulation; they have washed their robes and made them white in the blood of the Lamb. ¹⁵Therefore,
"they are before the throne of God
and serve him day and night in his temple;
and he who sits on the throne will spread his tent over them.
¹⁶Never again will they hunger;
never again will they thirst.
The sun will not beat upon them,
nor any scorching heat.
¹⁷For the Lamb at the center of the throne will be their shepherd;
he will lead them to springs of living water.
And God will wipe away every tear from their eyes."

Much of the symbolism used in this passage appears earlier in the book. The "throne" is the throne of God, the mark of his divine sovereignty (see comments on Rev 4:2). The "Lamb" who shares the throne is Jesus, the Davidic king, who died as the sacrifice for sin and was then raised and exalted by God (see on 5:6). The "elders" symbolize the church (see on 4:4) and the "four living creatures" represent all of creation (see on 4:6b,8). Together they offer to God the praise that is rightfully his.

The "great multitude" represents the 144,000 servants of God described in Revelation 7:1-8 (discussed above). We have seen that this symbolic number stands for the full number of the people of God — whatever that sum may be. The number "144,000" is not to be taken literally, for John reminds us that "no one could count" them.

The multitude comes "from every nation, tribe, people and language,"[12] which speaks of the universal nature of the church.[13] They wear "white robes," which elsewhere in Revelation symbolize "the

---

[12]Compare Rev 5:9.

[13]See the comments on the universal greeting formula used in Rev 1:4c.

righteous acts of the saints."[14] "Righteousness" refers to being in a covenant relationship with God and living a life consistent with covenant faithfulness. Christians can be "righteous" only because Jesus' blood sacrifice on the cross established the new covenant, thus making a covenant relationship with God available to us.[15] Apart from the Cross there is no covenant, and thus no righteousness. Here in chapter 7 John expresses this truth in a beautiful way: "They have washed their robes and made them white in the blood of the Lamb."

The saints are "holding palm branches in their hands" as a sign of joy and celebration.[16] What are they celebrating? First, they "have come out of the great tribulation" — that is, the period of "labor pains," the period of intense persecution of God's people immediately prior to the end of the "present evil age."[17] Their suffering is over, and now they stand on the far side of the final judgment in the presence of God and the Lamb. Second, they praise God for "salvation" — that is, resurrection to eternal life in the consummated kingdom of God. For those who oppose God, the Second Coming of Christ and final judgment bring only terror and condemnation and doom. In Revelation 6:16-17 they cry out to the mountains and the rocks, "Fall on us and hide us from the face of him who sits on the throne and from the wrath of the Lamb! For the great day of their wrath has come, and who can stand?" However, for those who serve God faithfully, that Day brings deliverance. Dressed in white robes, they stand before God's throne, wave their palm branches, and shout, "Salvation belongs to our God, who sits on the throne, and to the Lamb."

The vision includes several images of the kingdom rule of God come in its fullness. First, God and his Christ are on the "throne," and their people "worship" and "serve" them. Second, Christians are "before the throne of God" and in his "temple" — that is, constantly

---

[14]See the comment on Rev 3:4-5.

[15]See Part III.B.2.c.(4) of the Introduction: "The Kingdom of God and the Death of Jesus."

[16]Compare John 12:13, where the crowds wave palm branches at Jesus' "Triumphal Entry" into Jerusalem.

[17]See Parts III.B.2.b.(4) "The Shift of the Ages" and III.B.2.d.(3) "The 'Labor Pains'" of the Introduction, as well as the Commentary on Rev 1:9.

in the Lord's presence.[18] Third, the Lord Christ acts as their "shepherd"[19] by providing them with everything needed for eschatological life — here symbolized as food ("never again will they hunger"[20]), water ("never again will they thirst. . . . he will lead them to springs of living water"[21]), and shelter ("He who sits on the throne will spread his tent over them. . . . The sun will not beat upon them, nor any scorching heat"[22]). Fourth, the Lord "will wipe every tear from their eyes," erasing every sadness and healing every hurt.[23]

In the first interlude (Rev 7:1-17), John invites his first readers to lift up their eyes — to look beyond the hardships of their journey to the joys of their final destination. In the present, the forces of evil may seem to have the upper hand. However, in the future God will indeed triumph, and his servants will share in his victory. For a brief while they must pass through the "tribulation," but soon they will reign forever and ever. In prison or in exile, facing torture or even death, God has neither forgotten them nor abandoned them. He has marked them as his own and sealed them for salvation.

---

[18] Compare, for example, Rev 3:12 and 21:3,22. See also the comment on Rev 21:15-16.

[19] Note that, in the Old Testament, the prophet Ezekiel describes the Davidic king or "Messiah" as the "shepherd" of Israel (see, e.g., Ezek 34:23-24; 37:24). Others apply the title to God (Ps 23:1-6; 80:1; Isa 40:11) and to Jesus (John 10:1-18; Heb 13:20; 1 Pet 2:25; 5:4).

[20] Compare Rev 2:7; 22:2.

[21] Compare Rev 21:6; 22:1-2.

[22] Compare Rev 21:23 and 22:5, which use similar language to express a different idea.

[23] Compare Rev 21:4.

REVELATION 8-9

5. The Consummation of God's Kingdom: Seal Seven (8:1)

¹When he opened the seventh seal, there was silence in heaven for about half an hour.

8:1 Jewish apocalyptists describe the period before God's creation of the world as being absolutely silent. To illustrate, the "second Baruch" asks: "Will the universe return to its nature and the world go back to *its original silence*?" (2 Baruch 3:7). Likewise, the "fourth Ezra" writes:

> O Lord, you spoke at the beginning of creation, and said on the first day, "Let heaven and earth be made," and your word accomplished the work. And then the Spirit was hovering, and darkness and *silence embraced everything; the sound of man's voice was not yet there* (4 Ezra 6:38-39).

The latter author anticipates that, at the end of the present age, the world will be returned to its "original silence" before God recreates the universe as his eternal kingdom:

> And after these years my son the Messiah shall die, and all who draw human breath. And the world shall be turned back to primeval silence for seven days, as it was at the first beginnings; so that no one shall be left. And after seven days the world, which is not yet awake, shall be roused . . . (4 Ezra 7:29-31).

John draws upon this apocalyptic idea in Revelation 8:1. The "silence" implies that the "new creation" will come even though John does not describe it in this verse. He previews the coming of God's kingdom in the "interlude" of chapter 7. However, John saves his detailed description of the consummation for the climax of the book in Revelation 21:1-22:5.

Note that where 4 Ezra predicts seven days of silence, John predicts only "about half an hour." The Christian apocalyptist expects virtually no delay at all between the final judgment (i.e., the opening of the sixth seal in 6:12-17) and the consummation of God's kingdom. The Lord will hurry history along to his intended goal.

6. Summary: John's First Vision of the Future (6:1–8:1)

In Revelation 6:1–8:1, John offers the first of three visions of the future. He presents the future in terms of the opening of seven seals of a scroll containing God's will. Since "seven" is the apocalyptic number symbolizing completeness,[1] the seals signify the complete future from the writing of Revelation in A.D. 95-96 to the consummation of the kingdom of God. According to the vision, what course will the future take? First, beginning in John's own century, Christians will endure the hardships of the "labor pains," including the martyrdom of believers (seals one through five). In the meantime, God will take note of who belongs to him, thus "marking" them for salvation (the "interlude" of chapter 7). The "labor pains" will be followed by the final judgment, in which Christ returns to destroy all evil and vindicate the good (seal six). Finally, God will form a "new creation," bringing the whole universe under his kingdom rule (the implication of seal seven).[2]

C. THE SECOND VISION OF THE FUTURE (8:2–11:19)

1. The Structure of the Second Vision

John's second vision of the future appears in Revelation 8:2–11:19. It communicates the same basic picture of the future found in the first vision (summarized above). However, the prophet views his subject from a different angle and thereby allows us to see several facets of the future not revealed in the earlier chapters.[3]

---

[1]See the Introduction, Part III.B.1.d: "Symbolic Numbers."
[2]Compare the shape of Christian apocalyptic theology as outlined in Fig. 2.
[3]For a more detailed discussion of the Structure of Revelation, see Part V of the Introduction.

a. Seven Trumpets versus Seven Seals

Whereas the first vision takes the form of the opening of seven seals, the second vision centers on the sounding of seven trumpets. In apocalyptic literature, seven is the symbolic number for "fullness" or "completeness."[4] In the second vision, John again describes the *complete* future from the time he received the Revelation in A.D. 95-96 to the consummation of God's kingdom at the Second Coming of Christ. For further comment on the seven trumpets, see below.

b. Major Elements of the Vision

As in the first vision, John predicts three major events: First comes the latter part of the "present evil age." This period includes the "labor pains," a time of intense suffering and persecution for God's people that had already begun in the first century[5] (compare 6:1-11 with 8:2–9:21). Next comes the final judgment, and then finally the consummation of God's kingdom rule (compare 6:12-17 and 8:1 with 11:15-19). Like the first vision, the second also contains an "interlude" in which John considers the present state of Christians in light of their future salvation (compare 7:1-17 with 10:1–11:14).

c. The Dominant Image: God's Coming Kingdom as a "Second Exodus" for His People

In the second vision, John's controlling idea, or dominant image, is Israel's Exodus from captivity in Egypt. Through his prophet spokesman, Christ takes the same basic revelation of the future we saw in 6:1–8:1 and recasts it within the framework of the Exodus story. By comparing the future deliverance of Christians to the past

---

[4]See the Introduction, Part III.B.1.d: "Symbolic Numbers."
[5]On the "present evil age," see Parts III.B.2.b.(2), "The Present Evil Age and the Kingdom of Satan," and III.B.2.c.(2), "Adam and the Present Evil Age," of the Introduction. On the "labor pains," see Parts III.B.2.b.(4), "The Shift of the Ages," and III.B.2.d.(3), "The 'Labor Pains,'" of the Introduction. On the "labor pains" as a reality in John's own time, see the comment on Revelation 1:9. Note that the "labor pains" are the sufferings of the "present evil age" particularly as they apply to Christians. See also Fig. 2 The Shape of Christian Apocalyptic Theology, p. 41.

deliverance of Israel, John invites his readers to view the coming kingdom as a sort of "Second Exodus" for God's covenant people.[6] We sketch the main points of comparison below:

The Exodus Story	John's Second Vision (Revelation 8:2–11:19)
1. Israel, the People of God, suffer oppression in Egypt under the evil Pharaoh (Exod 1–6).	1. John portrays Christians as the "new Israel,"[7] the People of God, who are enslaved in the "present evil age" and oppressed by the powers of evil (the "labor pains") (Rev 8:2–11:14).
2. God sends ten great plagues on the Egyptians in order to force them to let his people go (Exod 7–12).	2. John describes the "present evil age"/"labor pains" in language reminiscent of the ten plagues (trumpets one through six in Rev 8:2–9:21).
3. Israel, God's people, are spared from the plagues – the plagues do not affect them (see Exod 8:22-23; 9:4-7,26; 10:23; 12:13,23,27).	3. John shows that there is a sense in which the church, God's people, are spared the "plagues" of the "present evil age"/"labor pains" (the measuring of the temple in Rev 11:1 and the resurrection of the two witnesses in 11:11).[8]
4. In the face of the ten plagues, the Pharaoh hardens his heart and refuses to let Israel go (see Exod 7:22-23; 8:15,19,32; 9:7,12,34-35; 10:10-11,20,27-28). Even when he finally does release them, he soon changes his mind and pursues them into the Red Sea (see Exod 14:5-23).	4. John shows that, even in the face of the struggles of the "present evil age," many people harden their hearts, refusing to repent of their sins and turn from false gods to serve the true God (Rev 9:20-21).

---

[6]In the third vision, John will portray God's coming kingdom as a "Second Return" from "Exile" in "Babylon."

[7]On the church as the "new Israel," see the discussion of "The Sealing of the 144,000" in Revelation 7:1-8.

[8]See Part III.C.3.b.(2) of the Commentary: "A Note on the 'Protection' of the 'New Israel' from the 'Plagues.'"

5. God destroys Pharaoh in the Red Sea, thereby giving his people deliverance. They respond by singing songs of praise, which proclaim that "The Lord will reign for ever and ever" (Exod 14:23-15:21, particularly 15:18).	5. John describes the final judgment and consummation of God's kingdom (which, in this framework, we are encouraged to think of as a sort of "Second Exodus" of God's people from slavery to freedom). This includes a song of praise that announces God's eternal reign (trumpet seven in Revelation 11:15-19, particularly verse 15).
6. At God's command, Israel builds a tabernacle containing the ark of the covenant, where God is present with his covenant people (Exod 25-40, particularly 25:22 and 29:44-46).	6. After the final judgment and consummation, God's people are given access to his temple and the ark of the covenant, signifying the Lord's presence with his covenant people (Rev 11:19).

d. Subordinate Imagery in Revelation 8:2-9:21

Having acquainted ourselves with the overall framework of John's vision, we will now make a closer examination of its individual elements. We begin with the sounding of the first six trumpets in Revelation 8:2-9:21. As noted above, these first trumpets represent the evils and hardships that the whole of humanity experiences during the latter part of the "present evil age." At the same time, they represent the "labor pains" — the additional persecution and oppression believers endure because of their commitment to Christ as Lord.

This portion of the second vision of the future contains a great deal of very subtle imagery drawn from many parts of the Old Testament and apocalyptic writings. We could fill many pages simply showing that nearly every line — nearly every phrase — has deep roots in ancient literature and culture. (For this kind of study, see, for example, the commentaries by Aune and Caird listed in the Bibliography.) In this case, however, knowing the history of John's images does not necessarily contribute much to our understanding of John's message. In this case, the prophet gathers up "building stones" from many older structures and puts them together to form an entirely new edifice. When studying chapters 8-9, then, we must take special care not to focus on the individual "leaves" and miss the beauty of the "tree." We may lean in close and look at a single "brush stroke," but then we must step back and look at the whole "painting." We must not get so caught up in the details that we miss John's point. His overall aim is to portray the coming salvation of Christians as a "Second Exodus" from bondage. The individual elements of the vision are subordinate to this overarching theme and must be interpreted in the context of that theme. In the paragraphs that follow, we will indeed analyze the key components of John's vision. However, we will make it our first priority to uncover the "big picture" by highlighting the major theological claims made in this portion of Revelation.

2. The "Present Evil Age/Labor Pains": Trumpets One through Six (8:2–9:21)

²And I saw the seven angels who stand before God, and to them were given seven trumpets.

³Another angel, who had a golden censer, came and stood at the altar. He was given much incense to offer, with the prayers of all the saints, on the golden altar before the throne. ⁴The smoke of the incense, together with the prayers of the saints, went up before God from the angel's hand. ⁵Then the angel took the censer, filled it with fire from the altar, and hurled it on the earth; and there came peals of thunder, rumblings, flashes of lightning and an earthquake.

⁶Then the seven angels who had the seven trumpets prepared to sound them.

⁷The first angel sounded his trumpet, and there came hail and fire mixed with blood, and it was hurled down upon the earth. A third of the earth was burned up, a third of the trees were burned up, and all the green grass was burned up.

⁸The second angel sounded his trumpet, and something like a huge mountain, all ablaze, was thrown into the sea. A third of the sea turned into blood, ⁹a third of the living creatures in the sea died, and a third of the ships were destroyed.

¹⁰The third angel sounded his trumpet, and a great star, blazing like a torch, fell from the sky on a third of the rivers and on the springs of water— ¹¹the name of the star is Wormwood.ᵃ A third of the waters turned bitter, and many people died from the waters that had become bitter.

¹²The fourth angel sounded his trumpet, and a third of the sun was struck, a third of the moon, and a third of the stars, so that a third of them turned dark. A third of the day was without light, and also a third of the night.

¹³As I watched, I heard an eagle that was flying in midair call out in a loud voice: "Woe! Woe! Woe to the inhabitants of the earth, because of the trumpet blasts about to be sounded by the other three angels!"

¹The fifth angel sounded his trumpet, and I saw a star that had fallen from the sky to the earth. The star was given the key to the shaft of the Abyss. ²When he opened the Abyss, smoke rose from it like the smoke from a gigantic furnace. The sun and sky were darkened by the smoke from the Abyss. ³And out of the smoke locusts came down upon the earth and were given power like that of scorpions of the earth. ⁴They were told not to harm the grass of the earth or any plant or tree, but only those people who did not have the seal of God on their foreheads. ⁵They were not given power to kill them, but only to torture them for five months. And the agony they suffered was like that of the sting of a scorpion when it strikes a man. ⁶During those days men will seek death, but will not find it; they will long to die, but death will elude them.

⁷The locusts looked like horses prepared for battle. On their heads they wore something like crowns of gold, and their faces resembled human faces. ⁸Their hair was like women's hair, and their teeth were like lions' teeth. ⁹They had breastplates like breastplates of iron, and the sound of their wings was like the thundering of many horses and chariots rushing into battle. ¹⁰They had tails and stings like scorpions, and in their tails they had power to torment people for five months. ¹¹They had as king over them the angel of the Abyss, whose name in Hebrew is Abaddon, and in Greek, Apollyon.ᵇ

¹²The first woe is past; two other woes are yet to come.

¹³The sixth angel sounded his trumpet, and I heard a voice coming from the hornsᶜ of the golden altar that is before God. ¹⁴It said to the sixth angel who had the trumpet, "Release the four angels who are bound at the great river Euphrates." ¹⁵And the four angels who had been kept ready for this very hour and day and month and year were released to kill a third of mankind. ¹⁶The number of the mounted troops was two hundred million. I heard their number.

¹⁷The horses and riders I saw in my vision looked like this: Their breastplates were fiery red, dark blue, and yellow as sulfur. The heads of the horses resembled the heads of lions, and out of their mouths came fire, smoke and sulfur. ¹⁸A third of mankind was killed by the three plagues of fire, smoke and sulfur that came out of their mouths. ¹⁹The power of the horses was in their mouths and in their tails; for their tails were like snakes, having heads with which they inflict injury.

²⁰The rest of mankind that were not killed by these plagues still did not repent of the work of their hands; they did not stop worshiping demons, and idols of gold, silver, bronze, stone and wood—idols that cannot see or hear or walk. ²¹Nor did they repent of their murders, their magic arts, their sexual immorality or their thefts.

ᵃ*8:11* That is, Bitterness   ᵇ*9:11* Abaddon *and* Apollyon *mean* Destroyer.   ᶜ*13* That is, projections

a. Hail, Blood, Bitter Waters, Darkness, Locusts, and Death: The "Present Evil Age" and "Labor Pains" as Eschatological "Plagues"

(1) Present Evils as "Plagues." As the first six trumpets are sounded, John describes *in apocalyptic symbolism* the evils that afflict humankind during the "present evil age" and the "labor pains." In chapter 9, verses 18 and 20, he characterizes these evils as "plagues." By choosing this term, he makes a purposeful comparison between these evils and the ten plagues God poured out against Pharaoh and Egypt in Exodus 7–12. Throughout this portion of Revelation, John uses language that reminds the reader of that formative event in Israel's history.[9]

(2) The First Trumpet. At the sounding of the first trumpet there come "hail and fire mixed with blood," which burns up "a third of the earth, a third of the trees, and all the green grass" (Rev 8:7). This is reminiscent of the seventh plague on Egypt in which thunder, hail, and lightning destroyed crops in the fields (see Exod 9:13-35).

---

[9]Note: Plagues not directly utilized in Revelation include the second plague of frogs (Exod 8:1-14), the third plague of gnats (Exod 8:16-19), the fourth plague of flies (Exod 8:20-32), and the fifth plague that killed the Egyptians' livestock (Exod 9:1-7).

(3) The Second Trumpet. At the sounding of the second trumpet, "something like a huge mountain, all ablaze, was thrown into the sea. A third of the sea turned into blood, a third of the living creatures in the sea died, and a third of the ships were destroyed" (Rev 8:8-9). This is reminiscent of the first plague on Egypt in which the water of the River Nile was turned to blood and the fish died (see Exod 7:14-24).

(4) The Third Trumpet. At the sounding of the third trumpet, "a great star, blazing like a torch, fell from the sky on a third of the rivers and on the springs of water — the name of the star is Wormwood. A third of the waters turned bitter, and many people died from the waters that had become bitter" (Rev 8:10-11). This calls to mind both the first plague on Egypt, in which the waters of the River Nile were turned to blood and made undrinkable (see Exod 7:14-24), and the tenth plague in which many Egyptians died (see Exod 11-12).

(5) The Fourth Trumpet. At the sounding of the fourth trumpet, a third of the sun, moon and stars turn "dark" (Rev 8:12). This reminds us of the ninth plague on Egypt, in which a darkness that could be felt descended on the land (see Exod 10:21-29).

(6) The Fifth Trumpet. At the sounding of the fifth trumpet, a star fallen from heaven to earth is given the key to the Abyss. When the Abyss is opened, smoke ascends out of it like a giant furnace and darkens the sun and sky.[10] Locusts then emerge from the smoke and sting those who do not bear the seal of God on their foreheads (Rev 9:1-12). The fifth trumpet calls to mind the sixth plague on Egypt, in which soot taken from a furnace becomes fine dust that spreads throughout the land, producing boils on men and animals (see Exod 9:8-12). It also resembles the eighth plague on Egypt in which locusts devour the plants left after the plague of hail (see Exod 10:1-20).

(7) The Sixth Trumpet. When the sixth trumpet sounds, four angels leading a demonic army are released to kill a third of mankind (Rev 9:13-19). This is reminiscent of the tenth plague on Egypt in which the angel of death kills the firstborn male offspring of every person and animal in Egypt (Exod 11-12). In the Book of Exodus, the plague of death is the last plague before Israel's Exodus from Egypt. In Revelation, the sixth trumpet is the last trumpet before the

---

[10]Compare Amos 5:18-20 and 8:9, where the "day of the Lord" brings "darkness, not light."

seventh, which marks the consummation of God's kingdom — the "New Exodus" of God's People.

(8) Heightened Imagery Portraying Eschatological Events: In describing the troubles of the present time, John uses language similar but not identical to that found in Exodus. To illustrate, the hail of Exodus is mixed with blood in Revelation. The locusts of Exodus become demon locusts in Revelation. Whereas normal locusts destroy vegetation, John's demon locusts ignore vegetation and destroy human beings (see Rev 9:4-5). The single angel of death in Exodus becomes an army of two hundred million in Revelation. Apocalyptic writers commonly use such heightened imagery to show that they are speaking of eschatological events associated with the coming transformation of the cosmos. We see it, for example, in Daniel 12:1, where the writer describes the "labor pains" as "a time of distress such as has not happened from the beginning of nations until then." Jesus uses similar language in Matthew 24:21, where he describes the same period as "great distress, unequaled from the beginning of the world until now — and never to be equaled again." By adopting this stereotypical manner of expression, John invites his Christian readers to think of their present troubles as more than common everyday events. Instead, they mark the "last times," the beginning of the "eschatological age," the "labor pains," the terrible time that immediately precedes the coming of God's kingdom in all its fullness.

(9) Partial Destruction versus Total Destruction. The plagues associated with the first six trumpets harm only a *portion* of the earth — "a third of the earth" (8:7), "a third of the trees" (8:7), the "grass" (8:7), "a third of the sea" (8:8), "a third of the living creatures in the sea" (8:9), "a third of the ships" (8:9), "a third of the rivers" (8:10), "a third of . . . the springs of water" (8:10), "a third of the waters" (8:11), "a third of the sun" (8:12), "a third of the moon" (8:12), "a third of the stars" (8:13), "a third of the day" (8:12), "a third of the night" (8:12), and "a third of mankind" (9:15,18). In chapter 9 the locusts are not allowed to kill *all* people, but only to harm a *limited* group (i.e., "those people who did not have the seal of God on their foreheads") for a *limited* time ("five months"[11]) (9:5,10).

---

[11]On the significance of the apocalyptic number "five," see Part III.B.1.d of the Introduction: "Symbolic Numbers."

In contrast, Revelation 11:13 describes how "seven thousand people were killed." Since seven and multiples of seven symbolize "completeness" in apocalyptic literature,[12] this number represents not just a portion, but *all* those who refuse to serve God (see the commentary on this passage given below). Why does John speak of *partial* destruction early in the vision, but *total* destruction later in the vision? The answer is that the first six trumpets represent the evils and suffering human beings typically experience during the "present evil age" and the "labor pains." The earthquake and *total* destruction of Revelation 11:13 symbolize the final judgment, when God destroys *all* evil and thereby ends the world as we know it.

b. Earth, Trees, Grass, Springs, Rivers, Sea, and Sea Creatures: The Effect of the "Present Evil Age" and "Labor Pains" on the Natural World

In John's first vision of the future, he names five specific evils present during the time of "labor pains" — namely, political struggle and conquest (symbolized by the first horseman in Rev 6:2); conflict and war (symbolized by the second horseman in 6:4); limited famine and economic hardship (the third horseman in 6:5-6); and death in its various forms (represented by the fourth horseman in 6:8), including the murder of Christians (symbolized by the souls of the martyrs under the altar in Rev 6:9-11). In his second vision John speaks of the evils of the present time using more general terms, such as "harm" (9:4), "torture" (9:5), "agony" (9:5), "torment" (9:10), and "death" (8:9,11; 9:15,18).

However, a new kind of evil appears in chapter 8, where John repeatedly mentions the harm inflicted on the natural world during the time of "labor pains." Trees and green grass are destroyed (8:7). Sea creatures die (8:9). The earth's water supplies become bitter (8:11). Are these mere symbols based on the Exodus plagues, or is John presenting humankind's abuse of the planet as one of the wrongs of the "present evil age" and "labor pains"? The latter seems to be the case, for this second vision of the future ends with a word of condemnation for those who misuse God's creation: "The time has come for judging the dead . . . and for destroying those who destroy the earth" (Rev 11:18).

---

[12]See Part III.B.1.d of the Introduction: "Symbolic Numbers."

Through such imagery, John communicates the fact that not just human beings, but the entire created order, have been warped by sin. Not just human beings, but the entire created order, are in need of redemption. Human beings, in their sin, pollute and exploit the earth. Human beings, in their sin, twist and pervert God's good creation to serve evil ends. Human beings, by their sin, turn the present age into the "present *evil* age" for the entire planet.[13] Many biblical writers express this truth, as the following texts illustrate:

> To Adam [God] said, "Because you listened to your wife and ate from the tree about which I commanded you, 'You must not eat of it,'
>
> *"Cursed is the ground because of you;*
>   through painful toil you will eat of it
>   all the days of your life.
> It will produce thorns and thistles for you,
>   and you will eat the plants of the field" (Gen 3:17-18).
>
> *The earth is defiled by its people;*
>   they have disobeyed the laws,
>   violated the statutes
>   and broken the everlasting covenant.
> Therefore a curse consumes the earth;
>   its people must bear their guilt.
> Therefore earth's inhabitants are burned up,
>   and very few are left (Isa 24:5-6).

> The creation waits in eager expectation for the sons of God to be revealed [at the resurrection and consummation of God's kingdom]. For the creation was subjected to frustration, not by its own choice, but by the will of the one who subjected it, in hope that the creation itself will be liberated from its bondage to decay and brought into the glorious freedom [from decay] of the children of God.
> We know that *the whole creation has been groaning as in the pains of childbirth* [the "labor pains"] right up to the present time (Rom 8:19-22).

---

[13]For further discussion of this point, see Part III.B.2.b.(2) of the Introduction: "The Present Evil Age and the Kingdom of Satan."

Revelation looks forward not just to the salvation of humans, but to the salvation of God's whole creation.

c. The "Present Evil Age" and "Labor Pains" as God's Judgment on Sin and Call to Repentance

Exodus portrays the ten plagues as God's judgment on Egypt's gods and on the Egyptians themselves for their idolatry. For example, God turns the life-giving Nile into blood (Exod 7:14-24) and blots out Ra, the sun god, from the sky (Exod 10:21-23). In promising the plague of death, God says: "On that same night I will pass through Egypt and strike down every firstborn—both men and animals—and I will bring judgment on all the gods of Egypt. I am the LORD" (Exod 12:12). The plagues were intended to bring Pharaoh and the Egyptians to repentance, but again and again they hardened their hearts against God, refusing to change their ways and acknowledge him as Lord (see Exod 5:2; 7:22-23; 8:15,19,32; 9:7,12,34-35; 10:10-11,20,27-28).

By likening the hardships of the "present evil age" to the plagues on Egypt, John invites his readers to view the world's current troubles as God's judgment on human sin. The Apostle Paul makes a similar point in Romans 1:18-32, where he declares that "The wrath of God is [presently] being revealed from heaven against all the godlessness and wickedness of men who suppress the truth [about God] by their wickedness."

Just as the ten plagues were intended to lead Pharaoh to repent of his opposition to Israel and Israel's God, John makes clear that the troubles of the present time are intended to impress upon human beings their need for God and their reliance on God. They are intended to lead people to repent and turn to the Lord. Seen in this light, the world's suffering and the delay of the consummation is an act of God's mercy toward sinners. Peter expresses a similar idea in his Second Epistle, chapter 3, verses 9-19:

> The Lord is not slow in keeping his promise [to come again], as some understand slowness. He is patient with you, not wanting anyone to perish, but everyone to come to repentance.
>
> But the day of the Lord will come like a thief. The heavens will disappear with a roar; the elements will be destroyed by fire, and the earth and everything in it will be laid bare.

Since everything will be destroyed in this way, what kind of people ought you to be? You ought to live holy and godly lives as you look forward to the day of God and speed its coming.

Sadly, John does not expect God's efforts to lead sinners to repentance to be entirely successful. In Revelation 9:20-21 he writes:

> The rest of mankind that were not killed by these plagues still did not repent of the work of their hands; they did not stop worshiping demons, and idols of gold, silver, bronze, stone and wood—idols that cannot see or hear or walk. Nor did they repent of their murders, their magic arts, their sexual immorality or their thefts.

d. The "Present Evil Age" and "Labor Pains" as a Source of Hope and a Call to Perseverance

The ten plagues — God's judgment on Pharaoh and the Egyptians — were immediately followed by the Exodus, the deliverance of God's people. By picturing our present circumstances as a series of plagues, John reminds his Christian readers that the ultimate "Exodus" — the final deliverance of God's people from the kingdom of Satan into the kingdom of God — is about to occur.[14] Christ's prophet intends for these chapters to be a word of hope and a call for perseverance in the face of impending deliverance. Jesus himself offers a similar word of encouragement in Luke 21:28-31:

> "When these things begin to take place, stand up and lift up your heads, because your redemption is drawing near."
>
> He told them this parable: "Look at the fig tree and all the trees. When they sprout leaves, you can see for yourselves and know that summer is near. Even so, when you see these things happening, you know that the kingdom of God is near.

e. The Blazing Mountain, Falling Stars, Wormwood, Demon Locusts from the Abyss, Abaddon, Apollyon, and a Demon Army: The "Present Evil Age" and "Labor Pains" as God's Unleashing Demonic Forces on the Earth

Throughout chapters 8 and 9, John emphasizes the demonic

---

[14]See Fig. 2, The Shape of Christian Apocalyptic Theology, p. 41.

nature of the suffering that presently afflicts the world. For example, at the sounding of the third and fifth trumpets, stars fall from the sky (Rev 8:10-11; 9:1). We have seen that, in apocalyptic literature, stars tend to represent angels,[15] while fallen stars tend to symbolize fallen angels — demons — who have turned to evil in rebellion against God.[16] Because the first falling star/demon turns the waters of the earth bitter, John calls it "Wormwood" (Greek ἄψινθος, *apsinthos*; Hebrew *laanah*), the name of a poisonous and bitter plant mentioned several times in the Old Testament.[17]

The second falling star/demon opens the Abyss (ἄβυσσος, *abyssos*) — that is, the "Deep," or the "Underworld." In the Greco-Roman culture of John's time, the Abyss was considered to be the dwelling place of the dead[18] or of demons.[19] Throughout Revelation, John uses the term in the latter sense as the reservoir of evil, a prison for demonic powers where they await the final judgment.[20] Here in chapter 9 God permits the angel to unlock this reservoir and unleash a swarm of demon locusts on the earth. This fierce demonic army is led by "the angel of the Abyss," which appears to be a reference to Satan, the "king" of the demons. John identifies him with the Hebrew name "Abaddon" and the Greek name "Apollyon," both of which mean "Destroyer" or "Killer."[21]

---

[15]See the comment on the "seven stars" in Revelation 1:12-13,16,20.

[16]See the discussion of "Rebellion in Heaven" in Part III.B.2.b.(1) of the Introduction. Compare Isaiah 14:12, where the prophet uses similar language to describe the humiliation of King Nebuchadnezzar: "How you have fallen from heaven, O morning star, son of the dawn! You have been cast down to the earth, you who once laid low the nations!"

[17]See Amos 5:6-7 and 6:12, where the fire of God's judgment devours those who turn justice into bitter wormwood. See also Jeremiah 9:15 and 23:15, where God promises to make sinful Israel drink poison water and eat bitter food. The term "wormwood" (*laanah*) also appears in Deuteronomy 29:18; Proverbs 5:4; and Lamentations 3:15,19.

[18]See, for example, Romans 10:7, where Paul asks: "'Who will descend into the deep [*abyssos*]?' (that is, to bring Christ up from the dead)."

[19]See, for example, Luke 8:31, where the "Legion" of demons beg Christ "not to order them into the Abyss."

[20]See Revelation 9:1-11; 11:7; 17:8; 20:1-3. For further discussion of the "imprisonment" of demons, see Part III.B.2.b.(1) of the Introduction: "Rebellion in Heaven."

[21]Compare Job 26:6; 28:22; Proverbs 15:11; Psalm 88:11, where "Destruction" (*Abaddon*) is equated with "Death" or the "Grave." Some

At the sounding of the second trumpet, "something like a huge mountain, all ablaze, was thrown into the sea," turning a third of its waters into blood (Rev 8:8). Like the falling stars, this blazing mountain probably represents demonic powers. John borrows the symbol from 1 Enoch 18:13, which describes evil angels as "burning mountains" kept in prison until the final judgment.[22]

When the sixth angel sounds his trumpet, "four angels" are "released to kill a third of mankind" (Rev 9:15). They lead an army of mounted demons numbering two hundred million.

Throughout chapters 8 and 9, John indicates that part of the sufferings of the "present evil age" and "labor pains" result from God's allowing the demonic powers to unleash chaos and evil on the earth. The horrible malice of the devil and his demon allies is illustrated by Job 1–2, where Satan desires to harm God's righteous servant by destroying his property, his family, his health, his faith, and even his life. Agreeing to test Job, the Sovereign Lord lets Satan have his way. However, he sets boundaries on the devil's power, commanding him to spare Job's life. (Imagine what Satan would do to us if a merciful God did not set limits on demonic activity!) Likewise, in Revelation, John sees God lifting his restraints, allowing the demonic powers to carry out a part of their malicious intent. Before he destroys them in his final judgment, God uses even the demons — even evil itself — as his servants in order to accomplish his good purposes. He uses them to punish his enemies and to move sinners to repentance.[23]

---

scholars suggest that the "king" of the demons symbolizes Domitian, the "king" of the Roman empire who made himself an instrument of evil by killing Christians. If this is the case, then "Apollyon" may be a pun on "Apollo," the divine name that Domitian sometimes applied to himself. For more on the relationship between Domitian and Apollo, see the comments on Revelation 12.

[22]For other possible sources of John's imagery, compare Jeremiah 51:24-25 (where Babylon appears as a "destroying mountain" that, after devastating "the whole earth," is "burned out" by God) and Amos 7:4 (which describes "judgment by fire" on land and sea).

[23]The "divine passive" verbs of Revelation 9:1 ("The star *was given* the key"), 3 ("locusts...*were given* power"), and 5 ("They *were not given* power to kill them, but only to torture them") identify God as the One who permits the demonic powers to carry out their destructive desires. For an explanation of the "divine passive" construction, see the comment on Revelation 6:2,4,8.

f. Fire from the Altar: The "Present Evil Age" and "Labor Pains" as an Answer to Prayer

In Revelation 8–9 John also portrays the "labor pains" and the sufferings of the "present evil age" as an answered prayer:

> And I saw the seven angels who stand before God, and to them were given seven trumpets.
> Another angel, who had a golden censer, came and stood at the altar. He was given much incense to offer, with the prayers of all the saints, on the golden altar before the throne. The smoke of the incense, together with *the prayers of the saints, went up before God* from the angel's hand. Then [in response to the saints' prayers] the angel took the censer, filled it with *fire* from the altar, and *hurled* it *on the earth*; and there came peals of thunder, rumblings, flashes of lightning and an earthquake[24] (Rev 8:2-5).

In answer to the prayers of his people, God causes fire to be hurled down onto the earth. The succeeding verses suggest that the plagues — that is, the sounding of the first six trumpets, the troubles of the "present time" — *are* that "fire."

> The first angel sounded his trumpet, and there came hail and *fire* mixed with blood, and it was *hurled down upon the earth* (Rev 8:7a).

> The second angel sounded his trumpet, and something like a huge mountain, all *ablaze*, was *thrown into the sea* (Rev 8:8a).

> The third angel sounded his trumpet, and a great star, *blazing like a torch, fell from the sky* on a third of the rivers and on the springs of water . . .(Rev 8:10).

John invites us to view the troubles of the "present time" as God's gracious answer to our prayers. The Lord is hurrying along the apocalyptic scenario — moving us through the "labor pains" — so that we may reach history's goal, the consummated kingdom of God.[25]

---

[24]Seen also in Revelation 4:5, the thunder, lightning, and earthquake are a theophany indicating that God is present and active. See the comment on the "loud voice like a trumpet" in Revelation 1:10,12.

[25]Compare Revelation 6:10-17 (where the final judgment and destruction of God's enemies comes in response to the prayers of the martyred saints) and 11:6 (where the "two witnesses" — symbolizing the church — "have power . . . to strike the earth with every kind of plague as often as they want").

g. The Sounding of Seven Trumpets: The "Present Evil Age" and "Labor Pains" as the Announcement of the Day of the Lord

John describes the future from his own time to the consummation as the sounding of seven trumpets — or perhaps (since "seven" is the apocalyptic number for completeness[26]) as the sounding of the trumpet in its completeness. In Jewish history and tradition, trumpets could carry a number of different meanings that would make good sense in the context of Revelation 8–9. First, trumpets were used as a call to celebration (see Num 10:10). If this is what John has in mind, then the prophet invites us to view the present time — when the "trumpets" are being "sounded" — as a call to the celebration of God's future kingdom rule.

Second, trumpets were used as a signal warning of danger (see Ezek 33:3; Amos 3:6; cf. Joel 2:15). Perhaps, then, John is inviting us to view the troubles of the present time as a warning of the impending final judgment, as a call for all to take shelter in Christ.

Third, trumpets were part of the theophany on Mount Sinai, an audible sign of God's invisible presence (see Exod 19:16). If this is the meaning of the trumpet in John's vision, then he is urging his Christian readers to view their present sufferings not as a time when God has abandoned his people, but as a time when God is present and active.

Fourth, trumpets were used to announce the crowning of a new king (see 2 Sam 15:10; 1 Kgs 1:39; 2 Kgs 9:13). Perhaps, then, John is calling on us to listen — to hear the long "trumpet blast" that is sounding even now, announcing that God's kingdom reign is about to come in its fullness.

All these interpretations of the seven trumpets are quite plausible, and the symbol may communicate multiple truths simultaneously. (Once again, apocalyptic symbolism proves to be evocative, tensive, and polyvalent.[27]) However, there is a fifth interpretation of the trumpets that should be considered, for it most likely captures John's intended meaning. In Revelation, we should probably understand the seven trumpets to be announcing the Day of the Lord.

---

[26]See Part III.B.1.d of the Introduction: "Symbolic Numbers."

[27]For an explanation of this terminology, see the comment on "someone 'like a son of man'" in Revelation 1:13.

In Old Testament prophecy, the term "day of the Lord" is used to refer to any time when God, the Mighty Warrior, judges his enemies and vindicates his people. Quite often, the prophets describe the day of the Lord using battle imagery, including the sounding of the battle trumpet. One fine example appears in Joel 2:1-2,10-11:

> Blow the trumpet in Zion;
>   sound the alarm on my holy hill.
> Let all who live in the land tremble,
>   for the day of the LORD is coming.
> It is close at hand—
>   a day of darkness and gloom,
>   a day of clouds and blackness.
> Like dawn spreading across the mountains
>   a large and mighty army comes,
> such as never was of old
>   nor ever will be in ages to come.
>
> Before them the earth shakes,
>   the sky trembles,
> the sun and moon are darkened,
>   and the stars no longer shine.
> The LORD thunders
>   at the head of his army;
> his forces are beyond number,
>   and mighty are those who obey his command.
> The day of the LORD is great;
>   it is dreadful.
>   Who can endure it?

Later apocalyptic writers use this same sort of imagery, including the trumpet, to describe the ultimate "Day of the Lord" — namely, the resurrection of the dead, the judgment, God's final victory over his enemies, and the coming of his kingdom in its fullness.[28] Jesus and his first disciples build on this tradition by identifying the "Day of the Lord" with the victorious Second Coming of Christ. The following New Testament passages illustrate:

---

[28]See the discussion of "The Shift of the Ages" in Jewish apocalyptic theology found in Part III.B.2.b.(4) of the Introduction.

Immediately after the distress of those days [i.e., the "labor pains"]
> "the sun will be darkened,
>   and the moon will not give its light;
> the stars will fall from the sky,
>   and the heavenly bodies will be shaken."

At that time the sign of the Son of Man will appear in the sky, and all the nations of the earth will mourn. They will see the Son of Man coming on the clouds of the sky, with power and great glory. And he will send his angels with a loud trumpet call, and they will gather his elect from the four winds, from one end of the heavens to the other (Matt 24:29-31).

I declare to you, brothers, that flesh and blood cannot inherit the kingdom of God, nor does the perishable inherit the imperishable. Listen, I tell you a mystery: We will not all sleep, but we will all be changed— in a flash, in the twinkling of an eye, *at the last trumpet*. For *the trumpet will sound*, the dead will be raised imperishable, and we will be changed. For the perishable must clothe itself with the imperishable, and the mortal with immortality. When the perishable has been clothed with the imperishable, and the mortal with immortality, then the saying that is written will come true: "Death has been swallowed up in victory."
> "Where, O death, is your victory?
>   Where, O death, is your sting?"

The sting of death is sin, and the power of sin is the law. But thanks be to God! He gives us the victory through our Lord Jesus Christ (1 Cor 15:50-57).

Brothers, we do not want you to be ignorant about those who fall asleep, or to grieve like the rest of men, who have no hope. We believe that Jesus died and rose again and so we believe that God will bring with Jesus those who have fallen asleep in him. According to the Lord's own word, we tell you that we who are still alive, who are left till the coming of the Lord, will certainly not precede those who have fallen asleep. For the Lord himself will come down from heaven, with a loud command, with the voice of the archangel *and with the trumpet call of God*, and the dead in Christ will rise first. After that, we who are still alive and are left will be caught up together with them in the clouds to meet the Lord in the air. And so we will be with the Lord forever. Therefore encourage each other with these words (1 Thess 4:13-18).

By presenting the future from his own time to the consummation as a series of trumpet calls, John is inviting his readers to view the time in which they live as one long trumpet blast announcing the coming Day of the Lord — the final triumph of God.

h. The Eagle and the Three "Woes"

Prior to the sounding of the last three trumpets, John writes:

> As I watched, I heard an eagle that was flying in midair call out in a loud voice: "Woe! Woe! Woe to the inhabitants of the earth, because of the trumpet blasts about to be sounded by the other three angels!" (8:13).

The Greek term here translated "eagle" (ἀετός, *aetos*) can refer not only to the eagle, but also to several other birds of prey. A good English translation would be "raptor." In this context, John is probably describing a circling vulture, with all the connotations of death normally associated with that creature.

"Woe" (οὐαί, *ouai*) is an exclamation of anger, sadness, and impending doom. The vulture pronounces three "woes," which John links to the sounding of the last three trumpets (see Rev 9:12 and 11:14). As the succession of trumpet blasts reaches its climax, the vulture and the three "woes" create an atmosphere of mounting terror leading up to the "wrath" of the final judgment in 11:18. In similar fashion, three series of "woes" will be pronounced over Babylon in Revelation 18:10,16, and 19.

REVELATION 10

3. Interlude: The Mighty Angel and the Two Witnesses (10:1-11:14)

As we noted above,[1] each of Revelation's three visions of the future contains a series of seven elements, and each series contains an "interlude" between the sixth and seventh elements. These interludes create suspense by causing readers to anticipate the climactic seventh element. They also lead John's readers to consider the positive outcome of their faith in contrast to the negative consequences for those who reject such faith. In this way, the interludes inspire hope and faithful endurance in those suffering for Jesus' sake.

In John's second vision of the future (Rev 8:2-11:19), the interlude appears in 10:1-11:14. This interlude has two main parts: The second part, which describes the murder and subsequent resurrection of God's "two witnesses," focuses on the persecution and deliverance of the church. The first part of the interlude, in which John sees a "mighty angel" holding a "little scroll," tells when this deliverance will take place. The angel declares, "There will be no more delay!"

a. The Mighty Angel with the Little Scroll (10:1-11)

[1]Then I saw another mighty angel coming down from heaven. He was robed in a cloud, with a rainbow above his head; his face was like the sun, and his legs were like fiery pillars. [2]He was holding a little scroll, which lay open in his hand. He planted his right foot on the sea and his left foot on the land, [3]and he gave a loud shout like the roar of a lion. When he shouted, the voices of the seven thunders spoke. [4]And when the seven thunders spoke, I

---

[1]See the discussion of Rev 7:1-17 in Part III.B.4 of the Commentary.

was about to write; but I heard a voice from heaven say, "Seal up what the seven thunders have said and do not write it down."

⁵Then the angel I had seen standing on the sea and on the land raised his right hand to heaven. ⁶And he swore by him who lives for ever and ever, who created the heavens and all that is in them, the earth and all that is in it, and the sea and all that is in it, and said, "There will be no more delay! ⁷But in the days when the seventh angel is about to sound his trumpet, the mystery of God will be accomplished, just as he announced to his servants the prophets."

⁸Then the voice that I had heard from heaven spoke to me once more: "Go, take the scroll that lies open in the hand of the angel who is standing on the sea and on the land."

⁹So I went to the angel and asked him to give me the little scroll. He said to me, "Take it and eat it. It will turn your stomach sour, but in your mouth it will be as sweet as honey." ¹⁰I took the little scroll from the angel's hand and ate it. It tasted as sweet as honey in my mouth, but when I had eaten it, my stomach turned sour. ¹¹Then I was told, "You must prophesy again about many peoples, nations, languages and kings."

(1) The Angel's Appearance. In describing the angel's appearance, John uses the kind of "glory" language seen earlier in the book. This heavenly being has "a rainbow above his head" similar to the rainbow that encircles God's throne in Revelation 4:3. His face shines "like the sun" and his legs glow "like fiery pillars" in a manner that recalls Christ's radiance in 1:15-16.[2] The angel is "robed in a cloud," just as the glory of God is often hidden by a cloud in the Old Testament.[3] By repeating the same symbols, John shows his readers that the person who speaks through the angel is God/Christ.[4]

(2) The Angel's Voice. The angel's voice is "like the roar of a lion," that majestic beast to which John compares Christ in Revelation 5:5.

---

[2]For interpretations of these symbols, see the comments on those earlier passages.
[3]See, e.g., Exodus 13:21; 14:24; 16:10; 19:9; 40:34-38; Numbers 9:15-23; 1 Kings 8:10-11; 2 Chronicles 5:13-14; Psalm 105:39.
[4]See the discussion of the "chain of revelation" found in the comment on Revelation 1:1.

In Amos 3:8, the "lion's roar" is the voice of God himself ("The lion has roared.... The Sovereign LORD has spoken"). Like Amos, John uses "the roar of a lion" to represent the words of God. This is confirmed by the fact that, when the angel shouts, "the voices of the seven thunders" speak. In the Old Testament, thunder often represents the voice of God.[5] The "loud shout like the roar of a lion" and "the voices of the seven thunders" are, then, two symbolic ways of showing that the angel speaks the words of God.

Since "seven" is the apocalyptic number for completeness,[6] the "seven thunders" symbolize the totality of God's words, a complete revelation. Yet John is not allowed to share this complete revelation with his readers: "When the seven thunders spoke, I was about to write; but I heard a voice from heaven say, 'Seal up what the seven thunders have said and do not write it down.'" Such prohibitions are common in ancient revelatory writings.[7] In this case, it shows that John's Revelation does not contain answers to every question about the future that we may ask.[8]

(3) The Little Scroll. The revelation that John *is* allowed to share takes the form of a "little scroll" that the angel gives to him. John takes the scroll and eats it, "digesting" its message so that he may "prophesy again about many peoples, nations, languages and kings." The scroll tastes "sweet as honey" in John's mouth, but it turns his stomach "sour" when he swallows it.[9] The prophecy contains a bittersweet message of salvation and judgment, as chapter 11 will show.

(4) Comparison with Daniel 12. John's description of what the angel says and does calls to mind Daniel 12:1-7. In this text, an angel who looks like a man dressed in linen (see 10:5) tells Daniel:

---

[5]See, e.g., Job 37:2-5; 40:9; Psalms 18:13; 29:3-9; 68:33; 103:7; Isaiah 30:30; cf. Exodus 19:16-19.

[6]See the Introduction, Part III.B.1.d: "Symbolic Numbers."

[7]Dr. Aune cites numerous examples in volume two, pages 562-563 of his commentary. See the Bibliography.

[8]As Dr. Stanley K. McDaniel, retired professor of Johnson Bible College, used to say: "The Bible does not contain all truth, but it contains true truth."

[9]The prophet Ezekiel consumes a similar scroll of "lament and mourning and woe" in Ezekiel 2-3.

"At that time Michael [i.e., the archangel in charge of the Jewish nation[10]], the great prince who protects your people, will arise. There will be a time of distress such as has not happened from the beginning of nations until then [i.e., the "labor pains" or "tribulation"]. But at that time your people—everyone whose name is found written in the book—will be delivered. Multitudes who sleep in the dust of the earth will awake: some to everlasting life, others to shame and everlasting contempt [a reference to the resurrection and final judgment]. Those who are wise will shine like the brightness of the heavens, and those who lead many to righteousness, like the stars for ever and ever [a reference to glorious resurrection existence in the consummated kingdom of God]. But you, Daniel, close up and seal the words of the scroll until the time of the end. Many will go here and there to increase knowledge."

Then I, Daniel, looked, and there before me stood two others, one on this bank of the river and one on the opposite bank. One of them said to the man clothed in linen, who was above the waters of the river, "How long will it be before these astonishing things are fulfilled?"

The man clothed in linen, who was above the waters of the river, lifted his right hand and his left hand toward heaven, and I heard him swear by him who lives forever, saying, "It will be for a time, times and half a time."

A comparison of Daniel 12 with Revelation 10 proves instructive:

Daniel 12	Revelation 10
1. The angel is located "above the waters of the river" (v. 6).f	1. The angel straddles the land and the sea (v. 2).
2. The angel predicts the final events of time from the "labor pains" through the resurrection and final judgment, to the consummation of God's kingdom (vv. 1-3).	2. The angel holds a "little scroll" containing prophecies of the end (vv. 2,8-11).

---

[10]For further discussion of this idea, see the interpretation of the "seven stars" in Revelation 1:12-13,16,20.

3. The angel commands Daniel to seal up this prophecy and hide it until "the time of the end" (v. 4).	3. The scroll is not sealed up, but "open." The angel commands John to eat it so that he may reveal its contents to others (vv. 2,8-11).
4. When asked "How long will it be before these astonishing things are fulfilled?" the angel raises his hands toward heaven and swears by the God "who lives forever" that the fulfilment will be *delayed*. It will take place in the *future* — after "a time, times and half a time"[12] have passed (vv. 6-7).	4. The angel raises his right hand toward heaven and swears by "him who lives for ever and ever" that "There will be *no more delay!*[11] But in the days when the seventh angel is about to sound his trumpet, the mystery of God will be accomplished" (vv. 5-7).

In Daniel's time, the eschatological events of the "labor pains," the resurrection of the dead, and God's final judgment had not yet arrived. These events still belonged to Daniel's *future*. However, in John's time, the eschatological scenario has already begun with the coming of the "labor pains."[13] Even the resurrection of the dead had begun with the resurrection of Christ.[14] For John, the eschatological age is *present*; there is "no more delay" in God's initiating the closing events of history. We are now living in the time of the "labor pains" — that is, during the "sounding" of the first six trumpets. We are living "in the days when the seventh angel is about to sound his trumpet." We are already witnessing "the mystery of God" — that is, the eschatological scenario "announced" by the prophets — being "accomplished" in our own time. Once the "labor pains" have ended, the "sounding" of the seventh trumpet will mark the final judgment and consummation of the kingdom (see below), the fulfillment of God's redemptive purpose.

---

[11]A quote from Habakkuk 2:3.

[12]The symbolic "time, times and half a time" also plays an important role in Revelation, as the comment on Rev 11:2 shows.

[13]See Fig. 2, "The Shape of Christian Apocalyptic Theology," p. 41.

[14]For an explanation, see Part III.B.c.(5) of the Introduction: "The Kingdom of God and the Resurrection of Jesus."

REVELATION 11

b. The Measuring of the Temple and the Two Witnesses (11:1-14)

¹I was given a reed like a measuring rod and was told, "Go and measure the temple of God and the altar, and count the worshipers there. ²But exclude the outer court; do not measure it, because it has been given to the Gentiles. They will trample on the holy city for 42 months. ³And I will give power to my two witnesses, and they will prophesy for 1,260 days, clothed in sackcloth." ⁴These are the two olive trees and the two lampstands that stand before the Lord of the earth. ⁵If anyone tries to harm them, fire comes from their mouths and devours their enemies. This is how anyone who wants to harm them must die. ⁶These men have power to shut up the sky so that it will not rain during the time they are prophesying; and they have power to turn the waters into blood and to strike the earth with every kind of plague as often as they want.

⁷Now when they have finished their testimony, the beast that comes up from the Abyss will attack them, and overpower and kill them. ⁸Their bodies will lie in the street of the great city, which is figuratively called Sodom and Egypt, where also their Lord was crucified. ⁹For three and a half days men from every people, tribe, language and nation will gaze on their bodies and refuse them burial. ¹⁰The inhabitants of the earth will gloat over them and will celebrate by sending each other gifts, because these two prophets had tormented those who live on the earth.

¹¹But after the three and a half days a breath of life from God entered them, and they stood on their feet, and terror struck those who saw them. ¹²Then they heard a loud voice from heaven saying to them, "Come up here." And they went up to heaven in a cloud, while their enemies looked on.

¹³At that very hour there was a severe earthquake and a tenth of the city collapsed. Seven thousand people were killed in the earthquake, and the survivors were terrified and gave glory to the God of heaven.

¹⁴The second woe has passed; the third woe is coming soon.

In the "interlude" of Revelation 10:1–11:14, John helps his Christian readers to view their present hardships in light of the glorious future God has planned for them. In the first part of the interlude (10:1-11, discussed above), John swallows a "little scroll" that enables him to "prophesy again about many peoples, nations, languages and kings" (10:9; compare 11:9). The scroll tastes "sweet as honey" in his mouth, but turns "sour" in his stomach (10:9-10). This signifies that his God-given message has both positive and negative elements. As John "prophesies again" in chapter 11, we find that the bitter aspect of his message concerns persecution and martyrdom endured by the church. The "sweet" component concerns the protection and deliverance God offers his suffering people.

11:1-2a I was given a reed like a measuring rod and was told, "Go and measure the temple of God and the altar, and count the worshipers there. ²But exclude the outer court; do not measure it, because it has been given to the Gentiles.

In Ezekiel 40–43, an angel shows Ezekiel a vision of the temple in Jerusalem and measures it with a measuring rod. John adapts this image for his own purposes here in Revelation 11.

In the first century A.D., the temple area was divided into several courts: First, there was the Court of Priests, just outside the temple building itself, which only priests from the tribe of Levi could enter. The Altar was located in this court. Just outside the Court of Priests was a second court, the Court of Israel, where only Jewish men could congregate. From the Court of Israel one passed through the Nicanor Gate to a third court, the Court of Women, where Jewish women could pray. These three inner courts, closest to the temple proper, were reserved for Jews alone, for those in covenant relationship with God. Only they could come near to the Most Holy Place, the inner room of the temple where the Presence of God dwelled.

Beyond these "Jewish" courts was an outer court called the Court of the Gentiles. The term "Gentiles" (ἔθνη, *ethnē*, which may also be translated "nations") refers to non-Jews, or to anyone not participating in the Mosaic covenant God gave Israel on Mount Sinai. The temple layout itself drew sharp boundaries between Jews and Gentiles, between "insiders" and "outsiders," between those in covenant relationship with God and those outside the covenant. A stone inscription on the temple grounds threatened death to any Gentile who entered the areas reserved for Jews.

In the vision of Revelation 11, John counts the worshipers in the inner court — that is, "Israel," the covenant people of God. However, he excludes the "Gentiles" in the outer court. He draws a sharp distinction between two groups of people — the "insiders" and the "outsiders." Do these symbols refer to literal Jews and Gentiles? No, in John's vision the "Israelites" in the inner court represent Christians — both Jews and Gentiles — who participate in the new covenant established by the sacrificial death of Christ.[1] The "Gentiles" outside represent non-Christians — both Jews and Gentiles — who have not embraced that new covenant. The vision of the measuring of the temple in John's second interlude parallels the vision of the sealing of the 144,000 in his first interlude in Revelation 7:1-8. The first interlude shows that, during the time of the "labor pains" (symbolized by the opening of the first five seals), God puts his seal of ownership on Christians, on the "new Israel," on his covenant people (symbolized by the 144,000 from all the tribes of "Israel"). He marks them for salvation. Likewise, the second interlude shows that, during the time of the "labor pains" (symbolized by the sounding of the first six trumpets), God takes note of who belongs to him (symbolized by the "new Israel" in the inner court of the temple) and who does not (symbolized by the "Gentiles" outside). He takes note of who participates in the new covenant through faith in Christ and who does not. God sets apart his covenant people for deliverance and a place in his eternal kingdom.

What are the present circumstances of God's people, and what will be their future? John offers answers to these questions in the next portion of the interlude, which concerns the trampling of the "holy city" and the prophetic work of the "two witnesses."

11:2b They [i.e., the "Gentiles"] will trample on the holy city

The "holy city" refers to Jerusalem, the city where the temple was

---

[1]On the new covenant, see Part III.B.2.c.(4) of the Introduction: "The Kingdom of God and the Death of Jesus."

located.² King David made Jerusalem the capital city of Israel a thousand years before the Advent of Christ. From that time forward, Jerusalem embodied and represented the Jewish nation just as Washington, D.C., for example, embodies the American nation. The term "holy" means "set apart" or "dedicated" to God's service. The "holy city," Jerusalem, was "set apart" from all other cities as the place where God caused his temple to be built and his presence to dwell. It was also "set apart" in the sense of being the city of the Israelites, God's "holy people," God's covenant community. In the context of Revelation 11, the "holy city" symbolizes Christians, God's "holy people," the new covenant community. According to the vision, the "Gentiles" will "trample on the holy city." In other words, non-Christians will mistreat Christians.

for 42 months.

This abuse will continue "for 42 months." "Forty-two months" is a very important symbolic number in Revelation. Variations on this symbol will appear again and again in John's Apocalypse, beginning with this verse. The symbol has its roots in Daniel 12, the text quoted above in our discussion of Revelation 10. In that Old Testament prophecy, an angel predicts the events of the end times, including the "distress" of the "labor pains," the resurrection of the dead, and the final judgment. When asked, "How long will it be before these astonishing things are fulfilled?" the angel offers the mysterious reply: "It will be for a time, times and half a time" (Dan 12:6-7). In Daniel, then, the phrase "time, times and half a time" refers to the length of time between the giving of the revelation to Daniel and the consummation of the kingdom of God. John adapts this symbol in his own apocalypse, giving it a similar meaning. In Revelation, "a time, times and half a time" is a symbolic number referring to the length of time between the giving of the Revelation to John in A.D. 95-96 and the consummation of the kingdom of God.

John understands the phrase "a time, times and half a time" to refer to "three and a half times." He apparently reasons that the

---

²See, e.g., Nehemiah 11:1,18; Isaiah 52:1; Joel 4:17; Matthew 4:5; 27:53. Compare Revelation 21:2,10,19, where John calls "the new Jerusalem," a symbol for the consummated kingdom of God, the "holy city."

word "time" is singular, referring to *one* "time." The word "times" is plural, referring to more than one "time" — that is, *two* "times." The word "half," of course, refers to *half* a "time." In other words, 1 ("time") + 2 ("times") + ½ ("time") = 3½ ("times"). For John, "three and a half" is a symbolic number equivalent in meaning to "a time, times and half a time."

The value of "three and a half times" depends, of course, on what measurement of "time" one is using, whether it be hours or days or months or years or millennia. In some parts of Revelation, John uses the symbol "three and a half days." In other parts of the Apocalypse, he is apparently thinking in terms of years. Three and a half years consist of 42 months. Three and a half years also consist of 1260 days — if, like John, one is using a lunar calendar in which a year consists of 12 months and each month includes 30 days (30×12×3½ = 1260).

Variations on the symbolic number "three and a half" appear often in John's third vision of the future. He speaks of (1) "a time, times and half a time" in Revelation 12:14; (2) "three and a half days" in 11:9 and 11:11; (3) "42 months" in 11:2 and 13:5; and (4) "1260 days" in 11:3 and 12:6. All are ultimately derived from Daniel 12, and all carry the same symbolic meaning. Grasping this truth is essential for understanding the latter chapters of John's Apocalypse: *In Revelation, the symbols "a time, times and half a time," "42 months," "1260 days," and "three and a half days" are equivalent in meaning. All are symbolic numbers referring to the length of time between the giving of the Revelation to John (A.D. 95-96) and the consummation of God's kingdom – whatever the actual length of that interval may be.*

Against this background, how should we interpret John's statement in Revelation 11:2: The Gentiles "will trample on the holy city for 42 months"? John means that non-Christians will persecute Christians throughout the entire period extending from the late first-century A.D. to Christ's Second Coming and the consummation of God's kingdom. John expresses a similar truth in Revelation 6:9-11, where he describes the opening of the fifth seal. The period between John's time and Christ's return will be marked by the "labor pains" — by the suffering and persecution and martyrdom of Christians at the hands of the enemies of God. John elaborates on this suffering in verses 3-6.

11:3-6 And I will give power to my two witnesses, and they will prophesy for 1,260 days, clothed in sackcloth." These are the two olive trees and the two lampstands that stand before the Lord of the earth. If anyone tries to harm them, fire comes from their mouths and devours their enemies. This is how anyone who wants to harm them must die. These men have power to shut up the sky so that it will not rain during the time they are prophesying; and they have power to turn the waters into blood and to strike the earth with every kind of plague as often as they want.

At this point, John introduces two new characters into his vision narrative — the "two witnesses." How should we interpret this symbol? Whom do the "two witnesses" represent? John identifies the character of the "witnesses" by likening them to four Old Testament heroes — namely, Moses, Elijah, Joshua, and Zerubbabel.

In Exodus 7–12, Moses brings ten terrible plagues on Egypt, including the plague of turning the Nile's waters into blood (Exod 7:14-24). Like Moses, the "two witnesses" have "power to turn the waters into blood and to strike the earth with every kind of plague as often as they want." In 1 Kings 17:1, Elijah, outraged over Israel's idolatry, prays that "there will be neither dew nor rain in the next few years except at my word." The drought persists until Elijah destroys the prophets of Baal, at which time he prays for the rains to come (1 Kgs 18:45). Like Elijah, the "two witnesses" have "power to shut up the sky so that it will not rain during the time they are prophesying." Both Moses and Elijah were mighty prophets, powerful spokesmen for God. By likening the "two witnesses" to these particular Old Testament figures, John identifies the "two witnesses" as prophets, as persons who speak for God.

Joshua[3] and Zerubbabel were leaders of the Jewish community that returned to Jerusalem from Babylonian exile. Zerubbabel, a descendant of King David, acted as governor or "king"[4] (under the

---

[3]This Joshua is to be distinguished from the man of the same name who served as Moses' assistant and led in the Conquest of Canaan.

[4]Zerubbabel is identified as "governor" in Haggai 1:1 and 2:2. In Haggai 2:23 the Lord promises to make Zerubbabel like a "signet ring," that is, a bearer of God's kingly authority. Zechariah 4:14 describes him as "anointed," the mark of both kings and priests. On the anointing of Davidic kings, see the comment on "Jesus Christ" in Rev 1:5.

emperor Darius) and led in the rebuilding of the temple. Joshua, a descendant of Aaron, served as High Priest at the new temple. In Zechariah 4:14, God sets these two men apart by declaring, "These are the two who are anointed to serve the LORD of all the earth." In the same context, the Lord refers to Joshua and Zerubbabel as "two olive trees" next to a golden "lampstand." In a similar fashion, John describes the "two witnesses" in Revelation 11 as "the two olive trees and the two lampstands that stand before the Lord of the earth." By likening the "witnesses" to Joshua and Zerubbabel, John identifies them as priests and kings.

Seen in this light, we should interpret the "two witnesses" as a symbolic representation of the church. At least four observations support this assertion: First, we have seen that the "two witnesses" bear the characteristics of a king (Zerubbabel), a priest (Joshua), and a prophet (Moses and Elijah). Throughout Revelation, Christians are portrayed as kings, priests, and prophets. To illustrate, they "rule" as kings in Revelation 2:26-27, share Christ's kingly "throne" in 3:21, and wear "crowns" like kings in 4:4. They bear the priestly number "twenty-four" in Revelation 4:4, carry "bowls of incense" like priests in 5:8, and approach the temple and altar like priests in 11:1. John praises Christ as the one "who has made us to be a kingdom and priests" in Revelation 1:6 and 5:10. Finally, Christians speak "the word of God" in 6:9 and offer "testimony" in 12:11, thereby acting as the Lord's spokesmen or "prophets."

Second, the "two witnesses" are called "witnesses" (μάρτυς, *martys*). Elsewhere in Revelation John applies this title to Christians – and particularly to believers who are killed because of their testimony to Christ.[5]

Third, John says in verse 6 that the "two witnesses" have power "to strike the earth with every kind of plague as often as they want." As we have seen, this statement links the "two witnesses" with the prophet Moses. At the same time, it may serve to identify the "two witnesses" with the Christian "saints" of Revelation 8:3, for it is the

---

[5]See Revelation 2:13; 17:6; cf. 1:2,9; 6:9; 12:11; 20:4. For a discussion of Christian "witness" or "martyrdom" in Revelation, see the comment on "the faithful witness" in Revelation 1:5.

prayers of those "saints" that unleash the "plagues" of the first six trumpets.[6]

Fourth, as we will see in the next few verses, the "two witnesses" are persecuted and killed by the forces of evil during the period between John's prophecy and the consummation of God's kingdom. This is exactly the situation faced by Christians throughout the Book of Revelation. It is the reason the "two witnesses" wear sackcloth, the black garment of mourning.[7] The evidence suggests, then, that the "two witnesses" in Revelation 11 should be understood as a symbol for Christians.

If John intends for the "two witnesses" to symbolize Christians, then why are there "two" witnesses? Why not one or twelve or one hundred and forty-four thousand witnesses? The number "two" is symbolic, and it is based on Deuteronomy 19:15: "A matter must be established by the testimony of two or three witnesses."[8] Two witnesses are required in order for testimony to be accepted as valid in a court of law. Two witnesses are required to ensure that a charge does not become "one man's word against another's." "Two," then, is the number for valid or reliable witness. By portraying the church as "two" witnesses, John communicates the fact that its testimony concerning Christ is valid, dependable, trustworthy, and true.

In verse 3 the Lord says, "I will give power to my two witnesses, and they will prophesy for 1,260 days." As explained above,[9] the "1,260 days" symbolize the entire period from the giving of the Revelation in A.D. 95-96 to the Second Coming of Christ. Throughout these centuries, Christians will be functioning as God's "prophets," empowered by his Holy Spirit to spread the gospel of Christ. When reading this verse, one cannot help but to recall the Lord's words to his disciples:

> You will receive power when the Holy Spirit comes on you; and you will be my witnesses in Jerusalem, and in all Judea and Samaria, and to the ends of the earth (Acts 1:8).

---

[6]See Part III.C.2.f of the Commentary: "Fire from the Altar: The 'Present Evil Age' and 'Labor Pains' as an Answer to Prayer" in Revelation 8-9.
[7]See, e.g., Genesis 37:34; 2 Samuel 3:31; Esther 4:1-3; Psalm 30:11; Isaiah 15:3; 22:12; Lamentations 2:10; Joel 1:13; Amos 8:10.
[8]Cf. Deuteronomy 17:6; Matthew 18:16; 2 Corinthians 13:1.
[9]See the explanation of the "42 months" in Revelation 11:2.

This gospel of the kingdom will be preached in the whole world as a testimony to all nations [or "all Gentiles"], and then the end will come (Matt 24:14).

Verse 5 says that, "if anyone tries to harm" the "two witnesses," then "fire comes from their mouths and devours their enemies. This is how anyone who wants to harm them must die." There is something about the message of the "two witnesses" — what "comes from their mouths" — that hurts and destroys the enemies of God. John is probably thinking of the gospel message, which is both a message of salvation for those who put their faith in Christ, as well as a message of condemnation and destruction for those who oppose him. The image has precedent in Old Testament passages such as Jeremiah 5:14: "Therefore this is what the LORD God Almighty says: 'Because the people have spoken these words, I will make my words in your mouth a fire and these people the wood it consumes.'" Compare John's statement in verse 10: "These two prophets had tormented those who live on the earth."

11:7 Now when they have finished their testimony, the beast that comes up from the Abyss will attack them, and overpower and kill them.

In Revelation, the "Abyss" is the reservoir of evil, the dwelling place of demons.[10] We have seen that, in apocalyptic literature, "beasts" usually symbolize political powers allied with Satan against God and His people.[11] "The beast that comes up from the Abyss" probably represents, then, political powers that have become "demonic" by opposing Christ and his church. (John will develop this theme later in chapter 13.) In John's time and place, they take the form of Roman authorities who persecute and kill Christians.[12]

John says that these enemies of Christ and the church "overpower" God's people. The Greek verb rendered "overpower" is the same word translated elsewhere as "overcome." A major theme in

---

[10]See the discussion of "Demon Locusts from the Abyss," etc., in Revelation 8–9.

[11]See Part III.B.1.b of the Introduction: "Symbolism."

[12]See Part IV.B.3 of the Introduction: "Persecution Related to Emperor Worship in Asia Minor."

Revelation is that Satan and his allies "overcome" by killing Christians, while Christians "overcome" evil by persisting in their witness to Christ and remaining faithful even to death.[13] According to John's vision, Christians die only after they "have finished their testimony." God will not allow the church to be erased from the earth; he will not allow the gospel message to be totally silenced. The church's prophetic witness to Christ will continue throughout the "1,260 days" (v. 3), or until its Lord returns.

11:8 Their bodies will lie in the street of the great city, which is figuratively called Sodom and Egypt, where also their Lord was crucified.

Some students of Scripture understand "the great city" to be a reference to the entire human community. In support of this view, verse 9 places "men from every people, tribe, language and nation" in the city. This interpretation is certainly plausible, and it may be correct. However, John also describes "the great city" as the place where the "Lord was crucified." This statement suggests that the symbol may carry a narrower meaning.

The city where the Lord Jesus was crucified is Jerusalem, the capital city of the Jewish nation. John figuratively calls Jerusalem "Sodom," which is the name of an ancient city destroyed by God for its outrageous sin.[14] He also calls it "Egypt," thereby likening it to the evil nation that held Israel in slavery for 400 years.[15] John is probably making a reference to Jewish participation in the persecution and killing of Christians.[16] Earthly Jerusalem claims to be the "holy city;" non-Christian Jews claim to be a "holy people."[17] However, since they oppose God's Christ and God's church, John uncovers their true character by calling them "Sodom" and "Egypt."

---

[13]See Part II.D of the Commentary: "'Overcomers' in Revelation."
[14]See Genesis 18–19.
[15]See Exodus 1–14; cf. Genesis 15:13.
[16]On Jewish opposition to early Christians, see Part IV.B.3 of the Introduction ("Persecution Related to Emperor Worship in Asia Minor"), as well as Part II.C.2 of the Commentary ("Pressures and Opposition from Outside the Christian Community").
[17]On Jerusalem as the "holy city," see the comment on Rev 11:2.

11:9-10 For three and a half days men from every people, tribe, language and nation will gaze on their bodies and refuse them burial. The inhabitants of the earth will gloat over them and will celebrate by sending each other gifts, because these two prophets had tormented those who live on the earth.

To refuse a person burial, to allow the dogs and vultures and other scavengers to mutilate his/her body, was a sign of tremendous dishonor and disrespect.[18] The point of the symbol is that people of all nations will hold Christians in contempt. Why? Because the church's message "torments those who live on the earth," pronouncing judgment on their idolatry and their sin.[19]

The "three and a half days" of verse 9 is equivalent in meaning to the "42 months" of verse 2 and the "1,260 days" of verse 3. These symbolic numbers refer to the period between the giving of the Revelation to John in A.D. 95-96 to the Second Coming of Christ and the consummation of God's kingdom.[20] During these centuries, the church will carry out its prophetic ministry of proclaiming the gospel of Christ (v. 3), all the while enduring persecution and scorn and martyrdom at the hands of Jews and Gentiles from every nation (vv. 2,9).

11:11 But after the three and a half days a breath of life from God entered them, and they stood on their feet, and terror struck those who saw them.

"After the three and a half days" (i.e., at the time of Christ's return — see above), the "breath of life from God" enters the "two witnesses" (i.e., Christians), and they stand "on their feet." This is a clear reference to the resurrection, when God raises and vindicates his people.[21] This event, of course, strikes "terror" in the hearts of those who have opposed Christ and his church. Compare Revelation

---

[18]See, e.g., 1 Samuel 31:8-13; 2 Samuel 21:9-14; 1 Kings 14:10-13; 2 Kings 9:34-37.

[19]See the comment on the similar statement in verse 5: "If anyone tries to harm [the 'two witnesses'], fire comes from their mouths and devours their enemies. This is how anyone who wants to harm them must die."

[20]For an explanation, see the comment on the "42 months" in Rev 11:2.

[21]For more on the subject of the resurrection, see Parts III.B.2.b.(4) "The Shift of the Ages" and III.B.2.c.(5) "The Kingdom of God and the Resurrection of Jesus" of the Introduction.

1:7: "Look, he is coming with the clouds, and every eye will see him, *even those who pierced him*; and *all the peoples of the earth will mourn because of him*. So shall it be! Amen."

11:12-13 Then they heard a loud voice from heaven saying to them, "Come up here." And they went up to heaven in a cloud, while their enemies looked on.

At that very hour there was a severe earthquake and a tenth of the city collapsed. Seven thousand people were killed in the earthquake, and the survivors were terrified and gave glory to the God of heaven.

As in the first vision of the future (Rev 6:2) and the third vision of the future (16:18), the "earthquake" symbolizes God's final judgment. This event marks the end of world as we know it and the end of the "present evil age."[22] The "seven thousand people" killed in the "earthquake" symbolize the full number of non-Christians, who are condemned by God at the judgment.[23] The "survivors" represent Christians, who are filled with the "fear of the Lord" upon witnessing this awesome event. When John says, "a tenth of the city collapsed" in the "earthquake," he means that a *portion* of the human community, Jew and Gentile, perishes at the final judgment.[24] As we will see in our discussion of Revelation 21-22, God does not intend to obliterate his good creation totally, but to redeem it by purging the evil from it.[25]

At the "very hour" that the final judgment occurs, the "two witnesses" — that is, the church — are caught "up to heaven in a cloud." This is John's way of saying that, at the final judgment, Christians will be "saved" — that is, raised from the dead, welcomed into the Lord's presence, and given a place in his eternal kingdom. The

---

[22]See Fig. 2, "The Shape of Christian Apocalyptic Theology," p. 41.

[23]On "seven thousand" as an apocalyptic number for "completeness," see Part III.B.1.d of the Introduction: "Symbolic Numbers." On the destruction of nonbelievers at the final judgment, compare the vision of the "lake of fire" in Rev 20:11-15.

[24]On the symbolic significance of the number "ten," see Part III.B.1.d of the Introduction: "Symbolic Numbers."

[25]Compare Revelation 16:19, where "the great city split into three parts" in the "earthquake" of the final judgment.

Apostle Paul speaks of this event using similar language in 1 Thessalonians 4:15-18:

> According to the Lord's own word, we tell you that we who are still alive, who are left till the coming of the Lord, will certainly not precede those who have fallen asleep [i.e., Christians who have died before Christ's Second Coming]. For the Lord himself will come down from heaven, with a loud command, with the voice of the archangel and with the trumpet call of God, and the dead in Christ will rise first. After that, we who are still alive and are left *will be caught up together with them in the clouds to meet the Lord in the air. And so we will be with the Lord forever.* Therefore encourage each other with these words.[26]

(1) A Note on the "Rapture." Some students of Scripture anticipate a time when most Christians will be caught up to heaven *prior* to the Second Coming of Christ and the final judgment. Non-Christians and Christian Jews will then remain to endure the "labor pains" or "tribulation."[27] This sudden removal of the church from the world is called the "Rapture." Two biblical passages are offered as the primary support for this view — namely, Revelation 11:12 and Matthew 24:36-41.

Revelation 11:12 does indeed speak of Christians (symbolized by the "two witnesses") being caught up into heaven to enter the presence of Christ. However, this "rapture" does not occur *prior* to the Lord's return. Instead, it occurs at the "very hour" of the "earthquake" (v. 13) — that is, at the time of Christ's Second Coming and the final judgment. Read in context, Revelation 11:12 offers no support for a pretribulation rapture of the church.

Matthew 24:36-41 reads as follows:

> No one knows about that day or hour, not even the angels in heaven, nor the Son, but only the Father. As it was in the days of Noah, so it will be at the coming of the Son of Man. For in the days before the flood, people were eating and drinking, marrying and giving in marriage, up to the day Noah entered the ark; and

---

[26]Compare also Matthew 24:31.

[27]Variations of this idea are characteristic of Dispensational Premillenialism, a view that will be discussed further in the commentary on Revelation 20.

they knew nothing about what would happen until the flood came and took them all away. That is how it will be at the coming of the Son of Man. Two men will be in the field; one will be taken and the other left. Two women will be grinding with a hand mill; one will be taken and the other left.

Some understand verses 40-41 to mean: "Two men will be in the field; [the Christian] one will be [suddenly] taken [up into heaven] and the other [non-Christian man will be] left [on earth to endure a period of tribulation prior to the Second Coming of Christ and the final judgment]. Two women will be grinding with a hand mill; [the Christian] one will be [suddenly] taken [up into heaven] and the other [non-Christian woman will be] left [on earth to endure a period of tribulation prior to the Second Coming and final judgment]." This kind of interpretation has captured the imagination of many modern-day Christians, inspiring books, movies, and even amusing bumper stickers that read: "WARNING: In case of Rapture, this vehicle will be unoccupied." However, a closer reading of Matthew's Gospel proves this understanding of Jesus' words to be unfounded.

First, the Lord is not talking about events that will happen *prior* to his Second Coming. In verse 37 he clearly indicates that he is talking about what will take place *"at the coming of the Son of Man"* — that is, his "coming on the clouds of the sky, with power and great glory" (Matt 24:30).

Second, one of the ongoing themes in the Gospel of Matthew concerns the *separation* between the righteous and the unrighteous, between Christians and non-Christians, that will take place at the final judgment. To illustrate, the two groups are likened to "wheat" separated from "chaff" in Matthew 3:12, "good trees" separated from "bad trees" in 7:19, "wheat" separated from "weeds" in 13:30, "good fish" separated from "bad fish" in 13:48, those wearing "wedding clothes" separated from those not wearing "wedding clothes" in 22:12-14, "wise virgins" separated from "foolish virgins" in 25:10-12, and "sheep" separated from "goats" in 25:32. The Lord's statement concerning the two men in the field and two women grinding meal simply represents another contribution to this theme. At the Second Coming of Christ and the final judgment, "one will be taken and the other left."

(2) A Note on the "Protection" of the "New Israel" from the "Plagues." We noted above[28] that, in his second vision of the future, John compares the suffering of the "labor pains" and "present evil age" to the ten plagues poured out against Egypt. In this way, he encourages his readers to think of Christ's return and the consummation of the kingdom as a sort of "Second Exodus" for God's covenant people.

In the Book of Exodus, the plagues that torment the Egyptians do not affect the people of Israel (see Exod 8:22-23; 9:4-7,26; 10:23; 12:13,23,27). In contrast to Israel, John makes clear that Christians — the "new Israel" — are certainly not exempt from the "plagues" of Revelation 8–9. Believers (symbolized by the "two witnesses") suffer hardship, persecution, and even death during the "labor pains" and "present evil age."

However, in the midst of their suffering, the Lord takes note of who belongs to him — a truth signified by the measuring of the temple in Revelation 11:1-2. In the end, God also raises his servants from the dead, undoing the evil work of their enemies. Christians endure the "plagues," but the "plagues" do them no *permanent* harm. In this sense, God protects and delivers his "new Israel," just as he delivered the first Israel centuries ago.

11:14 The second woe has passed; the third woe is coming soon.

For an interpretation of this text, see the comment on "The Eagle and the Three 'Woes'" in Revelation 8:13.

4. The Final Judgment and Consummation of God's Kingdom: Trumpet Seven (11:15-19)

¹⁵The seventh angel sounded his trumpet, and there were loud voices in heaven, which said:

> **"The kingdom of the world has become the**
> **kingdom of our Lord and of his Christ,**
> **and he will reign for ever and ever."**

¹⁶And the twenty-four elders, who were seated on their thrones before God, fell on their faces and worshiped God, ¹⁷saying:

---

[28]See Part III.C.1.c of the Commentary: "The Dominant Image: God's Coming Kingdom as a 'Second Exodus' for His People."

"We give thanks to you, Lord God Almighty,
 the One who is and who was,
because you have taken your great power
 and have begun to reign.
¹⁸The nations were angry;²⁹
 and your wrath has come.
The time has come for judging the dead,
 and for rewarding your servants the prophets
and your saints and those who reverence your
  name,
 both small and great—
and for destroying those who destroy the earth."³⁰

¹⁹**Then God's temple in heaven was opened, and within his temple was seen the ark of his covenant. And there came flashes of lightning, rumblings, peals of thunder, an earthquake and a great hailstorm.**

11:15-19 The sounding of the seventh trumpet announces the final judgment and the coming of God's kingdom reign in its fullness. In verse 18, John highlights the "separation" God makes at the final judgment between his servants and his enemies: Those who "reverence" God's name, "both small and great," receive a "reward." Those who oppose God's rule endure "wrath" and destruction.

With all opposition to God erased, "The kingdom of the world has become the kingdom of our Lord and of his Christ, and he will reign for ever and ever" (v. 15). This statement, which inspired the great "Hallelujah Chorus" of Handel's "Messiah," offers one of the best definitions of the consummated kingdom of God in Revelation. All worldly authorities must step aside as God and his Christ mount the throne, bringing everything in the universe under their sovereign will.

With his enemies destroyed, his people redeemed, and the Lord on the throne, "God's temple in heaven was opened, and within his

---

²⁹John here alludes to Psalm 2:1 ("Why do the nations rage?" LXX), a "Royal Psalm" discussed in the comment on the title "Christ" in Revelation 1:5.

³⁰On "those who destroy the earth," see the section of the commentary on Revelation 8–9 labeled "Earth, Trees, Grass, Springs, Rivers, Sea, and Sea Creatures: The Effect of the 'Present Evil Age' and 'Labor Pains' on the Natural World."

temple was seen the ark of his covenant. And there came flashes of lightning, rumblings, peals of thunder, an earthquake and a great hailstorm." The thunder, lightning, hail, and earthquake represent a theophany — a visible and audible sign that the invisible God is present and working in a powerful way.[31]

The symbol of the "ark of his covenant" within God's temple communicates at least three truths: First, the Ark of the Covenant is a model of God's heavenly throne.[32] The ark, then, signifies that God is sovereign, that his kingdom has come. Second, the ark is the place where God's presence dwells. Redeemed Christians enjoy not only God's beneficent kingship over them, but also his loving presence with them.[33] Third, the Israel of the Old Testament era came through the ten plagues, saw their enemies destroyed, and experienced God's presence in their camp over the ark in the tabernacle/temple. Likewise, John's vision portrays Christians passing through the "plagues" of the first six trumpets, seeing the destruction of their enemies at the Second Coming of Christ, and then experiencing God's presence symbolized by the Ark of the Covenant. The ark, then, forms a fitting conclusion to John's second vision of the future. It completes the dominant image of the vision by helping to portray the coming of God's kingdom as a "Second Exodus" for his covenant people.[34]

The second vision (Rev 8:2–11:19) takes the form of the sounding of seven trumpets, with seven being the apocalyptic number for "completeness."[35] In the vision, John presents the complete future from the giving of Revelation in A.D. 95-96 to the consummation of the kingdom of God. The consummation itself occurs with the sounding of the seventh trumpet in Revelation 11:15-19. Accordingly, the "twenty-four elders" (symbolizing the church[36])

---

[31]Compare Revelation 4:5. Other biblical examples of theophanies include Exod 19:16-19; 1 Kgs 19:11-12; and Matt 27:51-53.

[32]For an explanation, see the comment on Rev 4:6b,8, fn 10.

[33]See the preceding note, as well as the comment on Christ's eyes, feet, and face in Rev 1:14-16.

[34]For further discussion of this dominant image, see Part III.C.1.c of the Commentary.

[35]See the Introduction, Part III.B.1.d: "Symbolic Numbers."

[36]See the comment on Rev 4:4.

address the deity as "Lord God Almighty, the One who is and who was." John's more complete form of this title has been "the one who is, and who was, and who is to come."[37] He omits the third element in 11:17 because, at this point in the vision, the Lord has already "come" again.

5. Summary: John's Second Vision of the Future (8:2–11:19)

In Revelation 8:2–11:19, John offers the second of three visions of the future. He presents the future in terms of the sounding of seven trumpets that announce the approaching Day of the Lord. Since "seven" is the number symbolizing completeness, the trumpets also signify the complete future from John's time to the consummation of the kingdom.

How will the future unfold? According to the vision, it will resemble Israel's experience with Egypt. First, as Israel witnessed ten great plagues poured out against Egypt, so will the human race experience the hardships of the "labor pains" and the "present evil age" (trumpets one through six).

Through vivid imagery, John emphasizes aspects of the "labor pains" not seen in the first vision, such as the demonic nature of human suffering and the harmful effects of sin on the natural world.

During this period, Christians (the "two witnesses" described in the "interlude") will carry out a prophetic ministry of spreading the gospel. However, many people, both Jew and Gentile, will continue to reject this message. They will ridicule believers, persecute them, and even kill them because of their witness to Christ. In the midst of these hardships, God will take note of who belongs to him and who does not (the measuring of the temple).

Finally, the Lord will deliver the church from its enemies, just as he delivered Israel from Egypt (trumpet seven). Christ will return, raise the dead, carry out the final judgment, destroy those who oppose him, and welcome his redeemed people into his presence (the Ark of the Covenant). That Day will be like a "Second Exodus" for the covenant people of God.

---

[37]See Revelation 1:4,8; 4:8. On this title, as well as the title "Almighty," see the comment on Revelation 1:4.

REVELATION 12

D. THE THIRD VISION OF THE FUTURE (12:1-22:6)

1. The Structure of the Third Vision

John's third vision of the future appears in Revelation 12:1-22:6. It communicates the same basic picture of the future found in the first two visions — namely, a time of "labor pains" (12:1-13:18) followed by the final judgment and the consummation of God's kingdom (14:1-22:6).[1] Of the three visions, the third is by far the longest and most detailed. It uncovers important facets of the future not addressed in the earlier two visions.[2]

2. The "Labor Pains": The Dragon's War against the Saints (12:1-13:18)

a. The Dragon, the Woman, and the Male Child (12:1-17)

¹**A great and wondrous sign appeared in heaven: a woman clothed with the sun, with the moon under her feet and a crown of twelve stars on her head. ²She was pregnant and cried out in pain as she was about to give birth. ³Then another sign appeared in heaven: an enormous red dragon with seven heads and ten horns and seven crowns on his heads. ⁴His tail swept a third of the stars out of the sky and flung them to the earth. The dragon stood in front of the woman who was about to give birth, so that he might**

---

[1] For a discussion of these concepts, see Parts III.B.2.b-d of the Introduction. For a graphic representation, see Fig. 2, "The Shape of Christian Apocalyptic Theology," p. 41.

[2] For a more detailed discussion of the Structure of Revelation, see Part V of the Introduction.

devour her child the moment it was born. ⁵She gave birth to a son, a male child, who will rule all the nations with an iron scepter. And her child was snatched up to God and to his throne. ⁶The woman fled into the desert to a place prepared for her by God, where she might be taken care of for 1,260 days.

⁷And there was war in heaven. Michael and his angels fought against the dragon, and the dragon and his angels fought back. ⁸But he was not strong enough, and they lost their place in heaven. ⁹The great dragon was hurled down—that ancient serpent called the devil, or Satan, who leads the whole world astray. He was hurled to the earth, and his angels with him.

¹⁰Then I heard a loud voice in heaven say:

"Now have come the salvation and the power and
    the kingdom of our God,
and the authority of his Christ.
For the accuser of our brothers,
    who accuses them before our God day and night,
has been hurled down.
¹¹They overcame him
    by the blood of the Lamb
    and by the word of their testimony;
they did not love their lives so much
    as to shrink from death.
¹²Therefore rejoice, you heavens
    and you who dwell in them!
But woe to the earth and the sea,
    because the devil has gone down to you!
He is filled with fury,
    because he knows that his time is short."

¹³When the dragon saw that he had been hurled to the earth, he pursued the woman who had given birth to the male child. ¹⁴The woman was given the two wings of a great eagle, so that she might fly to the place prepared for her in the desert, where she would be taken care of for a time, times and half a time, out of the serpent's reach. ¹⁵Then from his mouth the serpent spewed water like a river, to overtake the woman and sweep her away with the torrent. ¹⁶But the earth helped the woman by opening its mouth and swallowing the river that the dragon had spewed out of his mouth. ¹⁷Then the dragon was enraged at the woman and went off to make war against the rest of her offspring—those who obey God's commandments and hold to the testimony of Jesus.

Three main characters fill John's narrative in chapter 12 — the "red dragon," the "woman," and the "male child." Below, we will seek to discern the identity of each.

(1) The Identity of the Male Child. The "male child" obviously symbolizes Jesus, the Messiah. The proof lies in verse 5, which says: "She gave birth to a son, a male child, who will rule all the nations with an iron scepter." John here alludes to Psalm 2:7-9, a "Royal Psalm" in which the Davidic king or "Messiah" says:

⁷I will proclaim the decree of the LORD:

He said to me, "You are my Son;
  today I have become your Father.
⁸Ask of me,
  and I will make *the nations* your inheritance,
  the ends of the earth your possession.
⁹*You will rule them with an iron scepter;*
  you will dash them to pieces like pottery."

For a discussion of this Psalm and its application to Jesus, see the comment on the title "Jesus Christ" in Revelation 1:5.

If the male child is Jesus, then the remainder of verse 5 ("And her child was snatched up to God and to his throne.") refers to Jesus' ascension into heaven to take a seat at God's right hand. In a single verse, John moves from Jesus' birth, through his earthly ministry, death, resurrection and ascension, to his exaltation by God.

(2) The Identity of the Red Dragon. In verse 9, John himself identifies the "red dragon" as "that ancient serpent called the devil, or Satan, who leads the whole world astray." A close examination of the prophet's description of Satan proves instructive:

First, "Satan" is the Hebrew term for "adversary" or "accuser." We see Satan performing the role of "accuser" in, for example, Job 1-2. In Revelation 12:10 John calls Satan "the accuser of our brothers, who accuses them before our God day and night." The term "devil" (διάβολος, *diabolos*), a Greek translation of "Satan," likewise means "adversary," "accuser," or "slanderer." By John's time, apocalyptic writers understand the biblical "Satan" to be a fallen angel, the leader of a group of demons bent on destroying the good works of God.[3]

---

[3]For further discussion of angels and demons, see Part III.B.2.b.(1) of the Introduction: "Rebellion in Heaven."

Second, John calls Satan a "serpent" (ὄφις, *ophis*). He thereby identifies him with the "serpent" (*ophis*) of Genesis 3, which tempted Adam and Eve to sin and thereby "led the whole world astray."

Third, John calls him a "dragon" (δράκων, *drakōn*, the noun form of the Greek verb δέρκομαι, *derkomai*, which means "to gleam or shimmer" like the scales of a reptile). The term "dragon" — or "shimmery thing" — can be used as a synonym for "serpent" since dragons were first conceived of as great shimmering serpents.

Fourth, the fact that the dragon has "seven heads" identifies him with a particular "serpent" — namely, Leviathan, the seven-headed sea serpent used in Jewish apocalyptic as a symbol for evil and chaos.[4]

Fifth, the dragon wears "seven crowns" — one for each head. It makes itself out to be a king — a king in the place of the rival king about to be born, the "male child" whom the dragon hopes to destroy.

Sixth, the dragon bears "ten horns." It thus resembles the "fourth beast" of Daniel 7:7. In Daniel, the fourth beast represents an evil empire that torments Israel, God's covenant people. After a time, the Lord slays the beast and replaces this human kingdom with the eternal kingdom of God (see Dan 7:11-14). The ten horns symbolize ten kings over this doomed empire. By adapting this image, John adds political connotations to his presentation of the dragon.

Seventh, John writes that the dragon's "tail swept a third of the stars out of the sky and flung them to the earth." This image is reminiscent of Daniel 8:10, in which a "little horn" (probably representing King Antiochus IV "Epiphanes"[5]) "threw some of the starry host down to the earth and trampled on them." In other words, he

---

[4]Compare Isaiah 27:1 (LXX), which describes Leviathan as both a *drakōn* ("dragon") and an *ophis* ("serpent"); Jeremiah 51:34, which calls Nebuchadnezzar a "serpent" to be destroyed by God; and Ezekiel 29:3-5 and 32:2-8, which likewise picture Pharaoh as a scaly "sea monster" killed by God. For further discussion of Leviathan, see Part III.E.3.a of the Commentary, which concerns Revelation 2:17: "The Hidden Manna, the Messianic Banquet, Behemoth and Leviathan."

[5]By taking the name "Epiphanes," this blasphemous king sought to identify himself as a manifestation, or "epiphany," of God on earth.

exalted himself over even the angels in heaven.[6] John's image also pictures Satan as the one who led a group of angels ("stars" in v. 4, "his angels" in vv. 7-9) to rebel against God and to be cast out of heaven — a common idea in apocalyptic literature.[7]

In Revelation 12, John seems to be presenting Satan not so much as an individual being (although that is not excluded), but as the leader or personification of all the forces of evil that oppose God and his Messiah. The dragon stands for Satan himself as the ancient corrupter of the human race and rival to Christ (Satan, the devil, seven crowns, the one "who leads the whole world astray"), demonic powers (stars flung from heaven), evil political powers (ten horns, the one who sweeps the stars from the sky), and the forces of evil and chaos in general (dragon, serpent, Leviathan, seven heads). Satan is the individual evil behind evil in its variety of forms. John will further develop this image later in the book.

(3) Five Theories Regarding the Identity of the Woman. Whereas the "male child" obviously represents Christ, and the "enormous red dragon" obviously symbolizes Satan, the identity of the "woman" is harder to discern. Let us begin by examining the specific statements John makes about her.

First, the woman is "clothed with the sun, with the moon under her feet and a crown of twelve stars on her head" (v. 1). Her "wondrous" appearance — with the sun, moon, and stars surrounding her — is reminiscent of the way ancient writers portray a goddess. Does John intend for us to view the woman as a goddess? Do the "twelve stars" of her crown represent the twelve tribes of Israel, associating her with the covenant people of God? Do they represent the twelve constellations of the zodiac (a popular decorative motif in John's time), associating the woman with the heavens, the dwelling place of deities?

Second, the woman is pregnant and crying out in pain as she struggles to give birth (v. 2).

Third, she gives birth to the Messiah — she is the mother of the Messiah (v. 5).

---

[6]On "stars" as a symbol for angels, see the comment on the "seven stars" in Revelation 1:12-13,16,20.
[7]See Part III.B.2.b.(1) of the Introduction: "Rebellion in Heaven."

Fourth, verse 17 shows that she is also the mother of Christians. "Those who obey God's commands and hold to the testimony of Jesus" are also her "offspring."

Fifth, the woman is "pursued" by Satan (v. 13).

Sixth, she flees to the desert on the wings of an eagle (vv. 6,14).

Seventh, God cares for the woman for "1,260 days" or for "a time, times and half a time" (vv. 6,14-16). As we have seen, these symbolic numbers represent the entire period from John's receipt of the Revelation in A.D. 95-96 to the consummation of the kingdom of God.[8] The woman, then, remains alive throughout the centuries leading up to the Second Coming of Christ.

What does this "wondrous sign" mean? What "woman" could possibly fit this description? Scholars have put forward a number of theories in an attempt to answer this question. We will examine the leading theories below.

First, some suggest that the woman symbolizes Mary, the wife of Joseph and the virgin mother of Jesus. Christians of certain traditions (e.g., Roman Catholics), with their exalted view of Mary, will have no difficulty seeing the Virgin in Revelation 12. Although Mary is certainly worthy of high honor and praise, other believers will conclude that this theory strains probability. Would John portray Mary, a mere human being, as a goddess? In what sense could Mary be viewed as the Mother of the whole church? How could a woman who died centuries ago be said to live on to the consummation? Did Christians of the late first century already view Mary in this light?[9]

A second group of scholars suggests that the "woman" of Revelation 12 symbolizes the church, the Body of Christ. This theory certainly explains many elements of the vision, including how Christians can be the woman's offspring, how she is pursued by

---

[8]For an explanation, see the comment on the "42 months" in Revelation 11:2.

[9]In brief, orthodox Catholics would respond that Mary is not being portrayed as a deity or goddess, but as exalted. She is the "Mother" of the church in the sense that she gives birth to the Messiah, who himself founds the church. She lives on through the "1,260 days" in the sense that she did not die, but was taken up bodily into heaven, where she now leads the saints in interceding for the church. The evidence that such a view of Mary was held in the first century is Revelation 12 itself.

Satan, and how she can live on to the Second Coming. However, it is difficult to see how John could describe the church as giving birth to Jesus!

A third group suggests that the "woman" is Eve, the wife of Adam. They base this theory on Genesis 3:1-16, particularly verse 15 which says that the serpent will wound Eve's "offspring" ("strike his heel"), but the "offspring" will kill the serpent ("crush your head").

Identifying the "woman" in Revelation 12 as Eve — and the "male child" as Eve's promised "offspring" — accounts for Jesus' destroying Satan later in the story (e.g., in Rev 20:10). However, this theory does not explain other important elements of the vision. For example, why would John portray sinful Eve as a goddess? In what sense does Eve enjoy protection by God throughout the "1,260 days"?

According to a fourth theory, the "woman" of Revelation 12 symbolizes Israel — first the Jews who received the Mosaic covenant, and then later Christians (the "new Israel," both Jews and Gentiles) who embrace the new covenant.[10] It may be difficult to explain why John portrays "Israel" as a goddess. However, this theory seems consistent with most of the other statements in the biblical text. The "crown of twelve stars" on the woman's head identifies her with the twelve tribes of "Israel," the covenant people of God. As Old Testament Israel, the woman "gives birth" to the Messiah. We find some precedent for this idea in the Dead Sea Scrolls.[11] As the "new Israel" or church, the woman "gives birth" to Christians, is pursued by Satan, and receives protection from God throughout the "1,260 days" leading up to the Second Coming of Christ. This is the most plausible interpretation of Revelation 12 we have considered thus far.

A fifth theory is similar to the fourth. According to this view, the woman symbolizes either the hill of Zion or Jerusalem, the city built on the hill of Zion. Evidence supporting this theory includes Isaiah 66:7-13 (which pictures Zion as a woman giving birth to a nation) and 4 Ezra 9:38–10:59 (which similarly pictures Zion as the mother of Jerusalem and all Israelites). Later in Revelation, John himself

---

[10]On the church as the "new Israel," see the discussion of "The Sealing of the 144,000" in Revelation 7:1-8.

[11]Israel, the People of God, is pictured as a mother bringing forth the Messiah in the Hymns Scroll (1QH 3:4 — see Vermes, p. 157).

portrays two other cities as women — namely, "Babylon" or Rome (the "great prostitute") in chapters 17-18 and the "new Jerusalem" (the Bride of Christ) in chapters 21-22. If John uses women to symbolize cities later in Revelation, then we have some precedent for thinking that the "woman" of Revelation 12 also represents a city. If this is the case, then the woman/Zion/Jerusalem should probably be understood as the embodiment of the people of Israel (first the "old" and then the "new Israel"). Accordingly, the fifth theory is virtually identical to the fourth.

A sixth theory views Revelation 12 as John's Christian adaptation of the Greek myth concerning the birth of Apollo. This theory avoids the pitfalls of the alternative explanations and, in the eyes of this author, appears correct.

(4) A Sixth Theory: John's Adaptation of the Apollo Myth. According to the myth,[12] Zeus, the highest god in the Greek pantheon, has sexual relations with the goddess Leto, who becomes pregnant with the sun god Apollo. Zeus then marries the goddess Hera. Zeus' new wife, Hera, becomes jealous of Leto, and so she forbids all the lands of the earth to give her rival a resting place for giving birth. She also sends Python to destroy Leto and her offspring. Python, a monstrous serpent that emerges from the waters of the Deluge, is the Greek version of Leviathan.

Taking pity on Leto, the sea god Poseidon sends a dolphin that conveys her to the floating island of Delos. Zeus fixes this island in the Aegean Sea, in a place not far from Patmos, and then floods it with shallow water so that Leto will not give birth on land. Clinging to a palm tree on the island, Leto endures nine days' labor before giving birth to Apollo, the sun god. When he is four days old, Apollo kills Python at Delphi. He then inaugurates a "golden age" among the gods, full of music and celebration.

Certain Roman emperors of the first century (e.g., Augustus, Nero, and Domitian) adapted the Apollo myth for purposes of political propaganda. Domitian, for example, liked to dress in the costume of Apollo and to be portrayed as the sun god in works of art. The emperor thus presented himself as a "new Apollo," the

---

[12]The Apollo story is a Greek version of an ancient Egyptian solar myth in which the dragon of darkness tries to kill the sun god, only to be killed by him when the new day dawns.

divine son of the goddess Roma (Rome[13]), who overcomes the "serpent" (that is, whatever obstacles are preventing the peace and prosperity of the Empire) and inaugurates a "golden age" for Rome.

The Apollo myth, which would have been well known to the first readers of Revelation, provides the key to understanding Revelation 12. Exiled on the island of Patmos — not far from Delos — John probably heard the story told again and again. He was no doubt familiar with how the Emperor Domitian used the myth to portray himself as the divine savior of the Empire. However, John knows that both Apollo and Domitian are "pretenders," mere parodies of Christ. In writing Revelation 12 John says, in effect, "Let me tell you about the one who truly overcomes the 'serpent' (Satan) and who truly launches a 'golden age' (the 'eschatological age' of the kingdom of God)." Finding common ground with his Hellenistic readers, John adapts the Apollo myth and Christianizes it, using the myth to express important truths concerning the Lord he serves.[14] The Apollo myth thus provides the overall "plot" or "story line" for this part of the Apocalypse.

Against this background, who, then, is the "woman" of Revelation 12? It may be that John has no one in particular in mind — that the mother of the "male child" is simply a literary device, a necessary part of the myth John uses to present Christ as the true destroyer of evil. If John does intend for her to represent a particular person or group of persons, then *the "woman" most likely represents Zion/Jerusalem/Israel (first Old Testament Israel and then later "true Israel," the church) pictured as the goddess Leto.* This theory easily explains all the statements John makes about the woman — including those concerning her appearance, which portray her more as a goddess than as a human being.

(5) Interpretation of Revelation 12. If the "red dragon" symbolizes Satan, and the "male child" symbolizes Christ, and the "woman" symbolizes the people of God portrayed as a goddess, then what is

---

[13]In worshiping the goddess Roma, the Romans were essentially worshiping themselves.

[14]Having presented a true picture of Christ in chapter 12, John will show the true nature of the Empire and the emperors in chapters 13 and 17. Roma/Rome is a "great prostitute," drunk on the blood of the saints, and the emperors are mere servants of Satan.

the meaning of Revelation 12? We will analyze John's message in the paragraphs below.

12:1-2 A great and wondrous sign appeared in heaven: a woman clothed with the sun, with the moon under her feet and a crown of twelve stars on her head. She was pregnant and cried out in pain as she was about to give birth.

As explained above,[15] the "woman" represents Zion or "Israel" (first Old Testament Israel and then the "new Israel," the church) dressed up as the goddess Leto. As Leto went through nine days' labor to give birth to the sun god Apollo, so does Old Testament Israel give birth to Jesus Messiah, the Son of God. John adapts the Greek myth concerning the birth of Apollo in order to express important truths concerning Christ.

12:3-4 Then another sign appeared in heaven: an enormous red dragon with seven heads and ten horns and seven crowns on his heads. His tail swept a third of the stars out of the sky and flung them to the earth. The dragon stood in front of the woman who was about to give birth, so that he might devour her child the moment it was born.

The "red dragon" symbolizes Satan as the head of all the forces of evil allied against God and his Messiah.[16] As the sea serpent Python tried to destroy Leto and her son Apollo, so does this "serpent" (v. 9) seek to destroy "Israel" (which now represents the church) and the Christ.

12:5 She gave birth to a son, a male child, who will rule all the nations with an iron scepter. And her child was snatched up to God and to his throne.

Just as Python failed to destroy Apollo, so did Satan fail to destroy Christ. Although Jesus died on the cross, God raised him from the dead, seated him on a heavenly throne, and gave him the rule over all nations.[17]

---

[15]See above under "(3) Five Theories Regarding the Identity of the Woman" and "(4) A Sixth Theory: John's Adaptation of the Apollo Myth."

[16]See above under "(2) The Identity of the Red Dragon."

[17]See above under "(1) The Identity of the Male Child."

12:6 The woman fled into the desert to a place prepared for her by God, where she might be taken care of for 1,260 days.

As Poseidon and Zeus cared for Leto and protected her from Python, so does God care for the church. For further discussion of this theme, see the comment on Revelation 12:13-17.

12:7-12 And there was war in heaven. . . . The great dragon was hurled down—that ancient serpent called the devil, or Satan, who leads the whole world astray. . . . Then I heard a loud voice in heaven say: "Now have come the salvation and the power and the kingdom of our God, and the authority of his Christ. For the accuser of our brothers, who accuses them before our God day and night, has been hurled down. They overcame him by the blood of the Lamb . . . . But woe to the earth and the sea, because the devil has gone down to you! He is filled with fury, because he knows that his time is short."

In Revelation 12:7-12, John elaborates on 12:4-5. Those earlier verses tell how Satan intended to destroy Christ, but instead Christ was crowned king. Verses 7-12 explain how Christ's victory was achieved.

According to verse 7, "there was war in heaven" — that is, "war" in the supernatural realm.[18] John pictures this "war" as a battle between God and Satan, who fight each other through their respective angels. Michael, the archangel responsible for Israel, serves as the commander of God's angelic army.[19] Verses 8-9 show that Satan loses the war, and John portrays his defeat by using an image common in Jewish apocalyptic writings: Satan and his demon allies are cast out of heaven to the earth.[20]

Verse 11 makes clear that this supernatural "war" took place on the cross. The key phrase is "by the blood of the Lamb." By his sacrificial death, Christ established the new covenant based on faith that carries the promise of eternal life in the consummated kingdom

---

[18]For a discussion of "heaven" as the supernatural sphere and "earth" as the natural sphere, see Part III.B.2.a.(1) of the Introduction: "Genesis 1–5."

[19]In the Christian canon, Michael appears in Daniel 10:13,21; 12:1; Jude 9; and Revelation 12:7. The archangel plays a much larger role in Jewish apocalyptic literature of the intertestamental period.

of God. In establishing this covenant, Christ provides everything human beings need to escape from sin and the "present evil age." On the cross, then, Christ wins the decisive battle against Satan and the forces of evil. He "overcomes" the "dragon" by inaugurating the "eschatological age" and the kingdom of God. As Apollo defeats Python, so Christ defeats Satan. Christians share in this victory "by the blood of the Lamb" (that is, by embracing the new covenant through faith), "by the word of their testimony" (that is, by sharing the "good news" of what Christ has done with others, so that they too may be saved), and by "not loving their lives so much as to shrink from death" (that is, by remaining faithful to Christ even at the cost of martyrdom). For detailed discussions of these important themes, see Part III.B.2.c(4) of the Introduction ("The Kingdom of God and the Death of Jesus") and Part II.D of the Commentary ("'Overcomers' in Revelation").

In verse 10 a heavenly voice proclaims: "*Now* have come the salvation and the power and the kingdom of our God, and the authority of his Christ." With the sacrificial death of Christ complete, "the kingdom of our God, and the authority of his Christ," have *already* begun. At the same time, the voice issues a word of warning in verse 12: "Woe to the earth and the sea, because the devil has gone down to you! He is filled with fury, because he knows that his time is short." Although Satan has been mortally "wounded," he is *not yet* "dead." Even though he has lost the "war," he nevertheless continues to fight. With these statements, John expresses "the already, but not yet" of Christian theology. By his death, Christ has *already* inaugurated the "eschatological age." However, the "present evil age" has *not yet* entirely passed away. The kingdom of Satan has *already* been broken, but it has *not yet* been abolished. The kingdom rule of God has *already* begun, but it has *not yet* been consummated. The two ages temporarily "overlap." The two kingdoms "coexist" until

---

[20]For a discussion of this apocalyptic theme, see Part III.B.2.a.(1) of the Introduction: "Genesis 1–5." Note that, whereas most apocalyptic writers describe the demons' fall from heaven as a defeat suffered *prior to the temptation of Adam and Eve or shortly thereafter,* John describes it as a defeat suffered *at the time of Christ's crucifixion.* The prophet adapts the apocalyptic image of fallen angels and uses it to communicate a different idea than it normally communicates.

Christ returns to complete his redemptive work. For further discussion of this important theme, see Part III.B.2.c(5) of the Introduction ("The Kingdom of God and the Resurrection of Jesus"). For a graphic representation, see Fig. 2, "The Shape of Christian Apocalyptic Theology" on page 41. For another example of the "already, but not yet" theme in John's Apocalypse, see the comment on Revelation 1:9.

12:13-17 When the dragon saw that he had been hurled to the earth, he pursued the woman . . . . from his mouth the serpent spewed water like a river, to overtake the woman and sweep her away with the torrent. But the earth helped the woman . . . . Then the dragon was enraged at the woman and went off to make war against the rest of her offspring—those who obey God's commandments and hold to the testimony of Jesus.

Verses 7-12 elaborated on verses 4-5 by showing how the "male child" (Christ) overcame the "dragon" (Satan). In similar fashion, verses 13-17 elaborate on verse 6, which describes the circumstances of the "woman" (the people of God) during the "1,260 days."

We have seen that the "1,260 days" of verse 6 and the "time, times and half a time" of verse 14 are symbolic numbers. Both refer to the period between John's receiving the Revelation in A.D. 95-96 and the consummation of God's kingdom at the Second Coming of Christ.[21] This period roughly coincides with the "overlap" of the ages, when Satan has *already* been defeated on the cross, but has *not yet* been totally destroyed. In John's apocalyptic scenario, this is the time of the "labor pains," when Satan — in desperation — makes one last attempt to defeat Christ by destroying the church.[22] It is the "labor pains" that John describes in Revelation 12:6 and 12:11-17.

The prophet shows that, during this period, Satan repeatedly attacks the church. As Python pursues Leto, so does Satan pursue God's covenant people. John expresses this truth in two ways: First, "from his mouth the serpent spewed water like a river, to overtake the woman and sweep her away with the torrent" (v. 15). The "water" probably symbolizes all the various evils Satan has at his disposal for threatening the church — sickness, disease, doubt, dissension, harassment,

---

[21]See the comment on the "42 months" in Revelation 11:2.
[22]See Fig. 2, "The Shape of Christian Apocalyptic Theology," p. 41.

persecution, and all the rest.[23] Second, verse 11 says that Christians "overcame" Satan because "they did not love their lives so much as to shrink from death." This implies that Satan makes war against Christians by killing them.[24] John and the first readers of Revelation were certainly experiencing the "dragon's" wrath.[25] Christians down through the centuries — throughout the "1,260 days" — have likewise experienced the suffering and hardship of the "labor pains."

John also shows that, in the midst of these trials, God cares for his people. As Poseidon and Zeus sheltered Leto from Python, so does God shelter the church from Satan:

> The woman fled into the desert to a place prepared for her by God, where she might be taken care of for 1,260 days (v. 6).

> The woman was given the two wings of a great eagle, so that she might fly to the place prepared for her in the desert, where she would be taken care of for a time, times and half a time, out of the serpent's reach (v. 14).

> The earth helped the woman by opening its mouth and swallowing the river that the dragon had spewed out of his mouth (v. 16).

The earth opens up and swallows the torrent, just as the earth is said to have opened up and swallowed Pharaoh and his army in Exodus 15:12. God delivers the woman on eagle's wings, just as he carried Israel "on eagle's wings" in Exodus 19:4. God cares for the woman in the desert for "1,260 days," just as he cared for Old Testament Israel in the desert for 40 years.

When John says that God "takes care" of his people, he certainly does not mean that Christians are exempt from all suffering. His point is that, although believers are often persecuted and killed, God will not allow the church to be completely destroyed. It will survive throughout the "1,260 days" to the Second Coming of Christ.

---

[23]For water as an ancient symbol for the forces of evil and chaos, see the comment on the "sea of glass" before God's throne in Revelation 4:6a.

[24]For more on this theme, see Part II.D.1 of the Commentary: "Satan as 'Overcomer.'"

[25]See Part IV.B.3 of the Introduction: "Persecution Related to Emperor Worship in Asia Minor."

John ends chapter 12 with these words: "Then the dragon was enraged at the woman and went off to make war against the rest of her offspring—those who obey God's commandments and hold to the testimony of Jesus" (12:17). In this chapter, the prophet describes how Satan "makes war" against the saints only in the most general of terms — that is, through a torrent of water in verse 15 and through killing Christians in verse 11. Next, in chapter 13, John will identify two very specific weapons Satan uses in his efforts to destroy the church. These weapons are symbolized by the "beast coming out of the sea" and the "beast coming out of the earth."

REVELATION 13

b. The Beast from the Sea (13:1-10)

¹And the dragon[a] stood on the shore of the sea. And I saw a beast coming out of the sea. He had ten horns and seven heads, with ten crowns on his horns, and on each head a blasphemous name. ²The beast I saw resembled a leopard, but had feet like those of a bear and a mouth like that of a lion. The dragon gave the beast his power and his throne and great authority. ³One of the heads of the beast seemed to have had a fatal wound, but the fatal wound had been healed. The whole world was astonished and followed the beast. ⁴Men worshiped the dragon because he had given authority to the beast, and they also worshiped the beast and asked, "Who is like the beast? Who can make war against him?"

⁵The beast was given a mouth to utter proud words and blasphemies and to exercise his authority for forty-two months. ⁶He opened his mouth to blaspheme God, and to slander his name and his dwelling place and those who live in heaven. ⁷He was given power to make war against the saints and to conquer them. And he was given authority over every tribe, people, language and nation. ⁸All inhabitants of the earth will worship the beast—all whose names have not been written in the book of life belonging to the Lamb that was slain from the creation of the world.[b]

⁹He who has an ear, let him hear.

¹⁰If anyone is to go into captivity,
  into captivity he will go.
If anyone is to be killed[c] with the sword,
  with the sword he will be killed.

This calls for patient endurance and faithfulness on the part of the saints.

[a]*1* Some late manuscripts *And I*   [b]*8* Or *written from the creation of the world in the book of life belonging to the Lamb that was slain*   [c]*10* Some manuscripts *anyone kills*

13:1a,11a And the dragon stood on the shore of the sea. And I saw a beast coming out of the sea. . . . Then I saw another beast, coming out of the earth.

As we saw in the commentary on chapter 12, the "dragon" symbolizes Satan, the leader and personification of the forces of evil allied against God and his church.[1] The "sea" is an ancient Middle Eastern symbol for the forces of evil and chaos.[2] From out of the sea, the reservoir of evil, the dragon summons a great "beast." Later, in verse 11, a second great beast appears — a beast from the earth. John probably intends for the two beasts to remind his readers of the sea monster Leviathan and the land monster Behemoth, two well-known apocalyptic symbols for the forces of evil and chaos.[3] With the "beast coming out of the sea" and the "beast coming out of the earth," John is introducing two new manifestations of evil into his vision of the future — two new weapons with which Satan "makes war" against the church. We will examine both of these symbols closely to discern exactly what kind of evils John has in mind.

13:1b-2,5-7 And I saw a beast coming out of the sea. He had ten horns and seven heads, with ten crowns on his horns, and on each head a blasphemous name. The beast I saw resembled a leopard, but had feet like those of a bear and a mouth like that of a lion. The dragon gave the beast his power and his throne and great authority. . . .

The beast was given a mouth to utter proud words and blasphemies and to exercise his authority for forty-two months. He opened his mouth to blaspheme God, and to slander his name and his dwelling place and those who live in heaven. He was given power to make war against the saints and to conquer them.

Much of the imagery used to describe the appearance of the beast in Revelation 13:1-8 is parallel to Daniel 7:1-8,23-25:[4]

---

[1]See the discussion of "The Identity of the Red Dragon" in the commentary on Revelation 12:1-17.

[2]See the comment on the "sea of glass" in Revelation 4:6a.

[3]For further discussion, see Part II.E.3.a of the Commentary, which concerns Revelation 2:17: "The Hidden Manna, the Messianic Banquet, Behemoth and Leviathan."

[4]John also draws on Daniel 7 for his description of the "enormous red dragon" in chapter 12. See the discussion of "The Identity of the Red Dragon" in the commentary on Rev 12:1-17.

In the first year of Belshazzar king of Babylon, Daniel had a dream, and visions passed through his mind as he was lying on his bed. He wrote down the substance of his dream.

Daniel said: "In my vision at night I looked, and there before me were the four winds of heaven churning up the great sea. Four great beasts, each different from the others, came up out of the sea.

"The first was like a lion, and it had the wings of an eagle. I watched until its wings were torn off and it was lifted from the ground so that it stood on two feet like a man, and the heart of a man was given to it.

"And there before me was a second beast, which looked like a bear. It was raised up on one of its sides, and it had three ribs in its mouth between its teeth. It was told, 'Get up and eat your fill of flesh!'

"After that, I looked, and there before me was another beast, one that looked like a leopard. And on its back it had four wings like those of a bird. This beast had four heads, and it was given authority to rule.

"After that, in my vision at night I looked, and there before me was a fourth beast—terrifying and frightening and very powerful. It had large iron teeth; it crushed and devoured its victims and trampled underfoot whatever was left. It was different from all the former beasts, and it had ten horns.

"While I was thinking about the horns, there before me was another horn, a little one, which came up among them; and three of the first horns were uprooted before it. This horn had eyes like the eyes of a man and a mouth that spoke boastfully.

"He gave me this explanation: 'The fourth beast is a fourth kingdom that will appear on earth. It will be different from all the other kingdoms and will devour the whole earth, trampling it down and crushing it. The ten horns are ten kings who will come from this kingdom. After them another king [the 'little horn'] will arise, different from the earlier ones; he will subdue three kings. He will speak against the Most High and oppress his saints and try to change the set times and the laws. The saints will be handed over to him for a time, times and half a time.

Daniel describes four separate beasts that emerge from the sea — the first like a lion, the second like a bear, the third like a leopard, and the fourth with ten horns. John combines the four into a single beast coming out of the sea. It resembles a lion, a bear, and a leopard, and it also has ten horns. Daniel's fourth beast has a little horn that speaks boastfully against the Most High God. In similar fashion, John's beast blasphemes God and the angels in heaven. Daniel's little horn oppresses the Lord's saints, exercising authority against them for a time, times and half a time. Likewise, John's beast makes war against the saints, exercising its authority for forty-two months.

In Daniel's vision, the four beasts symbolize four kingdoms, while the ten horns symbolize ten kings or rulers over those kingdoms. Seen in the light of Daniel 7, John's references to the ten horns, ten crowns, the leopard, the bear, and the lion make it very clear that *he is thinking of a political evil. The beast from the sea represents a manifestation of the forces of evil that takes the form of a kingdom(s) and/or king(s).*

13:1b And I saw a beast coming out of the sea. He had . . . seven heads

The beast's "seven heads" may be understood in two ways: First, the seven heads may serve to associate the beast with Leviathan, the seven-headed sea monster of Jewish mythology (see above). Since Leviathan is an ancient symbol for evil and chaos, the "seven heads" identify the beast from the sea — in general terms — as a manifestation of the forces of evil.

Second, in Revelation 17 John describes a "scarlet beast that was covered with blasphemous names and had seven heads and ten horns" (17:3). Later in the chapter, he explains that the seven heads represent the seven hills on which the city of Rome is built (17:9). In other words, the seven-headed, ten-horned beast in Revelation 17 symbolizes Rome. If John intends for the seven-headed, ten-horned beast in chapter 13 to represent the same reality, then he is picturing Rome as a "beast" and the Roman emperors as its "horns." In this case, the political evil described here in chapter 13 is specifically Rome — the particular manifestation of political evil on the scene in John's day.

13:1c,5-6,8 and on each head a blasphemous name. . . .

The beast was given a mouth to utter proud words and blasphemies . . . . He opened his mouth to blaspheme God, and to

slander his name and his dwelling place and those who live in heaven. . . . All inhabitants of the earth will worship the beast—all whose names have not been written in the book of life belonging to the Lamb that was slain from the creation of the world.

Like the "little horn" of Daniel 7, the beast from the sea speaks "blasphemies." The term "blasphemy" refers to any statement that shows disrespect for God or for the things of God. In Daniel's prophecy, the "little horn" probably refers to King Antiochus IV, a Seleucid ruler of the second century B.C. Antiochus tried to forcibly "hellenize" the Jewish people. In other words, he forbade the Jews to offer sacrifices to God, circumcise their children, keep the Sabbath, eat kosher foods, and otherwise follow the Mosaic Law.[5] Antiochus made such "crimes" punishable by death. He insisted that the Jews abandon their "Jewishness," and instead adopt Greek language and culture — including worship of the Greek gods. Such pressures on the Jewish community sparked the Maccabean Revolt.[6]

Antiochus IV committed "blasphemy" by showing disrespect for God's Law and God's covenant with the Jewish people. Furthermore, in an act of extreme arrogance, he took for himself the name "Epiphanes," which means "manifestation (of god on earth)." In this way also he blasphemed God by trying to put himself in God's place.

When John says that the beast from the sea — or Rome — wears "blasphemous names" and speaks "blasphemies," he is making a comparison between the Roman Caesars and Antiochus "Epiphanes." The resemblance applies to a number of different rulers. However, John is probably thinking first and foremost of Domitian, the emperor on the throne at the time he received the Revelation. Like Antiochus before him, Domitian claimed to be a god. He insisted that his subjects worship him as "lord," "god," "son of the gods," and "savior" of the Roman Empire. Those who refused he sentenced to death.[7] John views such divine claims as rank "blasphemy."

---

[5]This is what is meant by Daniel 7:25, in which the prophet predicts that Antiochus — the "little horn" — will speak against the Most High and oppress his saints and try to change the set times and the laws."

[6]First and Second Maccabees, which form part of the Old Testament Apocrypha, describe this terrible period in Jewish history.

[7]See Part IV.B.3 of the Introduction: "Persecution Related to Emperor Worship in Asia Minor."

Nevertheless, many participate in the "blasphemy." Verse 8 reads: "All inhabitants of the earth will worship the beast — all whose names have not been written in the book of life belonging to the Lamb that was slain from the creation of the world."[8] The "book of life" contains the names of all the faithful servants of Christ, who will receive a place in the consummated kingdom of God (see Rev 20:12,15). In John's time, some Christians were preaching compromise with the Roman authorities. They urged other believers to offer a sacrifice of incense to the emperor — without taking it seriously — as a means of saving their lives.[9] Here in Revelation 13 John insists that, if Christians do such things, then they are "worshiping the beast" and their names will *not* appear in the "book of life."

13:3 One of the heads of the beast seemed to have had a fatal wound, but the fatal wound had been healed. The whole world was astonished and followed the beast.

The symbol of the "fatal wound" that "had been healed" is probably based on the first-century idea of *Nero redivivus*, or "Nero come back to life." Nero was the Roman emperor who had persecuted Christians in such a terrible way in the mid-60s.[10] In A.D. 68, he committed suicide by cutting his own throat. Apparently, many Romans thought that the news of Nero's death was too good to be true, for they had difficulty believing that they were actually rid of him. Rumors spread that he was not really dead, but that he would one day return, leading an army of Parthians to conquer Rome.[11] A

---

[8]On Jesus as the "Lamb," see the comments on Revelation 5:6-14. Christ was "slain from the creation of the world" in the sense that God planned, far in advance, to redeem the world through his sacrificial death on the cross. Compare Matthew 25:34; Ephesians 1:4-10; 1 Peter 1:18-21.

[9]See Part IV.B.3 of the Introduction, "Occasion: Persecution Related to Emperor Worship in Asia Minor," and Part II.C.1 of the Commentary, "Pressures and Opposition from Within the Christian Community."

[10]For Tacitus' description of this persecution, see Part IV.B.2 of the Introduction: "Date."

[11]For examples of the *Nero redivivus* myth, see Sib. Or. 4:137-139; 5:94-110, 214-227, 361-385. After the end of World War II, similar fantasies spread about another evil ruler, Adolf Hitler. Since Hitler's body was not produced, rumors circulated for decades that he was alive in Argentina, plotting the revival of the Third Reich.

series of imposters, claiming to be the returned ruler, bolstered these stories.[12] Over time, the rumors were embellished and took many forms. Some even went so far as to say that Nero would come back from the dead, leading an army of demons against the Empire.[13]

By describing the beast from the sea as having a "fatal wound" that "had been healed," John draws a comparison between it and Nero. The "beast" — the political power of which he speaks — will be like "Nero returned," or like "Nero all over again." In other words, it will be a terrible persecutor of the church. Again, the resemblance applies to a number of different governments and a number of different rulers. However, when the first readers of Revelation heard about the "beast from the sea," they would certainly have thought of Domitian. Following the path blazed by Nero, Domitian carried out the second great persecution of Christians in the first century.[14] For believers in Asia in A.D. 95-96, Domitian was *Nero redivivus* — "Nero all over again."

By describing the beast from the sea as having a "fatal wound" that "had been healed," John also draws a comparison between it and Christ. The Lord Jesus received "fatal wounds" in his crucifixion, which led to his death. However, on the third day, God "healed" those wounds by raising him from the dead. People from the "whole world" have been impressed by this miracle and have decided to "follow" Jesus as his disciples. Similar ideas appear in Revelation 13:3, where John writes: "One of the heads of the beast seemed to have had a fatal wound, but the fatal wound had been healed. The whole world was astonished and followed the beast." In this way, John identifies the "beast" as an imitator or a parody of Christ, who tries to put himself in the Lord's place. Satan's parody of Christ is a major theme in Revelation 12–13, and a major theme in the book as a whole. We will discuss this subject in more detail in part "d," which appears below.

---

[12]See Tacitus, *History*, II.8-9; Dio Cassius, *Roman History*, LXIV.9; and Suetonius, *Lives of the Caesars*, Nero, LVII.

[13]See Sib. Or. 3:63-74; Ascension of Isaiah 4:1

[14]See the Introduction, Parts IV.B.1.b.(4), "The Testimony of Eusebius, Origen, and Papias," and IV.B.2, "Date."

13:2b,4-5,7 The dragon gave the beast his power and his throne and great authority. . . . Men worshiped the dragon because he had given authority to the beast, and they also worshiped the beast and asked, "Who is like the beast? Who can make war against him?" The beast was given . . . to exercise his authority for forty-two months. . . . He was given power to make war against the saints and to conquer them. And he was given authority over every tribe, people, language and nation.

In Revelation 12:17, John declares that Satan ("the dragon") "makes war" against Christians — against "those who obey God's commandments and hold to the testimony of Jesus." Here in chapter 13, John discloses one of the ways the devil does that. "The dragon" gives "the beast his power and his throne and great authority." In other words, Satan exercises his influence for evil through the agency of cooperative political powers. Writing in A.D. 56, the Apostle Paul urges Roman Christians to "submit to the governing authorities" because they act as "God's servants" (Rom 13:1-7; cf. 1 Pet 2:13-17; Matt 22:21). However, by A.D. 95-96, Satan has twisted those same governing authorities into a weapon for war against the church. John looks closely into the eyes of Domitian and sees the cold malice of the "dragon."

The threat is limited neither to Rome nor to the first century, for the "beast" is allowed "to exercise his authority for forty-two months" (v. 5). As explained above, this symbolic number refers to the entire period of time from the giving of the Revelation in A.D. 95-96 to the Second Coming of Christ.[15] Throughout these centuries, Satan continues to look for opportunities to turn rulers and governments into instruments of his evil will. Domitian and Rome were early examples of this demonic strategy. In more recent times, Hitler, Stalin, Mao, and so many others have been "Nero all over again" for the church.

The teachings of Jesus and Peter and Paul show that human governments are not inherently evil, that they are gifts from the Lord meant for our good. However, John's vision of the "beast from the sea" serves as a warning to God's people: Rulers and governments *tend* to try to put themselves in the place of God, demanding

---

[15]See the comment on the "42 months" in Revelation 11:2.

absolute loyalty. Satan will seek to use political powers to destroy Christians, who bow instead to the lordship of Christ. This is one of the realities that make the "labor pains" so "painful." John calls on believers to open their eyes to Satan's methods and be on their guard against his assaults.

13:9-10 He who has an ear, let him hear. If anyone is to go into captivity, into captivity he will go. If anyone is to be killed with the sword, with the sword he will be killed. This calls for patient endurance and faithfulness on the part of the saints.

The NIV incorrectly translates the final sentence of verse 10. The words "this calls for" do not appear in the Greek text. Instead, the verse literally reads: "Here is the patient endurance and the faith[fulness] of the saints" (Ὧδέ ἐστιν ἡ ὑπομονὴ καὶ ἡ πίστις τῶν ἁγίων, *Hōde estin hē hypomonē kai hē pistis tōn hagiōn*).

What is the proper response for believers under attack by godless political powers? In the case of the first readers of Revelation, what is the proper response if they are hauled into the Roman courts, and then ordered to renounce Christ and confess "Caesar is Lord"? Should they offer sacrifice to the emperor and save themselves? Should they proclaim Domitian "lord" and "god" to win their freedom? No, "If anyone is to go into captivity, into captivity he will go. If anyone is to be killed with the sword, with the sword he will be killed. *Here is the patient endurance and the faith[fulness] of the saints.*" When offered a choice between idolatry and captivity or death, then the Christian must choose captivity or death. This is the form that "patient endurance"[16] and "faith" must take as long as the "beast" still rules.[17]

c. *The Beast from the Land (13:11-18)*

[11]Then I saw another beast, coming out of the earth. He had two horns like a lamb, but he spoke like a dragon. [12]He exercised all the authority of the first beast on his behalf, and made the earth and its inhabitants worship the first beast, whose fatal wound had

---

[16]For a discussion of "patient endurance" as the attribute required of Christians during the "labor pains," see the comment on Revelation 1:9.

[17]See the discussion of "The Christians' Choice" in Part IV.B.3.f of the Introduction.

been healed. ¹³And he performed great and miraculous signs, even causing fire to come down from heaven to earth in full view of men. ¹⁴Because of the signs he was given power to do on behalf of the first beast, he deceived the inhabitants of the earth. He ordered them to set up an image in honor of the beast who was wounded by the sword and yet lived. ¹⁵He was given power to give breath to the image of the first beast, so that it could speak and cause all who refused to worship the image to be killed. ¹⁶He also forced everyone, small and great, rich and poor, free and slave, to receive a mark on his right hand or on his forehead, ¹⁷so that no one could buy or sell unless he had the mark, which is the name of the beast or the number of his name.

¹⁸This calls for wisdom. If anyone has insight, let him calculate the number of the beast, for it is man's number. His number is 666.

13:11a Then I saw another beast, coming out of the earth.

The second beast, the "beast coming out of the earth," calls to mind the great land monster Behemoth (see the comment on 13:1a, given above). John is using apocalyptic symbolism to describe another manifestation of the forces of evil that will be a part of the future his readers must face.

13:11b-12a He had two horns like a lamb, but he spoke like a dragon. He exercised all the authority of the first beast on his behalf,

At first glance, the beast resembles Christ, the "Lamb."[18] (See the discussion of "Satan's Parody of Christ" that appears below.) However, the beast's words reveal it to be something quite different.

Later in Revelation, John refers to the second beast as the "false prophet" (see Rev 16:13; 19:20; 20:10). As we read through chapter 13, we see that its primary function is to serve as the prophet, or spokesman, or representative, or advocate for the first beast — that is, the beast from the sea representing political powers opposed to Christ and his people. The beast from the land "speaks like a dragon" (v. 11). In other words, it serves as a mouthpiece for Satan, who, in turn, exercises his power and authority through the beast from the sea. The beast from the land "exercises all the authority of

---

[18]For a discussion of Christ as the "Lamb," see the comment on Rev 5:6.

the first beast on his behalf" (v. 12). In other words, it serves as the agent or representative for the first beast.

13:12b-17 [The beast from the land] made the earth and its inhabitants worship the first beast, whose fatal wound had been healed. And he performed great and miraculous signs . . . . deceived the inhabitants of the earth. He ordered them to set up an image in honor of the beast who was wounded . . . . and cause all who refused to worship the image to be killed. He also forced everyone, small and great, rich and poor, free and slave, to receive a mark . . . which is the name of the beast or the number of his name.

John here pictures the beast from the land as a "priest" for the beast from the sea. In other words, the second beast sets up the first beast (the political power) as a "god and then forces others to worship it on the threat of death or economic ruin. Whom does this second beast – this "spokesman" and "priest" for the first beast – represent? Some believe John is thinking of Roman provincial governors,[19] or other government officials, who serve as representatives for the emperor and the Empire throughout the Mediterranean world. This interpretation explains the "spokesman" idea, but not the religious imagery used by John. It seems more likely that the beast from the land symbolizes two other groups.

First, John's description of the beast immediately calls to mind the priests of the Caesar cult, who presided over emperor worship in the temples at Ephesus, Smyrna, Pergamum, and elsewhere in the Roman world. This interpretation accounts for all the imagery used in Revelation 13:12-17. The beast from the land sets up an "image" in honor of the political power, the beast from the sea (v. 14). Likewise the priests of the Caesar cult set up idols or images representing Caesar, the goddess Roma (i.e., Rome itself), and the other Roman deities. The beast from the land performs "great and miraculous signs" that promote the worship of the beast from the sea. It "causes fire to come down from heaven" and causes the idol to speak (vv. 13,15). Likewise, the priests of the Caesar cult used ventriloquism to make the gods' images pronounce oracles. Furthermore, they performed sophisticated magic tricks — including impressive displays of

---

[19]Such as Pliny in Bithynia — see the Introduction, Part IV.B.3.e.: "Correspondence of Pliny and Trajan."

"lightning" — to deceive worshipers into thinking that the images exhibited divine powers.[20] The beast from the land prevents anyone who does not receive the "mark" of the first beast — the political power — from buying or selling. Likewise, the priests of the Caesar cult built emperor worship into nearly every aspect of Roman civil, social, and political life. In doing so, they made it virtually impossible for anyone to participate in society, or participate in the Roman economy, without worshiping the "divine Caesar."[21]

Second, the beast from the land could also symbolize another type of religious power — namely, Christians who preached accommodation with Roman culture, ideology and cult. This would include people like "Jezebel," the prophetess mentioned in Revelation 2:20, and those who held to the "teaching of Balaam" mentioned in Revelation 2:14. These so-called servants of Christ were urging believers to participate in emperor worship in order to save themselves from economic hardship and social ostracism.[22] In doing so, they were acting as priests, spokesmen, representatives, and advocates for the beast from the sea — for political powers allied with Satan against Christ.

We have seen that the "beast from the land" symbolizes religious persons who support political authorities (the "beast from the sea") allied with Satan (the "dragon") against Christ and his church. In John's day, this second beast immediately called to mind the priests of the Caesar cult and "heretics" like "Jezebel." However, the symbol should not be limited to these two groups. Revelation 13:5 indicates that the "beast from the sea" and its "false prophet" will be active for the full "forty-two months" — that is, for the entire period of "labor pains" extending from A.D. 95-96 to the Second Coming of Christ.[23] The imperial priests and "Jezebel" were two historical manifestations

---

[20]For a description of their ingenious techniques, see Steven J. Scherrer, "Signs and Wonders in the Imperial Cult: A New Look at a Roman Religious Institution in the Light of Rev 13:13-15," *Journal of Biblical Literature* 103 (1984): 599-610.

[21]See Part IV.B.3.b of the Introduction: "Emperor Worship in Daily Life."

[22]See Part II.C.1 of the Commentary: "Pressures and Opposition from Within the Christian Community."

[23]See the comment on Revelation 13:2b,4-5,7, as well as the discussion of the "42 months" in Revelation 11:2.

of Satan's "religious weapon" against the church. In our own time, Satan uses his religious allies to attack believers in other ways. To illustrate, religious authorities in some Muslim countries bar Christians from educational opportunities, prohibit them from participating in civic life, and permit them to hold only the most menial of jobs. In the United States, so-called "Christian" groups actively support governmental efforts to promote the homosexual lifestyle against the clear commands of Scripture. They encourage the murder of innocent children in the womb while claiming to worship the God who hates the shedding of innocent blood. They join with the social and political elites in heaping ridicule on the practice of holiness. They promote the idolatrous idea that all religions lead to God, denying that Jesus alone is "the way and the truth and the life" — that "no one comes to the Father except through" him (John 14:6). John invites us to look beneath the Christian veneer of such persons and see them as instruments of Satan. He invites us to penetrate beyond their religious-sounding rhetoric to hear the voice of the "dragon."

13:18 This calls for wisdom. If anyone has insight, let him calculate the number of the beast, for it is man's number. His number is 666.

According to verses 16-17, the beast from the land

> also forced everyone, small and great, rich and poor, free and slave, to receive a mark on his right hand or on his forehead, so that no one could buy or sell unless he had the mark, which is the name of the beast or the number of his name.

In verse 18, this "mark" takes the form of a number — namely, the number of the beast, which is "666."[24]

In the Greco-Roman world of John's time, there were no Arabic numerals (1,2,3,4,5 . . .). Instead, letters of the alphabet were assigned numerical values, so that numbers could be written using letters. Figure 3 (overleaf) shows the numerical values of Greek letters as they were used in the first century.

---

[24]A few ancient copies of Revelation identify the beast's number as "616." On the significance of this alternative number, see below.

Under this system, the numerical value of any Greek word could be "calculated" by simply adding up the sum of its letters. For example, the numerical value of the name of the Apostle Paul (*Paulos* or Παῦλος) is 781 (Π = 80, α = 1, υ = 400, λ = 30, ο = 70, ς = 200).

A α	(Alpha)	=	1	Π π	(Pi)	=	80
B β	(Beta)	=	2	Ϙ	(Koppa)	=	90
Γ γ	(Gamma)	=	3	P ρ	(Rho)	=	100
Δ δ	(Delta)	=	4	Σ σ,ς	(Sigma)	=	200
E ε	(Epsilon)	=	5	T τ	(Tau)	=	300
Ϝ	(Vau)	=	6	Υ υ	(Upsilon)	=	400
Z ζ	(Zeta)	=	7	Φ φ	(Phi)	=	500
H η	(Eta)	=	8	X χ	(Chi)	=	600
Θ θ	(Theta)	=	9	Ψ ψ	(Psi)	=	700
I ι	(Iota)	=	10	Ω ω	(Omega)	=	800
K κ	(Kappa)	=	20	ϡ	(Sampi)	=	900
Λ λ	(Lambda)	=	30	͵α		=	1000
M μ	(Mu)	=	40	͵β		=	2000
N ν	(Nu)	=	50	͵γ		=	3000
Ξ ξ	(Xi)	=	60	͵δ		=	4000
O o	(Omicron)	=	70		etc.		

Fig. 3 Numerical Values of Greek Letters[25]

Ancient people enjoyed toying with the numbers of words and of names. They did it for fun, as illustrated by a bit of graffiti discovered in the ruins of Pompeii that reads: "I love her whose number is 545." However, they also used numbers for more serious purposes, such as writing theology in the form of mysterious apocalyptic visions. An example appears in the Sibylline Oracles, Book V, Lines 1-51 (an Egyptian Jewish document dating to the late first or early second century A.D.), in which the author provides a brief overview of Roman history. The text reads, in part:

---

[25]Three of the letters shown (vau [also called digamma], koppa and sampi) belonged to the primitive Greek alphabet. By the time of the writing of the New Testament, they had become obsolete as letters but were still used as numbers.

In a Greek numerical expression, the final letter has an accent above it. To illustrate, ͵αωξή = 1868; ͵δκέ = 4025; ͵βγ́ = 2003; and ρδ΄ = 104.

... there will be the first prince who will sum up twice ten with his initial letter. He will conquer long in wars. He will have his first letter of ten (i.e., Iulius Kaisar, or Julius Caesar, where I = 10 and K = "twice ten" or 20), so that after him will reign whoever obtained as initial the first of the alphabet (i.e., Augustus Caesar) . . . . After a long time he will hand over sovereignty to another, who will present a first letter of three hundred, and the beloved name of a river (i.e., Tiberius Caesar, where T = 300) . . . (Sib. Or. 5:12-15, 20-22).

The numerical value of the name "Jesus" (*Iēsous* or 'Ιησοῦς) is 888 (I = 10, η = 8, σ = 200, ο = 70, υ = 400, ς = 200). That early Christians were acquainted with this fact is shown, for example, by Sibylline Oracles, Book I (a Jewish book reworked by a Christian editor in the early second century A.D.). Lines 324-330 read as follows:

Then indeed the son of the great God will come, incarnate, likened to mortal men on earth, bearing four vowels (I,η,ο,υ), and the consonants in him are two (σ,ς). I will state explicitly the entire number for you. For eight units, and equal number of tens in addition to these, and eight hundreds (i.e., [8×1] + [8×10] + [8×100] = 888) will reveal the name to men who are sated with faithlessness."[26]

The fact that the number for "Jesus" happens to be 888 created all sorts of possibilities for early Christian "number artists." To illustrate, there are 7 days in a week. Sunday is the 1st day of the week; but one could also think of it as the 8th day — the beginning of a new week. Sunday, the 8th day, is the "Lord's Day" — the day of him whose number is 888. Sunday, the 8th day, is also the day on which Christ rose from the dead and began a new "week" or new age — the "eschatological age" of the kingdom of God. So 8 is the number of Christ and also the number of the new age, the new Creation that he inaugurated.[27] It is for reasons such as these that 8 became the symbolic number for Jesus in early Christian apocalyptic.[28]

---

[26]Charlesworth, *Pseudepigrapha*.

[27]It was on the 8th day that Jesus, whose number is 888, won a victory over Satan by rising from the dead. It is also interesting to note that it was on the 6th day that Satan (whose number is 666? — see below) had his apparent triumph over Christ by killing him on the cross.

[28]For a discussion of the symbolic meaning of other numbers, see Part III.B.1.d of the Introduction.

In Revelation 13:18, John says that 666, the number of the beast, is "man's number" (ἀριθμὸς ἀνθρώπου, *arithmos anthrōpou*, which could also be translated "a human's number" or "a human number"). This statement may be understood in two ways: First, the writer may be saying that 666 is the number for an individual human being's name. Second, John may be identifying 666 as a "human number" in the sense that it is computed in the normal "human" way — that is, according to the system presented in Figure 3. In other words, it is a number that has meaning beyond expressing the quantity six hundred sixty-six.[29]

If John is thinking of 666 as the number of an individual human being, then the reference is probably to Nero. However, to derive the name "Nero" from the number 666 requires an unusual spelling of that name. First, we must use the name "Nero Caesar," rather than simply "Nero." Second, we must spell the name in Hebrew, rather than Greek. Third, we must add an extra letter to the name. The result is "Neron Caesar," which has a numerical value of 666 (i.e. נרון קסר, where נ = 50, ר = 200, ו = 6, ן [נ] = 50, ק = 100, ס = 60, ר = 200).

One may question whether John's Greek readers would have grasped this hidden meaning. However, the churches of Asia probably did include Jewish believers with some knowledge of Hebrew.[30] At least one occurrence of "Nero" spelled with the extra letter has been found in the Dead Sea Scrolls.[31] Furthermore, in a few ancient manuscripts of Revelation, scribes have changed the number "666" to "616," which is the numerical value of "Nero Caesar" without the extra letter. This shows that at least some early Christians understood the number of the beast to refer to "Nero" and that they were trying to help readers see the connection. Therefore it is possible (if not probable) that the number "666" in Revelation 13:18 is intended to link the "beast" with the Emperor Nero. If this is the case, then John most likely does not mean Nero alone, or Nero individually,

---

[29]Compare Revelation 21:17, where an angel measures the heavenly city using "man's measurement" (μέτρον ἀνθρώπου, *metron anthrōpou*) — that is, the normal "human" system of measurement.

[30]See Part IV.A.1 of the Introduction: "First Readers."

[31]See *Discoveries in the Judaean Desert*, Vol. II (Oxford: Clarendon Press, 1961), Plate 29, Line 1 (p. 101).

because that emperor had been long dead. Instead, by giving the beast from the sea the number for Nero, John again identifies it as *Nero redivivus* — that is, a terrible persecutor of the church after the example set by Nero himself.[32]

While it is indeed possible that the number 666 identifies the beast with Nero, this author finds a different interpretation more convincing. We saw earlier that the number of "Jesus" is 888, which consists of three identical digits. Using three identical digits to identify the beast may simply be another way for John to say that the beast parodies Christ, or imitates Christ, or tries to put itself in the place of Christ. (For a discussion of this major theme in Revelation, see below under "Satan's Parody of Christ.") If so, then why use 666 as the number for the beast? Why not 333 or 555 or 999? Perhaps the Spirit directs John to use the number 6 because it is the apocalyptic number for "incompleteness," or "imperfection," or even "evil." A multiple of 6 (such as 666) symbolizes the fullness of that idea — namely, "complete incompleteness" or "imperfection perfected."[33] If this is the case, then *the number "666" is not intended to communicate the beast's name, but its character. It is an imitator of Christ (signified by the three identical digits) and an embodiment of the forces of evil (signified by the number "6" intensified).*

d. Satan's Parody of Christ

A "parody" is a weak imitation of something else. Throughout his apocalypse, John presents Satan and his allies as ones who parody, or imitate, or try to put themselves in the place of God/Christ. That Satan's parody of Christ is an important aspect of the theology of Revelation becomes especially clear in chapter 13. The following comparison draws together examples of this theme for the reader's consideration:

---

[32]On the *Nero redivivus* idea, see the comment on the "fatal wound that had been healed" in Revelation 13:3.

[33]On the meaning of various symbolic numbers, see Part III.B.1.d of the Introduction.

God	Satan
A. The "Trinity":	A. The "Evil Trinity" (a unit in Rev 16:3):
1. God, the Creator	1. Satan, the Destroyer
2. Christ the Lamb through whom God acts/makes war against Satan	2. The Beast from the Sea — i.e., political powers through which Satan makes war against Christ and his saints
3. The Holy Spirit by whom God speaks through the prophet John and calls all people to worship him	3. The Beast from the Land/False Prophet — i.e., religious powers through which Satan speaks and calls all people to worship him
B. God:	B. Satan:
1. Sits on the throne of the universe (4:2)	1. Wears crowns as a usurper of God's throne (12:3)
C. The Lamb:	C. The Beast from the Sea:
1. Wears many crowns (19:12)	1. Wears crowns (13:1)
2. Has seven horns signifying complete power (5:6)	2. Has ten horns signifying power (13:1)
3. Wears names such as "King of kings" and "Lord of lords" (19:16)	3. Wears blasphemous names — i.e., takes to itself names that rightfully belong to Christ (13:1,5-6)
4. Has authority over all nations (12:5)	4. Has authority over all nations (13:7)
5. Receives power, throne, and authority from God; shares God's throne (5:6)	5. Receives power, throne, and authority from Satan; shares the dragon's throne (13:2)
6. Dies and is then raised from the dead (1:5; 5:6)	6. Seems to have a fatal wound that has been healed (13:3)
7. "Overcomes" Satan and his allies by dying as a sacrifice (12:11)	7. Seems to "overcome" Christ and his people by killing them (13:7)
8. Reigns for 1000 years — and this is only the beginning of an eternal reign (20:4; 11:15)	8. Reigns for 42 months (13:5)
9. His number is "888" (not explicitly stated in Revelation)	9. His number is "666" (13:18)

D. The Holy Spirit:
   1. The Spirit of God/Christ (3:1)
   2. Empowers John to speak for God/Christ (1:10; 2:7; 19:10; etc.)
   3. "The testimony of Jesus is the Spirit of prophecy" (19:10)
   4. Gives resurrection life to Christ and Christians (11:11)
   5. Through the Revelation, calls all nations to worship God/Christ

E. The People of God:
   1. "Overcome" Satan by dying (12:11)
   2. Worship both God and his Christ (5:13)
   3. Are "measured" and "counted" by God (11:1), and sealed with the seal of God (7:3-4; 14:1)

D. The Beast from the Land:
   1. Has two horns like a lamb — a parody of Christ (13:11)
   2. Speaks like the dragon (13:11)
   3. Exercises the authority of the beast from the sea (13:12)
   4. Gives life (lit. "spirit") to the image of the beast from the sea (13:15)
   5. Makes all the earth worship the beast from the sea (13:12,14)

E. The People of Satan:
   1. "Overcome" Christ and his servants by killing them (13:7,15)
   2. Worship both the beast from the sea — and the dragon that gives it power — as if they were God and Christ. They ask, "Who is like the beast?" (13:4), which is a parody of Exodus 15:11: "Who among the gods is like you, O LORD?"
   3. Are marked with "666," the number of the beast from the sea (13:17-18)

As the above comparison shows, John characterizes Satan and his allies as those who try to usurp God's sovereignty, who attempt to put themselves in the place that rightfully belongs to God/Christ/the Holy Spirit/the People of God. "Playing god" has been the agenda of Satan — and the essence of sin — from the beginning. We see it in the words with which Satan tempted Adam and Eve in Genesis 3:4-5:

> "You will not surely die," the serpent said to the woman. "For God knows that when you eat of it your eyes will be opened, and *you will be like God*, knowing good and evil."

e. Summary of Revelation 12–13: The "Labor Pains"

In summary, Revelation 12–13 describes the "labor pains" — the period of intense suffering and persecution of God's people immediately preceding the consummation of his kingdom rule.[34] One of the reasons Christians suffer during this time is that our enemy Satan — defeated and desperate — continues to "make war" against the saints (Rev 12:17). Chapter 13 describes two "weapons" that Satan commonly uses in his efforts to destroy the church. The "beast from the sea" represents political powers allied with Satan against Christ. The symbol of the "beast from the land" shows that, in his diabolical cunning, the devil uses even religious powers to further his evil agenda. John witnessed the first attempts at this demonic strategy in the form of hostile Roman authorities, the supportive imperial cult, and accommodating "Christians." He warns contemporary readers to be on the lookout for similar threats.

---

[34]For a more detailed discussion of this concept, see Parts III.B.2.b-d of the Introduction. For a graphic representation, see Fig. 2, "The Shape of Christian Apocalyptic Theology" p. 41.

REVELATION 14

3. The Final Judgment and Consummation of God's Kingdom (14:1–22:6)

a. *The Relationship between Salvation and Condemnation, Final Judgment and Consummation*

Revelation 12-13 describes the "labor pains," or the time of intense suffering and persecution for God's people immediately prior to the Second Coming of Christ. During this period, Satan (symbolized by the "red dragon") will continue to make war against the saints through both political and religious powers (symbolized by the two "beasts" from land and sea). After the "labor pains" will come the final judgment and the consummation of God's kingdom, which are the subject of Revelation 14:1-22:6.

The final judgment involves *separation* of the righteous from the wicked (i.e., separation of those who participate in the new covenant from those who do not), *condemnation* and punishment of the wicked, and *salvation* and reward for the righteous. Salvation takes the form of a place in God's consummated kingdom — that is, eternal life in a universe purged from evil and brought totally into conformity with God's good and beneficent will. Condemnation takes the form of exclusion from this kingdom.[1]

It is very important to understand that salvation and condemnation, the final judgment and consummation, are two sides of a single event. If God's plan is to establish his own kingship or sovereignty or lordship over all creation, then that means that he must, of necessity, put down all opposing lordships. To illustrate, Adolf Hitler desired a

---

[1] For a discussion of these concepts, see Parts III.B.2.b-d of the Introduction. For a graphic representation, see Fig. 2, "The Shape of Christian Apocalyptic Theology," p. 41.

world without Jews. God desires a world community made up of Jews and persons "from every nation, tribe, people and language." The two visions are totally incompatible. Both cannot be realized. The slaveholder's system of fear and oppression cannot coexist with God's designs for freedom and loving servanthood. The pedophile's vision of an ideal world is very different from God's vision. The spinmeister's smokescreen of lies and deception is incompatible with God's desire for "the truth" to "set us free" (John 8:32). John Lennon's call to "imagine there's no heaven" is quite different from what God imagines for the future of his creation. It comes down to this question: What kind of world do we want it to be? Whose vision of the world do we want to prevail? Jesus teaches us to pray, "May *God's* kingdom come; may *his* will be done on earth as it is in heaven" (Matt 6:10). May *God's* vision prevail! The "good news" of the gospel — and the "good news" of Revelation — is that *God's vision will indeed prevail.* God will both establish his eternal kingdom (salvation and consummation) *and* destroy the opposing kingdom of Satan and his allies (judgment and condemnation). The two, of necessity, go together. Both are essential aspects of the gospel. "The kingdom of the world" will "become the kingdom of our Lord and of his Christ, and he will reign for ever and ever" (Rev 11:15).

The alternative to destroying the kingdom of Satan would be to leave creation in its fallen state — to leave the "present evil age" intact. This would require the good and holy God to give his approval and consent to evil. God has shown remarkable patience and mercy by offering everyone an opportunity to repent. However, he will not consent to the permanent ruin of the universe. The One who created the world "very good" (Gen 1:31) will not deny his own character by redefining "goodness." He will not give Satan the final word, but will destroy him and his evil works forever.

Throughout Revelation, John draws a very sharp line between Christians destined for salvation and non-Christians destined for destruction. However, this is not an uncrossable line. The "good news" of the gospel is that those who oppose Christ may repent,[2] "wash their robes in the blood of the Lamb," and become a part of the "144,000" sealed with the mark of God's ownership.[3] This is the

---

[2]See, for example, Rev 2:21-22; 9:20-21; 16:9-11.
[3]See Revelation 7, particularly verses 3, 4, and 14.

aim of the faithful witness of the church, which will continue to the end of the "1,260 days" and the return of Christ in glory.[4] The words of doom in Revelation are not intended to be a "death sentence" for nonbelievers, but a warning for them to turn to the Lord before it is too late. The kingship of God is offered as a free gift to any sinner who wants it — that is, to anyone willing to live under the kingship of God. (The Bible calls such willingness "faith" — that is, commitment to him as Lord.) The kingdom of God is the shape of the future, and he graciously offers this wonderful future to everyone. Those who reject God's future will have no future at all.

b. The Structure of Revelation 14:1–22:6

Since the final judgment and consummation of God's kingdom are two aspects of the same event, John treats them together in Revelation 14:1–22:6. These chapters are filled with images of the condemnation of the wicked and the salvation of the righteous.

The first section (14:1–19:4) focuses primarily on the punishment of God's enemies, with an occasional glimpse of the redemption of his people. After introducing the theme of judgment (14:1-13), John likens the destruction of the wicked to the harvest of the earth (14:14-20) and the emptying of seven bowls filled with God's wrath (15:1–16:21). He describes the fall of "Babylon" as representative of the final outcome for all who oppose God.

The second section (19:5–22:6) focuses primarily on the salvation of God's servants, with an occasional look backward to the destruction of his enemies. It includes a variety of images of God's Final Triumph, such as the wedding supper of the Lamb (19:5-10) and a mounted Christ victorious over Satan's armies (19:11-21). It concludes with an elaborate vision describing the final judgment and consummation of God's kingdom as the deliverance of God's people from Babylonian Captivity (20:1–22:5).

c. Announcement of the Final Judgment (14:1-13)

In chapter 14 John begins moving toward the climax of Revelation, where he shows that — in spite of Satan's efforts — Christ and the church will ultimately be victorious. Verses 1-13 introduce the

---

[4]See Rev 11:3.

theme of the final judgment by describing the two groups that will emerge from it — first the "144,000" servants of God sealed for salvation, and then the worshipers of the beast marked for destruction. The focal point of the text is verse 7, where an angel declares: "The hour of [God's] judgment has come."

¹Then I looked, and there before me was the Lamb, standing on Mount Zion, and with him 144,000 who had his name and his Father's name written on their foreheads. ²And I heard a sound from heaven like the roar of rushing waters and like a loud peal of thunder. The sound I heard was like that of harpists playing their harps. ³And they sang a new song before the throne and before the four living creatures and the elders. No one could learn the song except the 144,000 who had been redeemed from the earth. ⁴These are those who did not defile themselves with women, for they kept themselves pure. They follow the Lamb wherever he goes. They were purchased from among men and offered as firstfruits to God and the Lamb. ⁵No lie was found in their mouths; they are blameless.

(1) The 144,000 (14:1-5). This paragraph describes the people of God, who will inherit eternal life in his kingdom. Most of the symbols appear earlier in the book.

14:1 Then I looked, and there before me was the Lamb,

The Lamb represents Jesus Christ as the one who died on the cross as a sacrifice for sin. He is the one who delivers his people not through military force, but by dying for them. For further discussion of Christ as the "Lamb," see the comment on Revelation 5:6.

standing on Mount Zion,

In Revelation 13:1, John pictures Satan, the "dragon," as standing "on the shore of the sea," the great reservoir of evil. Here in 14:1 he pictures Jesus "standing on Mount Zion." Zion is the hill on which King David built Jerusalem, the capital city of Israel. By placing Jesus here, John may be alluding to Psalm 2:6, a "Royal Psalm" in which God declares: "I have installed my King on Zion, my holy hill." In other words, John is identifying Jesus as the Messiah, or Davidic King, who has been crowned by God himself. For a discussion of Psalm 2 and its application to Jesus, see the comment on the title "Jesus Christ" in Revelation 1:5.

and with him 144,000

The "144,000" represent the totality of the church pictured as the "new Israel," God's covenant people. For further discussion of this symbolic number, see the comment on Revelation 7:1-8. An examination of the various images used to describe the 144,000 (see below) tells us much about John's conception of the church.

who had his name and his Father's name written on their foreheads.

In contrast to the allies of the beast, who wear the number "666" on their foreheads (see Rev 13:16-18), Christians bear the names of God and his Christ. The names are the seal of ownership showing that the church belongs to the Lord. For further discussion, see the comments on Revelation 7:1-8, as well as the promise to "him who overcomes" in 3:12.

14:2 And I heard a sound from heaven like the roar of rushing waters and like a loud peal of thunder. The sound I heard was like that of harpists playing their harps.

The sound "like the roar of rushing waters" calls to mind the voice of the risen Christ in Revelation 1:15. Both this sound and the sound "like a loud peal of thunder" symbolize the voice of the heavenly multitude in 19:6. Here in Revelation 14:2 they represent the loud music of harps.

The harp is the instrument of redeemed saints in 15:2 and of the twenty-four elders (symbolizing the redeemed saints) in 5:8. Accompanied by the harps, the 144,000 sing a "new song" in verse 3.

14:3 And they sang a new song before the throne and before the four living creatures and the elders. No one could learn the song except the 144,000

As in Revelation 4, the "throne" is the throne of God, which is shared by Christ the Lamb.[5] The "four living creatures" symbolize the whole of creation.[6] The "elders" symbolize the church.[7]

---

[5]See the comment on Rev 4:2. Concerning the Lamb on the throne, see the comment on Rev 5:6.
[6]See the comments on Rev 4:6b-8.
[7]See the comment on Rev 4:4.

In the presence of God, his Christ, the whole church, and all creation, the "144,000" redeemed saints sing "a new song." The Greek term translated "new" is καινός (*kainos*). Throughout Revelation, John uses this term to speak of eschatological "newness" — that is, the "new" realities of the "eschatological age" and the emerging kingdom of God.[8] Only Christians may learn the "new song" because only Christians may participate in the kingdom.

The phrase "new song" also has Old Testament antecedents to which John may consciously allude here. See, for example, Psalm 33:2-3 (where "Sing to him a new song" is linked with "Praise the LORD with the harp") and Psalm 98:1 (where the psalmist calls on people to "Sing to the LORD a new song" because he has "worked salvation").

who had been redeemed from the earth.

The Greek verb translated "redeemed" is ἀγοράζω (*agorazō*). The NIV translates the same verb as "purchased" in verse 4. The basic idea communicated by this verb is "paying a price in order to gain someone's release from prison or slavery." In the context of Revelation, John is describing Christians as persons who — at the "cost" of Christ's sacrificial death — gain release from the kingdom of Satan and the "present evil age." Out of all the people "from the earth," only Christians receive this blessing.

14:4 These are those who did not defile themselves with women, for they kept themselves pure.

In considering this verse, note that the term "women" is plural. The "144,000" do not "defile themselves" with *multiple women* – that is, they are not promiscuous. Note also that the Greek term translated "pure" is παρθένοι (*parthenoi*), which literally means "virgins" (male or female).

Verse 4 does not mean that all of the "144,000" redeemed saints are celibate males, or that sex itself is sinful. We have seen that, throughout Revelation, adultery, fornication, prostitution, and sexual promiscuity are common images for idolatry — that is, for relationships with gods other than the true creator and Lord of all.

---

[8]For a discussion of this topic, see Part II.E.3.c of the Commentary: "The Secret Name" in Rev 2:17.

By calling them "pure/virgins," John characterizes Christians as persons who shun the kind of idolatry involved in Roman emperor worship and other pagan religions. They do not give in to the temptations placed before them by people like "Jezebel," those promoting the "teaching of Balaam,"[9] or the "beast from the land."[10]

By describing Christians as "pure," John is also laying the groundwork for a powerful contrast that will appear later in the book — namely, the contrast between "Babylon" as a "great prostitute" (17:1) and the church as the pure, chaste, virginal "Bride" of Christ (21:9).

They follow the Lamb wherever he goes.

The Greek term translated "follow" is ἀκολουθέω (*akoloutheō*). It can mean "follow" in the sense of "walking behind someone else." However, in the New Testament this is also a technical term for "following *as a disciple*," which is John's meaning here. Christians, by definition, "follow" Christ as his faithful disciples — even if that path leads them to a martyr's death.

They were purchased from among men

See the comment on the phrase "who had been redeemed from the earth" in verse 3.

and offered as firstfruits to God and the Lamb.

Under the Mosaic covenant, the "firstfruits" of each season's agricultural produce, the firstborn of all livestock, and all firstborn sons were presented to God in token acknowledgement that the entire crop, the entire herd, and all children truly belong to him.[11] By characterizing Christians as "firstfruits," John acknowledges that they are God's possession. Believers also represent the entirety of humanity, which truly belongs to God.

---

[9]On "Jezebel" and the "teachings of Balaam," see Part II.C.1 of the Commentary: "Pressures and Opposition from Within the Christian Community."

[10]See the comment on Revelation 13:12b-17.

[11]See, e.g., Exod 13:1-16; 23:19; Lev 23:10-11; 27:26-28; Num 15:20-21; 18:12-19; Deut 15:19; 18:4; 26:1-11.

14:5 No lie was found in their mouths; they are blameless.

The Old Testament uses similar language to describe the "Servant of the Lord" in Isaiah 53:9 and the "remnant of Israel" in Zephaniah 3:13. By adopting such language, John identifies Christians as "servants" of the Lord and the "true Israel," or new covenant people of God. In contrast to Satan and his allies, Christians speak the truth about God and live accordingly.

⁶Then I saw another angel flying in midair, and he had the eternal gospel to proclaim to those who live on the earth—to every nation, tribe, language and people. ⁷He said in a loud voice, "Fear God and give him glory, because the hour of his judgment has come. Worship him who made the heavens, the earth, the sea and the springs of water."

⁸A second angel followed and said, "Fallen! Fallen is Babylon the Great, which made all the nations drink the maddening wine of her adulteries."

⁹A third angel followed them and said in a loud voice: "If anyone worships the beast and his image and receives his mark on the forehead or on the hand, ¹⁰he, too, will drink of the wine of God's fury, which has been poured full strength into the cup of his wrath. He will be tormented with burning sulfur in the presence of the holy angels and of the Lamb. ¹¹And the smoke of their torment rises for ever and ever. There is no rest day or night for those who worship the beast and his image, or for anyone who receives the mark of his name." ¹²This calls for patient endurance on the part of the saints who obey God's commandments and remain faithful to Jesus.

¹³Then I heard a voice from heaven say, "Write: Blessed are the dead who die in the Lord from now on."

"Yes," says the Spirit, "they will rest from their labor, for their deeds will follow them."

(2) Threefold Announcement of the Judgment (14:6-13). Verses 6-13 contain a threefold announcement of the final judgment. The multiple announcements create an atmosphere of increasing terror leading up to the visions of the judgment itself, which begins in verse 14. The threefold announcement thus functions in a manner similar to the vulture's three "Woes!" in 8:13[12] and the three pairs of "Woes!" pronounced against Babylon in 18:10, 16, and 19.

---

[12]See Part III.C.2.h of the Commentary: "The Eagle and the Three 'Woes.'"

John introduced the "144,000," who will receive a positive verdict at the judgment, in verses 1-5. Now, in verses 6-13, he introduces those who will receive a negative verdict — namely, "Babylon the Great" and "those who worship the beast and his image, or . . . anyone who receives the mark of his name."

14:6-7 Then I saw another angel flying in midair, and he had the eternal gospel to proclaim to those who live on the earth—to every nation, tribe, language and people. He said in a loud voice, "Fear God and give him glory, because the hour of his judgment has come. Worship him who made the heavens, the earth, the sea and the springs of water."

In the first announcement of the final judgment, an angel proclaims the "eternal gospel" — a message intended for "every nation, tribe, language and people." The Greek term translated "gospel" (εὐαγγελιον, *euangelion*) literally means "good news." Note that the "good news" of the gospel includes the announcement that "the hour of [God's] judgment has come." The judgment, condemnation, and destruction of God's enemies is "good news" because that alone will permit the coming of God's kingdom rule and the salvation of his people. (See the discussion of "The Relationship between the Final Judgment and Consummation" that appears above.) The Lord's enemies perish because of their idolatry — that is, because of their refusal to "fear God and give him glory," and their refusal to acknowledge him as the true creator (see v. 7) and Lord of all.

14:8 A second angel followed and said, "Fallen! Fallen is Babylon the Great, which made all the nations drink the maddening wine of her adulteries."

The second announcement of the final judgment focuses on the doom of "Babylon the Great." Like other apocalyptists of his era, John uses "Babylon" as a symbol for Rome.[13] King Nebuchadnezzar's Babylon destroyed Jerusalem and the temple in 587 B.C. Rome did the same in A.D. 70, becoming a "second Babylon" in the eyes of Jews and Christians.

---

[13]See the discussion of the "Date" for Revelation in Part IV.B.2 of the Introduction. John clearly identifies symbolic "Babylon" as Rome in Revelation 17:9, which refers to the "seven hills" on which Rome was built.

Rome's "adulteries" are a reference to its idolatry, or unfaithfulness to God.[14] In place of the true creator and Lord, Rome worships the emperor and other Roman deities. The "maddening wine" associated with Rome's idolatry is the shed blood of martyred Christians, who die because they refuse to participate in Rome's sin (see 17:4,6). By promoting idolatry among "the nations" under its control, Rome encourages them to drain the same evil cup. John will develop these ideas further in chapter 17, where he portrays Rome as drunk on the blood of the saints.

The twofold "Fallen! Fallen!" announcing Rome's doom is patterned after Isaiah 21:9b: "Babylon has fallen, has fallen! All the images of its gods lie shattered on the ground!" As historical Babylon perished for its idolatry, so will God judge the "new Babylon" for its sin. The final judgment of Rome exemplifies the condemnation of all human powers that refuse to bow before God. John will describe the fall of Babylon in more detail in 18:1–19:4.

14:9-11 A third angel followed them and said in a loud voice: "If anyone worships the beast and his image and receives his mark on the forehead or on the hand, he, too, will drink of the wine of God's fury, which has been poured full strength into the cup of his wrath. He will be tormented with burning sulfur in the presence of the holy angels and of the Lamb. And the smoke of their torment rises for ever and ever. There is no rest day or night for those who worship the beast and his image, or for anyone who receives the mark of his name."

The third announcement of the final judgment focuses on "those who worship the beast and his image" and "anyone who receives the mark of his name." These symbols, which were introduced in 13:11-18 (see above), refer to anyone who makes government into a god, as Rome did in the first century. John describes the ultimate condemnation of such idolaters using two powerful images:

First, he likens God's eschatological "wrath" and "fury" to a "cup" filled with "wine" (cf. Rev 16:19). In doing so, John imitates several Old Testament prophets from the time of the Babylonian Exile, including the prophet Jeremiah:

---

[14]On adultery as a symbol for idolatry, see Part II.c.1.b of the Commentary: "The Teaching of Balaam."

This is what the Lord, the God of Israel, said to me: "Take from my hand this cup filled with the wine of my wrath and make all the nations to whom I send you drink it. When they drink it, they will stagger and go mad because of the sword I will send among them" (Jer 25:15-16; cf. Isa 51:17,22; Ezek 23:31-34).[15]

In the ancient world, people generally diluted their wine with water. John says that the "wine" of God's wrath will not be diluted. Instead, his enemies will be forced to drink it "full strength."

Second, John likens God's final judgment against idolaters to the annihilation of Sodom and Gomorrah, two classic examples of evil. In Genesis 19:24, God rains down "burning sulfur" on Sodom and Gomorrah. Likewise, the wicked are "tormented with burning sulfur" in Revelation 14:10. Looking toward Sodom and Gomorrah, Abraham sees "dense smoke rising from the land" in Genesis 19:28. Likewise, in Revelation 14:11, "the smoke of their torment rises for ever and ever," giving them "no rest."[16]

14:12-13 This calls for patient endurance on the part of the saints who obey God's commandments and remain faithful to Jesus. Then I heard a voice from heaven say, "Write: Blessed are the dead who die in the Lord from now on." "Yes," says the Spirit, "they will rest from their labor, for their deeds will follow them."

Those who "worship the beast" will perish like Sodom and Gomorrah. And yet those who refuse to worship the beast may find themselves in a Roman law court being sentenced to death for treason. What is a Christian to do in such an "impossible" situation? John gives his answer in verse 12: "This calls for patient endurance[17] on the part of the saints." In other words, Christians must firmly resist the pressure to embrace idolatry — even if that resistance does

---

[15]Compare also Jesus' prayer in Gethsemane as he faces the cross: "My Father, if it is possible, may *this cup* be taken from me. . . . My Father, if it is not possible for *this cup* to be taken away unless I drink it, may your will be done." (Matt 26:39,42//Mark 14:36//Luke 22:42; cf. Matt 20:22-23//Mark 10:38-39; John 18:11).

[16]Compare the "rest" the saints enjoy in verse 13.

[17]See the discussion of "patient endurance" in the comment on Rev 1:9.

indeed lead to death. This is the only way for Christians to "overcome" the forces of evil.[18]

In verse 13 a "voice from heaven" and the Holy Spirit himself strengthen the readers' resolve with important reminders: Those who die "in the Lord" — that is, within the sphere of Christ's lordship — will be "blessed" (μακάριοι, *makarioi*) by God. "Their deeds will follow them," for God will remember their obedience and their faith. Unlike the wicked, who will have "no rest" (v. 11), God's servants "will rest from their labor."

d. The Harvest of Earth (14:14-20)

¹⁴I looked, and there before me was a white cloud, and seated on the cloud was one "like a son of man"[a] with a crown of gold on his head and a sharp sickle in his hand. ¹⁵Then another angel came out of the temple and called in a loud voice to him who was sitting on the cloud, "Take your sickle and reap, because the time to reap has come, for the harvest of the earth is ripe." ¹⁶So he who was seated on the cloud swung his sickle over the earth, and the earth was harvested.

¹⁷Another angel came out of the temple in heaven, and he too had a sharp sickle. ¹⁸Still another angel, who had charge of the fire, came from the altar and called in a loud voice to him who had the sharp sickle, "Take your sharp sickle and gather the clusters of grapes from the earth's vine, because its grapes are ripe." ¹⁹The angel swung his sickle on the earth, gathered its grapes and threw them into the great winepress of God's wrath. ²⁰They were trampled in the winepress outside the city, and blood flowed out of the press, rising as high as the horses' bridles for a distance of 1,600 stadia.[b]

[a]*14* **Daniel 7:13**   [b]*20* **That is, about 180 miles (300 kilometers)**

14:14-20 With these verses, John launches a series of major visions depicting God's final judgment against his enemies. Christ appears as "one 'like a son of man,'" a Messianic title used of the Lord in Revelation 1:13 (see above). Here in chapter 14, he performs one of the major functions of the Messiah/Son of Man by carrying out God's eschatological judgment.

---

[18]See the discussion of "Christians as 'Overcomers'" in Part II.D.3 of the Commentary.

John pictures the final judgment as a "harvest" of the earth. Similar ideas appear elsewhere in the Bible (e.g., Isaiah 63:1-6) — notably in the teachings of Jesus (e.g., Matt 13:24-30,36-43). However, the primary source for John's imagery is Joel 3:13:

> Swing the sickle,
>   for the harvest is ripe.
> Come, trample the grapes,
>   for the winepress is full
>   and the vats overflow—
> so great is their wickedness!

The imagery is frightening. John first envisions the Lord's enemies as standing "grain." Just as harvesters reap the grain, so will God *cut down* the wicked.

The prophet then portrays God's "wrath" as a great "winepress" and the wicked as "grapes." Just as grapes are thrown into a winepress and trampled until the juice runs out, so are the wicked thrown into God's "wrath" and crushed until their blood runs out. The blood rises "as high as the horses' bridles for a distance of 1,600 stadia." In other words, it flows six or seven feet deep for nearly two hundred miles.

The Old Testament sometimes portrays Israel, God's covenant people, as a "vine" or "vineyard" (see, e.g., Isa 5:1-7; Jer 2:21; Ezek 19:10-14). Jesus describes the church, God's new covenant community, in similar terms (see John 15:1-8). If John is thinking of such texts, then the action of cutting the "grapes" off the vine may express the idea of *separating* the wicked from God's people — an important element in the final judgment.[19] The image of the "grapes" being trampled "outside the city" certainly communicates this truth.

---

[19]See above under Part a: "The Relationship between the Final Judgment and Consummation."

REVELATION 15

e. The Seven Last Plagues or Seven Bowls of God's Wrath (15:1-16:21)

¹I saw in heaven another great and marvelous sign: seven angels with the seven last plagues—last, because with them God's wrath is completed. ²And I saw what looked like a sea of glass mixed with fire and, standing beside the sea, those who had been victorious over the beast and his image and over the number of his name. They held harps given them by God ³and sang the song of Moses the servant of God and the song of the Lamb:

"Great and marvelous are your deeds,
 Lord God Almighty.
Just and true are your ways,
 King of the ages.
⁴Who will not fear you, O Lord,
 and bring glory to your name?
For you alone are holy.
All nations will come
 and worship before you,
for your righteous acts have been revealed."

⁵After this I looked and in heaven the temple, that is, the tabernacle of the Testimony, was opened. ⁶Out of the temple came the seven angels with the seven plagues. They were dressed in clean, shining linen and wore golden sashes around their chests. ⁷Then one of the four living creatures gave to the seven angels seven golden bowls filled with the wrath of God, who lives for ever and ever. ⁸And the temple was filled with smoke from the glory of God and from his power, and no one could enter the temple until the seven plagues of the seven angels were completed.

(1) The Structure of Revelation 15-16. Chapters 15 and 16 form a self-contained vision of God's final judgment against his enemies. The vision portrays the judgment as the unleashing of seven terrible

"plagues" or the pouring out of seven bowls filled with God's "wrath." The seven plagues are first mentioned in 15:1, and the final plague concludes in 16:21.

Like John's second vision of the future in 8:2–11:19,[1] this vision of the judgment is *loosely* based on the story of Israel's Exodus from Egypt. We sketch the main points of comparison below:

The Exodus Story	**The Final Judgment (Revelation 15-16)**
1. God devastates Egypt with ten terrible "plagues" (Exod 7:14–12:30).	1. & 3. God completely destroys his enemies with a series of seven "plagues" (Rev 16:1-21)
2. Israel crosses the Red Sea (Exod 13:17–14:22).	2. & 4. Redeemed saints stand beside "a sea of glass mixed with fire" and sing a song of redemption called "the song of Moses the servant of God and the song of the Lamb" (Rev 15:2-4).
3. God completely destroys the Egyptian army in the sea (Exod 14:23-31).	
4. Israel stands beside the Red Sea as Moses leads the people in singing a song of redemption (Exod 15:1-18).	
5. Israel later builds a tabernacle in the wilderness where the glory of God is present (Exod 25–40).	5. John anticipates that Christians will later enter a "tabernacle" where the glory of God is present (Rev 15:8).

By likening God's destruction of his enemies to the devastation of Egypt, and by likening the salvation of God's servants to the deliverance of Israel, John again encourages his readers to think of the final judgment as a "Second Exodus" for God's covenant people. Below, we will examine more closely the various elements of the vision.

(2) The Sea of Glass and Fire (15:1-4). The vision opens with an image of the redeemed saints standing by a "sea," just as Israel stood by the Red Sea so many centuries ago. In the vision, John draws a comparison between the circumstances of Christians at the time of Christ's Second Coming and the circumstances of the Israelites at the time of their Exodus from Egypt.

---

[1]See Part III.C.1.c of the Commentary: "The Dominant Image: God's Coming Kingdom as a 'Second Exodus' for his People."

15:1 I saw in heaven another great and marvelous sign: seven angels with the seven last plagues—last, because with them God's wrath is completed.

John reminds us that the seven bowls of "plagues" are a "sign" — that is, a symbol pointing to the deeper reality of God's impending judgment.[2] By calling them the "last plagues," he informs his readers that the frightening images to come do not portray the hardships of the "labor pains" (as did the "plagues" of Revelation 8 and 9 — see particularly 9:20). Nor do they symbolize God's common, everyday punishments for sin. The judgment of which John speaks in Revelation 15-16 is the *final* judgment.

15:2a And I saw what looked like a sea of glass mixed with fire and, standing beside the sea, those who had been victorious over the beast and his image and over the number of his name.

As explained in the comment on 4:6a, the "sea" symbolizes evil and chaos. John portrays it as a "sea of glass" — that is, perfectly calm, perfectly still — because the forces of evil have been subdued by God through the sacrificial death of Christ. Evil still exists, but it suffered a decisive defeat on the Cross as the kingdom of God began to supplant the kingdom of Satan. The "present evil age" persists, but the "eschatological age" has begun with the victory of the Lamb.[3] At the consummation of God's kingdom described in 21:1, evil will cease to exist entirely — there will be "no longer any sea."

"Those who had been victorious over the beast" are the Christians mentioned in 14:12 — "the saints who obey God's commandments and remain faithful to Jesus." They have displayed "patient endurance"; they have persistently refused to worship the "beast" by putting Caesar, or any other power, on the throne of God.[4] John pictures them "standing beside the sea," just as Israel stands by the Red Sea in Exodus 14.

---

[2]See the comment on "He made it known" in Revelation 1:1.

[3]For further discussion of these truths, see Part III.B.2.c.(4) of the Introduction, "The Kingdom of God and the Death of Jesus"; Part III.B.2.d(2) of the Introduction, "The Coming of God's Kingdom"; and Part II.D.2 of the Commentary, "Christ as 'Overcomer'". For a graphic representation of the "overlap" of the two ages, see Fig. 2, "The Shape of Christian Apocalyptic Theology," p. 41.

[4]For a discussion of the "beast" and his "image," see the comments on Revelation 13 — particularly verses 4-10 and 12-17.

Like Israel, these Christians have passed through the waters — that is, they have passed through the "present evil age." It has been a painful, difficult journey, full of trouble, persecution, and even martyrdom. The "sea" has been "mixed with fire," but now at last they stand safe and dry on the far "shore," at the end of time. Like Israel, they will witness the destruction of their enemies.

15:2b-3a They held harps given them by God and sang the song of Moses the servant of God and the song of the Lamb:

In Exodus 15, Moses leads Israel in singing a song of praise to God for "shattering" the Egyptians. Similarly, in Revelation 15, the church sings a song of praise to God for defeating their enemies through Christ. John explicitly draws a connection between this "Second Exodus" and the first by calling their hymn "the song of Moses the servant of God and the song of the Lamb."

Concerning the "harps" used to accompany the singing, see the comment on Revelation 14:2. The fact that the harps are "given them by God" signifies that it is the Lord alone who gives redemption — who enables his people to sing the song of victory.

15:3b-4 "Great and marvelous are your deeds, Lord God Almighty. Just and true are your ways, King of the ages. Who will not fear you, O Lord, and bring glory to your name? For you alone are holy. All nations will come and worship before you, for your righteous acts have been revealed."

In its song, the church praises God as "Lord," as "King,"[5] and as the "Almighty."[6] At this point in John's narrative, God is destroying his enemies and exerting his kingly authority in its fullness. The King displays his "holiness" by showing himself to be "set apart" from all others as unique, the one and only God, without rival. He displays his "righteousness" by keeping his new covenant promises to destroy the forces of evil and save his faithful saints. He displays his "justice" by giving his enemies the punishment they deserve.[7]

---

[5]Some manuscripts read "King of the nations," rather than "King of the ages."

[6]On this divine title, see the comment on "him who is, and who was, and who is to come" in Revelation 1:4.

[7]For further discussion of how God is "just" in his judgments, see the comment on Revelation 16:5-7.

In adapting the Exodus story, John slightly changes the order of events. Israel *first* sees the destruction of the Egyptians in the Red Sea, and then *afterwards* sings a song of redemption. In contrast, the saints in Revelation *first* sing a song of redemption in chapter 15, and then *afterwards* witness the destruction of their enemies in chapter 16. How can this be? Christians are able to sing songs of redemption *before* the final judgment because their final victory is assured. Christ won the decisive battle against evil on the cross. All that remain are the "mopping up operations."[8]

(3) The Heavenly Tabernacle (15:5-8). After the Israelites crossed the Red Sea, they built a tabernacle where God caused his presence to dwell. After Christians cross the "sea" in Revelation 15, a heavenly "tabernacle" appears.

15:5-8 After this I looked and in heaven the temple, that is, the tabernacle of the Testimony, was opened. Out of the temple came the seven angels with the seven plagues. They were dressed in clean, shining linen and wore golden sashes around their chests. Then one of the four living creatures gave to the seven angels seven golden bowls filled with the wrath of God, who lives for ever and ever. And the temple was filled with smoke from the glory of God and from his power, and no one could enter the temple until the seven plagues of the seven angels were completed.

John calls the structure "the tabernacle of the Testimony." The term "Testimony" refers to the stone tablets on which the Ten Commandments were inscribed. As the heart of the Mosaic Law and the basis for the Mosaic covenant between God and Israel, these tablets were placed in the Ark of the Covenant within the tabernacle's inner room. By mentioning the "Testimony" in verse 5, John is linking the heavenly tabernacle with the tabernacle of Exodus as the place of God's glorious presence.[9]

---

[8] See Part III.B.2.c.(4) of the Introduction: "The Kingdom of God and the Death of Jesus."

[9] See, for example, Exodus 31:18 ("When the LORD finished speaking [the Law] to Moses on Mount Sinai, he gave him the two tablets of the Testimony, the tablets of stone inscribed by the finger of God.") and 25:21-22 ("Place the cover on top of the ark and put in the ark the Testimony, which I will give you. There, above the cover between the two cherubim that

The angels, robed in priestly garments[10] and carrying the seven bowls of God's wrath, exit from the tabernacle — that is, from the presence of God. When they empty the bowls, and thus carry out the final judgment, they will be acting as God's agents.

Verse 8 implies that, after the judgment, Christians will be able to enter the heavenly temple and draw near to God. John describes this event later in the book, in Revelation 21:22. As in Exodus, God's victory over evil comes first. Only then may the redeemed enter his presence.

---

are over the ark of the Testimony, I will meet with you and give you all my commands for the Israelites.").

[10]Compare the angels' "golden sashes" with the "golden sash" worn by the risen Christ in Revelation 1:13. Compare the "clean, shining linen" worn by the angels with the "clean white" garments worn by the angelic army in 19:14, and the "shining and clean" garments of the Bride of Christ in 19:8.

REVELATION 16

¹Then I heard a loud voice from the temple saying to the seven angels, "Go, pour out the seven bowls of God's wrath on the earth."

²The first angel went and poured out his bowl on the land, and ugly and painful sores broke out on the people who had the mark of the beast and worshiped his image.

³The second angel poured out his bowl on the sea, and it turned into blood like that of a dead man, and every living thing in the sea died.

⁴The third angel poured out his bowl on the rivers and springs of water, and they became blood. ⁵Then I heard the angel in charge of the waters say:

"You are just in these judgments,
   you who are and who were, the Holy One,
   because you have so judged;
⁶for they have shed the blood of your saints and
     prophets,
   and you have given them blood to drink as they
     deserve."

⁷And I heard the altar respond:

"Yes, Lord God Almighty,
   true and just are your judgments."

⁸The fourth angel poured out his bowl on the sun, and the sun was given power to scorch people with fire. ⁹They were seared by the intense heat and they cursed the name of God, who had control over these plagues, but they refused to repent and glorify him.

¹⁰The fifth angel poured out his bowl on the throne of the beast, and his kingdom was plunged into darkness. Men gnawed their tongues in agony ¹¹and cursed the God of heaven because of their pains and their sores, but they refused to repent of what they had done.

¹²The sixth angel poured out his bowl on the great river Euphrates, and its water was dried up to prepare the way for the kings from the East. ¹³Then I saw three evil[a] spirits that looked like frogs; they came out of the mouth of the dragon, out of the mouth of the beast and out of the mouth of the false prophet. ¹⁴They are spirits of demons performing miraculous signs, and they go out to the kings of the whole world, to gather them for the battle on the great day of God Almighty.

¹⁵"Behold, I come like a thief! Blessed is he who stays awake and keeps his clothes with him, so that he may not go naked and be shamefully exposed."

¹⁶Then they gathered the kings together to the place that in Hebrew is called Armageddon.

¹⁷The seventh angel poured out his bowl into the air, and out of the temple came a loud voice from the throne, saying, "It is done!" ¹⁸Then there came flashes of lightning, rumblings, peals of thunder and a severe earthquake. No earthquake like it has ever occurred since man has been on earth, so tremendous was the quake. ¹⁹The great city split into three parts, and the cities of the nations collapsed. God remembered Babylon the Great and gave her the cup filled with the wine of the fury of his wrath. ²⁰Every island fled away and the mountains could not be found. ²¹From the sky huge hailstones of about a hundred pounds each fell upon men. And they cursed God on account of the plague of hail, because the plague was so terrible.

[a]*13* Greek *unclean*

16:1 Then I heard a loud voice from the temple saying to the seven angels, "Go, pour out the seven bowls of God's wrath on the earth."

(4) The Meaning of the Seven Bowls of God's Wrath (16:1). The bowls contain God's "wrath," or his anger expressed against sin and evil. John refers to the contents of the bowls as "plagues" (15:1,8; 16:9,21). As we will see, the terrible judgments poured out from the bowls loosely resemble specific "plagues" that God unleashed against Egypt. This has theological significance: Just as the ten "plagues" were the means by which God delivered Israel from Egypt, so will the seven bowls of wrath deliver the church from the forces of evil. They effect a "Second Exodus" for the people of God.

The bowls of wrath symbolize not merely God's judgment, but his *final judgment*. John expresses this truth in two primary ways:

First, the prophet envisions "seven" bowls of wrath (rather than "ten," which would make the connection with Exodus even clearer). "Seven" is the apocalyptic number for "fullness" or "completeness,"[1] so the seven bowls represent God's wrath poured out undiluted, without restraint, with nothing held in reserve, with nothing left for the future. A clear statement of this idea appears in Revelation 15:1:

> I saw in heaven another great and marvelous sign: seven angels with the seven last plagues — last, because with them God's wrath is completed.

The "It is done!" of 16:17 reiterates this point.

Second, we have seen that, in Revelation 8–9, John compares the hardships of the "present evil age" and "labor pains" with the plagues unleashed against Egypt. The "plagues" of these earlier chapters cause only *partial* destruction. For example, only "a third of the trees were burned up" (8:7) and "a third of the living creatures in the sea died" (8:9).[2] These "plagues" do not represent the end of the world, but only God's punishment of sin during the period leading up to the Second Coming of Christ.[3] In contrast to chapters 8 and 9, the "plagues" of chapter 16 wreak *total* destruction: "*Every* living thing in the sea" dies (v. 3). *All* the "islands" and "mountains" (v. 20), *all* the "rivers and springs of water" (v. 4), and *all* the "cities of the nations" are affected. Revelation 16 portrays the *total* destruction of God's *final judgment.*

Since the "plagues" of chapters 8 and 9 symbolize the "present evil age" and "labor pains," they affect Christians and non-Christians alike. In contrast, the "plagues" of chapter 16 symbolize God's eschatological condemnation of his enemies. They affect only "the people who had the mark of the beast and worshiped his image" (v. 2), those who have "shed the blood of [God's] saints and prophets" (v. 6), "the beast and his kingdom" (v. 10), and "Babylon the Great" (v. 19).

---

[1]See the Introduction, Part III.B.1.d: "Symbolic Numbers."

[2]See Part III.C.2.a.(9) of the Commentary: "Partial Destruction versus Total Destruction."

[3]See Part III.C.2.c of the Commentary: "The 'Present Evil Age' and 'Labor Pains' as God's Judgment on Sin and Call to Repentance."

What form does the final judgment take? Revelation 16 presents it in terms of God releasing all sorts of destructive forces against those who oppose him — sickness and disease, powerful forces of nature, evil spirits, war and death. The Almighty removes his sustaining hand and plunges the world into chaos. God's condemnation is the opposite of creation; it is the uncreation of his enemies.

16:2 The first angel went and poured out his bowl on the land, and ugly and painful sores broke out on the people who had the mark of the beast and worshiped his image.

(5) The First Bowl of Wrath (16:2). The first bowl of wrath reminds us of the plague of boils in Exodus 9:8-12. God removes his protective hand and the very bodies of his enemies begin to deteriorate. He hammers them with sickness and disease.

16:3 The second angel poured out his bowl on the sea, and it turned into blood like that of a dead man, and every living thing in the sea died.

(6) The Second Bowl of Wrath (16:3). The second bowl calls to mind both the turning of the Nile to blood in Exodus 7:14-24 and the final plague of death in Exodus 11:1-12:30. Whereas the Egyptian plagues affect only the Nile and only the firstborn sons, the plague of Revelation 16 affects the larger waters of the sea and "every living thing" dies.

It is possible that John intends for the term "sea" to be understood here in its symbolic sense.[4] In this case, the angel pours out his bowl on all forces of evil and chaos (represented by the "sea"). The result is that evil itself "dies."

16:4-7 The third angel poured out his bowl on the rivers and springs of water, and they became blood. Then I heard the angel in charge of the waters say: "You are just in these judgments, you who are and who were, the Holy One, because you have so judged; for they have shed the blood of your saints and prophets, and you have given them blood to drink as they deserve." And I heard the altar respond: "Yes, Lord God Almighty, true and just are your judgments."

---

[4]For an explanation, see the comment on the "sea of glass" in Rev 4:6a.

(7) The Third Bowl of Wrath (16:4-7). The plague of water turned to blood calls to mind the similar plague in Exodus 7:14-24. Again, the final judgment is more comprehensive, for it affects not only the Nile, but all "the rivers and springs of water."

The angel refers to the Lord as "you who are and who were." He leaves off the traditional third element in the title ("and who is to come") because, at this point in Revelation, the Lord *has* come. John is describing God's final judgment, which occurs at the Second Coming of Christ. For further discussion of this threefold designation for God and the related title "Almighty," see the comment on Revelation 1:4c.

The angel declares that God is "just" (or "righteous," δίκαιος, *dikaios*) in carrying out these judgments, and a voice from the altar (where the souls of the martyred saints lay in 6:9) agrees. When biblical writers speak of "just" or "righteous" judges, they mean persons who render "appropriate" judgments, or who judge in accordance with the "truth." They mean judges who consistently, and without partiality, acquit those who are truly innocent and condemn those who are truly guilty.[5] The several books of the Maccabees call a judgment "appropriate" or "righteous" if it fits the crime. We find an example of such "poetic justice" in 2 Maccabees 9:6, where God "righteously" afflicts Antiochus with a terrible bowel disease "since he had tormented others' bowels with many unusual calamities." Another example appears in 13:7, where Menelaus smothers in a tower full of ashes "inasmuch as he had committed many sins about the altar, whose fire and ashes were holy."

In Revelation 16, John presents the Lord God as a righteous Judge. His judgments are "just" and "true" (vv. 5,7). They are "deserved" by his enemies (v. 6). Furthermore, God's judgments fit the crime: "They have shed the blood of your saints and prophets, and you have given them blood to drink as they deserve."

16:8-9 The fourth angel poured out his bowl on the sun, and the sun was given power to scorch people with fire. They were seared by the

---

[5]See Proverbs 17:15: "Acquitting the guilty and condemning the innocent — the LORD detests them both." Cf. 24:23-26; Exodus 23:2-3,6-8; Leviticus 19:15; Deuteronomy 1:16-17; 16:18-20; 25:1.

intense heat and they cursed the name of God, who had control over these plagues, but they refused to repent and glorify him.

(8) The Fourth Bowl of Wrath (16:8-9). The fourth angel offers up the opposite of the plague of darkness in Exodus 10:21-29. Instead of depriving human beings of the light of the sun, God — in his final judgment — is pictured unleashing the destructive powers of nature against sinners.

16:10-11 The fifth angel poured out his bowl on the throne of the beast, and his kingdom was plunged into darkness. Men gnawed their tongues in agony and cursed the God of heaven because of their pains and their sores, but they refused to repent of what they had done.

(9) The Fifth Bowl of Wrath (16:10-11). The fifth bowl of wrath calls to remembrance the plague of darkness in Exodus 10:21-29. Again, the plague is directed against God's enemies — "the beast and his kingdom," those who "curse the God of heaven" and "refuse to repent" of their sins.

16:12-14,16 The sixth angel poured out his bowl on the great river Euphrates, and its water was dried up to prepare the way for the kings from the East. Then I saw three evil spirits that looked like frogs; they came out of the mouth of the dragon, out of the mouth of the beast and out of the mouth of the false prophet. They are spirits of demons performing miraculous signs, and they go out to the kings of the whole world, to gather them for the battle on the great day of God Almighty. . . . Then they gathered the kings together to the place that in Hebrew is called Armageddon.

(10) The Sixth Bowl of Wrath (16:12-14,16). The sixth bowl of wrath recalls the plague of frogs described in Exodus 8:1-15. As in the parallel sixth plague of Revelation 9:13-21, the imagery is intensified. The frogs become demon frogs to show that John is not speaking of normal, everyday occurrences, but of earthshaking eschatological events.[6]

The demons come forth from the mouths of the "dragon" (i.e., Satan), the "beast" (i.e., political powers allied with Satan), and the

---

[6]See Part III.C.2.a.(8) of the Commentary: "Heightened Imagery Portraying Eschatological Events."

"false prophet" (i.e., religious authorities who give their support to political powers allied with Satan).[7] Together they incite "the kings of the whole world" to gather for "battle" against God and his Christ.[8] In other words, John envisions Satan and the other demonic powers (the "dragon" and "evil spirits") using their human allies (the "beast" and "false prophet," or political and religious authorities such as those in Rome) to turn the nations to idolatry and hostility toward God and his people.[9]

However, God is gathering his forces to meet them: "The sixth angel poured out his bowl on the great river Euphrates, and its water was dried up to prepare the way for the kings from the East." John's first readers would have understood "the kings from the East" to refer to nations such as the Parthians, who lived in what is now northeastern Iran. The Parthians were fierce warriors, and the Romans lived in constant fear that they would one day cross the Euphrates River and invade the Empire. As God once dried up the Jordan River to allow Israel to cross and conquer the idolatrous Canaanites (see Josh 3:15-17), so John envisions him now drying up the Euphrates River to allow his chosen instruments to cross and destroy his enemies.

God's enemies gather together "to the place that in Hebrew is called Armageddon." In Hebrew, the term *Har* means "mountain." *Har-Mageddon,* or "Armageddon," means, then, "Mountain of Mageddon." There is no such place in Scripture, and no such place in the world. What, then, does John mean by this symbol? As we have seen,[10] the prophet's symbolism is evocative, tensive, and polyvalent. In other words, it evokes in the mind of the reader a number of possible interpretations. It sets up a tension between the various possible meanings, forcing the reader to consider which interpretations apply. Finally, it is possible for John's symbols to communicate

---

[7]For a detailed analysis of these symbols, see the commentary on Revelation 12–13.

[8]Compare Revelation 17:12-14, where John says more explicitly that the "beast" and the "kings" of the earth "make war against the Lamb."

[9]Compare Revelation 17:2: "*With* [the great prostitute, or Rome] the kings of the earth committed adultery [i.e., unfaithfulness to God] and the inhabitants of the earth were intoxicated with the wine of her adulteries."

[10]See the comment on "someone 'like a son of man'" in Revelation 1:13.

multiple meanings simultaneously. In the case of "Armageddon," three possible meanings come to mind.

First, some scholars[11] suggest that *Har-Mageddon* sounds like *Har-Mōēd*, the term translated "mount of assembly" in Isaiah 14:13. The "mount of assembly" refers to a mountain north of Babylon that was thought to be the assembly place of the gods. Isaiah uses the term as part of an oracle against Babylon and a taunt against Nebuchadnezzar, the king of Babylon. Nebuchadnezzar is so powerful, so exalted, that he begins to think of himself as a god, deserving a place among the gods. However, Isaiah predicts that both he and his kingdom will fall:

> How you have fallen from heaven,
>   O morning star, son of the dawn!
> You have been cast down to the earth,
>   you who once laid low the nations!
> You said in your heart,
>   "I will ascend to heaven;
> I will raise my throne
>   above the stars of God;
> I will sit enthroned on the *mount of assembly*,
>   on the utmost heights of the sacred mountain.
> I will ascend above the tops of the clouds;
>   I will make myself like the Most High."
> But you are brought down to the grave,
>   to the depths of the pit (Isa 14:12-15).

Interpreting *Har-Mageddon* as "mount of assembly" fits beautifully in the context of Revelation 16. John is describing the "fall" of "Babylon the Great," which symbolizes Rome and any other human power that attempts to put itself in the place of God. John envisions the kings of the idolatrous nations being gathered together to *Har-Mōēd*, the very height from which Nebuchadnezzar was cast down. Like Nebuchadnezzar before them, these enemies of God will be "brought down to the grave, to the depths of the pit."

This is an intriguing theory. However, in the judgment of this writer, *Har-Mōēd* does not sound enough like *Har-Mageddon* to make

---

[11]Such as Matthias Rissi in *The Future of the World: An Exegetical Study of Revelation 19:11–22:15*, Studies in Biblical Theology, Second Series, 23 (London: SCM Press, Ltd., 1972), pp. 84-85.

the theory plausible. It does not seem likely that John's readers would have drawn the necessary connection between *Har-Mageddon* and Isaiah 14.

Second, *Har-Mageddon* sounds very much like *Har-Megiddo*, or "Mount of Megiddo." Located in northern Israel, the city of Megiddo (sometimes pronounced *Mageddo* or *Mageddon*[12]) held great strategic importance in the ancient world. It lay along one of the primary trade routes running between Egypt in the south, and Asia and Europe to the north. Furthermore, Megiddo was situated on the edge of the Plain of Esdraelon (otherwise known as the "Plain of Jezreel" or the "Plain of Megiddo"), which bisected Israel from east to west. Whoever controlled the Plain and the fortress of Megiddo controlled the trade routes and the whole country of Israel. For this reason, many important battles were fought in this area.[13]

There was no mountain at Megiddo, but only the small artificial mound on which the city was built. What, then, are we to make of John's reference to *Har-Megiddo*, or "Mount of Megiddo"? *It may be that the prophet calls up images of Megiddo to cause his readers to think of a place of battle or war.* He manufactures the name *Har-Megiddo* as a way of reminding his readers that this is not a real place, but a symbol. In other words, Revelation 16:14 and 16 should be "heard" as follows:

> [The demons] go out to the kings of the whole world, to gather them *for the battle* on the great day of God Almighty.... Then they gathered the kings together to *the place of battle*.

This interpretation of Revelation 16:14,16 seems quite plausible in light of the historical connection between Megiddo and Esdraelon, the plain of battle.

Third, while there is no mountain at Megiddo itself, a prominent mountain stands nearby — namely, Mount Carmel. This mountain was the site of one of the most dramatic events in Old Testament history. First Kings 18 describes how the prophet Elijah, at this very place, delivered a challenge to the people of Israel:

---

[12]See, for example, the Hebrew text of Zechariah 12:11. Such matters are complicated by the fact that biblical Hebrew is written without vowels.

[13]For example, Deborah and Barak versus the Canaanite king Sisera in Judges 5:19, Jehu versus King Joram of Israel and King Ahaziah of Judah in 2 Kings 9:27, and King Josiah of Judah versus Pharaoh Neco in 2 Kings 23:29.

Elijah went before the people and said, "How long will you waver between two opinions? If the LORD is God, follow him; but if Baal is God, follow him."

But the people said nothing.

Then Elijah said to them, "I am the only one of the LORD's prophets left, but Baal has four hundred and fifty prophets. Get two bulls for us. Let them choose one for themselves, and let them cut it into pieces and put it on the wood but not set fire to it. I will prepare the other bull and put it on the wood but not set fire to it. Then you call on the name of your god, and I will call on the name of the LORD. The god who answers by fire—he is God" (1 Kgs 18:21-24).

The prophets of Baal build their altar and lay the sacrifice on it. They cry out to Baal all morning and afternoon, but nothing happens. That evening Elijah builds his own altar of twelve stones, lays the sacrifice on it, digs a trench around the altar, and pours water over the whole until it even fills the trench.

At the time of sacrifice, the prophet Elijah stepped forward and prayed: "O LORD, God of Abraham, Isaac and Israel, let it be known today that you are God in Israel and that I am your servant and have done all these things at your command. Answer me, O LORD, answer me, so these people will know that you, O LORD, are God, and that you are turning their hearts back again."

Then the fire of the LORD fell and burned up the sacrifice, the wood, the stones and the soil, and also licked up the water in the trench.

When all the people saw this, they fell prostrate and cried, "The LORD—he is God! The LORD—he is God!"

Then Elijah commanded them, "Seize the prophets of Baal. Don't let anyone get away!" They seized them, and Elijah had them brought down to the Kishon Valley and slaughtered there (1 Kings 18:36-40).

Against this background, we may offer a second quite plausible interpretation of Revelation 16:15. It may be that, when John describes the kings of the earth gathering for battle at the "Mount of Megiddo," he intends for his readers to think of Mount Carmel. As Elijah slaughtered the prophets of Baal at Carmel, so will God slaughter those who oppose him at *Har-Megiddo*. The mysterious

"Armageddon" serves, then, as a symbol for the total defeat of God's enemies at the final judgment.

In light of the preceding analysis, how should we understand the symbol of the sixth bowl of wrath in Revelation 16? John indicates that Satan, the demons, and their human allies incite the "kings of the whole world" to battle against God. If they want war, then God will give them war! The nations gather together at "Armageddon," which may be understood simply as the symbolic place of battle (drawing a connection with Megiddo and the Plain of Esdraelon), or – more ominously – as the place where God annihilates his foes (drawing a connection with Mount Carmel). The Lord sends in his own forces, symbolized by the fearsome "kings from the East." He dries up the river before them, allowing them to cross. The last time God did such a thing, he was preparing the way for Joshua and Israel to destroy the idolatrous Canaanites. Watching God's armies likewise cross on dry land does not bode well for the idolaters waiting at Armageddon. Even more foreboding is the date chosen for the battle. It will occur on "the great day of God Almighty." This is a variation of the biblical idea of the "Day of the Lord,"[14] which refers to any day on which God defeats his enemies and saves his people. The final judgment promises to be the ultimate "Day of the Lord."[15]

In the case of the sixth bowl, God's eschatological "wrath" takes the form of war or total annihilation in battle. Here is yet another "weapon" God will wield against the wicked. Disease, death, blood, the burning sun, poisoned water, war – the list becomes overwhelming. In contemplating these powerful images, the reader must not lose sight of John's basic idea in chapter 16: At the final judgment, God will release every destructive force imaginable against his enemies.

---

[14]For a discussion of this concept, see Part III.C.2.g of the Commentary: "The Sounding of the Seven Trumpets: The 'Present Evil Age' and 'Labor Pains' as the Announcement of the Day of the Lord."

[15]It is striking that Revelation 16 never describes an actual *battle* at Armageddon. John only implies what its outcome will be. The final "battle" occurs as part of a later vision in Revelation 19:21. We will discuss this very one-sided contest at the appropriate point in the Commentary.

16:15 "Behold, I come like a thief! Blessed is he who stays awake and keeps his clothes with him, so that he may not go naked and be shamefully exposed."

(11) Interlude (16:15). Each of John's three visions of the future includes a series of seven elements — namely, seven seals in 6:1–8:1, seven trumpets in 8:2–11:19, and seven bowls in 12:1–22:6. Between the sixth and seventh elements in each series, John includes an "interlude" that, for a moment, interrupts the flow of the narrative. These interludes appear in 7:1-17; 10:1–11:14; and here again in 16:15. In Revelation the interludes serve to build suspense leading up to the climactic seventh elements. Furthermore, they encourage Christian readers to reflect on their present conduct in light of the future glory God has prepared for them.

In the middle of John's description of the coming final judgment, the voice of Jesus suddenly breaks in with a warning: "Behold, I come like a thief![16]" — that is, suddenly, unexpectedly, as a surprise. Since the time of Christ's Second Coming and final judgment are unknown, Christians must remain constantly alert and constantly prepared for that Day. Blessed are those not "caught with their pants down" at the Lord's return.

Why does the Lord speak in the middle of John's description of the sixth plague, rather than between the descriptions of the sixth plague and the seventh? In other words, why does the interlude fall between verses 14 and 16, rather than between verses 16 and 17? Perhaps the intent is to associate the Second Coming of Christ mentioned in the interlude with the Day of the Lord, or "the great day of God Almighty" mentioned at the end of verse 14.

16:17-21 The seventh angel poured out his bowl into the air, and out of the temple came a loud voice from the throne, saying, "It is done!" Then there came flashes of lightning, rumblings, peals of thunder and a severe earthquake. No earthquake like it has ever occurred since man has been on earth, so tremendous was the quake. The great city split into three parts, and the cities of the nations collapsed. God remembered Babylon the Great and gave her the cup filled with the wine of the fury of his wrath. Every

---

[16]Compare Matthew 24:43 // Luke 12:39; 1 Thessalonians 5:2,4; 2 Peter 3:10; Revelation 3:3.

island fled away and the mountains could not be found. From the sky huge hailstones of about a hundred pounds each fell upon men. And they cursed God on account of the plague of hail, because the plague was so terrible.

(12) The Seventh Bowl of Wrath (16:17-21). The seventh and final bowl of wrath calls to mind the plague described in Exodus 9:13-35: "The LORD sent thunder and hail, and . . . lightning flashed back and forth" (vv. 23-24). Again John employs heightened imagery ("huge hailstones of about a hundred pounds each," "no earthquake like it has ever occurred") to show he is speaking of end-time events.[17]

The thunder, hail, and lightning are accompanied by a "tremendous earthquake" unprecedented in its strength. The Old Testament roots of this image may be traced to passages such as Haggai 2:6-7:

> This is what the LORD Almighty says: "In a little while I will once more shake the heavens and the earth, the sea and the dry land. I will shake all nations, and the desired of all nations will come . . . .

The Hebrews writer interprets this text as a prophecy of the final judgment and the consummation of God's eternal kingdom. He writes:

> [God] has promised, "Once more I will shake not only the earth but also the heavens. The words "once more" indicate the removing of what can be shaken—that is, created things [such as human kingdoms]—so that what cannot be shaken [the kingdom of God] may remain.
>
> Therefore, since we are receiving a kingdom that cannot be shaken, let us be thankful, and so worship God acceptably with reverence and awe, for our "God is a consuming fire" (Heb 12:26b-29).

Like the Hebrews writer, John uses the "earthquake" to symbolize God's final judgment. He did the same in both of his earlier visions of the future (see Rev 6:12-17; 11:13). When the "earthquake" comes, the islands flee, the mountains disappear, and the nations collapse. God shouts, "It is done!" thus declaring the end of the world as we know it.

---

[17]See Part III.C.2.a.(8) of the Commentary: "Heightened Imagery Portraying Eschatological Events."

When the end comes, "Babylon the Great" — the "great city" symbolizing Rome[18] and all other human powers opposed to God — "splits into three parts" and passes away. The Lord forces Babylon to drain dry the "cup" filled with his wrath.[19] John will describe the fall of Babylon in more detail in his next vision (Rev 17:1-19:4).

---

[18]For discussions of Rome as the second "Babylon," see the comments on Rev 14:8 and 17:9.

[19]On the image of the "cup" of God's wrath, see the comment on Rev 14:8.

REVELATION 17

f. God's Final Judgment against Babylon (17:1-19:4)

We now turn to John's vision of the final judgment against Babylon in Revelation 17:1-19:4. As we will see, "Babylon" symbolizes Rome. However, the vision has broader application, for the condemnation of Rome is representative of the condemnation that awaits any human authority that opposes God. We begin by examining the symbols of the "great prostitute" and the "scarlet beast" in chapter 17.

¹One of the seven angels who had the seven bowls came and said to me, "Come, I will show you the punishment of the great prostitute, who sits on many waters. ²With her the kings of the earth committed adultery and the inhabitants of the earth were intoxicated with the wine of her adulteries."

³Then the angel carried me away in the Spirit into a desert. There I saw a woman sitting on a scarlet beast that was covered with blasphemous names and had seven heads and ten horns. ⁴The woman was dressed in purple and scarlet, and was glittering with gold, precious stones and pearls. She held a golden cup in her hand, filled with abominable things and the filth of her adulteries. ⁵This title was written on her forehead:

MYSTERY
BABYLON THE GREAT
THE MOTHER OF PROSTITUTES
AND OF THE ABOMINATIONS OF THE EARTH.

⁶I saw that the woman was drunk with the blood of the saints, the blood of those who bore testimony to Jesus.

When I saw her, I was greatly astonished. ⁷Then the angel said to me: "Why are you astonished? I will explain to you the mystery of the woman and of the beast she rides, which has the seven heads and ten horns. ⁸The beast, which you saw, once was, now is not, and will come up out of the Abyss and go to his destruction. The inhabitants of the earth whose names have not been written in the book of life from the creation of the world will be astonished when they see the beast, because he once was, now is not, and yet will come.

⁹"This calls for a mind with wisdom. The seven heads are seven hills on which the woman sits. ¹⁰They are also seven kings. Five have fallen, one is, the other has not yet come; but when he does come, he must remain for a little while. ¹¹The beast who once was, and now is not, is an eighth king. He belongs to the seven and is going to his destruction.

¹²"The ten horns you saw are ten kings who have not yet received a kingdom, but who for one hour will receive authority as kings along with the beast. ¹³They have one purpose and will give their power and authority to the beast. ¹⁴They will make war against the Lamb, but the Lamb will overcome them because he is Lord of lords and King of kings—and with him will be his called, chosen and faithful followers."

¹⁵Then the angel said to me, "The waters you saw, where the prostitute sits, are peoples, multitudes, nations and languages. ¹⁶The beast and the ten horns you saw will hate the prostitute. They will bring her to ruin and leave her naked; they will eat her flesh and burn her with fire. ¹⁷For God has put it into their hearts to accomplish his purpose by agreeing to give the beast their power to rule, until God's words are fulfilled. ¹⁸The woman you saw is the great city that rules over the kings of the earth."

17:1a One of the seven angels who had the seven bowls came and said to me, "Come, I will show you the punishment of the great prostitute. . . ."

(1) The Great Prostitute (17:1-18). The angel announces a vision of "the punishment of the great prostitute." This is the subject of 17:1–19:4. Who exactly is this "great prostitute"? The angel identifies her in verse 18.

17:18 The woman you saw is the great city that rules over the kings of the earth.

The prostitute is Rome, the "great city" of Italy that ruled over the entire Mediterranean world. In John's time, the Roman Empire stretched from what is now France and Belgium in the north to Egypt in the south, and from Spain and Portugal in the west to the Caspian Sea in the east.

By picturing Rome as a woman, John may simply be following the Old Testament tradition of portraying cities as females.[1] However, his intention may be to picture the city as the goddess Roma, the patron goddess and "mother" of the Roman Empire. John's "astonishment" at seeing the woman (v. 6) is a typical human reaction to an encounter with deity.[2]

17:1b,4a,15 the great prostitute, who sits on many waters. . . . The woman was dressed in purple and scarlet, and was glittering with gold, precious stones and pearls. She held a golden cup in her hand . . . . Then the angel said to me, "The waters you saw, where the prostitute sits, are peoples, multitudes, nations and languages."

The image of the woman straddling "many waters" refers to Rome's dominance of the Mediterranean basin. Through organizational genius, naval supremacy, and brutal military force, the Romans grew rich on tribute from the surrounding nations. The woman's fine clothing, jewelry, and golden cup reflect this fabulous wealth.

At the same time, the "many waters," the "golden cup," and the great wealth link Rome with the prophecy found in Jeremiah 51:6-14:

> Flee from Babylon!
> > Run for your lives!
> > Do not be destroyed because of her sins.
> It is time for the LORD's vengeance;
> > he will pay her what she deserves.
> Babylon was *a gold cup* in the LORD's hand;
> > she made the whole earth drunk.
> The nations drank her wine;
> > therefore they have now gone mad.
> Babylon will suddenly fall and be broken
> > Wail over her!

---

[1]To illustrate, the Lord accuses Jerusalem of being an "adulterous wife" in Ezekiel 16. He condemns Nineveh for being a "harlot" and "mistress of sorceries" in Nahum 3.

[2]See, e.g., Isa 6:5; Dan 8:27; Luke 5:8-9; Acts 9:7. Compare the reaction to the beast from the sea, a false god, in Rev 13:3. The "scarlet beast" evokes a similar response in Rev 17:7.

> Get balm for her pain;
>> perhaps she can be healed.
> "We would have healed Babylon,
>> but she cannot be healed;
> let us leave her and each go to his own land,
>> for her judgment reaches to the skies,
>> it rises as high as the clouds."
> "The LORD has vindicated us;
>> come, let us tell in Zion
>> what the LORD our God has done."
> Sharpen the arrows,
>> take up the shields!
> The LORD has stirred up the kings of the Medes,
>> because his purpose is to destroy Babylon.
> The LORD will take vengeance,
>> vengeance for his temple.
> Lift up a banner against the walls of Babylon!
>> Reinforce the guard,
> station the watchmen,
>> prepare an ambush!
> The LORD will carry out his purpose,
>> his decree against the people of Babylon.
> You who live by *many waters* [a reference to the Euphrates River, which passed through the city of Babylon, and to the Tigris River, which passed nearby]
>> and are *rich in treasures*,
> your end has come,
>> the time for you to be cut off.
> The LORD Almighty has sworn by himself:
>> I will surely fill you with men, as with a swarm of locusts,
>> and they will shout in triumph over you.

By describing Rome using language from this prophecy, John communicates at least two truths concerning that great empire: First, Rome is a "Second Babylon." As Babylon destroyed Jerusalem and the Jewish temple in 587 B.C. (an event alluded to in Jer 51:11), so did Rome destroy the same city and temple in A.D. 70.[3]

---

[3]For this reason, non-Christian Jewish apocalyptists also use "Babylon" as a symbol for Rome. See, e.g., 2 Baruch and 4 Ezra, two Jewish apocalypses written in the early second century A.D.

Furthermore, Rome has persecuted and killed Christians. Like Babylon, Rome has been an enemy of the covenant people of God.

Second, the prophecy speaks of Babylon as the object of God's wrath and judgment. By identifying the prostitute with Babylon, John predicts that Rome, too, will perish in the wrath of God's final judgment.

17:2,4b-6 With [the great prostitute] the kings of the earth committed adultery and the inhabitants of the earth were intoxicated with the wine of her adulteries." . . . She held a golden cup in her hand, filled with abominable things and the filth of her adulteries. This title was written on her forehead: MYSTERY / BABYLON THE GREAT / THE MOTHER OF PROSTITUTES / AND OF THE ABOMINATIONS OF THE EARTH. I saw that the woman was drunk with the blood of the saints, the blood of those who bore testimony to Jesus. When I saw her, I was greatly astonished.

John presents the Empire as a beautiful, attractive, seductive woman, bedecked with gold, jewels, and rich garments. But then he tells his readers that dear "mother Rome" is a whore! (If this is the sort of thing John was saying in his preaching in Asia Minor, then it is no wonder that the Romans exiled him to Patmos!) The prophet is laying the groundwork for contrasting the adulterous prostitute "Babylon" with the pure, chaste "New Jerusalem" or "Bride of Christ" described in chapters 19-22.

We have seen that, throughout the Book of Revelation, prostitution, adultery and other forms of sexual immorality symbolize idolatry or unfaithfulness to God.[4] As adulterers break their marriage covenants with their spouses, so do idolaters break covenant with God. The prostitute Rome seduces "the kings of the earth" to "commit adultery" with her. In other words, she promotes emperor worship and other forms of pagan idolatry among the various subject peoples that make up the Empire. She uses her power, her influence, and her position of world leadership to turn other nations away from God.

The "title" on the whore's forehead emphasizes this truth. The first words of this title are: "Mystery: Babylon the Great." In apocalyptic literature, the term "mystery" tends to refer to "something

---

[4]See the comment on "The Teaching of Balaam" in Rev 2:14.

once hidden that is now revealed (through God's prophets)."[5] The term is also used of "symbols," which are not to be taken literally but which communicate a hidden truth.[6] Here in Revelation 17, John identifies the title "Babylon the Great" as a "mystery" or symbol. He thus emphasizes that the "great prostitute" should not be understood as literally referring to Babylon. Instead, she represents the "Second Babylon," the City of Rome (see above).

He calls Rome "the mother of prostitutes and of the abominations of the earth." In this context, "prostitutes" refer to idolaters, who refuse to recognize the true and living God. "Abominations" are things that God finds hateful or disgusting.

The phrase "mother of" may be interpreted in two ways, both of which make good sense in Revelation 17. First, a mother is the *source* of her children in the sense that they come forth from her womb. Rome is the source of idolaters and things detestable to God in the sense that she promotes sin and idolatry among the nations (see above). Second, a mother is a *full-grown, adult* version of her offspring. If John is thinking of the "prostitute" in this second sense, then he is saying that Rome is the biggest idolater and abominator on earth.

What sort of "abominations" does Rome commit? To find out, we must look in her cup: "She held a golden cup in her hand, *filled with abominable things* and the filth of her adulteries." What is the whore drinking? "The blood of the saints"! This is the filthy "wine of her adulteries" — the cup that her idolatry leads her to drink. And Rome does not merely sip from the cup. Instead, she is *"drunk* with the blood of the saints;" she gorges herself with the lives of martyred Christians. Furthermore, she passes the cup to others, encouraging them to drink as well. As a result, "the inhabitants of the earth" are also "intoxicated with the wine of her adulteries." Chapters 18 and 19 will show that, to the Lord God Almighty, the murder of his faithful servants is an "abomination" for which Rome will pay with her life.

---

[5]See, e.g., Dan 2:29 and 1 Cor 15:51.

[6]Compare Rev 1:20: "The *mystery* (i.e., symbol) of the seven stars that you saw in my right hand and of the seven golden lampstands is this: The seven stars are the angels of the seven churches, and the seven lampstands are the seven churches."

When John sees the prostitute, he is "greatly astonished." As noted above, this statement may be intended to show that John is viewing a "deity" — the goddess Roma. However, it may be that John is simply taken aback at seeing the true nature of the Empire that is admired and worshiped by so many.

(2) The Scarlet Beast (17:1-18). In John's vision, the "great prostitute" is mounted on a "scarlet beast." The beast's appearance resembles that of the "beast coming out of the sea" described in Revelation 13:1-8. We have seen that the beast from the sea symbolizes political powers used by Satan to make war on the saints. These political authorities include, but are not limited to Rome and its Caesars. The symbol of the "scarlet beast" also points to Rome, but it moves beyond the symbol of the beast from the sea to communicate additional truths.

17:3 Then the angel carried me away in the Spirit into a desert. There I saw a woman sitting on a scarlet beast that was covered with blasphemous names and had seven heads and ten horns.

Like the beast from the sea, the scarlet beast has "seven heads." These seven heads immediately evoke images of Leviathan, the seven-headed sea serpent that symbolizes the forces of evil and chaos.[7] However, verses 9-11 show that John also intends for the heads on the scarlet beast to symbolize "seven kings" (see below).

Like the beast from the sea, the scarlet beast also has "ten horns" and wears "blasphemous names." These symbols are drawn from Daniel 7, where the "ten horns" represent individual kings[8] and the "blasphemies" are spoken by Antiochus Epiphanes.[9] The political powers symbolized by the scarlet beast are "covered with blasphemous names" in this sense: They take for themselves names that rightfully belong only to God and to Christ ("God," "Lord," "Son of God," etc.). They put themselves in the place of the Deity.[10] John interprets the "ten horns" in verses 12-14 and 16-17 (see below).

---

[7] See the comment on Rev 13:1b.
[8] See the comment on Rev 13:1b-2,5-7.
[9] See the comment on Rev 13:1c,5-6, 8.
[10] See the comment on Rev 13:1c,5-6,8.

17:7-11 Then the angel said to me: "Why are you astonished? I will explain to you the mystery of the woman and of the beast she rides, which has the seven heads and ten horns. The beast, which you saw, once was, now is not, and will come up out of the Abyss and go to his destruction. The inhabitants of the earth whose names have not been written in the book of life from the creation of the world will be astonished when they see the beast, because he once was, now is not, and yet will come.

"This calls for a mind with wisdom. The seven heads are seven hills on which the woman sits. They are also seven kings. Five have fallen, one is, the other has not yet come; but when he does come, he must remain for a little while. The beast who once was, and now is not, is an eighth king. He belongs to the seven and is going to his destruction."

According to verse 9, "the seven heads are seven hills on which the woman sits." This statement identifies the scarlet beast as the city of Rome, which was widely known to be built on seven hills.[11]

According to verse 10, the seven heads "are also seven kings" — that is, seven emperors of the Roman Empire. Note the flexibility of the imagery: Both the prostitute and the scarlet beast she rides represent Rome in its various aspects — Rome as city ("Babylon," "the great city"), geographical location ("seven hills"), empire ("sits on many waters," "peoples, multitudes, nations and languages," "rules over the kings of the earth"), goddess ("woman"), emperors ("ten horns," "seven kings," "an eighth king"), and promoter of idolatry ("prostitute," "adulterer"). Again, apocalyptic symbolism is polyvalent, capable of communicating multiple meanings simultaneously.[12]

Concerning the seven kings, John writes:

> Five have fallen, one is, the other has not yet come; but when he does come, he must remain for a little while (Rev 17:10).

Some scholars think John is referring to eight specific Roman emperors, with the sixth being the ruling emperor at the time

---

[11]See, e.g., Juvenal, *Satires* 9.130; Propertius 3.11.57; Horace *Carmen saeculare* 5; Ovid *Tristia* 1.5.69; Pliny *Hist. nat.* 3.66-67; Claudian *Bell. Gild.* 104; *VI cons. Hon.* 617.

[12]For a discussion of this point, see the comment on "someone 'like a son of man'" in Rev 1:13.

Revelation is written ("one is"). This approach is problematical because John's description of the eight kings does not seem to match what we know about Roman emperors from historical sources. However, if we read the prophet's numbers as symbolic, apocalyptic numbers,[13] then the text yields its meaning.

Since "seven" is the symbolic number for "completeness," the phrase "seven kings" refers to the entire series of Roman emperors from beginning to end — whatever the literal number may be. When John writes, "Five have fallen, one is, the other has not yet come," he is saying that he and his first readers live during the time of the sixth emperor. "Six," being one less than "seven," is the symbolic number for "incompleteness." If John is writing during the reign of the "sixth" emperor, then the end or "completion" of the Roman Empire has not yet come.

John speaks of an "eighth king" in verses 8 and 11:

> The [scarlet] beast, which you saw, once was, now is not, and will come up out of the Abyss and go to his destruction. The inhabitants of the earth whose names have not been written in the book of life from the creation of the world will be astonished when they see the beast, because he once was, now is not, and yet will come (Rev 17:8).
>
> The beast who once was, and now is not, is an eighth king. He belongs to the seven and is going to his destruction (Rev 17:11).

Who is this "eighth king"? He "belongs to the seven," which shows that he is part of the complete line of Roman emperors. He "comes up out of the Abyss," the reservoir of evil and place of demons,[14] which shows that he is a tool of Satan. Furthermore, the eighth king is a "beast," or a particular manifestation of political evil (see above).

The emperor of whom John speaks is an "eighth king." This symbolic number identifies him as a parody of Christ, whose number is also "eight."[15] This evil emperor is someone who tries to put himself in the place of Christ, usurping his heavenly throne.

---

[13]See Part III.B.1.d of the Introduction: "Symbolic Numbers."

[14]See the discussion of "Demon Locusts from the Abyss" (Rev 9:1-2) in Part III.C.2.e of the Commentary.

[15]For a discussion of "eight" as the symbolic number for Christ, see the

John also describes the eighth king as someone who "once was, now is not, and yet will come." In the context of Revelation, this description carries two meanings: First, John identifies the eighth king as a parody of God, whom the prophet elsewhere describes as him "who is, and who was, and who is to come" (Rev 1:8). Second, John identifies the eighth king as *Nero redivivus*.[16] Nero supposedly died and then returned to life. Likewise, the eighth king dies ("once was, now is not") and then returns to life ("yet will come"), causing non-Christians who see him to be "astonished" as in the presence of a god. The eighth king is like Nero returned from the dead — that is, he is a great persecutor of the church. As a rival to God and persecutor of his people, the eighth king will eventually go "to his destruction." He will endure the wrath of God's final judgment.

Who, then, is the "eighth king"? If John has a particular individual in mind, then the most logical choice would be Domitian, the emperor on the throne at the time John wrote Revelation. As an emperor who claimed to be divine, and a persecutor of Christians, Domitian fits every element in John's description of the "eighth king."[17] However, John may intend for the "eighth king" to represent *any* future ruler who tries to put himself in the place of Christ.

17:12-14,16-17 "The ten horns you saw are ten kings who have not yet received a kingdom, but who for one hour will receive authority as kings along with the beast. They have one purpose and will give their power and authority to the beast. They will make war against the Lamb, but the Lamb will overcome them because he is Lord of lords and King of kings—and with him will be his called, chosen and faithful followers."

". . . The beast and the ten horns you saw will hate the prostitute. They will bring her to ruin and leave her naked; they will eat her flesh and burn her with fire. For God has put it into their

---

comment on Rev 13:18. For a discussion of "Satan's Parody of Christ," see Part III.D.2.d of the Commentary.

[16] For an explanation of the *Nero redivivus* idea, see the comment on the beast's "fatal wound" that "had been healed" in Rev 13:3.

[17] For a discussion of Domitian, see Part IV.B.3 of the Introduction, which describes "Persecution Related to Emperor Worship in Asia Minor."

hearts to accomplish his purpose by agreeing to give the beast their power to rule, until God's words are fulfilled."

The scarlet beast's "ten horns" represent rulers of various nations, who are subservient to Rome and who cooperate with Rome in "making war against the Lamb" and his followers. Two examples from John's past would be Herod Antipas and Herod Agrippa I. Both served as "King of the Jews" in Palestine, and both cooperated with the Roman authorities in crucifying Jesus, beheading the Apostle James, and imprisoning the Apostle Peter.[18] In Revelation 17 John is speaking of *future* rulers ("kings who have *not yet* received a kingdom") who will behave in a similar manner.

In verses 16-17 John predicts that such kings will eventually turn against Rome and destroy her. They "accomplish [the Lord's] purpose" by carrying out God's judgment against Rome for her sins. In the fifth century, Rome finally did fall to foreign invaders. John had already predicted it in the first century.

In destroying Rome, the "ten horns" will have help from the "beast" itself. Strangely enough, the "beast," which symbolizes Rome (see v. 9), will destroy the "prostitute," which also symbolizes Rome (see v. 18). This is an image of the self-destructive power of evil. We see this power at work in individuals every day. For example, those who center their lives on alcohol, drugs, illicit sex, hatred, and violence, often destroy themselves by their sinful behavior. Romans 1:18-32 shows that one instrument God will use to carry out his judgment against sinners is sinners themselves. He will "give them over" to their sinful desires, allowing them to reap the consequences of their own behavior:

> *The wrath of God is [presently] being revealed from heaven against all the godlessness and wickedness of men who suppress the truth [about God]* by their wickedness, ...
>
> Therefore *God gave them over* in the sinful desires of their hearts to sexual impurity for the degrading of their bodies with one another. . . .
>
> Because of this, *God gave them over* to shameful lusts. Even their women exchanged natural relations for unnatural ones. In the same way the men also abandoned natural relations with women

---

[18]See Luke 23:6-11 and Acts 12:1-5.

and were inflamed with lust for one another. Men committed indecent acts with other men, and *received in themselves the due penalty* for their perversion.

Furthermore, since they did not think it worthwhile to retain the knowledge of God, *he gave them over* to a depraved mind, to do what ought not to be done. They have become filled with every kind of wickedness, evil, greed and depravity. They are full of envy, murder, strife, deceit and malice. They are gossips, slanderers, God-haters, insolent, arrogant and boastful; they invent ways of doing evil; they disobey their parents; they are senseless, faithless, heartless, ruthless. Although they know God's righteous decree that those who do such things deserve death, they not only continue to do these very things but also approve of those who practice them (Rom 1:18,24,26-32).

As it is with individuals, so it is with empires. One of the ways God exercises his righteous judgment against sinful nations is by letting them have their own way — by "giving them over" to themselves. This is God's "punishment of the great prostitute" (Rev 17:1). The only escape comes through repentance, righteousness, abandoning idolatry, and a seeking after God. The Lord says to Israel in 1 Chronicles 7:14:

If my people, who are called by my name, will humble themselves and pray and seek my face and turn from their wicked ways, then will I hear from heaven and will forgive their sin and will heal their land.

REVELATION 18

(3) The Fall of Babylon (18:1-19:4). Having introduced Rome as "Babylon the Great" in chapter 17, John announces the fall of "Babylon" in 18:1-19:4. This part of Revelation is reminiscent of the oracle against Babylon in Jeremiah 50-51 and the lament for idolatrous Tyre in Ezekiel 27.

In these verses, John focuses specifically on God's final judgment against Rome. However, the condemnation experienced by Rome illustrates the kind of punishment that will confront any nation that opposes God.

¹After this I saw another angel coming down from heaven. He had great authority, and the earth was illuminated by his splendor. ²With a mighty voice he shouted:

> **"Fallen! Fallen is Babylon the Great!**
> **She has become a home for demons**
> **and a haunt for every evil[a] spirit,**
> **a haunt for every unclean and detestable bird.**
> **³For all the nations have drunk**
> **the maddening wine of her adulteries.**
> **The kings of the earth committed adultery with her,**
> **and the merchants of the earth grew rich from her**
> **excessive luxuries."**

[a] 2 Greek *unclean*

A mighty angel, radiant with glory,[1] announces the fall of Rome. For an explanation of why Rome is called "Babylon the Great," see the comment on Revelation 17:1b,4a,15.

---

[1] Concerning the "glory" of angelic beings, see the comment on "someone 'like a son of man'" in Rev 1:13.

The Scriptures speak of the uninhabited wilderness or desert as the home of demons,[2] jackals and owls, and other wild animals.[3] When John describes fallen Babylon as "a home for demons" and "a haunt for every unclean and detestable bird," he is saying that God will turn the heavily populated city of Rome into an abandoned "ghost town." This part of Revelation resembles the oracle against Babylon found in Isaiah 13:19-22 (cf. Jer 51:37):

> Babylon, the jewel of kingdoms,
>> the glory of the Babylonians' pride,
> will be overthrown by God
>> like Sodom and Gomorrah.
> She will never be inhabited
>> or lived in through all generations;
> no Arab will pitch his tent there,
>> no shepherd will rest his flocks there.
> But desert creatures will lie there,
>> jackals will fill her houses;
> there the owls will dwell,
>> and there the wild goats will leap about.
> Hyenas will howl in her strongholds,
>> jackals in her luxurious palaces.
> Her time is at hand,
>> and her days will not be prolonged.

18:1-3 The kings of the earth have "committed adultery" with Rome in the sense that they share in Rome's idolatry, her unfaithfulness to God. The "maddening wine of her adulteries" refers to the blood of the saints shed by Rome and by other nations under Rome's influence. For further discussion of these symbols, see the comment on Revelation 17:6.

⁴Then I heard another voice from heaven say:

"Come out of her, my people,
so that you will not share in her sins,
so that you will not receive any of her plagues;
⁵for her sins are piled up to heaven,
and God has remembered her crimes.

---

[2]See, e.g., Matt 12:43//Luke 11:24.
[3]See, e.g., Isa 34:11-15; Jer 9:10-12; Zeph 2:13-15; Mal 1:3.

> ⁶**Give back to her as she has given;**
>   **pay her back double for what she has done.**
>   **Mix her a double portion from her own cup.**
> ⁷**Give her as much torture and grief**
>   **as the glory and luxury she gave herself.**
> **In her heart she boasts,**
>   **'I sit as queen; I am not a widow,**
>   **and I will never mourn.'**
> ⁸**Therefore in one day her plagues will overtake her:**
>   **death, mourning and famine.**
> **She will be consumed by fire,**
>   **for mighty is the Lord God who judges her."**

18:4-5 In verses 4-5, the voice of God or Christ[4] shouts a command for Christians in view of the impending destruction of Babylon. The call to "Come out of her, my people" echoes Jeremiah 51:45, where the Lord urges Israel to flee before he punishes Babylon of old. (For more on this command, see the comment on verses 9-20.)

18:6-8 In verses 6-8 the Lord pronounces his righteous verdict against the idolatrous nation. He will pour out on Babylon all the "plagues" described in chapter 16. He will "give back to her as she has given," carrying out a "just judgment" for her sins.[5] The command to "mix her a double portion from her own cup" is a death sentence, for Babylon's "cup" contains the blood of murdered saints (see Rev 17:4,6). The "one day" of Babylon's doom will be the promised "Day of the Lord," when God destroys his enemies and saves his people.[6]

> ⁹**"When the kings of the earth who committed adultery with her and shared her luxury see the smoke of her burning, they will weep and mourn over her. ¹⁰Terrified at her torment, they will stand far off and cry:**

---

[4]Note that the voice calls Christians "my people."

[5]For a discussion of "justice" in God's judgments, see the comment on "The Third Bowl of Wrath" in Rev 16:4-7.

[6]For a discussion of the "Day of the Lord," see Part III.C.2.g of the Commentary: "The Sounding of the Seven Trumpets: The 'Present Evil Age' and 'Labor Pains' as the Announcement of the Day of the Lord." See also the comment on Rev 16:12-14,16.

"'Woe! Woe, O great city,
  O Babylon, city of power!
In one hour your doom has come!'
¹¹"The merchants of the earth will weep and mourn over her because no one buys their cargoes any more—¹²cargoes of gold, silver, precious stones and pearls; fine linen, purple, silk and scarlet cloth; every sort of citron wood, and articles of every kind made of ivory, costly wood, bronze, iron and marble; ¹³cargoes of cinnamon and spice, of incense, myrrh and frankincense, of wine and olive oil, of fine flour and wheat; cattle and sheep; horses and carriages; and bodies and souls of men.
¹⁴"They will say, 'The fruit you longed for is gone from you. All your riches and splendor have vanished, never to be recovered.' ¹⁵The merchants who sold these things and gained their wealth from her will stand far off, terrified at her torment. They will weep and mourn ¹⁶and cry out:

"'Woe! Woe, O great city,
  dressed in fine linen, purple and scarlet,
  and glittering with gold, precious stones and pearls!
¹⁷In one hour such great wealth has been brought to ruin!'

"Every sea captain, and all who travel by ship, the sailors, and all who earn their living from the sea, will stand far off. ¹⁸When they see the smoke of her burning, they will exclaim, 'Was there ever a city like this great city?' ¹⁹They will throw dust on their heads, and with weeping and mourning cry out:

"'Woe! Woe, O great city,
  where all who had ships on the sea
  became rich through her wealth!
In one hour she has been brought to ruin!
²⁰Rejoice over her, O heaven!
Rejoice, saints and apostles and prophets!
God has judged her for the way she treated you.'"

18:9-20 As the Lord continues his pronouncement, he pictures a group of people standing "far off" and seeing "the smoke of [Babylon] burning." In like manner, Abraham stood at a distance and watched the smoke rising from the destruction of the wicked cities of Sodom and Gomorrah (Gen 19:28; cf. Rev 14:11).

It is very important to note who is speaking in this text: They are "the kings of the earth" in verses 9-10, "the merchants of the earth" in verses 11-17a, and mariners in verses 17b-19. All cry out, "Woe! Woe!" in grieving over the loss of Rome and the "great wealth" she brings to them. "Woe" is an expression of anger, sadness, and impending doom.

There is nothing inherently evil about commerce, or even great wealth. (The New Jerusalem of chapters 21–22 is not a cluster of tar paper shacks!) Rome is condemned not for her wealth, but for the sins of idolatry and mistreatment of Christians. (See verses 3,5-6,20,23-24. There may be an implied rebuke for "excessive luxuries" in verse 3.) The wealth perishes because of the sin. The merchants and sailors, who have invested their lives in Babylon, mourn bitterly her destruction. Those who turn wealth into a "god," who pursue it as an end in itself, will likewise lose everything at the final judgment.

In the Roman Empire of the first century, commerce was thoroughly intertwined with the imperial cult. As John notes in Revelation 13:17, "No one could buy or sell unless he had the mark, which is the name of the beast or the number of his name." It was nearly impossible to participate in the Roman economy without bowing to Caesar as "lord and god."[7] In these circumstances, Christ calls on his people not to participate in this idolatrous commercial system. The Lord rejects the kind of compromise urged by "Jezebel" and by the "people who hold to the teaching of Balaam."[8] His command for the church is: "Come out of her, my people, so that you will not share in her sins" (v. 4)!

The reference to "cargoes of . . . bodies and souls of men" in verse 13 refers to the slave trade carried on by Rome. In John's time there were about ten million slaves in the Empire. They comprised 16-20% of the entire population.

²¹Then a mighty angel picked up a boulder the size of a large millstone and threw it into the sea, and said:
"With such violence

---

[7]See Part IV.B.3.b of the Introduction: "Emperor Worship in Daily Life." Another helpful resource is J. Nelson Kraybill, "Cult and Commerce in Revelation 18," Ph.D. diss., Union Theological Seminary in Virginia, 1992.

[8]See Part II.C.1 of the Commentary: "Pressures and Opposition from Within the Christian Community."

> the great city of Babylon will be thrown down,
> never to be found again.
> ²²The music of harpists and musicians, flute players and
> trumpeters,
> will never be heard in you again.
> No workman of any trade
> will ever be found in you again.
> The sound of a millstone
> will never be heard in you again.
> ²³The light of a lamp
> will never shine in you again.
> The voice of bridegroom and bride
> will never be heard in you again.
> Your merchants were the world's great men.
> By your magic spell all the nations were led astray.
> ²⁴In her was found the blood of prophets and of the
> saints,
> and of all who have been killed on the earth."

18:21-24 Throughout Scripture, the Lord's prophets often combine a word from God with a symbolic action designed to illustrate that message. For example, Jeremiah breaks a clay jar and declares:

> This is what the LORD Almighty says: "I will smash this nation and this city just as this potter's jar is smashed and cannot be repaired" (Jer 19:11).

The Christian prophet Agabus

> took Paul's belt, tied his own hands and feet with it and said, "The Holy Spirit says, 'In this way the Jews of Jerusalem will bind the owner of this belt and will hand him over to the Gentiles'" (Acts 21:11).[9]

Here in Revelation 18:21, an angel performs the same kind of symbolic action and then interprets its meaning:

> Then a mighty angel picked up a boulder the size of a large millstone and threw it into the sea, and said: "With such violence the

---

[9]For further examples, see 1 Kings 11:29-32; Isaiah 8:1-4; 20:1-6; Jeremiah 32:6-15; Hosea 1:2-9; 3:1-5.

great city of Babylon will be thrown down, never to be found again."

This action and word of judgment are patterned after Jeremiah 51:60-64:

> Jeremiah had written on a scroll about all the disasters that would come upon Babylon—all that had been recorded concerning Babylon. He said to Seraiah, "When you get to Babylon, see that you read all these words aloud. Then say, 'O LORD, you have said you will destroy this place, so that neither man nor animal will live in it; it will be desolate forever.' When you finish reading this scroll, tie a stone to it and throw it into the Euphrates. Then say, 'So will Babylon sink to rise no more because of the disaster I will bring upon her. And her people will fall.'"

God condemns Rome not out of caprice, and not because he hates the prosperous. Rather, God condemns Rome because "in her was found the blood of prophets and of the saints, and of all who have been killed on the earth." Rome's punishment is deserved and entirely just. The phrase "never again" — repeated six times — expresses the finality of God's final judgment against his enemies.

REVELATION 19

¹After this I heard what sounded like the roar of a great multitude in heaven shouting:

"Hallelujah!
Salvation and glory and power belong to our God,
 ²for true and just are his judgments.
He has condemned the great prostitute
 who corrupted the earth by her adulteries.
He has avenged on her the blood of his servants."

³And again they shouted:

"Hallelujah!
The smoke from her goes up for ever and ever."

⁴The twenty-four elders and the four living creatures fell down and worshiped God, who was seated on the throne. And they cried:

"Amen, Hallelujah!"

19:1-4 John hears the sound of a heavenly multitude offering praise to the divine King, who is seated on his throne. The chorus includes "twenty-four elders," who symbolize the church, and "four living creatures," which symbolize the whole of creation.[1] Together they shout "Hallelujah," the Hebrew term for "Praise the LORD!"

Once again, the text highlights the justness of God's sentence against Rome. "Babylon" falls not due to some irrational divine whim, but because she has "corrupted the earth" with the "adultery" of idolatry. Furthermore, she has murdered the saints of God.[2] At

---

[1] See the comments on "The Throne of God and the Twenty-Four Elders" in Rev 4:2-6a and on "The Four Living Creatures" in Rev 4:6b-8.

[2] On Rome as a murderous "prostitute" promoting "adultery," see comments on Rev 17:2,4b-6.

the final judgment, God has rightly and justly "avenged on her the blood of his servants."[3]

The smoke of Babylon's destruction "goes up for ever and ever," signifying that Rome's final condemnation is unending and irreversible.[4] The whole church and the whole of creation voice their approval of what God has done by shouting "Amen," a Hebrew term meaning "So be it!" or "Truly!"

Verses 1 and 2 find a close connection between God's "salvation" and his "judgments." Salvation "belongs" to God only because he carries out the final judgment. We have seen that, in reality, redemption and condemnation are two sides of the same event. The kingdom of God cannot come until the Lord first destroys the kingdom of Satan. The Lord cannot consummate his own beneficent kingship without eliminating all opposing kingships. He cannot establish the good without destroying evil.[5]

g. Announcement of the Wedding Supper of the Lamb (19:5-10)

In Revelation 14:1–22:6, John offers a kaleidoscope of images depicting the final judgment and the consummation of God's kingdom — two facets of a single event. The early images (14:1–19:4) focus primarily on the condemnation of God's enemies with an occasional look forward to the salvation of his servants. However, beginning in 19:5, the prophet shifts his emphasis. From this point forward, the majority of images will concern the salvation of God's servants with only an occasional look back at the destruction of his enemies. Chapter 19, verses 5-10, includes an announcement of the wedding supper of the Lamb.

⁵Then a voice came from the throne, saying:
"Praise our God,
    all you his servants,

---

[3]On "true and just judgments," see the comment on "The Third Bowl of Wrath" in Rev 16:4-7.

[4]Compare Rev 14:11: "And the smoke of their torment rises for ever and ever. There is no rest day or night for those who worship the beast and his image, or for anyone who receives the mark of his name."

[5]See Part III.D.3.a of the Commentary: "The Relationship between Salvation and Condemnation, Final Judgment and Consummation."

you who fear him,
    both small and great!"

⁶Then I heard what sounded like a great multitude, like the roar of rushing waters and like loud peals of thunder, shouting:

"Hallelujah!
    For our Lord God Almighty reigns.
⁷Let us rejoice and be glad
    and give him glory!
For the wedding of the Lamb has come,
    and his bride has made herself ready.
⁸Fine linen, bright and clean,
    was given her to wear."

(Fine linen stands for the righteous acts of the saints.)

⁹Then the angel said to me, "Write: 'Blessed are those who are invited to the wedding supper of the Lamb!'" And he added, "These are the true words of God."

19:5-9 *(1) The Wedding of the Lamb.* With one voice all God's servants shout: "Hallelujah! (a Hebrew term meaning 'Praise the LORD!') For our Lord God Almighty reigns!" They thus announce the consummation of God's kingdom rule — the extension of his sovereign reign over the whole universe.⁶ In verses 7-9 the Lord's servants use a different image to proclaim the same truth: "The wedding of the Lamb has come! . . . Blessed are those who are invited to the wedding supper of the Lamb!" The "Lamb" refers to Jesus Christ, whose sacrificial death on the cross destroys the kingdom of Satan and establishes the kingdom of God.⁷ The "wedding supper of the Lamb" is a combination of two biblical and apocalyptic metaphors — namely, the Messianic Banquet and Israel as the "bride" of God.

We have seen that early Jewish and Christian writers often picture the consummated kingdom of God as a great banquet hosted by the Messiah — a "Messianic Banquet."⁸ Banquets are times

---

⁶For discussions of the "Kingdom of God" concept, see the Introduction, Parts III.B.2.b-d.

⁷See Parts II.D.2 ("Christ as 'Overcomer'") and III.A.7 ("The Lamb Who Was Slain [5:6-14]") of the Commentary, as well as Part III.B.2.c.(4) of the Introduction ("The Kingdom of God and the Death of Jesus").

⁸See Part II.D.3.a of the Commentary: "The Hidden Manna, the Messianic Banquet, Behemoth and Leviathan."

of joy and togetherness. The "Messianic Banquet" metaphor communicates the truth that God's final victory over evil will likewise be an occasion for celebration. Jesus makes frequent use of the Messianic Banquet idea in his teaching. One example appears in Luke 14:12-24. Here the Lord speaks of the surprising variety of people who are "invited" to participate in God's kingdom "Banquet," including Gentiles and the outcasts of society. He also warns that, even though the Jews were the first to hear of the kingdom "Feast," some (particularly some of the Jewish leaders) will lose their place because they do not accept God's "invitation."

> Then Jesus said to his host, "When you give a luncheon or dinner, do not invite your friends, your brothers or relatives, or your rich neighbors; if you do, they may invite you back and so you will be repaid. But when you give a banquet, invite the poor, the crippled, the lame, the blind, and you will be blessed. Although they cannot repay you, you will be repaid at the resurrection of the righteous."
>
> When one of those at the table with him heard this, he said to Jesus, "Blessed is the man who will eat at the feast in the kingdom of God."
>
> Jesus replied: "A certain man was preparing a great banquet and invited many guests. At the time of the banquet he sent his servant to tell those who had been invited, 'Come, for everything is now ready.'
>
> "But they all alike began to make excuses. The first said, 'I have just bought a field, and I must go and see it. Please excuse me.'
>
> "Another said, 'I have just bought five yoke of oxen, and I'm on my way to try them out. Please excuse me.'
>
> "Still another said, 'I just got married, so I can't come.'
>
> "The servant came back and reported this to his master. Then the owner of the house became angry and ordered his servant, 'Go out quickly into the streets and alleys of the town and bring in the poor, the crippled, the blind and the lame.'
>
> "'Sir,' the servant said, 'what you ordered has been done, but there is still room.'
>
> "Then the master told his servant, 'Go out to the roads and country lanes and make them come in, so that my house will be full. I tell you, not one of those men who were invited will get a taste of my banquet.'"

In his Parable of the Wedding Banquet (Matt 22:1-14) and Parable of the Ten Virgins (Matt 25:1-13; cf. Luke 12:35-38), Jesus likens the kingdom of God to a marriage celebration. In other words, he transforms the "Messianic Banquet" into a *wedding* banquet.

A second metaphor that lies behind Revelation's "wedding supper of the Lamb" is the Old Testament idea of Israel, the people of God, being the Lord's "bride."[9] As a bride enters into a covenant relationship with her husband, so did Israel enter into the Mosaic covenant with God. For Israel, being "betrothed" or "married" to God carried the idea of forsaking idolatry — that is, being faithful to God, obeying his commandments, and not having relationships with other gods. In the prophecy of Hosea, God denounces Israel for being an unfaithful "wife" because she is forsaking the true God and carrying on "adulterous affairs" with the Baals, the Canaanite fertility gods. How does the Lord respond to this painful betrayal? He could devastate the land, but his deep love for Israel will not allow him to do so (see, e.g., Hosea 11:8-11). He therefore resolves once again to woo Israel, to draw his "bride" back to himself through gentleness and compassion. In Hosea 2:13-23 the Lord says:

> "I will punish her for the days
>   she burned incense to the Baals;
> she decked herself with rings and jewelry,
>   and went after her lovers,
>   but me she forgot,"
>   declares the LORD.
>
> "Therefore I am now going to allure her;
>   I will lead her into the desert
>   and speak tenderly to her.
> There I will give her back her vineyards,
>   and will make the Valley of Achor a door of
>   hope.
> There she will sing as in the days of her youth,
>   as in the day she came up out of Egypt.
>
> "In that day," declares the LORD,
>   "you will call me 'my husband';

---

[9]See, e.g., Isa 62:5; Jer 2:1-3.

> you will no longer call me 'my master' [lit. 'my
> Baal' — 'Baal' means 'lord' or 'master'].
> I will remove the names of the Baals from her lips;
> no longer will their names be invoked.
> In that day I will make a covenant for them
> with the beasts of the field and the birds of the air
> and the creatures that move along the ground.
> Bow and sword and battle
> I will abolish from the land,
> so that all may lie down in safety.
> I will betroth you to me forever;
> I will betroth you in righteousness and justice,
> in love and compassion.
> I will betroth you in faithfulness,
> and you will acknowledge the LORD.
>
> "In that day I will respond,"
> declares the LORD—
> "I will respond to the skies,
> and they will respond to the earth;
> and the earth will respond to the grain,
> the new wine and oil,
> and they will respond to Jezreel.
> I will plant her for myself in the land;
> I will show my love to the one I called 'Not my loved one.'
> I will say to those called 'Not my people,' 'You are my people';
> and they will say, 'You are my God.'"[10]

New Testament writers apply this "bride of God" metaphor to the "new Israel," the church. Jesus is called the "bridegroom" in Mark 2:19-20 and John 3:29. The Apostle Paul compares the relationship between Christ and the church to that between a husband and wife in 2 Corinthians 11:2-5 and Ephesians 5:22-33.

---

[10]Note the similarity between Hos 2:23b ("I will say to those called 'Not my people,' 'You are my people'; and they will say, 'You are my God.'") and the vision of the bride of Christ in Rev 21:3 ("Now the dwelling of God is with men, and he will live with them. They will be his people, and God himself will be with them and be their God.").

Building on this tradition, John employs the "Messianic Banquet" as a symbol of the consummated kingdom of God. Like Jesus, he transforms it into a wedding banquet. Then, adding the church as the "bride of Christ" idea, he creates the beautiful image of "the wedding supper of the Lamb." As the virginal "bride of Christ," the church is portrayed as free from idolatry (i.e., "adultery") and wholly committed to the Lord. Her wedding garment is "fine linen, bright and clean," which John interprets as "the righteous acts of the saints" (v. 8). "Righteousness" is participation in a covenant. Christians become "righteous," or put on the "wedding garment," or become the "bride of Christ," by embracing the new covenant based on faith and established by the Lamb's sacrificial death.[11] John further develops the image of the church as the "bride of Christ" in chapters 21–22 (see 21:2,9).

¹⁰At this I fell at his feet to worship him. But he said to me, "Do not do it! I am a fellow servant with you and with your brothers who hold to the testimony of Jesus. Worship God! For the testimony of Jesus is the spirit of prophecy."

19:10 *(2) The Testimony of Jesus.* The Christian Scriptures maintain a sharp distinction between creatures (such as angels and humans) and the creator, between finite beings and the infinite deity. It is appropriate to worship only God and never his handiwork, for worshiping the created thing in place of the creator is idolatry.[12] Accordingly, the angel in Revelation 19:10 (and again in 22:8-9) reminds John not to worship him, but to "worship God" alone.[13] Although human beings are created "a little lower than the angels" (Ps 8:5), the angels still fall in the same general class with humans as mere creatures of God. John's readers may have needed this reminder because angel worship was practiced in the Roman province of Asia and, at times, had infiltrated the churches.[14]

---

[11]See Part III.B.2.c.(4) of the Introduction: "The Kingdom of God and the Death of Jesus."

[12]See, e.g., Isa 44:1-20; Jer 10:1-16; Rom 1:18-25.

[13]Similar rebukes appear, for example, in Acts 10:25-26; 14:11-15.

[14]Note Paul's warning to the church at Colossae in southern Asia: "Do not let anyone who delights in false humility and the worship of angels disqualify you from the prize" (Col 2:18a). Compare Hebrews 1–2, where the writer

According to the structure of the Greek sentence, the enigmatic statement at the end of verse 10 gives the reason John should worship God rather than the angel: "Worship God! For [or 'because,' γάρ, *gar*] the testimony of Jesus is the spirit of prophecy." A "prophecy" is an intelligible message, such as that spoken by the church as a whole,[15] by Christian prophets in general,[16] by the prophet John in particular,[17] and by some of the angels in Revelation.[18] The phrase "Spirit of prophecy" refers to the Holy Spirit of God, who enables prophets (such as John) to speak.[19] "The testimony of Jesus" is a specific type of "prophecy" — namely, a "witness" to who Jesus is and what God is doing through him.[20] Against this background, how should we understand the angel's statement in verse 10? The angel has just spoken "the true words of God" to John (v. 9). John responds by bowing down to worship the angel. Perhaps the angel is reminding John that he is merely a messenger[21] — a "fellow servant" with John and with everyone who testifies to Jesus Christ. Behind the message and behind the messenger stands the Spirit of God himself. He is the one who should be worshiped — not his agents. The angel says, "The testimony of Jesus is the Spirit of prophecy." In other words, remember that the "testimony of Jesus" is ultimately attributable to

---

argues that Christ is superior to the angels — a point that some apparently questioned. See also Gal 1:8-9, which may reflect the influence of "gospels" spoken by angels.

[15]See Rev 11:3,6,10, where the "two witnesses" symbolize the church.

[16]See Rev 10:7; 11:18; 16:6; 18:20,24; 22:6,9.

[17]See Rev 1:3; 10:11; 22:7,10,18,19.

[18]See Rev 1:1; 5:11-12; 10:5-7; 14:6-11 (where an angel proclaims the "gospel"); 17:7-18; 18:1-3,21-24; 22:6,16 (where an angel gives "testimony for the churches").

[19]See Rev 1:10; 2:7,11,17,29; 3:6,13,22; 4:2; 14:13; 17:3; 21:10; 22:17. Compare 1 Corinthians 12–14 (where the ability to "prophesy" is a gift that the Holy Spirit gives to some Christians), as well as Eph 2:20 and 3:5 (where the church is "built on the foundation of the apostles and prophets" as those who carry out a ministry of "prophecy" or proclamation).

[20]See, e.g., Rev 1:9; 6:9; 12:11,17; 17:6; 19:10; 20:4.

[21]Note how angels play the role of mediators between God and Christian prophets in Rev 1:1-4 and 22:6. The angels' testimony enables the testimony of Christians. However, the Spirit of God himself stands behind the angel mediators." Cf. Rev 1:1-4.

the "Spirit" of God, who gives the "prophecy." Therefore "worship God" — not his messenger!

h. The Victorious Christ (19:11-21)

In Revelation 19:11-21 John sees a vision of Christ and his people victorious over their enemies. Most of the symbols that make up this vision appear earlier in the book.

> ¹¹**I saw heaven standing open and there before me was a white horse, whose rider is called Faithful and True. With justice he judges and makes war. ¹²His eyes are like blazing fire, and on his head are many crowns. He has a name written on him that no one knows but he himself. ¹³He is dressed in a robe dipped in blood, and his name is the Word of God. ¹⁴The armies of heaven were following him, riding on white horses and dressed in fine linen, white and clean. ¹⁵Out of his mouth comes a sharp sword with which to strike down the nations. "He will rule them with an iron scepter."ᵃ He treads the winepress of the fury of the wrath of God Almighty. ¹⁶On his robe and on his thigh he has this name written:**
>
> **KING OF KINGS AND LORD OF LORDS.**

ᵃ*15 Psalm 2:9*

19:11-16 *(1) The King of Kings.* John pictures Jesus as a conquering king, majestically mounted on a white horse at the head of a heavenly army. Several of the symbols speak of his sovereign authority. First, "he has a name written on him that no one knows but he himself" (v. 12). This signifies that no one else has power over Jesus, but that he enjoys complete self-determination. See the discussion of the similar symbol that appears in Revelation 2:17.[22]

Second, John quotes Psalm 2:9, which reads: "He will rule them with an iron scepter" (v. 15). By applying this "Royal Psalm" to Jesus, the prophet identifies him as the Messiah, the Christ, the Anointed One chosen by God to rule as king over all nations. For further discussion of this Psalm and its application to Jesus, see the comment on the title "Jesus Christ" in Revelation 1:5.

---

[22]See Part II.E.3.c of the Commentary: "The Secret Name."

Third, Christ bears the title "King of kings and Lord of lords," (v. 16),[23] which means "King over all other kings and Lord over all other lords." In the ancient world, similar titles are used of human potentates — particularly in the Middle East — who exercise authority over lesser rulers throughout a vast empire. To illustrate, Nebuchadnezzar of Babylon bears the title "king of kings" in Ezekiel 26:7 and Daniel 2:37. The Persian king Artaxerxes carries the same title in Ezra 7:12. By calling Christ "King of kings and Lord of lords," John identifies him as the only ruler who truly bears this universal authority — not Caesar and not any other earthly king.

In Jewish and Christian literature, such titles are applied to God as the divine King of all creation. He is called "Lord of lords" in Deuteronomy 10:17 and Psalm 136:3. In 1 Enoch 9:4 (part of a first century B.C. Jewish apocalypse), He is "Lord of lords, and the God of gods, and the King of kings." The Apostle Paul refers to God as "the King of kings and Lord of lords" in 1 Timothy 6:15. By applying this divine title to Jesus, John may be stressing his deity. At the very least, the prophet identifies him as the "Messiah" or "Christ," who wields divine authority as the one seated at God's right hand.[24]

The title appears on Christ's "robe and on his thigh." The location is something of a puzzle. However, since Greeks and Romans sometimes carved titles on the thighs of statues, we speculate that John's readers were accustomed to seeing authoritative titles on images of the Roman Caesar. Here in Revelation 19, John shows them that the ultimate kingly authority belongs only to Christ.

Fourth, the eyes "like blazing fire" (v. 12) are an image of Christ's radiant glory. As in Revelation 1:14, they speak of his deity and his identity as the risen and exalted Lord.

Fifth, the Messiah's "many crowns" (v. 12) again testify to his authority over many peoples, tribes, languages and nations. God has made him Lord of all, but his kingship will not be fully realized until he puts down all opposing kingships. The next set of symbols show Christ doing just that.

---

[23]Compare Rev 17:14, where the Lamb is called "Lord of lords and King of kings."

[24]For further discussion of this idea, see the comment on "Jesus Christ" in Rev 1:5.

In addition to presenting Christ as a king, Revelation 19:11-16 portrays him as a conquering warrior. "He is dressed in a robe dipped in blood" (v. 13). The bloody garment calls to mind Isaiah 63:1-6, which describes God as the One who brings "salvation" and "redemption" to his people by executing "wrath" and "vengeance" against his enemies:

> Who is this coming from Edom,
>   from Bozrah, with his garments stained crimson?
> Who is this, robed in splendor,
>   striding forward in the greatness of his strength?
>
> "It is I, speaking in righteousness,
>   mighty to save."
>
> Why are your garments red,
>   like those of one treading the winepress?
>
> "I have trodden the winepress alone;
>   from the nations no one was with me.
> I trampled them in my anger
>   and trod them down in my wrath;
> their blood spattered my garments,
>   and I stained all my clothing.
> For the day of vengeance was in my heart,
>   and the year of my redemption has come.
> I looked, but there was no one to help,
>   I was appalled that no one gave support;
> so my own arm worked salvation for me,
>   and my own wrath sustained me.
> I trampled the nations in my anger;
>   in my wrath I made them drunk
>   and poured their blood on the ground."

John declares that Christ "judges and makes war." (v. 11). Elsewhere in Revelation, we see that the way Christ "makes war" is by dying on the cross as the sacrificial "Lamb." Through this sacrifice, he "overcomes" the forces of evil, executing God's judgment and condemnation against the kingdom of Satan. On this subject, see Part III.B.2.c.(4) of the Introduction ("The Kingdom of God and the Death of Jesus") and Part II.D.2 of the Commentary ("Christ as 'Overcomer'").

John calls the Lord "Faithful and True" (v. 11). These titles appear in Revelation 1:5, where Jesus is "the faithful witness," and

3:14, where he is "the faithful and true witness." Jesus is "Faithful and True" in the sense that he faithfully testified to the truth about God even though this witness led to his death. For further discussion of this idea, see the comment on 1:5.

Out of Jesus' mouth comes "a sharp sword with which to strike down the nations" (v. 15). The sword symbolizes the word of God, or the gospel of the kingdom, which is both a word of salvation for God's people and a word of condemnation for his enemies. Since Christ implements God's authoritative word, John calls him "the Word of God" (v. 13) — the very embodiment of God's spoken will. See the comment on the "sharp double-edged sword" in Revelation 1:16.

In Revelation 14:17-20, John pictures the final judgment as a great "winepress." As grapes are thrown into a winepress and trampled until their juice runs out, so are God's enemies thrown into the "winepress" of God's judgment and "trampled" until their blood runs out.[25] In Revelation 19:15, Jesus is identified as the one who does the "trampling" — the one who carries out God's final judgment.

Verse 11 declares that he carries out God's judgment "with justice," giving God's enemies exactly what they deserve. For further discussion of the "justice" of God, see the comment on "The Third Bowl of Wrath" in Revelation 16:4-7.

The conquering Christ leads "the armies of heaven," which are "riding on white horses and dressed in fine linen, white and clean" (v. 14). John may be envisioning angel armies expected to accompany Christ at his Second Coming.[26] However, four considerations lead us to believe that these are instead armies of Christians: First, they wear the kind of garments associated with believers throughout the Book of Revelation.[27] Second, they "follow" Christ, just as the 144,000 redeemed saints follow the Lamb in 14:4.[28] Third, Satan

---

[25]See Part III.D.3.d of the Commentary: "The Harvest of the Earth (14:14-20)."

[26]See Matthew 13:39-41; 16:27; 24:31; 25:31; Mark 8:38; 13:27; Luke 9:26; 2 Thessalonians 1:7-8.

[27]The saints wear "fine linen" in Rev 19:8, "white" garments in 3:4,5,18; 4:4; 6:11; 7:9,13,14, and "clean" clothing in 19:8.

[28]Note: Throughout the New Testament, the verb "follow" (ἀκολουθέω, *akoloutheō*) is very often used as a technical term for *following Jesus as his disciples*. See, e.g., Matthew 16:24.

and his allies "make war" against this army (see v. 19), just as they "make war" against the saints in Revelation 11:7; 12:17; and 13:7. Fourth, in verses 17-21 (discussed below), they share in Christ's final victory, just as Christians share in Christ's victory elsewhere in Revelation.[29] John's point is that the final judgment will be a day of victory not only for Christ, but for his faithful followers as well. As the prophet says in 17:14:

> [Satan and his allies] will make war against the Lamb, but the Lamb will overcome them because he is Lord of lords and King of kings—*and with him will be his called, chosen and faithful followers.*

[17]And I saw an angel standing in the sun, who cried in a loud voice to all the birds flying in midair, "Come, gather together for the great supper of God, [18]so that you may eat the flesh of kings, generals, and mighty men, of horses and their riders, and the flesh of all people, free and slave, small and great."

[19]Then I saw the beast and the kings of the earth and their armies gathered together to make war against the rider on the horse and his army. [20]But the beast was captured, and with him the false prophet who had performed the miraculous signs on his behalf. With these signs he had deluded those who had received the mark of the beast and worshiped his image. The two of them were thrown alive into the fiery lake of burning sulfur. [21]The rest of them were killed with the sword that came out of the mouth of the rider on the horse, and all the birds gorged themselves on their flesh.

19:17-21 *(2) The Great Supper of God.* In Revelation 13, John identifies the "beast coming out of the sea" (symbolizing political powers allied with Satan) and the "false prophet" (or "beast coming out of the earth," which symbolizes religious powers who give their support to evil political powers) as two instruments Satan uses to make war against the saints. In 16:12-16, he describes how these evil powers work together to incite the kings of all nations to battle Christ and the church. Here in 19:17-21, John reintroduces these characters into the narrative as part of his vision of Christ as conquering king. He portrays Christ as victor in the final judgment by allowing us to see those over whom the Lord is victorious.

---

[29]See, e.g., Rev 2:28; 3:21; 12:11; 17:14.

The prophet describes a great field of battle, covered with the bodies of the slain. An angel calls for the vultures and other scavenger birds to come and feast on the dead. The image calls to mind Ezekiel 39 (a text to which we will return in our examination of Revelation 20), which describes God's victory over the enemies of Israel:

> On the mountains of Israel you will fall, you and all your troops and the nations with you. I will give you as food to all kinds of carrion birds and to the wild animals. You will fall in the open field, for I have spoken, declares the Sovereign LORD. . . .
>
> Son of man, this is what the Sovereign LORD says: Call out to every kind of bird and all the wild animals: "Assemble and come together from all around to the sacrifice I am preparing for you, the great sacrifice on the mountains of Israel. There you will eat flesh and drink blood. You will eat the flesh of mighty men and drink the blood of the princes of the earth as if they were rams and lambs, goats and bulls—all of them fattened animals from Bashan. At the sacrifice I am preparing for you, you will eat fat till you are glutted and drink blood till you are drunk. At my table you will eat your fill of horses and riders, mighty men and soldiers of every kind," declares the Sovereign LORD.
>
> "I will display my glory among the nations, and all the nations will see the punishment I inflict and the hand I lay upon them. From that day forward the house of Israel will know that I am the LORD their God" (Ezek 39:4-5,17-22; cf. Zeph 1:7-9).

In our comment on Revelation 2:17, we explain that apocalyptic writers sometimes imagine the consummated kingdom of God as a great "banquet" hosted by the Messiah — the "Messianic Banquet." The Jewish writer "Second Baruch" says that the land monster Behemoth and the sea monster Leviathan will be eaten on this occasion. Behemoth and Leviathan are ancient symbols for the forces of evil and chaos. Baruch's point is that, when God's kingdom comes in its fullness, the Lord and his people will "have their enemies for lunch." They will enjoy total victory over those who tried to destroy them.[30]

John expresses essentially the same idea here in Revelation 19:17-21. The beast, the false prophet, the wicked kings of the earth, and their armies symbolize the forces of evil and chaos. At the final

---

[30] See Part II.E.3.a of the Commentary: "The Hidden Manna, the Messianic Banquet, Behemoth and Leviathan."

judgment and the consummation of God's kingdom, they are killed and then served up as "the great supper of God." Rather than being eaten by God's people, they become "buzzard bait," a feast for carrion birds.

In a sense, then, Revelation 19 provides two very different versions of the "Messianic Banquet" image. For God's faithful servants, the consummation of God's kingdom is "the wedding supper of the Lamb" (v. 9) — a celebration of the church's covenant union with Christ. For the enemies of Christ and his church, the coming kingdom becomes "the great supper of God" — a gruesome debacle of death.

In Revelation 16:14, the dragon, the beast from the sea, and the false prophet gather the kings of the earth to Armageddon for "battle" against the Lord. In 19:19, they assemble to "make war" against Christ and his saints. However, it appears that no real "battle" — no real "war" — ever takes place. The beast and false prophet are captured and thrown into the "lake of burning sulfur," which is an image of eschatological condemnation that reappears in chapters 20–21 (see below).[31] Their armies are killed with the sword that proceeds from the mouth of Christ — the sword that symbolizes the word of God (see above). Perhaps the "battle" is assumed. Perhaps this death by Christ's "sword" is itself the anticipated "battle." However, John describes no clash of arms. Christ simply declares his enemies vanquished by his authoritative word, and they are vanquished. One moment God's enemies gather for war. The next moment we see the vultures picking over their corpses. Yet we never see any fighting. The Lord's soldiers never draw their weapons. They take no casualties. There is no "Battle of Armageddon" as popularly conceived. The final judgment is "no contest."

There may be theological significance to this fact. From John's point of view, Christ wins the decisive battle against Satan and the forces of evil not through force of arms and not at the time of his Second Coming and final judgment. Instead, Christ "overcame" Satan two thousand years ago, on the hill of Golgotha, by dying as the sacrificial "Lamb."[32]

---

[31]See Rev 20:10,14-15; 21:8.

[32]For further discussion of this point, see Part III.B.2.c.(4) of the Introduction: "The Kingdom of God and the Death of Jesus"; and Part II.D.2 of

> . . . you were slain,
>> and with your blood you purchased men for God
>> from every tribe and language and people and
>>> nation.
>> You have made them to be a kingdom and priests to serve
>>> our God,
>>> and they will reign on the earth (Rev 5:9b-10).

From John's point of view, Christians have no need to raise a weapon at the time of the final judgment. Their struggle is over and their victory is already secured.[33]

> They overcame him
>> by the blood of the Lamb
>> and by the word of their testimony;
> they did not love their lives so much
>> as to shrink from death (Rev 12:11).

---

the Commentary: "Christ as 'Overcomer.'" See also the symbolic description of Christ's decisive victory in Rev 12:7-12.

[33]For further discussion of this point, see Part II.D.3 of the Commentary: "Christians as 'Overcomers.'"

REVELATION 20

i. Deliverance from Babylonian Captivity (20:1-22:6)

Revelation 20:1-22:5 consists of a very beautiful and very elaborate network of symbols patterned after Ezekiel 37-48. Through these symbols, John presents the final judgment and consummation of God's kingdom as a sort of second deliverance of the Lord's people from Babylonian Captivity. We will first examine the individual elements of John's vision, focusing primarily on chapter 20. Next, we will compare John's vision to the prophecy of Ezekiel and draw conclusions concerning John's intended meaning. Finally, we will examine more closely the climactic vision of the New Jerusalem in 21:1-22:5.

¹And I saw an angel coming down out of heaven, having the key to the Abyss and holding in his hand a great chain. ²He seized the dragon, that ancient serpent, who is the devil, or Satan, and bound him for a thousand years. ³He threw him into the Abyss, and locked and sealed it over him, to keep him from deceiving the nations anymore until the thousand years were ended. After that, he must be set free for a short time.

20:1-3 *(1) Element One: The Binding of Satan.* John begins with an image of God subduing Satan prior to the "fire" of the final judgment (see v. 10). For a discussion of the various titles used for the Evil One ("dragon," "serpent," "the devil," "Satan"), see Part III.D.2.a.(2) of the Commentary, which concerns "The Identity of the Red Dragon" in Revelation 12.

Satan has been "deceiving the nations," or leading them astray, ever since he first misrepresented God to Adam and Eve in Genesis 3. Accordingly, Jesus calls him "a liar and the father of lies" in John 8:44. Throughout Revelation, John describes how Satan uses political authorities, false prophets, and other human agents to turn the nations against Christ and the church.¹ Jesus and his Apostles predicted that it would be so.²

The angel temporarily imprisons Satan in the "Abyss," the dwelling place of demons,³ for "a thousand years" (see the comment below on vv. 4b-6). The binding of Satan is a familiar theme in Jewish apocalyptic literature, as 1 Enoch 10:4-6 illustrates:

> And secondly the Lord said to Raphael [an angel], "Bind Azaz'el [i.e., Satan] hand and foot [and] throw him into the darkness!" And he made a hole in the desert which was in Duda'el and cast him there; he threw on top of him rugged and sharp rocks. And he covered his face in order that he may not see light; and in order that he may be sent into the fire on the great day of judgment.⁴

A Christian example appears in 2 Peter 2:4:

> . . . God did not spare angels when they sinned, but sent them to hell [Greek "Tartarus"], putting them into gloomy dungeons to be held for judgment.⁵

John includes such an image in Revelation 20 for purposes discussed below in Part (7).

⁴I saw thrones on which were seated those who had been given authority to judge. And I saw the souls of those who had been beheaded because of their testimony for Jesus and because of the word of God. They had not worshiped the beast or his image and had not received his mark on their foreheads or their hands. They came to life . . . .

20:4a *(2) Element Two: The Resurrection of Christian Martyrs.* To his image of the binding of Satan, John now adds an image of the

---

¹See Rev 12:9; 13:14; 18:23; 19:20; 20:8,10.
²See, e.g., Matt 24:4-5,11,24; Mark 13:5-6; Luke 21:8; 2 Thess 2:11-12; 1 Tim 4:1-2; 2 John 7.
³See Part III.C.2.e of the Commentary, which discusses "Demon Locusts from the Abyss" in Rev 9:1-11.
⁴Charlesworth, *Pseudepigrapha*. Cf. Isaiah 24:21-22; 1 Enoch 18:12–19:1; 21:1-10; 54:1-6; 67–69; Test. Levi 18:12; Jubilee 5:10.
⁵Cf. Mark 3:26-27; Jude 6.

resurrection of Christians, or the "new Israel," or the new covenant people of God. They have "not worshiped the beast or his image" and have "not received his mark." In other words, they have not yielded to pressure from political and religious authorities to worship Caesar or other false gods. They have accepted social and economic hardship in order to avoid idolatry. (See the commentary on Revelation 13, the source of these symbols.) As a result, they have suffered martyrdom. They have been "beheaded because of their testimony for Jesus and because of the word of God."[6]

Jewish and Christian writers describe the souls of the righteous being raised up to share in God's eternal reign. They sit on thrones, are given authority over the nations and over angels, and exercise judgment. To illustrate, the Wisdom of Solomon (a part of the Apocrypha dating to the first century B.C. or first century A.D.) maintains that:

> The souls of the righteous are in the hand of God, and no torment will ever touch them. In the eyes of the foolish they seem to have died, and their departure was thought to be an affliction, and their going from us to be their destruction; but they are at peace. For though in the sight of men they were punished, their hope is full of immortality. Having been disciplined a little, they will receive great good, because God tested them and found them worthy of himself; like gold in the furnace he tried them, and like a sacrificial burnt offering he accepted them. In the time of their visitation they will shine forth, and will run like sparks through the stubble. *They will govern nations and rule over peoples*, and the Lord will reign over them for ever (Wisd Sol 3:1-8, RSV).[7]

Jesus says to his disciples:

> I tell you the truth, at the renewal of all things, when the Son of Man sits on his glorious throne, you who have followed me will also sit on twelve thrones, judging the twelve tribes of Israel (Matt 19:28).

---

[6]The souls of the martyrs last appeared in Rev 6:9-11, where they cry out to God for vengeance from under the heavenly altar.

[7]Compare Daniel 7:9-10, where *multiple* "thrones" are set up before the "court" is seated and the "books" of judgment are opened.

The Apostle Paul asks the Corinthians:

> Do you not know that the saints will judge the world? . . . Do you not know that we will judge angels? (1 Cor 6:2-3)

Following this tradition, John pictures Christian martyrs being raised to "life," seated on "thrones," given "authority to judge," and "reigning" with Christ (vv. 4-6).[8] Below, we will explain how this image of resurrection functions within the larger vision of Revelation 20:1–22:5.

and reigned with Christ a thousand years. ⁵(The rest of the dead did not come to life until the thousand years were ended.) This is the first resurrection. ⁶Blessed and holy are those who have part in the first resurrection. The second death has no power over them, but they will be priests of God and of Christ and will reign with him for a thousand years.

20:4b-6 *(3) Element Three: The Millennial Reign of Christ.* In this unusual text, John speaks of two deaths and two resurrections. The first death is the physical demise common to all mortals — the kind of death experienced, for example, by martyrs who have been "beheaded because of their testimony for Jesus" (v. 4a). The "second death" is the eschatological condemnation, or damnation, symbolized by the "lake of fire" in Revelation 20:14 and 21:8. While Christians may experience the first death, no Christian will experience the "second death." "He who overcomes will not be hurt at all by the second death" (Rev 2:11). "The second death has no power over them" (20:6). Only those whose names are "not found in the book of life" are "thrown into the lake of fire" (20:15).

In Revelation, the "first resurrection" refers to the resurrection of Christian martyrs mentioned in 20:4-6. They enjoy the special privilege of coming to life and reigning with Christ for a thousand years (i.e. a "millennium") before the rest of the church is raised.[9]

---

[8]Compare Rev 3:21: "To him who overcomes, I will give to sit with me on my throne." The twenty-four elders, which symbolize the church, are also pictured sitting on thrones in Rev 4:4 and 11:16. Christians "reign" with the Lord in Rev 5:10 and 22:5.

[9]John describes the martyrs as "blessed and holy," and as "priests of God and of Christ." Priests are "holy" in the sense that they are "set apart" by

The second resurrection is when "the rest of the dead," Christian and non-Christian, come to life after the thousand years have ended (20:5). At that time, God judges all the dead, both "great and small" (20:12-15).

The idea of eschatological condemnation — what John calls "the second death" — appears often in the New Testament. However, the notion of two separate resurrections — one for Christian martyrs and another for everyone else — is unique in the Christian canon. The idea of a temporary, earthly reign of the Messiah prior to the final judgment appears in Jewish apocalyptic writings, such as 4 Ezra.[10] However, a millennial reign of Christ appears nowhere in the Christian Bible apart from Revelation 20. How, then, should we understand this difficult text?

One of the major interpretive approaches to Revelation 20 is called *Historic Premillennialism*, a view first put forward in the early centuries of the Christian Era. Adherents generally believe that the kingdom of God has not yet come in its fullness though many concede that the reign of Christ begins with the church. At some point in the future, the church will endure a seven-year period of tribulation or "labor pains," during which Christians are persecuted by an individual antichrist. The tribulation will end with the Second

---

God to be different, with a distinctive commitment to serving the Lord. John may be alluding to Exodus 19:6: "Now if you obey me fully and keep my covenant, then out of all nations you will be my treasured possession. Although the whole earth is mine, you will be for me a kingdom of priests and a holy nation." Compare Rev 1:6 and 5:10.

[10]Fourth Ezra 7:26-33a reads: "For behold, the time will come, when the signs which I have foretold to you will come to pass; the city which now is not seen shall appear, and the land which now is hidden shall be disclosed. And everyone who has been delivered from the evils that I have foretold shall see my wonders. For my son the Messiah shall be revealed with those who are with him, and those who remain shall rejoice *four hundred years*. And after these years my son the Messiah shall die, and all who draw human breath. And the world shall be turned back to primeval silence for seven days, as it was at the first beginnings; so that no one shall be left. And after seven days the world, which is not yet awake, shall be roused, and that which is corruptible shall perish. And the earth shall give up those who are asleep in it; and the chambers shall give up the souls which have been committed to them. And the Most High shall be revealed upon the seat of judgment . . . ." From Charlesworth, *Pseudepigrapha*.

Coming of Christ, the binding of Satan, and the "rapture" of Christians to meet Christ in the air. He will then set up a thousand-year reign on earth, during which his deity and lordship will be publicly revealed to all nations. The millennium will be followed by the final judgment and consummation of God's kingdom. This view is called "premillennialism" because Christ's Second Coming occurs pre-millennium, or prior to his millennial reign.

A second interpretive approach to Revelation is called *Amillennialism*. Popularized by St. Augustine, this view is prevalent among Roman Catholics and many mainline Protestants (e.g., Reformed, Presbyterians, Lutherans). Adherents generally believe that the millennium is a symbol for the "Church Age" — that is, the entire period between the First and Second Comings of Christ, when Satan's power is limited and the Lord reigns as king in the hearts of his people. Many holders of this view see the "first resurrection" as an individual's introduction into the kingdom after putting the "old man" to death. The "Church Age" is also the time of tribulation, or "labor pains." Persecution of Christians will grow increasingly severe and may, in the view of some, culminate with an individual antichrist establishing a worldwide kingdom, though many others emphasize John's own statement (1 John 2:18) that there are many antichrists. The millennium and tribulation will end with Christ's Second Coming, the "rapture" of Christians into his presence, the final judgment, and the consummation of God's kingdom. This view is called "Amillennialism" because advocates do not believe in a literal, *earthly* reign of Christ prior to the consummation.

Postmillennialism is a third approach to Revelation that was particularly popular among nineteenth-century evangelicals. Adherents generally believe that the tribulation, or "labor pains," occurred roughly between A.D. 64 and 70. It included the persecution of Christians by Nero and the destruction of Jerusalem by Rome. The world will become better and better (although not perfect) as people from all nations come to Christ and his spiritual influence gradually spreads. This leads into the millennium, which will end with Christ's Second Coming, the "rapture" of Christians into his presence, the final judgment, and the consummation of God's kingdom. This view is called "postmillennialism" because Christ's Second Coming occurs post-millennium, or after his millennial reign.

A fourth interpretive approach to Revelation is *Dispensational Premillennialism*, a view held by many fundamentalists and conservative evangelicals. Adherents display a strong tendency to interpret John's Apocalypse literally. They generally believe that Israel and Gentile Christians are separate and distinct peoples of God. The Lord's plan to establish his kingdom at the First Coming of Christ was thwarted when many Jews rejected their Messiah. Therefore the kingdom is in no sense present now. Faced with Israel's rejection, God "paused" in his dealings with Jews in order to build the Gentile church. However, the church will eventually grow corrupt and fail in its mission to evangelize the world. At some point in the future, the world will endure a seven-year period of tribulation, or "labor pains." Prior to (or during) the tribulation, Christians will be "raptured" out of the world. Jews and Gentiles who come to Christ after the rapture will remain to face an individual antichrist, who becomes world dictator and persecutes believers. The tribulation will end with the Second Coming of Christ and the binding of Satan. Christ will then set up a primarily Jewish kingdom on earth, with its capital in Jerusalem, which will last for a thousand years. The temple will be rebuilt and the sacrificial system restored. The final judgment and consummation of God's kingdom will follow this millennial reign. This view is called "Premillennialism" because Christ's Second Coming occurs pre-millennium, or prior to his millennial reign. It is called "Dispensational" because God deals with human beings through a series of "dispensations." In other words, He sets up certain commands and promises (e.g., the Mosaic covenant versus the new covenant), that apply to certain groups of people (e.g., Jews versus Gentiles), during certain periods of time (e.g., Adam to Noah, Noah to Abraham, etc.).

Each of these four views represents a serious attempt to understand the word of God, and each is worthy of careful consideration. However, *this author holds a different understanding of Scripture, which is reflected in this commentary.*[11] God has always reigned as king over creation, holding ultimate power over the universe. However, Satan and his allies have introduced evil into God's good world. They have

---

[11]See Part III.B.2 of the Introduction: "Common Features of Apocalyptic Theology." For a graphic representation, see Fig. 2, "The Shape of Christian Apocalyptic Theology," p. 41.

transformed the world into the "kingdom of Satan" — a place where God permits Satan and other evildoers to exercise a certain degree of power and influence.

At his First Coming, Christ began to do away with evil and once again establish the good. He began the work of destroying the kingdom of Satan and establishing the kingship of God. He cast out demons and healed the sick. He called on people to forsake sin and submit to God. He died on the cross as the sacrifice that established the new covenant. Through a faith commitment to Christ, both Jews and Gentiles may enter into this covenant relationship with God. They begin to live under God's kingship now, and in the future they gain the sure hope of resurrection to eternal life in a world purged from evil and conformed to God's will.

Between the First and Second Comings of Christ, the two kingdoms coexist. Satan's influence continues, but more and more people are released from his grasp through participating in the new covenant and embracing the kingdom of God. We (like Jesus himself in Matt 12:29 // Mark 3:27 // Luke 11:21-22) may describe this as a "binding of Satan." However, this is not necessarily the same idea John has in mind in Revelation 20:1-3.

Between the First and Second Comings of Christ, Christians will also endure the tribulation or "labor pains," a time of intense suffering and persecution for God's people as Satan and his allies desperately try to regain control. Satan will "make war" against the saints using political authorities (symbolized by the beast from the sea in Revelation 13), religious authorities (symbolized by the beast from the land in Revelation 13), and whatever other weapons are at his disposal. There will not necessarily be a single great antichrist, for any "man who denies that Jesus is the Christ . . . is the antichrist" and "many antichrists have come" (1 John 2:22,18; cf. 4:3). The tribulation will endure until the Second Coming of Christ. However, it will not necessarily grow progressively worse. When Jesus speaks of "great distress unequaled from the beginning of the world until now" (Matt 24:21), he is saying that the period of "labor pains" — viewed as a whole — will be worse than the period preceding it. Persecution of Christians will, of course, be worse in certain places at certain times. However, Christ declares that his Second Coming will catch people by surprise, just as the Flood caught people by surprise in the days of Noah. People will be "eating and drinking, marrying and giving in marriage," going about their normal everyday business (see Matt 24:37-39). In other words, the times will not get so bad that society ceases to function and everyone realizes that the Lord *must* come now.

The tribulation will end at the Second Coming of Christ, when the dead are raised, Christians are "raptured" into the presence of the Lord,[12] Christ carries out the final judgment, the kingdom of Satan is destroyed, and the kingdom of God comes in its fullness. There will be no thousand year physical reign of Christ on earth prior to his Second Coming.

The view sketched above seems consistent with the whole of Scripture and consistent with the Book of Revelation. If the so-called "millennium" were an essential aspect of the Christian gospel, then we would expect to find it elsewhere in Scripture. If the millennium were an essential part of John's eschatological scenario, then we would expect to find it in his first two visions of the future in Revelation 6:1-8:1 and 8:2-11:19. Instead, he consistently describes only the "labor pains," the final judgment, and the consummation of God's kingdom. What, then, are we to make of the millennial reign of Christ in Revelation 20? This author holds that the images of Revelation 20 must be read *in context*. They are symbols that serve an important function within the *self-contained* climactic vision of Revelation 20:1-22:5. We will explain the function of these symbols and the meaning of John's vision in Part (7) below.

⁷When the thousand years are over, Satan will be released from his prison ⁸and will go out to deceive the nations in the four corners of the earth—Gog and Magog—to gather them for battle. In number they are like the sand on the seashore. ⁹They marched across the breadth of the earth and surrounded the camp of God's people, the city he loves. But fire came down from heaven and devoured them. ¹⁰And the devil, who deceived them, was thrown into the lake of burning sulfur, where the beast and the false prophet had been thrown. They will be tormented day and night for ever and ever.

---

[12]For a discussion of the "rapture" idea, see Part III.C.3.b.(1) of the Commentary: "A Note on the 'Rapture.'"

¹¹Then I saw a great white throne and him who was seated on it. Earth and sky fled from his presence, and there was no place for them. ¹²And I saw the dead, great and small, standing before the throne, and books were opened. Another book was opened, which is the book of life. The dead were judged according to what they had done as recorded in the books. ¹³The sea gave up the dead that were in it, and death and Hades gave up the dead that were in them, and each person was judged according to what he had done. ¹⁴Then death and Hades were thrown into the lake of fire. The lake of fire is the second death. ¹⁵If anyone's name was not found written in the book of life, he was thrown into the lake of fire.

20:7-15 *(4) Element Four: God's Judgment of Gog and Magog.* Earlier in Revelation, John spoke of "Satan," the "beast" from the sea (symbolizing political powers allied with Satan), and the "false prophet" (symbolizing religious figures who support the political powers allied with Satan) inciting the nations to oppose Christ and his church.¹³ These symbols appear again, in 20:7-11, in yet another vision of God's final judgment against his enemies. A new element is "Gog and Magog," which John defines as "the nations in the four corners of the earth" that do "battle" against the Lord and his people. As we will see below, the symbol of Gog and Magog parallels Ezekiel 38–39.

Two images of eschatological condemnation appear in verses 7-10. First, fire comes down from heaven and devours God's enemies. This symbol calls to mind Ezekiel 39:6, where God sends fire on Magog (see below), and 2 Kings 1:9-15, where fire comes down from heaven and consumes one hundred soldiers who try to arrest God's prophet Elijah.

Second, those who try to destroy God's people are thrown into a "lake of burning sulfur," where they are "tormented day and night for ever and ever." The "lake," which also appears in Revelation 19:20 and 21:8, symbolizes eternal and irreversible punishment.

Verses 11-15 contain perhaps the most well known image of the final judgment in Scripture. The Almighty God, so awesome that

---

¹³See Rev 13:7,11-17; 16:12-16; 17:12-14; 19:17-21, along with the corresponding parts of the Commentary.

earth and sky flee from his presence, mounts his judgment seat like a Middle Eastern king. He calls for the "books" — the records from the royal archives — so that he may dispense justice with accuracy.[14] The dead are then "judged according to what they had done as recorded in the books." The image of God using record books to carry out his final judgment evokes the same scene as that in Daniel 7:9-10:

> As I looked,
>
> "thrones were set in place,
> > and the Ancient of Days took his seat.
> His clothing was as white as snow;
> > the hair of his head was white like wool.
> His throne was flaming with fire,
> > and its wheels were all ablaze.
> A river of fire was flowing,
> > coming out from before him.
> Thousands upon thousands attended him;
> > ten thousand times ten thousand stood before him.
> The court was seated,
> > *and the books were opened.*"[15]

The "book of life" is a list of faithful Christians who will receive eternal life in God's kingdom through their relationship with Jesus Christ. John employs this image in Revelation 3:5; 13:8; 17:8; 20:12,15; and 21:17. A similar "book" appears in 1 Enoch 47:3, and perhaps also in Exodus 32:32.

"Hades" is the Greek place of the dead. The term could be translated "death," or "grave," or perhaps "cemetery." In John's vision, the "cemetery" is emptied as all the dead are raised to appear before God's judgment throne. After the final judgment, "death and Hades" themselves are "thrown into the lake of fire." In other words, death itself "dies" as God abolishes the grave and grants his redeemed people eternal life.

(5) Element Five: The New Jerusalem (21:1–22:5). The final image in John's final vision is "the Holy City, the new Jerusalem, coming down out of heaven from God" (21:2). The heavenly city symbolizes the

---

[14]Compare Ezra 4:15 and Esth 6:1.
[15]Cf. Ps 56:8; Jer 22:30; Mal 3:16; 4 Ezra 6:20; 1 Enoch 90:20; 2 Apoc. Baruch 24:1.

consummated kingdom of God, the community of God's redeemed people. The imagery is reminiscent of texts such as Isaiah 65:17 ("Behold, I will create new heavens and a new earth."). We will examine Revelation 21-22 more closely later in this volume. For our present purposes, it is important to note that John describes the "new Jerusalem" as a "temple" where God is present. Chapter 21, verse 22 and verse 3, communicate this truth most clearly:

> I did not see a temple in the city, because the Lord God Almighty and the Lamb are its temple (Rev 21:22).

> Now the dwelling of God is with men, and he will live with them. They will be his people, and God himself will be with them and be their God (Rev 21:3).

(6) Comparison of Revelation 20:1-22:5 with Ezekiel 37-48. We have seen that, in Revelation 20:1-22:5, John presents a series of five primary images: First, he describes the binding of Satan in a manner reminiscent of 1 Enoch 10 and other apocalyptic texts (20:1-3). Second, he describes the resurrection of Christians, the new covenant people of God (20:4a). Third, he envisions a millennial reign of Christ and Christians similar to the temporary reign of the Messiah portrayed in 4 Ezra 7 (20:4b-6). Fourth, he sees God's judgment of Gog and Magog in an image like that in Ezekiel 39 (20:7-15). Fifth, he describes a "New Jerusalem," where God is present, using similar language to that in texts such as Isaiah 65 (21:1-22:5). Drawing on his tradition, John presents five major images arranged in a particular sequence. What is his purpose? How can we explain the meaning of his vision – particularly the unusual elements, such as the binding of Satan, Gog and Magog, and the millennium?

Earlier in Revelation, we have seen John pattern parts of his Apocalypse after the Exodus story (e.g., Rev 8:2–11:19 and Rev 15–16) and the Greek myth concerning the birth of Apollo (Rev 12). We suggest that, in like manner, the climactic vision of Revelation 20:1-22:5 is patterned after Ezekiel 37-48. Ezekiel, then, provides the key to understanding Revelation 20-22. Below, we will acquaint ourselves with Ezekiel's prophecy. Then we will explain John's use of the prophecy and the message he intends to convey.

Ezekiel lived and worked at the time of Israel's Babylonian Exile. In 587 B.C. King Nebuchadnezzar of Babylon invaded Judah, destroyed Jerusalem and the temple built by Solomon, and took most of the Jewish people into captivity in Babylon. God had warned the people that he would send this disaster upon them because of their disobedience and idolatry. For example, he spoke through the prophet Jeremiah and said:

> "I will make Jerusalem a heap of ruins,
>   a haunt of jackals;
> and I will lay waste the towns of Judah
>   so no one can live there."

The LORD said, "It is because they have forsaken my law, which I set before them; they have not obeyed me or followed my law. Instead, they have followed the stubbornness of their hearts; they have followed the Baals, as their fathers taught them." Therefore, this is what the LORD Almighty, the God of Israel, says: "See, I will make this people eat bitter food and drink poisoned water. I will scatter them among nations that neither they nor their fathers have known, and I will pursue them with the sword until I have destroyed them" (Jer 9:11,13-16).

In Babylon, the captive Jews were in despair. They had lost their land, much of the Jewish population, their capital city, their temple — everything that made them a distinct, sovereign nation. Even God had turned against them because of their sin, leaving them no hope and no future. Judah as a nation had "died," and there was nothing left but mourning.

But then God speaks to the people, through the prophet Ezekiel, and gives them some wonderful promises. In one of the most thrilling texts in all of Scripture, Ezekiel sees a vision of the "dead" Jewish nation as a valley full of dry bones. The Lord promises that the nation will not pass away forever. Instead, he will "raise it from the dead." The Lord will return the Jewish people to their own land and give them new life as a nation (Ezekiel 37:1-14).[16] Ezekiel 37 begins, then, with a vision of the "resurrection" of Israel after the "death" of the nation in Babylonian Captivity.

---

[16]In this text, the NIV translates the single Hebrew word *ruach* with three different English words — namely, "Spirit" (vv. 1,14), "breath" (vv. 6,8-10), and "wind" (v. 9).

As the chapter continues, Ezekiel receives another word from the Lord. To understand this part of the prophecy, the reader should know that, after the death of Kings David and Solomon, the kingdom of Israel was divided into two kingdoms as the result of a tax revolt. This occurred in 922 B.C.[17] The southern kingdom included the tribes of Judah and Benjamin. It was called "Judah" after the dominant tribe. The northern kingdom included the remaining ten Jewish tribes. This kingdom was called "Israel" after the great Jewish patriarch, or "Ephraim" after the dominant tribe (in turn named for Ephraim, the son of Joseph, the son of Jacob or "Israel"). The northern kingdom endured until 722 B.C., when it was destroyed by Assyria. The southern kingdom continued until 587 B.C., when its population was taken into Babylonian Captivity.

In Ezekiel 37:15-28, the Lord promises to rejoin the northern and southern kingdoms into a single Jewish nation, like two sticks rejoined as one. As king, God will set over them "David" — that is, a Davidic king or anointed "messiah" descended from King David.[18]

Thus far, God has promised to give new life to the Jewish people by returning them to their own land (Ezek 37:1-14). Furthermore, he has promised to form them into a single, united nation, ruled by a Davidic king (Ezek 37:15-28). In Ezekiel 38-39, the Lord promises to defend the new nation from all its enemies. In this prophecy, Gog, king of the land of Magog, becomes a symbol for all the enemies of the Jewish people, whoever they may be. The Lord declares that he will judge Gog of Magog, destroying his enemies and saving his people.[19]

One more magnificent vision completes the prophecy of Ezekiel. In chapters 40-48, God promises that the temple at Jerusalem will be rebuilt, and the Lord will once again dwell in the midst of his covenant people. The passage contains a long, detailed description of the temple, including its gates, its courts, the rooms of the temple itself, some of the regulations governing the temple worship, and even the division of the land surrounding the temple where the

---

[17]See 1 Kings 12.

[18]For a discussion of Davidic kings, see the comment on the title "Jesus Christ" in Rev 1:5.

[19]Compare Revelation, chapters 8, 9, and 16; also compare the calling of the birds to feast in Ezek 39:17-20 with Rev 19:17-21.

Israelites will live. This extended vision ends with the Lord giving a new name to Jerusalem, the city where he will be present with Israel in the temple's Holy of Holies:

> And the name of the city from that time on will be:
> THE LORD IS THERE (Ezek 48:35b).

Against this background, it becomes clear that John's prophecy in Revelation 20:1–22:5 has been patterned after Ezekiel's prophecy in Ezekiel 37–48. We sketch the main points of comparison below:

Ezekiel 37–48	Revelation 20:1–22:5
1. Ezekiel's prophecy is given in the context of the Babylonian Captivity. God's covenant people, Israel, are suffering oppression under Babylon.	1. John's prophecy appears in the context of a sort of second "Babylonian Captivity." God's covenant people, the church or "new Israel," are suffering oppression under a second "Babylon" — namely, Rome and/or other enemies of Christ and his saints (see Rev 12–19, esp. 14:8; 16:19; 17:5; 18:2,10,21).
	2. John envisions a temporary binding of Satan prior to the "fire" of the final judgment (Rev 20:1-3).
3. In his vision of the dry bones, Ezekiel sees the "resurrection" of Israel, the people of God, after the "death" of the nation in Babylonian Captivity (Ezek 37:1-14).	3. In his vision, John sees the resurrection of Christians, the "new Israel" and people of God, after their deaths at the hand of "Babylon" (Rev 20:4a).
4. Ezekiel receives a vision of the reign of a Davidic king over Israel (Ezek 37:15-28).	4. John receives a vision of the reign of Christ, the Davidic king, over the "new Israel" or church (Rev 20:4b-6).
5. Ezekiel witnesses God's defeat and judgment of Gog, king of Magog, who symbolizes all the enemies of his people Israel (Ezek 38–39).	5. John witnesses God's defeat and final judgment of Gog and Magog, which symbolize all the enemies of the church or "new Israel," his covenant people (Rev 20:7-15).[20]

---

[20]In rabbinical commentaries on Ezekiel, Gog, king of Magog, becomes Gog and Magog. John apparently adopts this convention in Revelation.

Ezekiel	Revelation
6. Ezekiel sees the new temple to be built in Jerusalem, where God will be present with his people Israel (Ezek 40-48).	6. John sees the "new Jerusalem," which is a "temple" where God is present with his people the church, or "new Israel" (Rev 21:1-22:5).

(7) Conclusions Regarding the Meaning of Revelation 20:1–22:5. In Revelation 20:1-22:5, John draws five images from his tradition (the binding of Satan, the resurrection, the millennial reign of Christ, the judgment of Gog and Magog, and the new Jerusalem) and arranges them in such a way that they conform to the sequence of visions in Ezekiel 37-48. What is his purpose for doing so? Why did the Lord inspire John to structure Revelation in this way? What message does he seek to convey?

The prophet Ezekiel offers a vision of the deliverance of Israel (God's covenant people) from captivity in Babylon (literal Babylon) to their own city (literal Jerusalem). Imitating Ezekiel, John offers a vision of the final judgment and consummation pictured as the deliverance of the "new Israel" (the church, God's new covenant people) from captivity in "Babylon" (Rome and other powers that make war against the saints) to their own city (the "new Jerusalem"). As John presented the final judgment and consummation as a "Second Exodus" earlier in Revelation,[21] he presents these eschatological events as a second deliverance from Babylonian Captivity in chapters 20-22.

How, then, should we explain John's references to the binding of Satan and the millennium, which are normally not a part of his eschatological vision? In Revelation, the normal sequence of events includes the resurrection (found in Rev 20:4a), the final judgment (found in 20:7-15), and the consummation of God's kingdom (found in 21:1-22:5). Adding the millennium (20:4b-6) between the resurrection and judgment enables John's vision to conform to the sequence of events in Ezekiel (resurrection – reign – judgment – Jerusalem), thus drawing the desired connection to that Old Testament prophecy. Adding the binding of Satan (20:1-3) to the

---

[21]See the Commentary, Parts III.C.1.c, "The Dominant Image [in Revelation 8:2-11:19]: God's Coming Kingdom as a 'Second Exodus' for His People") and III.D.3.e.(1), "The Structure of Revelation 15-16."

beginning of the sequence allows the reign of Christ to take place prior to the final judgment and consummation — that is, *before* the forces of evil are destroyed. It thereby makes the sequence of events in John's vision more logical. In this author's view, the binding of Satan and millennium are literary devices designed to make this specific vision conform to the sequence of events in Ezekiel. John's overall aim is to express an important theological truth: The final judgment and consummation will be like a second deliverance from Babylonian Captivity for the oppressed people of God. The verses concerning the binding of Satan and the millennium *must* be understood in that context and in light of that aim.

REVELATION 21–22

^{21:1}Then I saw a new heaven and a new earth, for the first heaven and the first earth had passed away, and there was no longer any sea. ²I saw the Holy City, the new Jerusalem, coming down out of heaven from God, prepared as a bride beautifully dressed for her husband. ³And I heard a loud voice from the throne saying, "Now the dwelling of God is with men, and he will live with them. They will be his people, and God himself will be with them and be their God. ⁴He will wipe every tear from their eyes. There will be no more death or mourning or crying or pain, for the old order of things has passed away."

⁵He who was seated on the throne said, "I am making everything new!" Then he said, "Write this down, for these words are trustworthy and true."

⁶He said to me: "It is done. I am the Alpha and the Omega, the Beginning and the End. To him who is thirsty I will give to drink without cost from the spring of the water of life. ⁷He who overcomes will inherit all this, and I will be his God and he will be my son. ⁸But the cowardly, the unbelieving, the vile, the murderers, the sexually immoral, those who practice magic arts, the idolaters and all liars—their place will be in the fiery lake of burning sulfur. This is the second death."

⁹One of the seven angels who had the seven bowls full of the seven last plagues came and said to me, "Come, I will show you the bride, the wife of the Lamb." ¹⁰And he carried me away in the Spirit to a mountain great and high, and showed me the Holy City, Jerusalem, coming down out of heaven from God. ¹¹It shone with the glory of God, and its brilliance was like that of a very precious jewel, like a jasper, clear as crystal. ¹²It had a great, high wall with twelve gates, and with twelve angels at the gates. On the gates were written the names of the twelve tribes of Israel. ¹³There were three gates on the east, three on the north, three on the south and three on the west. ¹⁴The wall of the city had twelve

foundations, and on them were the names of the twelve apostles of the Lamb.

¹⁵The angel who talked with me had a measuring rod of gold to measure the city, its gates and its walls. ¹⁶The city was laid out like a square, as long as it was wide. He measured the city with the rod and found it to be 12,000 stadia^a in length, and as wide and high as it is long. ¹⁷He measured its wall and it was 144 cubits^b thick,^c by man's measurement, which the angel was using. ¹⁸The wall was made of jasper, and the city of pure gold, as pure as glass. ¹⁹The foundations of the city walls were decorated with every kind of precious stone. The first foundation was jasper, the second sapphire, the third chalcedony, the fourth emerald, ²⁰the fifth sardonyx, the sixth carnelian, the seventh chrysolite, the eighth beryl, the ninth topaz, the tenth chrysoprase, the eleventh jacinth, and the twelfth amethyst.^d ²¹The twelve gates were twelve pearls, each gate made of a single pearl. The great street of the city was of pure gold, like transparent glass.

²²I did not see a temple in the city, because the Lord God Almighty and the Lamb are its temple. ²³The city does not need the sun or the moon to shine on it, for the glory of God gives it light, and the Lamb is its lamp. ²⁴The nations will walk by its light, and the kings of the earth will bring their splendor into it. ²⁵On no day will its gates ever be shut, for there will be no night there. ²⁶The glory and honor of the nations will be brought into it. ²⁷Nothing impure will ever enter it, nor will anyone who does what is shameful or deceitful, but only those whose names are written in the Lamb's book of life.

²²⁻¹Then the angel showed me the river of the water of life, as clear as crystal, flowing from the throne of God and of the Lamb ²down the middle of the great street of the city. On each side of the river stood the tree of life, bearing twelve crops of fruit, yielding its fruit every month. And the leaves of the tree are for the healing of the nations. ³No longer will there be any curse. The throne of God and of the Lamb will be in the city, and his servants will serve him. ⁴They will see his face, and his name will be on their foreheads. ⁵There will be no more night. They will not need the light of a lamp or the light of the sun, for the Lord God will give them light. And they will reign for ever and ever.

^a*16* That is, about 1,400 miles (about 2,200 kilometers)   ^b*17* That is, about 200 feet (about 65 meters)   ^c*17* Or *high*   ^d*20* The precise identification of some of these precious stones is uncertain.

(8) Climax: The Consummated Kingdom of God (21:1–22:5). In Revelation 21:1–22:5, John concludes his third vision of the future with a symbolic description of the consummated kingdom of God. Below, we will analyze the symbols to uncover the nature of that kingdom.

22:3b The throne of God and of the Lamb will be in the city, and his servants will serve him.

First, the consummated kingdom of God will be just that — the *kingdom* of God.[1] Everything in the universe will be brought into conformity with God's good and beneficent will. He will be king. He will be sovereign. He will exercise rule. He will have the dominion. He will be Lord. John expresses this truth by picturing God on the "throne" and saying that "his servants will serve him."

The "throne," or kingship of God, is shared by "the Lamb" Jesus Christ. Jesus is called "the Lamb" because he died on the cross as the sacrifice that destroys the kingdom of Satan and establishes the kingdom of God.[2] He shares God's kingly authority by virtue of the fact that God has made him "Messiah" or "Christ," God's "right hand man."[3] God exercises his sovereign rule through Jesus Christ, the man in whom he became incarnate. The God we know through Jesus Christ will reign forever, determining the shape of the universe and the course of the future.

21:1b,4,8,27; 22:3a for the first heaven and the first earth had passed away, and there was no longer any sea. . . . "He will wipe every tear from their eyes. There will be no more death or mourning or crying or pain, for the old order of things has passed away."

". . . But the cowardly, the unbelieving, the vile, the murderers, the sexually immoral, those who practice magic arts, the idolaters and all liars—their place will be in the fiery lake of burning sulfur. This is the second death."

---

[1] For further discussion of the "kingdom of God" concept, see Part III.B.2 of the Introduction: "Common Features of Apocalyptic Theology."

[2] For an explanation, see Part III.B.2.c.(4) of the Introduction, "The Kingdom of God and the Death of Jesus," as well as Parts II.D.2, "Christ as 'Overcomer'" and III.A.7, "The Lamb Who Was Slain," of the Commentary.

[3] For a discussion of this point, see the comment on the title "Jesus Christ" in Revelation 1:5.

> . . . **Nothing impure will ever enter it, nor will anyone who does what is shameful or deceitful, but only those whose names are written in the Lamb's book of life.**
> . . . **No longer will there be any curse.**

Second, the consummation of God's kingdom will bring the destruction of evil and the end of the "present evil age." When Adam and Eve sinned, God said to Adam in Genesis 3:17-19:

> "Because you listened to your wife and ate from the tree about which I commanded you, 'You must not eat of it,'
>
> "Cursed is the ground because of you;
> through painful toil you will eat of it
> all the days of your life.
> It will produce thorns and thistles for you,
> and you will eat the plants of the field.
> By the sweat of your brow
> you will eat your food
> until you return to the ground [i.e., until you die],
> since from it you were taken;
> for dust you are
> and to dust you will return."

We have seen that apocalyptic writers mark this event as the beginning of the "present evil age" — that is, a world fallen away from its original goodness, a world characterized by pain, suffering, hardship, and death.[4]

When John, in Revelation 22:3, says, "No longer will there be any curse," he is describing the consummation of God's kingship as the end of the "curse" pronounced in Genesis 3. In other words, the coming of God's kingdom rule will mark the end of the "present evil age" — not the end of God's creation, but the end of creation in its sinful, fallen state. This is also the force of Revelation 21:1 ("The first heaven and the first earth had passed away.") and 21:4 ("He will wipe every tear from their eyes. There will be no more death or mourning or crying or pain, for the old order of things has passed away.").

In describing the coming kingdom, John also says that there will "no longer" be "any sea" (21:1). Throughout Revelation, the

---

[4]See Part III.B.2.b.(2) of the Introduction: "The Present Evil Age and the Kingdom of Satan."

prophet uses the "sea" as a symbol for evil and chaos. In Revelation 4:6, he pictures it "before the throne" of God as "a sea of glass, clear as crystal." He thus portrays the forces of evil as subdued or "overcome" by the Cross of Christ.[5] In Revelation 15:2 John envisions Christians as having passed through "a sea of glass mixed with fire." The sea is calm like glass because the decisive battle over evil has already been won at the Cross. Nevertheless, in the last days of the "present evil age," Christians still experience the world as a sea "mixed with fire" because Satan, in desperation, makes war against the saints.[6] Now, in Revelation 21:1, John describes the complete end of the "sea" as God consummates his kingdom and expels all evil from creation.

John also describes the purging of evil from creation in terms of the removal of evildoers from God's kingdom:

> But the cowardly, the unbelieving, the vile, the murderers, the sexually immoral, those who practice magic arts, the idolaters and all liars—their place will be in the fiery lake of burning sulfur. This is the second death (Rev 21:8).
>
> Nothing impure will ever enter it, nor will anyone who does what is shameful or deceitful, but only those whose names are written in the Lamb's book of life (Rev 21:27).

When the Lord establishes his kingdom in its fullness, He will tolerate sin no more. Everything that robs life of its intended meaning and fulfillment, its beauty and joy, will be eliminated. God will restore creation to its original goodness (see Gen 1:31).

On the "fiery lake of burning sulfur" and "the second death," see Part III.D.3.(1) of the Commentary: "Element Three: The Millennial Reign of Christ (20:4b-6)." On "the Lamb's book of life," see Part III.D.3.(4): "Element Four: God's Judgment of Gog and Magog (20:7-15)."

---

[5]See Part III.A.2 of the Commentary: "The Throne of God and the Twenty-Four Elders."

[6]See Part III.D.3.e.(2) of the Commentary: "The Sea of Glass and Fire (15:1-4)."

21:1a,5,6a,24b,26 **Then I saw a new heaven and a new earth . . . . He who was seated on the throne said, "I am making everything new!" Then he said, "Write this down, for these words are trustworthy and true." He said to me: "It is done. I am the Alpha and the Omega, the Beginning and the End." . . . the kings of the earth will bring their splendor into it. . . . The glory and honor of the nations will be brought into it.**

Third, not only does the consummation of God's kingdom mean the destruction of evil. It also brings the transformation of creation and the establishment of the good. In describing this coming transformation, John writes: "Then I saw a new heaven and a new earth . . . . He who was seated on the throne said, 'I am making everything new!'" The prophet here adapts language and ideas from Isaiah 65:17-19:

> Behold, I will create
>   new heavens and a new earth.
> The former things will not be remembered,
>   nor will they come to mind.
> But be glad and rejoice forever
>   in what I will create,
> for I will create Jerusalem to be a delight
>   and its people a joy.
> I will rejoice over Jerusalem
>   and take delight in my people;
> the sound of weeping and crying
>   will be heard in it no more.

Dr. Eugene Boring states the matter well when he says, "God does not make 'all new things,' but 'all things new.'"[7] The consummation of the kingdom does not mark the end of God's creation, but the transformation of creation so that it conforms to his sovereign will. God created the universe and pronounced it "good" (Gen 1:31). He loves his creation and does not want to destroy it. Instead, he wants to redeem it by removing the "cancer" of evil and restoring it to health.

God will renew all things, or "make everything new." Yet there will still be continuity between the old heaven and earth, and the

---

[7]Boring, *Revelation*, 220.

new heaven and earth. For example, Christians, who are a part of the present creation, will also be a part of the New Creation. This is the meaning of the biblical doctrine of the resurrection of the "body" or "person" (σῶμα, *sōma*).[8] When Jesus was raised from the dead, he was transformed. For example, he could now enter rooms with locked doors (John 20:19) and alter his appearance at will (Luke 24:13-35). At the same time, he was still essentially the same Jesus — still essentially the same "person" (*sōma*). The risen Jesus recognized his disciples, and they recognized him. Their relationship continued. In the same way, Christians will be raised to eternal life with our "selves" intact. We will retain our memories, our personalities — everything that makes us who we are. At the same time, we will be transformed and purified and renewed, so that we conform to God's will in every way.

Likewise, everything good in this world will be incorporated into God's eternal kingdom and made a part of the "new heaven and new earth." Every thought that has been thought, every deed that has been done, every creative contribution that brings glory to God will have a part in his New Creation. The Apostle Paul expresses this kind of an idea in 1 Corinthians 3:10-15:

> By the grace God has given me, I laid a foundation as an expert builder, and someone else is building on it. But each one should be careful how he builds. For no one can lay any foundation other than the one already laid, which is Jesus Christ. If any man builds on this foundation using gold, silver, costly stones, wood, hay or straw, his work will be shown for what it is, because the Day [i.e., the Day of the Lord — the Second Coming of Christ, the final judgment, and the consummation of God's kingdom[9]] will bring it to light. It will be revealed with fire, and the fire will test the quality of each man's work. If what he has built survives, he will receive his reward. If it is burned up, he will suffer loss; he himself will be saved, but only as one escaping through the flames.

---

[8]See Part III.B.2.c.(5) of the Introduction: "The Kingdom of God and the Resurrection of Jesus."

[9]On the "Day of the Lord," see Part III.C.2.g of the Commentary: "The Sounding of Seven Trumpets: The 'Present Evil Age' and 'Labor Pains' as the Announcement of the Day of the Lord."

In the context of 1 Corinthians 3, Paul is thinking specifically about building churches. However, his conception of the final judgment has broader application. Christians are people who build their lives on the "foundation" of Jesus Christ. At the final judgment, everything in our lives that does not conform to the will of God (the "wood, hay or straw") will be "burned up." Praise God, for all our character flaws and all our failures will be removed! They will not be a part of the New Creation. However, Christians themselves will be "saved," and whatever good we have accomplished (the "gold and silver") will be incorporated into God's eternal kingdom.

This is the meaning of Revelation 21:24 and 26: "The kings of the earth will bring their splendor into [God's kingdom]. . . . The glory and honor of the nations will be brought into it."[10] The Greek term translated "nations" (ἔθνη, *ethnē*) refers not to nation states, but to all the various ethnic groups that make up the human race. John is saying that the "new heaven and new earth" will include people "from every tribe and language and people and nation" (see Rev 5:9; 7:9). Each ethnic group will make its unique contributions to the richness and beauty of God's New Creation. The consummated kingdom of God will be a community based on the best theology and best philosophy, the best city planning and best social theory, the best science and best technology. The "new heaven and new earth" will include the best art, the best architecture, and the best landscaping from every culture. We will enjoy the best music, the best drama, the best literature, and the best food from every

---

[10]The scriptural basis for this image comes from the Book of Isaiah, chapters 2 ("In the last days the mountain of the LORD's temple will be established . . . and all nations will stream to it," v. 2) and 60 ("Nations will come to your light, and kings to the brightness of your dawn. . . . the riches of the nations will come. . . . Your gates will always stand open, they will never be shut, day or night, so that men may bring you the wealth of the nations — their kings led in triumphal procession. For the nation or kingdom that will not serve you will perish; it will be utterly ruined," vv. 3,5,11-12). Isaiah predicts that, when Jerusalem is rebuilt, God will cause all the Gentile nations to serve the Jews and bring tribute money to Jerusalem. In Revelation, John does not picture the Gentiles coming into the "new Jerusalem" as captives or as second-class citizens. Instead, all nations, all peoples, and all cultures are equal sharers in the New Creation. All make their own contributions to the glory and honor and goodness of God's kingdom.

nation. Over time, we will learn every language so that we may share with each of the redeemed saints in his or her "heart language." This will be necessary because there are aspects of the glory of God that can only be communicated in Navaho or Hmong or Chibemba. We will have minds that can understand and retain the finer points of molecular biology and quantum theory, so that we may grasp all the wonders God wants to show us. We will have resurrection bodies that will not grow weary if we dance for joy for the first million years. And this will be only the beginning. We will have all eternity to grow beyond what we can even imagine, for "no eye has seen, no ear has heard, no mind has conceived what God has prepared for those who love him" (1 Cor 2:9)!

In Revelation 16:17, an angel pours out the last Bowl of Wrath on Babylon the Great. Afterwards, the Lord shouts, "It is done," signifying the completion of God's final judgment against his enemies. The corresponding "It is done" of 21:6 signals the consummation of God's kingdom, the salvation of his covenant people. We have seen that salvation and condemnation are two aspects of the same event.[11] This is the purpose that motivates God, his aim for all creation. In 21:6 the Lord declares: "I am the Alpha and the Omega, the Beginning and the End."[12] God is the one who gives creation both its origin and its goal, and the goal toward which he is directing history is the destruction of evil and the establishment of good.

21:2a,10,12-14,17-21 I saw the Holy City, the new Jerusalem, coming down out of heaven from God . . . . And he carried me away in the Spirit to a mountain great and high, and showed me the Holy City, Jerusalem, coming down out of heaven from God . . . . It had a great, high wall with twelve gates, and with twelve angels at the gates. On the gates were written the names of the twelve tribes of Israel. There were three gates on the east, three on the north, three on the south and three on the west. The wall of the city had twelve foundations, and on them were the names of the twelve apostles of the Lamb. . . . He measured its wall and it

---

[11]See Part III.D.3.a of the Commentary: "The Relationship between Salvation and Condemnation, Final Judgment and Consummation."

[12]For a discussion of these divine titles, see the comment on "him who is, and who was, and who is to come," in Rev 1:4.

was 144 cubits thick, by man's measurement, which the angel was using. The wall was made of jasper, and the city of pure gold, as pure as glass. The foundations of the city walls were decorated with every kind of precious stone. The first foundation was jasper, the second sapphire, the third chalcedony, the fourth emerald, the fifth sardonyx, the sixth carnelian, the seventh chrysolite, the eighth beryl, the ninth topaz, the tenth chrysoprase, the eleventh jacinth, and the twelfth amethyst. The twelve gates were twelve pearls, each gate made of a single pearl. The great street of the city was of pure gold, like transparent glass.

Fourth, John presents the consummated kingdom of God as a "city," or a *community* made up of the Lord's people. His description of the city's foundations and walls and gates does not reveal the physical appearance of the city's architecture as much as it reveals the kind of people who make up the redeemed *community*.

John calls the city "the new Jerusalem," after the capital city of Israel. The old Jerusalem embodied Israel, the group of people who entered into the Mosaic covenant with God. In like manner, the "new Jerusalem" symbolizes Christians, the "new Israel," the group of people who have entered into the new covenant with God.[13]

John describes the city as "coming down out of heaven from God." Note that the city is not located somewhere in the sky on the clouds. Instead, it comes down "from God" to the earthly sphere.[14] This is a community created not by human beings, but by God himself. Its founder and builder is the Heavenly One.

The "new Jerusalem" has twelve foundations with the names of the twelve Apostles of the Lamb written on them. In other words, this new covenant community is built on the foundation of the apostles' witness, just as the church is in Ephesians 2:20.

The heavenly city has twelve gates with the names of the twelve tribes of Israel written on them. Elsewhere in Revelation, the twelve tribes of Israel symbolize the full number of Christians, the totality

---

[13]See the comment on "the holy city" in Rev 11:2. On a "heavenly Jerusalem" as the future home of the people of God, compare Gal 4:26 and Heb 12:22.

[14]For a discussion of the earthly and heavenly spheres, see Part III.B.2.b.(1) of the Introduction: "Rebellion in Heaven."

of the church.¹⁵ The twelve gates therefore represent an entryway for every part of the people of God. The consummated kingdom of God includes *all* the Lord's people.

The city is twelve thousand stadia long, twelve thousand stadia wide, and twelve thousand stadia high (literally about 1400 miles or 2200 kilometers long, wide, and high). We have seen that, in Jewish and Christian apocalyptic literature, "twelve" is the symbolic number for the people of God. Multiples of twelve symbolize the full number of the people of God.¹⁶ The dimensions of the city (12×1000, 12×1000, and 12×1000) therefore symbolize the fact that the kingdom community will include everyone who belongs to the Lord.

The city's walls are one hundred and forty-four cubits thick (literally about 200 feet or 65 meters thick). Again, John uses a multiple of twelve (12×12), showing that the "new Jerusalem" is a community consisting of all Christians. It has People of God "written all over it."

According to verses 19-20,

> The foundations of the city walls were decorated with every kind of precious stone. The first foundation was jasper, the second sapphire, the third chalcedony, the fourth emerald, the fifth sardonyx, the sixth carnelian, the seventh chrysolite, the eighth beryl, the ninth topaz, the tenth chrysoprase, the eleventh jacinth, and the twelfth amethyst.¹⁷

The twelve stones of the city's foundations are probably intended to remind us of the twelve stones mounted on the breastpiece worn by Aaron, the High Priest. According to Exodus 28:15-21, these twelve stones symbolize the twelve tribes of Israel, the whole of God's covenant people.

The names of the twelve stones given in Revelation 21 do not match all of the names of the stones given in Exodus 28 (which in the NIV are ruby, topaz, beryl, turquoise, sapphire, emerald, jacinth,

---

¹⁵See, for example, Part III.B.4.a of the Commentary: "The Sealing of the 144,000 (7:1-8)."

¹⁶See Part III.B.1.(d) of the Introduction: "Symbolic Numbers."

¹⁷Like Revelation, Isa 54:11-12 and Tobit 13:16-18 anticipate a new Jerusalem built from precious stones.

agate, amethyst, chrysolite, onyx, and jasper). However, since the Greek equivalents for the Hebrew names of jewels were not standard, this does not rule out the possibility that John is alluding to the breastpiece worn by the High Priest. If this is the case, then not only the number of jewels (twelve), but the jewels themselves serve to identify the heavenly city with the people of God.

The name of the city, its dimensions, the number of its gates and foundations, the thickness of its walls, and the materials from which it is constructed – all serve to identify the heavenly kingdom as the community of God's people. It is a "Holy City" – that is, a group of people wholly committed to God as Lord. Furthermore, it is a "city" – not a group of independent individualists, but an interdependent *community*. Salvation will not take the form of isolated individuals contemplating their creator. Salvation will involve a network of relationships with both God *and* our fellow believers.

21:3,11,15-16,22-24a,25; 22:4-5a And I heard a loud voice from the throne saying, "Now the dwelling of God is with men, and he will live with them. They will be his people, and God himself will be with them and be their God." . . . It shone with the glory of God, and its brilliance was like that of a very precious jewel, like a jasper, clear as crystal. . . . The angel who talked with me had a measuring rod of gold to measure the city, its gates and its walls. The city was laid out like a square, as long as it was wide. He measured the city with the rod and found it to be 12,000 stadia in length, and as wide and high as it is long. . . . I did not see a temple in the city, because the Lord God Almighty and the Lamb are its temple. The city does not need the sun or the moon to shine on it, for the glory of God gives it light, and the Lamb is its lamp. The nations will walk by its light . . . . On no day will its gates ever be shut, for there will be no night there. . . . They will see his face, and his name will be on their foreheads. There will be no more night. They will not need the light of a lamp or the light of the sun, for the Lord God will give them light.

Fifth, John shows that, at the consummation of his kingdom, God will be directly present with his people. In the Book of Exodus, God commanded Moses and the Israelites to build a tabernacle or tent. This tabernacle consisted of two rooms – namely, an outer room called the Holy Place and an inner room called the Most Holy Place. The inner room contained a wooden box, covered with gold, called the Ark of the Covenant, or Ark of the Testimony. The lid for the box was formed of a slab of pure gold on which were mounted two golden cherubim. This lid was called the Atonement Cover. Above the Atonement Cover hovered the glory of God, a bright light serving as a visible manifestation of the invisible God's presence. The Lord told Moses:

> [H]ave [Israel] make a sanctuary for me, and I will dwell among them. . . . There, above the cover between the two cherubim that are over the ark of the Testimony, I will meet with you and give you all my commands for the Israelites (Exod 25:8,22).

> So I will consecrate the Tent of Meeting and the altar and will consecrate Aaron and his sons to serve me as priests. Then I will dwell among the Israelites and be their God. They will know that I am the LORD their God, who brought them out of Egypt so that I might dwell among them. I am the LORD their God (Exod 29:44-46).

At the tabernacle, then, God was present with his covenant people Israel. The priests who served in the tabernacle could draw closer to God than the rest of the Israelites. However, only the High Priest could enter the Holy of Holies, the direct presence of God. He could do so only once per year on the Day of Atonement (see Leviticus 16).

Years later, King Solomon built a temple in Jerusalem, a more permanent structure to replace the older tabernacle. At the dedication of the new temple, God spoke to Solomon and declared his intention to "take up residence" there:

> I have consecrated this temple, which you have built, by putting my Name there forever. My eyes and my heart will always be there (1 Kgs 9:3).

> When the priests withdrew from the Holy Place, the cloud filled the temple of the LORD. And the priests could not perform their service because of the cloud, for the glory of the LORD filled his temple (1 Kgs 8:10-11).

So the temple, too, was a place where God was uniquely present with his covenant people. The temple signifies the presence of God.

In Revelation 21–22, John declares that the "new Jerusalem" is a "temple;" it is a place where God is present with his people. In verse 22 he writes: "I did not see a temple in the city, because the Lord God Almighty and the Lamb are its temple." In other words, there is no single building in the kingdom where God and Christ are present, because they are directly present everywhere. The entire city — the entire redeemed community — is a "temple."

In verses 15-16 an angel measures the heavenly city — just as an angel measures the *temple* in Ezekiel 40–42 (the Old Testament text which parallels this vision[18]) and John measures the *temple* in Revelation 11:1. The act of measuring itself implies that the "new Jerusalem" is a temple where God is present.

When the angel measures the city, he finds that it is "laid out like a square, as long as it was wide." He finds it to be "12,000 stadia in length, and as wide and high as it is long." In other words, the city is shaped like a perfect cube. This has theological significance, for 1 Kings 6:20 states that the Holy of Holies was also shaped like a perfect cube: "The inner sanctuary was twenty cubits long, twenty wide and twenty high" (cf. 2 Chron 3:8-9). The meaning of the symbol is that living in the consummated kingdom of God will be something like living in the Most Holy Place forever. All God's people will be "High Priests" in the sense that they will have direct access to the Lord — not just once per year, but always.[19] John emphasizes this truth with two other statements:

> And I heard a loud voice from the throne saying, "Now the dwelling [lit., 'tent'] of God is with men, and he will live with them. They will be his people [lit., 'peoples'], and God himself will be with them and be their God (Rev 21:3).[20]

---

[18]See Part III.D.3.i.(6) of the Commentary: "Comparison of Revelation 20:1–22:5 with Ezekiel 37–48."

[19]Compare Matthew 27:51, which shows that, at the moment of Jesus' death, the curtain blocking access to the Most Holy Place was "torn in two from top to bottom." This signifies that it is the sacrificial death of the Lamb that gives believers access to the presence of God.

[20]Compare this verse to Ezekiel 48:35, which John consciously imitates in this last series of visions: "And the name of the city from that time on will be: THE LORD IS THERE." For further discussion, see Part III.D.3.i.(6) of the Commentary: "Comparison of Revelation 20:1–22:5 with Ezekiel 37–48."

They will see his face,[21] and his name will be on their foreheads[22] (Rev 22:4).

In the Old Testament tabernacle and temple, the presence of God took the form of "glory," a visible bright light showing that the invisible Deity was there.[23] John pictures the same divine glory filling the heavenly city — again showing the Lord's constant presence with his people:

> It shone with the glory of God, and its brilliance was like that of a very precious jewel, like a jasper, clear as crystal (Rev 21:11).[24]

> The city does not need the sun or the moon to shine on it, for the glory of God gives it light, and the Lamb is its lamp. The nations will walk by its light . . . . On no day will its gates ever be shut, for there will be no night there (Rev 21:23-24a,25).[25]

> There will be no more night. They will not need the light of a lamp or the light of the sun, for the Lord God will give them light (Rev 22:5a).

21:2b,7,9 prepared as a bride beautifully dressed for her husband. . . . "He who overcomes will inherit all this, and I will be his God and he will be my son." . . . One of the seven angels who had the seven bowls full of the seven last plagues came and said to me, "Come, I will show you the bride, the wife of the Lamb."

---

[21]Compare 1 John 3:2: "We know that when he appears, we shall be like him, for we shall see him as he is." Contrast Exodus 33:18-23, where Moses is not allowed to see God's face, but only his back.

[22]The name on the forehead is a mark of belonging. Compare Rev 3:12.

[23]For further discussion of this phenomenon, see the comment on the risen Christ's eyes, feet, and face in Rev 1:14-16.

[24]On sparkling jewels signifying the radiant glory of God, see the comment on Rev 4:3.

[25]Since the city's gates remain open, a significant number of scholars argue that verse 25 implies universal salvation — the damned may leave the lake of fire and enter the "new Jerusalem." However, John clearly interprets the significance of the symbol of the open gate: "On no day will its gates ever be shut, *for there will be no night there.*"

Sixth, John shows that, when the kingdom comes, God's people will not only be in his presence. They will also enjoy the deepest, most personal, most intimate relationship with him. In 21:7 the Lord says: "He who overcomes[26] will inherit all this, and I will be his God and *he will be my son*." Christians will enjoy the same kind of relationship with God that adoring children share with their loving father.

In 21:2 and 9, John refers to the redeemed community as "the bride, the wife of the Lamb."[27] The church will enjoy the same sort of intimate fellowship with Christ that a wife shares with her husband. As the Lord's "bride," the Christian community is "beautifully dressed" in righteousness (see 19:7-8). In contrast to the "great prostitute" of chapter 17, she is wholly committed to her "husband," free from the "adultery" of idolatry.

21:6b; 22:1-2,5b "To him who is thirsty I will give to drink without cost from the spring of the water of life." . . . Then the angel showed me the river of the water of life, as clear as crystal, flowing from the throne of God and of the Lamb down the middle of the great street of the city. On each side of the river stood the tree of life, bearing twelve crops of fruit, yielding its fruit every month. And the leaves of the tree are for the healing of the nations. . . . And they will reign for ever and ever.

Finally, John portrays the consummated kingdom of God as *life eternal* in intimate fellowship with the Lord. The prophet draws imagery from Genesis 2, which describes the Garden of Eden as a place where many trees grew and from which a river flowed:

> Now the LORD God had planted a garden in the east, in Eden; and there he put the man he had formed. And the LORD God made all kinds of trees grow out of the ground—trees that were pleasing to the eye and good for food. In the middle of the garden were the tree of life and the tree of the knowledge of good and evil.
>
> A river watering the garden flowed from Eden . . . (Gen 2:8-10a).

---

[26]For an explanation, see Part II.D.3 of the Commentary: "Christians as 'Overcomers.'"

[27]Compare the parallel imagery in Rev 19:5-10.

John also makes use of Ezekiel 47:1-12, which describes the temple, the place of God's presence, as a source of life:[28]

> The man brought me back to the entrance of the temple, and I saw water coming out from under the threshold of the temple toward the east . . .
> I saw a great number of trees on each side of the river. He said to me, "This water flows toward the eastern region and goes down into the Arabah, where it enters the Sea [i.e., the Dead Sea, which is so salty that fish cannot live in it]. When it empties into the Sea, the water there becomes fresh. Swarms of living creatures will live wherever the river flows. There will be large numbers of fish, because this water flows there and makes the salt water fresh; so where the river flows everything will live. . . . Fruit trees of all kinds will grow on both banks of the river. Their leaves will not wither, nor will their fruit fail. Every month they will bear, because the water from the sanctuary flows to them. Their fruit will serve for food and their leaves for healing (Ezek 47:1a,7b-9,12; cf. Zech 14).

By comparing the heavenly Jerusalem to Eden, John defines the consummated kingdom of God as Paradise restored — as the world returned to its original goodness (see Gen 1:31). According to Genesis, the Garden of Eden held the "tree of life" — a tree bearing fruit that could sustain human life forever.[29] John declares that, in the coming kingdom community, this "fruit" — this gift of life — will always be available in abundance. The writer seems to be imagining multiple "trees of life," for they stand "on each side of the river." The trees bear "twelve crops of fruit, yielding its fruit every month," so life is never "out of season."[30]

In 21:6b, John employs a similar symbol — namely, the "water of life," or the water that gives life. The Lord says: "To him who is thirsty I will give to drink without cost (or "as a gift," δωρεάν, *dōrean*) from the spring of the water of life." Since God continually gives the gift of life to his people, "they will reign *for ever and ever.*"

---

[28]Revelation 20:1-22:5 is patterned after Ezekiel 37-48. See Part III.D.3.i.(6) of the Commentary.
[29]See Part II.B.2.a.(1) of the Introduction: "Genesis 1-5."
[30]Compare Rev 2:7; 1 Enoch 24-25; and Testament of Levi 18:11.

22:6"The angel said to me, "These words are trustworthy and true. The Lord, the God of the spirits of the prophets, sent his angel to show his servants the things that must soon take place."

22:6 *(9) Conclusion of the Third Vision of the Future.* With these words, John concludes his third and final vision of the future. In Revelation 1:19, Christ promises to reveal to his servant the present ("what is now") and also the future ("what will take place later"). John's vision of the present takes the form of the letters to the seven churches of Asia found in chapters 2–3. The three-part vision of the future begins with the transitional sentence in 4:1 ("Come up here, and I will show you *what must take place after this*" – i.e., after the "present" described in chapters 2–3) and ends with the closing statement in 22:6. For a more detailed discussion of the "Structure of Revelation," see Part V of the Introduction.

The angel refers to the Lord as "the God of the spirits of the prophets." In other words, he is the God who stands behind the prophets as the ultimate source of their prophecy. Compare Revelation 19:10.

Through the prophet John, the Lord has revealed to his church the shape of the future from the late first century to the Second Coming of Christ. According to this revelation, God's people must first face the "labor pains," a time of suffering and persecution fueled by Satan and his allies. However, the "labor pains" will not last forever. Christ will one day return, carry out God's final judgment, purge the world from evil, establish the good, and thereby bring the entire universe under his beneficent sovereignty. His people will be raised up to eternal life in a redeemed, renewed creation, where they will enjoy intimate fellowship with one another and with their loving creator. This message is neither wishful thinking nor blind speculation. The angel reminds us that these are the words of God himself, and they "are trustworthy and true."

IV. EPILOGUE (22:7-21)

7"Behold, I am coming soon! Blessed is he who keeps the words of the prophecy in this book."
8I, John, am the one who heard and saw these things. And when

I had heard and seen them, I fell down to worship at the feet of the angel who had been showing them to me. ⁹But he said to me, "Do not do it! I am a fellow servant with you and with your brothers the prophets and of all who keep the words of this book. Worship God!"

¹⁰Then he told me, "Do not seal up the words of the prophecy of this book, because the time is near. ¹¹Let him who does wrong continue to do wrong; let him who is vile continue to be vile; let him who does right continue to do right; and let him who is holy continue to be holy."

¹²"Behold, I am coming soon! My reward is with me, and I will give to everyone according to what he has done. ¹³I am the Alpha and the Omega, the First and the Last, the Beginning and the End.

¹⁴"Blessed are those who wash their robes, that they may have the right to the tree of life and may go through the gates into the city. ¹⁵Outside are the dogs, those who practice magic arts, the sexually immoral, the murderers, the idolaters and everyone who loves and practices falsehood.

¹⁶"I, Jesus, have sent my angel to give you[a] this testimony for the churches. I am the Root and the Offspring of David, and the bright Morning Star."

¹⁷The Spirit and the bride say, "Come!" And let him who hears say, "Come!" Whoever is thirsty, let him come; and whoever wishes, let him take the free gift of the water of life.

¹⁸I warn everyone who hears the words of the prophecy of this book: If anyone adds anything to them, God will add to him the plagues described in this book. ¹⁹And if anyone takes words away from this book of prophecy, God will take away from him his share in the tree of life and in the holy city, which are described in this book.

²⁰He who testifies to these things says, "Yes, I am coming soon."

Amen. Come, Lord Jesus.

²¹The grace of the Lord Jesus be with God's people. Amen.

ᵃ*16* The Greek is plural.

Revelation 22:7-21 forms a short epilogue that concludes the Apocalypse of John. Since most of the ideas appear earlier in the book, the epilogue primarily serves to reinforce important themes. It begins with a word from Christ himself.

22:7 "Behold, I am coming soon! Blessed is he who keeps the words of the prophecy in this book."

Much of Revelation has focused on the imminent Second Coming of Christ, which will bring the final judgment and the consummation of God's kingdom rule. As if to emphasize the reality of these events and the urgency of preparing for them, Christ says: "Behold, I *am* coming soon!" The Greek word translated "behold" (ἰδού, *idou*) literally means "Look!" It carries the force of "Listen closely!" or "Pay attention!" The Lord declares that the person who pays attention to Revelation, who takes it to heart and "keeps the words of the prophecy," will be "blessed" (μακάριος, *makarios*). In other words, that person will be "happy" or "fortunate" or "thriving."

After two thousand years of waiting, Christians may wonder how the Lord could truthfully say, "I am coming *soon!*" However, we have seen that the major events in God's apocalyptic scenario are the First Coming of Christ, then the "Labor Pains," then the Second Coming of Christ, and then the final judgment and consummation of God's Kingdom Rule.[31] The Messiah has already appeared and the "labor pains" are well underway. The very next item on God's eschatological agenda is the Second Coming of Christ. When viewed from within Revelation's apocalyptic framework, the return of Christ will indeed come very soon.

22:8-9 I, John, am the one who heard and saw these things. And when I had heard and seen them, I fell down to worship at the feet of the angel who had been showing them to me. ⁹But he said to me, "Do not do it! I am a fellow servant with you and with your brothers the prophets and of all who keep the words of this book. Worship God!"

On "John," the author of Revelation, see Parts IV.A.2 and IV.B.1 of the Introduction. On the warning to worship God rather than angels, see the comment on the parallel episode in Revelation 19:10.

22:10 Then he told me, "Do not seal up the words of the prophecy of this book, because the time is near.

In Daniel 12, an angel reveals to Daniel the future events of the

---

[31]For a graphic representation of these events, see Fig. 2, "The Shape of Christian Apocalyptic Theology," p. 41.

"labor pains," the resurrection, the final judgment, and the consummation of the kingdom of God (vv. 1-4). He then commands Daniel to "close up and seal the words of the scroll" because these events belong to the distant future, to "the time of the end" (v. 4). In the Book of Revelation, John sees visions of the same events. However, the angel commands him *not* to seal up the prophecy "because the time is near." In fact, the eschatological events have already begun because the "labor pains" are already in progress. This conscious imitation of the Book of Daniel highlights the fact that John's readers live in the time of the fulfillment of God's promises. It therefore adds urgency to the need to prepare for the Second Coming of Christ. John imitates Daniel 12 in a similar manner in Revelation 10.[32]

22:11 Let him who does wrong continue to do wrong; let him who is vile continue to be vile; let him who does right continue to do right; and let him who is holy continue to be holy."

This statement appears to be an adaptation of yet another verse from Daniel, chapter 12 (see above) — namely, Daniel 12:10:

> Many will be purified, made spotless and refined, but the wicked will continue to be wicked. None of the wicked will understand, but those who are wise will understand.

It is not surprising that an angel from the Lord would say: "Let him who does right continue to do right; and let him who is holy continue to be holy." It is quite surprising that a spokesman for the Holy God should say: "Let him who does wrong continue to do wrong; let him who is vile continue to be vile." This latter exhortation may be interpreted in several ways: First, it could simply be an acknowledgment that some will hear and heed Revelation, while others will not. In this case, the meaning would be similar to Ezekiel 3:27:

> But when I speak to you, I will open your mouth and you shall say to them, "This is what the Sovereign LORD says. 'Whoever will listen let him listen, and whoever will refuse let him refuse; for they are a rebellious house.'"[33]

---

[32]See Part III.C.3.a.(4) of the Commentary: "Comparison with Daniel 12."
[33]Compare Jesus' exhortation, "He who has ears, let him hear" — which implies that some will refuse to hear.

Second, it could be understood as an encouragement to believers facing persecution. In this case, the force of the statement would be: Let the wicked continue to do their worst because, in the end, Christ and his people will nevertheless "overcome"!

Third, the exhortation may be intended to startle readers into recognizing the seriousness of their conduct and, if necessary, move them to repentance. In other words, if Christian readers are involved in sinful behavior, then the Lord's invitation to continue in it until the Second Coming and final judgment may shock them into changing their ways.

Whatever the case, the angel's word should *not* be understood to mean that it is impossible for sinners to change their ways. In verse 14 Christ says: "Blessed are those *who wash their robes*, that they may have the right to the tree of life and may go through the gates into the city." It is possible for even the worst offenders to hear the gospel, believe it, turn from sin, embrace the Lord, and thereby gain the kingdom. Praise the Lord for his marvelous grace!

22:12-16 "Behold, I am coming soon! My reward is with me, and I will give to everyone according to what he has done. I am the Alpha and the Omega, the First and the Last, the Beginning and the End. Blessed are those who wash their robes, that they may have the right to the tree of life and may go through the gates into the city. Outside are the dogs, those who practice magic arts, the sexually immoral, the murderers, the idolaters and everyone who loves and practices falsehood. I, Jesus, have sent my angel to give you this testimony for the churches. I am the Root and the Offspring of David, and the bright Morning Star."

Christ again breaks into the narrative to warn of his impending return and final judgment. For each individual, the outcome of the judgment will be either eternal doom or eternal life. The determination will be made "according to what he has done" — that is, according to his response to Jesus Christ and the manner of life that flows from that response.

The Lord pronounces a blessing on those who "wash their robes." Earlier in Revelation, clean robes symbolize "the righteous acts of the saints" (19:8) — that is, behavior consistent with a new covenant relationship with God. Those who "wash their robes" — who enter into the new covenant through a faith commitment to Christ — receive the right to eat from "the tree of life." The tree, a symbol first introduced in Genesis 2:9, represents eternal life given by God.[34] The righteous are also given admittance to the heavenly city, the "new Jerusalem," a symbol for the consummated kingdom of God.[35]

Those who reject God's kingship over their lives and instead cling to sin will be barred from that "city." The Lord calls such people "dogs," which was a common first century Jewish slur against Gentiles, or non-Jews (see Matt 15:21-28//Mark 7:24-30; Phil 3:2). The Jews drew a sharp distinction between themselves and other ethnic groups because they were given the Mosaic covenant while other nations were not. They were "insiders" enjoying a close relationship with God, while the Gentiles were "outsiders" having no knowledge of God. Here in Revelation 22, the Lord calls non-Christians "dogs" not so much as an insult to them (not that it's a compliment!), but as a way of identifying his people as "insiders," participants in the new covenant, the "new Israel."[36]

The various titles applied to Christ have appeared earlier in the book. "The Alpha and the Omega (i.e., the 'A' and the 'Z'), the First and the Last, the Beginning and the End" identifies the Lord as the one who gives creation both its origin and its ultimate goal.[37] "The Root and the Offspring of David" identifies Jesus as the "Messiah," the "Christ," the King descended from David who rules as God's vicar over all creation.[38] "The bright Morning Star" identifies Jesus with the planet Venus, an ancient symbol for victory.[39] Jesus is the Victor, who will "overcome" God's enemies and establish God's eternal kingdom.

---

[34]See Part II.E.1 of the Commentary: "The Tree of Life (2:7)." See also the comments on Revelation 21:6b; 22:1-2,5b given above.

[35]For an analysis of this elaborate symbol, see the comments on Rev 21:1–22:5.

[36]On the Church as the "new Israel," see the comment on the "Sealing of the 144,000" in Rev 7:1-8. John draws a similar distinction between Christians and non-Christians in Rev 11:1-2a, as explained in our analysis of that text.

[37]See the comment on "him who is, and who was, and who is to come" in Rev 1:4c.

[38]See the comment on Rev 5:5. See also the explanation of the title "Jesus Christ" in Rev 1:5.

[39]See Part II.E.4 of the Commentary: "Authority over the Nations and the Morning Star."

22:17 The Spirit and the bride say, "Come!" And let him who hears say, "Come!" Whoever is thirsty, let him come; and whoever wishes, let him take the free gift of the water of life.

More than any other part of Revelation, this verse communicates the "good news" of the Christian gospel. More than any other part of Revelation, this verse expresses the grace of God. The kingdom is not limited to the rich, or the talented, or the beautiful, or the powerful, or the educated, or the famous, or the intelligent, or the witty, or the wellborn, or the successful, or the healthy, or the strong, or the innocent, or the flawless. Eternal life with the Lord, in a redeemed and transformed universe, under the beneficent kingship of God, is offered to *"whoever"* wants such a gift. *"Whoever* is thirsty" may freely "drink" of the "water of life"![40]

"Come!" The Spirit of God himself delivers the invitation. "Come!" The "bride" — the Lord's church — delivers the invitation as God's witnesses on earth.[41] Oh do come!

22:18-19 I warn everyone who hears the words of the prophecy of this book: If anyone adds anything to them, God will add to him the plagues described in this book. And if anyone takes words away from this book of prophecy, God will take away from him his share in the tree of life and in the holy city, which are described in this book.

Christ himself pronounces a curse on anyone who tampers with the revelation from God preserved in John's book. In the Letter of Aristeas 310-311 (cf. Deut 4:1-2), Jewish leaders take similar precautions after preparing a Greek translation of the Hebrew Old Testament (i.e., the Septuagint or "LXX"):

> As the books were read, the priests stood up, with the elders from among the translators and from the representatives of the "Community," and with the leaders of the people, and said, "Since this version has been made rightly and reverently, and in every respect accurately, it is good that this should remain exactly so, and that there should be no revision." There was general approval of

---

[40]For an explanation of the "water of life" symbol, see the comments on Revelation 21:6b; 22:1-2,5b.

[41]Compare, for example, Rev 11:3, where the "two witnesses" symbolize the church that bears testimony to Christ.

what they said, and they commanded that a curse should be laid, as was their custom, on anyone who should alter the version by any addition or change to any part of the written text, or any deletion either. This was a good step taken, to ensure that the words were preserved completely and permanently in perpetuity.[42]

22:20-21 He who testifies to these things says, "Yes, I am coming soon." Amen. Come, Lord Jesus. The grace of the Lord Jesus be with God's people. Amen.

Verse 21 represents the benedictory wish, in the writer's own hand, common in Hellenistic letters of the first century.[43] After a final reminder from Christ that he is indeed coming soon, John voices the only appropriate word with which to end this book: "Amen. (So be it!) Come, Lord Jesus."

Amen! Come, Lord Jesus!

---

[42]Charlesworth, *Pseudepigrapha*.
[43]See Part V.A of the Introduction: "The First Century Hellenistic Letter Form in Revelation."